Exploration & Exchange

"The GENIUS of the Work instructing YOUTH in the Conduct of those illustrious Circumnavigators &c. whose medallions are here exhibited and whose Important Discoveries & Exploits (amongst others) are recorded in our Collection." Frontispiece to John Hamilton Moore, *A New and Complete Collection of Voyages and Travels* (London, 1778).

Exploration & Exchange

A SOUTH SEAS ANTHOLOGY ❊ 1680–1900

Edited by

Jonathan Lamb, Vanessa Smith, and

Nicholas Thomas

The University of Chicago Press

Chicago and London

JONATHAN LAMB is professor of English at Princeton University. VANESSA SMITH is a U2000 postdoctoral fellow in the School of English, Art History, Film and Media at the University of Sydney. NICHOLAS THOMAS is a professor of anthropology at Goldsmith College, University of London.

The University of Chicago Press, Chicago 60637
The University of Chicago Press, Ltd., London
© 2000 by The University of Chicago
All rights reserved. Published 2000
Printed in the United States of America

09 08 07 06 05 04 03 02 01 00   1 2 3 4 5

ISBN: 0-226-46845-3 (CLOTH)
ISBN: 0-226-46846-1 (PAPER)

Research for this publication has been supported by the Centre for Cross-Cultural Research, an Australian Research Council Special Research Centre, The Australian National University, Canberra, ACT 0200, www.anu.edu.au/culture.

Library of Congress Cataloging-in-Publication Data
Lamb, Jonathan, Vanessa Smith, and Nicholas Thomas
    Exploration and Exchange: a South Seas anthology, 1680–1900
    / edited by Jonathan Lamb, Vanessa Smith, and Nicholas Thomas.
        p.   cm.
    Includes bibliographical references and index.
    ISBN 0-226-46845-3. (cloth: alk. paper) —ISBN 0-226-46846-1 (pbk.)
    1. Oceania—Discovery and exploration. 2. Travel writing—Oceania.
    I. Lamb, Jonathan, 1945– II. Smith, Vanessa. III. Thomas, Nicholas.

DU19. E95 2000
995—dc21   00-029930

Contents

Illustrations

Preface and Acknowledgments

Recent years have seen a new wave of scholarship on voyagers and travel writings. Formerly an area of relatively limited interest (primarily to maritime historians and specialists in travel literature), these narratives have emerged as focal areas for interdisciplinary work drawing on anthropology, literary studies, cultural history, and art history. Yet while an increasing critical and interpretative literature focuses on the complexities of exploratory and travel writings, and the fraught encounters that travel entailed, significant travel texts remain in many cases relatively inaccessible. Many older works have either never been republished or are available only in expensive facsimiles. This anthology provides a set of extracts from key texts arising from contacts in the Pacific, from the late seventeenth to the late nineteenth centuries. It is intended to serve as a resource to enable teachers and students to engage with primary materials, some of which are otherwise difficult to obtain.

Exploration and Exchange aims to be broadly representative of the writings of British and American explorers, mariners, missionaries, and visitors to the Pacific. All of the extracts are in some sense based upon or derived from actual experiences in Oceania. The texts have been selected to illuminate the complexities of representation and narrative in the liminal zones of culture contact. More specifically, they relate to a number of persistently significant themes—including those of mutiny, utopia, cannibalism, taboo, and hybridity—and to problems of the plausibility of travel narratives, linguistic comprehension and confusion, and the degeneration of European bodies in the Tropics. The book does not include writings by Herman Melville, whose works set in the Pacific are very easily obtained; otherwise, we have aimed to include both very well-known figures, such as James Cook, Joseph Banks, John Williams, William Ellis, Mark Twain, and Robert Louis Stevenson; and some texts like those of George Keate and Louis Becke, which were very widely read, but slipped into subsequent obscurity; as well as material that was not composed for immediate publication, by Edward Robarts and David Darling, among others. The extracts are presented here, essentially in chronological order, with commentaries and guides to further reading.

Much of the work on this volume coincided with an intensive four-week seminar, "Writing Voyages and Encounters," the first of a program of such seminars for graduate students visiting the Centre for Cross-Cultural Research at the Australian National University. We are grateful to the participants: Vanessa Agnew, Paul Arthur, Anette Bremer, Tony Brown, Greg Dening, Bronwen Douglas, Stephen Gapps, Padhraid Higgins, Anna Johnston, Ewan Johnston, Peter Kirkup, Catarina Krizancic, Maria Nugent, Michael Schlitz, Nancy Stockdale, Philippa Tucker, Paul Turnbull, Geoff Watson, and Ian Wilkins; their contributions to an exhausting but stimulating series of discussions provided the ideal context for the preparation of this anthology.

Our most substantial debt is to Hilary Ericksen, who transcribed some extracts, coordinated the scanning of many others, and helped with editing, permissions, bibliographic searches, and a host of other matters. Jonathan Lamb would also like to thank the Committee on Research in the Humanities and Social Sciences, Princeton University, for its generous contribution toward the costs of his research. He thanks Laura Sayre and Julie Park for their help in gathering background material and in preparing the first draft. Vanessa Smith would like to thank the University of Sydney U2000 Fellowship Scheme for supporting her research.

Introduction

In recent years, travel has emerged as a key topic in the humanities. The framework of a journey has always been important to the main genres of literature—epic, romance, bildungsroman, and satire—but since the advent of new historicism in the American academy, and cultural studies in the British, encounters with the strange and exotic have been the focus of increasingly specialized attention. Canonical works such as *The Tempest* and *Paradise Lost* have been reread in the light of exploration and settlement in the New World. And in the process, histories of travel—such as Hakluyt's *Voyages*, Heylyns's *Cosmographie,* and Knolles and Rycaut's *Turkish Historie*—have been scrutinized with the care previously bestowed on works of imagination, largely because they are reflections of the ways in which an imagined community mapped and made sense of its relation to the rest of the world. With the eighteenth century the interdependence of literature and travel is clearly manifest in *Gulliver's Travels* and *Robinson Crusoe*, which closely question the perceived foundations of civil society through narratives of voyages to remote places. Such works invite the modern reader to revisit the journals of mariners and castaways with an appreciation of the doubts and anxieties with which representatives of one world enter another. As confidence in notions of cultural centrality have begun to wane, and English Literature is giving way to literatures in English, the doubtfulness implicit in the traveling part of literary genres has become accordingly the prime point of interest: it defines the material conditions of a moment of cultural crisis.

For its part, anthropology has shifted away from classical ethnographic inquiry. The discipline is now concerned to join intensive work in and on local cultures with the historical analysis of local and global cultural flows. The self-conscious production of cultural difference in zones of interaction has received increasing attention, as have the activities of travelers who mediate differences, who are makers of cross-cultural understandings and misunderstandings. It is now appreciated that the practices of ethnography are not distinctive to twentieth-century professional anthropology, but belong to a much longer history of descriptions of foreign manners and customs. We can say that this began with the systematization of travel in the sixteenth century, or with Caesar, or with Herodotus. If cross-cultural encounters are highly salient to anthropological inquiry for many reasons, those attendant upon European travel are especially crucial, since they can be said to constitute the discipline's history.

For students of literature and anthropology alike, Oceania has loomed large. The South Seas has been the preferred site of utopias ever since Thomas More invented the genre in 1516; and the myth of a terrestrial paradise there was rather confirmed than dispatched by voyagers from de Quiros to Bougainville. The great expeditions to the Pacific mounted by the French and English in the 1760s and 1770s coincided with the Enlightenment tracings of society's original outlines; and the islands around Tahiti, named the Society Islands, provided not only apparent proof that utopias had a material existence, but also gave students of the history of cultures—such as Gottfried Herder and Adam Ferguson—data for their theories. In the twentieth century the Pacific islands seemed to offer anthropologists like Malinowski and Mead ideally restricted fields for developing the practice of ethnographic fieldwork, yet they also became sites where the limitations of fieldwork methodology were exposed.

The wide coverage given recently to the debate between Gananath Obeyesekere and Marshall Sahlins concerning the circumstances surrounding Cook's death at Kealakekua Bay on the island of Hawaii in 1779 attests not only to the enduring significance of the Pacific and the history of its navigation, but also to a conflict between postcolonial criticism and historical anthropology. Obeyesekere's *The Apotheosis of Captain Cook* took issue with a series of books and articles in which Sahlins argued that Cook was identified during his visits to Hawaii with Lono, god of peace and fertility. Sahlins claimed that Cook's reception and eventual assassination at the island were mediated by the rituals of Lono's investiture and deposition celebrated in the Hawaiian Makahiki festival. According to Obeyesekere, this thesis belonged within a widespread tradition of European myth-making in which a fantasy of the deified white explorer was projected onto indigenous subjects. Obeyesekere, a distinguished anthropologist of South Asian religions, adduced his knowledge of Sri Lankan cultural politics to his discussion of Hawaiian history, claiming subaltern status for the Hawaiians and finding that their culture had been irrevocably destroyed by Cook. Though augmented by categories such as "resistance," this account could be seen as little more than an update of Alan Moorhead's evocation of the "fatal impact" made on Pacific cultures by contact with Europeans, the ramifications of which were as lamentable as they were pervasive. The propositions that Pacific historians of the "islander-oriented" school of the 1960s had labored to establish—that European goods, persons, practices, and institutions were consistently subject to local manipulation if not appropriation—were passed over by Obeyesekere. Sahlins in response did not seek to vindicate Cook, but rather to draw attention to the activity and versatility of Polynesian and Melanesian cultures, from so-called first contacts through to the present day.

The pressure of attention focused on the Pacific archive by such debate would seem to indicate the urgency of fashioning a distinctive historical perspective, apt for the voyaging, settler, and indigenous cultures of Oceania, that is not awkwardly transposed to that region from postcolonial discourses stimulated by the wholly different histories of diasporic South Asian and American identities. In this book, we focus on the variable politics of encounter, rather than seeking to describe the operations of a monolithic discourse of imperialism. We are less interested in articulating common denominators—in locating the stereotypical or formulaic—than in identifying moments in accounts of cross-cultural contact that challenge our own postcolonial complacencies. We do not present any ready-made model or theory but aim instead to provide students with a set of readings that might open a fresh theoretical perspective upon the problems these texts raise.

The Beach

The accomplishment of Cook's second voyage was to find nothing. Cook had been charged with testing the ancient belief in the existence of a great southern continent, and he ventured far into the frigid south, meeting with much ice but no land. In representing what Daniel Boorstin has called "the ardours of negative discovery" (Boorstin 1985, 278), Cook was preserving a long tradition of Oceanic rhetoric. Gulliver praises the land of the Houyhnhnms for the things it does not contain; William Dampier describes the coast of New Holland (Australia) as a series of absent amenities; More delivers an account of Utopia by means of the figure of litotes, as Elizabeth McCutcheon (1977) and Stephen Greenblatt (1980) have pointed out, affirming things only by denying their opposites. Such negative methods of representation are an index of the profound uncertainty of navigators, travelers, and settlers in the Pacific. Europeans were frequently unsure of where they were, who they were, and what they knew. The accounts of voyaging, contact, and exchange in the Pacific that we present in this volume exhibit confusions of many kinds in many registers. The extracts we reproduce, ranging from the late seventeenth to the late nineteenth centuries, concern themselves with various alternatives to civility: isolation, mutiny, cannibalism, infanticide, paradise, utopia, romance, voluptuousness, and a distinct mood whose mildest manifestation is reverie or curiosity, and whose most turbulent is frenzy.

The emphasis we place upon the degree to which Europeans were "at sea" in multiple senses is at odds with widely held assumptions concerning colonial expansion in the eighteenth and nineteenth centuries. An insistence upon the calculated force of imperial agency forms a discursive continuity between more conventional maritime histories and much postcolonial critique, which postulates that the British exploration of the South Pacific was a deliberately conceived and executed imperial gambit. Voyages were disguised as projects of scientific curiosity, but in fact paved the way for mercantile imperialism and territorial expansion. This effort was enabled or accompanied by colonialism in the domains of culture and knowledge, thought to emerge from a consistent European ideology now often characterized as Enlightenment rationalism. Taxonomic, hierarchizing, and universalist habits of mind are seen to have appropriated Oceanic places, environments, and peoples. Through voyages, European reason fashioned itself as a historicized Self against a variety of primitive Others; in the nineteenth century racialized othering is harnessed to practical efforts of colonial intervention and exploitation. The editors of this volume seek to deny neither the scope of imperial ambition nor the mutual implication of racial science and colonial domination. Still less would we want to pass over the violence of exploration and subsequent colonization. But ambition is not accomplishment: metropolitan aspirations foundered in many ways, on the high seas as well as on the reefs and beaches of the Pacific. Like a number of scholars working in diverse postcolonial fields, who have become increasingly attendant to the particular rather than the universal aspects of colonial encounter, we find ourselves suspicious of gross totalities that blur the specificity of each enterprise and the distinctness of its outcome.[1] We do not dispute that significant epochal shifts in European thought and culture coincided with the penetration of the Pacific, but

---

1. We might mention here interventions as varied in their cultural, geographical, and political subject matter as those of Mitchell (1998), Lazarus (1990), Escobar and Alvarez (1992), and Lloyd (1993), which stress the importance of attending to distinct contexts of colonial encounter. However, unlike these theorists, the editors of this volume do not seek to articulate forms of countercultural resistance or to oppose a model of "minority discourse" to the hegemony of "colonial discourse."

texts of the kind we present in this anthology do not belong to a tightly delineated philosophical tradition that can be usefully periodized and labeled in this way. The accounts compiled here belong to a cultural history in the broadest sense, that certainly exhibits philosophical and political antinomies but, most vitally, reveals the ways in which these relations and contradictions were played out on the beach.

All the texts we present here were written in or from the Pacific, in a more or less immediate sense. They therefore register, often in vivid and compelling terms, the drama and risk of actual encounters. Even though these interactions were typically misunderstood; even though the accounts of them incorporate, to varying degrees, concocted incidents and overt or covert fictions, they were shaped by situations of cross-cultural conflict and exchange. They are therefore unlike the whole array of metropolitan texts that lacked any basis in an author's experience—utopias, anthropological syntheses, juvenile adventure stories—in which projections of European knowledge and fantasy survived armchair voyagings relatively intact. Writings from the beach, no matter how complacently they might invoke the moral, political, religious, and literary certitudes of home, were subject to the risks of encounter, and their narratives are motivated by the consequences (terrifying or pleasurable) of chances being taken.

If this anthology does little to sustain postcolonial orthodoxy, it points similarly to the shortcomings of a much longer tradition of commentary on European perceptions of Oceania, and the non-European world in general. No one with the most cursory acquaintance with this literature can have failed to have been impressed by the centrality of the notion of the "noble savage," which has been frequently juxtaposed with that of the "ignoble savage." The characterization of Oceanic peoples as "noble savages" is supposed to follow from Rousseauian primitivism, and broadly to typify late eighteenth- and early nineteenth-century discourses. Following closer colonial contacts and incidents of violent indigenous resistance, this romanticization is seen to have given way to denigrating representations that emphasized racial inferiority rather than social simplicity. The material presented here makes it evident that both the conventional idea of the "image" (of the Pacific Islander, or the Other) and the more theorized notion of the "stereotype" are far too static to account for the varying values and narratives that enter into renderings of particular indigenous peoples. These are, moreover, one-sided notions, that either forget that representations of encounters were about Europeans as well as natives, or presume that the former are simply marked as "civilized" in relation to "savages" who are either noble or ignoble. Many of the texts we present evince the extent to which civility was in no sense a secure term, nor one that could simply be bolstered through juxtaposition with savagery. Scurvy (the predominant maritime disease in voyages over the Pacific) was well-known to cause acute psychological as well as physiological symptoms, summed up by one expert as "scorbutic nostalgia," a state of enlarged sensibility that inclined the victims to form exquisite ideas of island paradises, and to behave with peculiar abandon when a beach appeared. A range of accounts, from early mutiny histories to the stories of Louis Becke, draw on developing discourses of degeneration to portray white males brutalized by long sea journeys and the circumstances of the beach, whose alienation from "civilized" values finds expression in their defection from the mini–civil society of the ship and incorporation into the indigenous realm. These forms of mutation and hybridity did not simply represent the points between poles that were themselves well-defined, since the failure of civility on the beach tended to prejudice the attributes and operations of European culture in an unconstrained way. The expression "gone native" is widely if jocularly known, but the cross-cultural shifts that it refers to have entered popular and scholarly writing on a few of the famous and infamous, such as Melville and Gauguin, rather than any more encompassing or contextualized account of European identities in Oceania.

While this anthology does not attempt to document or represent indigenous constructions of cross-cultural encounters, it is worth noting in passing that what is awkwardly described as "acculturation" or "Europeanization" stands as a complex counterpart to "going native." From the chiefs who embraced European names, clothes, and guns, to the native missionaries who became very numerous in the second half of the nineteenth century, islanders who personally adopted foreign ways were, like indigenized beachcombers, described in terms that ranged from ambivalent admiration to censure.

Insofar as terms such as the "noble savage" suggest a play of oppositional identifications in cross-cultural representation, the mutual definition of self and other, it may be suggested that the content of European (and, incidentally, indigenous) rhetoric is impoverished. Much travel writing and colonial discourse is indeed captivated by the exotic, and many expressions of Orientalism and primitivism no doubt did accentuate the difference and distance of other peoples from European subjects. However, contrary familiarizing tendencies are no less important in the history of exploratory and colonial writing. In their ethnographic remarks, eighteenth-century voyage writers frequently described Oceanic manners and institutions through a European political vocabulary, postulating dispositions shaped by climates and modes of government, suspended between virtue and corruption like European states both ancient and modern. Metropolitan political arguments proceeded between the lines of ethnographic description and interpretation as, conversely, those who wrote on the evolution of European polities cited or presumed an awareness of the travelers' writings on the non-European world. Later in our period, evangelical missionaries consistently wrote in a familiarizing fashion, emphasizing the common humanity of prospective Christian peoples while deploring their particular barbarisms. This discourse too, was reflexive, in several senses. Accounts of conversion in the Pacific and in early Britain (in Hume's *History of England*, for instance) resonated closely with one another; no opportunity was lost to draw attention to affinities between heathen and Catholic superstitions; and much the same rhetoric licensed missionary work among the benighted urban poor of Britain as among those in darkness in the South Seas. The literature of encounter, in sum, was richly paradoxical; it might stress sheer strangeness at one moment, while relentlessly assimilating novel terms at another.

Our discussion returns regularly to the beach, "a South Seas expression," Robert Louis Stevenson writes, "for which there is no exact equivalent" (1900, 64). In a series of publications beginning with an edition of one of the most remarkable of Pacific beachcomber books, *The Marquesan Journal of Edward Robarts* (1974), Dening has explored and retraversed the space of the beach as metaphor and as theater. The beach is, he suggests, above all a liminal space, in which two social orders intersect and neither is sovereign. If one of these orders, perforce the intrusive one, is represented not by a collectivity such as a ship's crew but by just one man, the gestures and ritualized interactions that sustain his symbolic world desert him, and he is suddenly in a space in which all action is provisional. Dening characterizes beachcombers—the deserters and resident castaways who take their name from the space of the beach—in these terms:

> Beachcombers were those who crossed beaches alone. They crossed the beach without the supports that made their own world real into other worlds that were well-established and self-sufficient. They were strangers in their new societies and scandals to their old. They left behind them the roles that made their world orderly and its gestures meaningful. On the beach they were no longer the sailors, the husbands or even the men that those roles made. In their new world there were none to recognize them as such. If they came from some fo'c's'le of a whaler or man-o'war, they left behind the rituals of obeisance which told them their status, the signals of friendship that mapped the limits

of their obligations and rights, the structures of the days that gave them times of work and leisure. On the beach, they needed to assume roles recognizable to their new world. They confronted, as few other men confront, the relativity of everything that made them what they were: their values, their judgements, the testimony of their senses. Whatever they did on the beach, they had to carve out a new world for themselves. The new world could not be the one they left: it lacked all the essential ingredients. It could not be the world on which they had intruded: none could be born again so radically. So on the beach they experimented. They made wives, children, relations, property in new ways. The beach that was the boundary between the old world and the new ran down the very centre of their lives. (1980, 129)

Cultural values, elsewhere taken for granted, are here meaningless, or at least highly susceptible to misrecognition. Dening draws on notions of symbolic worlds and roles loosely derived from the interpretative sociology of Berger and Luckman and the anthropology of Geertz and Turner, but he puts these to use not in pursuit of a quasi-functional account of cultural coherence, but in order to define an engagement with improvisation. The beachcomber's displacement into a radically different world leaves him without symbols, but with the need to deploy them; as he needs also to produce relations and invent rituals. Performances, in this context, are substantially unscripted.

Dening's concerns do not amount to a theory, but rather to an inspiring set of orientations that do much to draw attention to the uncertainties and to the sheer novelty of beach culture. As is no doubt already apparent, we find his emphasis upon the provisional nature of meaning and culture on the liminal ground of the beach especially productive. Because the beach is a site of loss as well as gain and risk as well as profit, we must anticipate that metropolitan values (of both the moral and commercial kind) are likely to be prejudiced here. And this is also why the European self may be a knowing subject, but also an object of indigenous knowledge and even appropriation—hence by no means necessarily an imperial agent with the capacity to call the shots.

This anthology, however, departs from Dening's project in a number of respects. His writing has been directed by an interest in evoking the beach-like dimensions of all practice; it has in other words been pitched toward universals, whereas we are concerned more specifically with the historical and cultural conditions of particular encounters. Anyone who walks a coastline knows that beaches come and go; the littoral may be broader or narrower, it may be devastated by a storm, it may be artificially reconstructed (as at Waikiki), or it may sustain an environmental, seasonal rhythm of accumulation and reduction, yet be covered with garbage. The figurative beaches of cross-cultural interaction begin by being different and are absolutely subject to changes of these kinds. The Tahitian beaches of the eighteenth century were broad enough to encompass much sociality on both sides, and Europeans entered Polynesian society to varying degrees and in varying ways, just as Polynesians entered the social orders of European vessels and even those of the European cities. In western Oceania over the same period, interaction was far more constrained: indigenous people, in Vanuatu for example, were generally unwilling to venture onto ships, and they obstructed Europeans who sought to visit interior gardens or villages. There the domain of interaction, of cross-cultural exchange, was almost wholly confined to the beach in a literal sense.

As beaches differed with the indigenous polities that attempted to structure the terms of interactions, so they did too with varying groups of Europeans, who from the beginning of the nineteenth century sought more than peripheral interaction, aspiring rather to install themselves on the landward side of the beach and to impose terms of trade, a rule of authority and property, and religious reform. If no initial contact had been exempt from some overt contest, the question of in whose interest contact proceeded would be continually negotiated, when it was not violently disputed. Although intrusions were nothing if not uneven, it becomes inappropriate to speak of a beach, since we can no longer postulate a scene of liminality situated between cultures that retain integrity. This is not to suggest that the distinctiveness of indigenous culture collapses with colonial government and that there is no longer a domain of practice beyond interaction. It is rather to acknowledge the limits of the spatial and topographical metaphor itself.

We have attempted to draw attention to the textual as well as the experiential aspects of the encounters reproduced in this volume. The transformation of the trajectory of the journey into that of a narrative, the publishing of voyage accounts for metropolitan audiences, involved other kinds of cultural and linguistic crossings and contacts. Historically variable conditions dictated the ways in which travelers might appear as authors, and in some cases excluded them from the task. The stories of disreputable narrators such as beachcombers, whose journeys into degeneracy disturbed convention and who lacked access to the world of publication or indeed to basic literacy skills, were frequently assembled or ventriloquized by more socially acceptable compositors—for instance, William Mariner's Dr. John Martin or George Vason's clergymen Solomon Pigott and James Orange.

Following a model established in eighteenth-century criminal biography, this editorial presence provided readers with a reassuring letter of introduction to a potentially scandalous literary sojourn outside the realm of civility. Even in unmediated first-person accounts, a sensitivity to codes of language, an awareness of pressures of interest, and imposed silences inevitably shaped the presentation of travel as text. In attempting to untangle disparate voices subsumed in the finished document, we have looked to framing histories—prefaces and apologia, manuscripts or related correspondence—and reviewed national contexts of reception, types of readership, and the degrees of popularity and influence that different accounts achieved within metropolitan literary culture. If travel participates in the crises that menace cultural confidence, undoing identities at their moment of extension, reports of foreign encounter are fashioned to bring dislocation and defamiliarization into the purview of the familiar. Like the traveler at the periphery, the text in the literary marketplace was implicitly reconstituted.

Contexts: Pacific Cultures and Histories

The capacity for innovation that Sahlins emphasized in his response to Obeyesekere is attested to over the long run in Oceania. Human settlement, especially of the more remote islands in the central and eastern Pacific, has a short prehistory in global terms. The ancestors of the Hawaiians, Easter Islanders, and Maori formed a single population in central Polynesia before these marginal islands were settled between 400 and 900 A.D., and the differences between the languages, social institutions, cultural practices, and art on those islands at the time of European contact thus arose quite late, in the course of relatively short separate histories that saw rapid changes and diverse adaptations.

The pre-European history of the western Pacific is more complex. Most of New Guinea is occupied by speakers of Papuan languages and has been inhabited for more than forty thousand years; this early phase of settlement extended into neighboring archipelagoes to the north and east, including parts of the Solomon Islands. Most of the other Pacific island groups, on the other hand, were settled much later by speakers of Austronesian languages who moved into the region from insular Southeast Asia between four and three thousand years ago. Archaeological evidence tells us that these peoples already practiced tattooing, which in its diversified forms at the time of contact astonished European visitors. Their hierarchically structured societies, organized around some form of chiefly leadership, would undergo much transformation. In parts of Polynesia, societies became more stratified, and prominent individuals of high rank were readily recognized as "kings" and "queens" by Europeans. In many cultures, however, complex rank structures emerged that attached importance to more differentiated priestly and warrior roles, and in some places to structures of titles and grades that were virtually unintelligible from the perspective of short-term visitors. The leaders with whom Europeans sought to deal were often thus elusive, or their roles were misunderstood.

Brief meetings between islanders and Europeans took place from the late sixteenth century onward, with the Spanish visits to the Marquesas, Espiritu Santo in north Vanuatu, and parts of the Solomon Islands. Dampier, following the Dutch, touched on the northwest Australian coast in the late seventeenth century, and over this period privateers and buccaneers entered the Pacific from the east to cruise against the French and Spanish; they rarely ventured far westward and thus had only the most limited contacts with the indigenous peoples of the Pacific. This period culminated with Anson's almost disastrous voyage of 1741–44; out of a fleet of seven vessels, only the flagship, the *Centurion*, returned, but the eventual capture of a Manilla galleon loaded with coin made the expedition in the end a sort of triumph.

More sustained interaction began in the last decades of the eighteenth century. Wallis's discovery of Tahiti in 1767 was swiftly followed by the visits of Bougainville, several Spanish vessels that established a short-lived mission, and Cook. Though Cook's voyages may have received a disproportionate measure of scholarly attention, the sheer range of his Pacific cruises was remarkable, specifically because the second and third voyages were so protracted and sought not merely to cross the Pacific, but required that it be crossed and re-crossed in the intervals between summer investigations in the southern and northern high latitudes respectively. What is especially significant, moreover, is that participants in Cook's voyages acquired unprecedented levels of cumulative familiarity with Oceanic environments, places, populations, and (in the Society Islands at least) particular people. Some measure of linguistic competence, and cross-cultural experience on both sides, meant that transactions on the beach ceased to be one-off events that seemed to lack a past or a future. Polynesians began to know who Europeans were and began to imagine what might be gained by dealings with them.

Though several navigators (including Cook and Bougainville) had made contacts in the western Pacific, in Vanuatu and New Caledonia, intrusions in this region—later known as Melanesia—were very limited until well into the nineteenth century. In the 1790s, however, New England traders initiated a trans-Pacific commerce and then discovered the value of Pacific resources such as sandalwood, tortoiseshell, and bêche-de-mer for the Chinese markets. In Polynesia and Micronesia it was not long before their visits became frequent; whalers as well as traders sought provisions, water, and sexual contacts. The beachcomber phenomenon that looms large in this collection is primarily, but not exclusively, a by-product of this activity; although some beachcombers were deserters from naval vessels, renegade missionaries, or escaped convicts, most abandoned trading vessels for one reason or another or were survivors of wrecks or attacks upon vessels by islanders.

From the end of the eighteenth century, the London Missionary Society was active, unsuccessfully in Tonga and the Marquesas, and to greater effect in Tahiti, which subsequently became a base for evangelism westward into the Cook Islands (from the 1820s), Samoa (from 1830), and elsewhere. American Protestants settled in Hawaii from 1820, and the Wesleyan Methodist Missionary Society began work in Tonga in the 1820s and Fiji from 1835. From 1827 Catholic orders followed: the Congregation of the Sacred Hearts of Jesus and Mary in Hawaii, the Marquesas, and Tahiti; and later the Marists in the western Pacific. These mainly French missionaries were often engaged in bitter competition with the Protestants, and in some cases indigenous peoples vigorously turned such rivalries to advantage. The theater of conversion was consistently one of disingenuous compliance, or at least of layered and complex motivations.

During the early nineteenth century, iron tools, cloth, and guns were widely introduced, access to European trade articles became a new source of power and prestige for warrior-chiefs, and islanders themselves traveled on ships and encountered other Pacific peoples and their artifacts. It was a dynamic period, when there were suddenly new resources and new opportunities for indigenous leaders, while colonial authorities were not yet in a position to attempt to control circumstances beyond the beach—and there only partially and for the duration of their visits. To varying degrees, indigenous warfare and other domains of cultural and political competition, such as feasting and the accumulation of prestige valuables, saw dramatic efflorescence. The intensification of conflict also, of course, created dangerous situations and situations of spectacular violence that may have been inflated in beachcomber and early missionary accounts, but are unlikely to have been entirely invented.

Although voyagers took possession of many islands at many times, most claims were neither officially recognized nor actively prosecuted. The French, however, annexed the Society Islands, the Marquesas, the Austral Islands, and the Tuamotus in 1842, just after the Treaty of Waitangi effected New Zealand's cession to Britain. France took control of New Caledonia in 1853, but most of the other tropical island groups remained autonomous until the late nineteenth century. Although a few extracts relate to places that had been formally colonized, this anthology is generally concerned with interactions prior to the establishment of foreign rule. The introduction of the colonial state meant that operations of government were more or (typically) less effectually prosecuted. The attendant discourses of governmentality belong essentially in a different epoch than the transactions and narratives that constitute the substance of this volume. While many Europeans on the beach practiced a sort of ethnography, administrators conducted more systematic inquiries that informed the regulation and often the appropriation of land, the establishment of taxation systems, and the policing of customs. These projects and the efforts of indigenous people to resist them are best understood through specific historical accounts (and there are many fine studies) rather than the textual sampling that we engage in here. This is to acknowledge that the conditions that constitute the beach have their own historical specificity. There are liminal conditions and situations of awkward transculturation in virtually all societies and periods, and there are ways in which the situations of voyaging, confusion, and curiosity that marked early contacts may resonate for those nonindigenous and indigenous people who travel through Oceania or inhabit it today. But the topographical and cultural scene of overlap that the beach constitutes is no longer constitutive of sociality, as it was in the eighteenth and nineteenth centuries. Over the period from which these texts speak, the site of liminality was paradoxically encompassing.

part one

Adventurers & Explorers

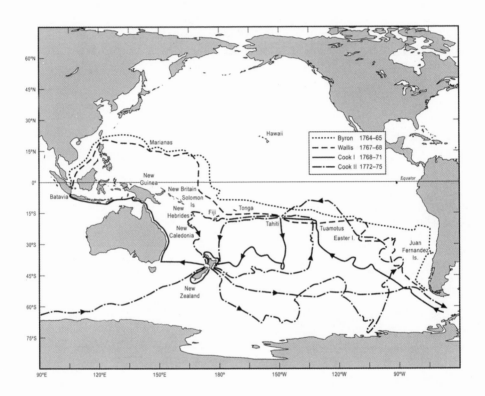

MAP I Voyagers' routes.

Introduction

The period extending from 1680 to 1800 saw successful challenges by the British and French to Dutch control of the Indian Ocean trade routes and to Spanish predominance in the Pacific. By the end of the eighteenth century both Britain and France had laid the basis of future claims to the largest of the island territories in the South Pacific, including New Zealand, Fiji, Tahiti, Vanuatu, New Caledonia, the Marquesas, and the continent of Australia. Although it may seem like a smooth accomplishment of the goals of national policy, it was in fact an extemporization upon a series of discrete events, some of which are described in the following section. These arise from motives of greed, curiosity, scientific inquiry, aggression, nostalgia, desire, and Christian benevolence: they embrace feats of endurance, violence, ethnography, cartography, acquisitiveness, utopian fantasy, and cross-cultural blending that were sometimes hard to frame in a coherent narrative—and even harder to believe. As far as British exploration and settlement were concerned, the Admiralty and the government reacted to developments rather than concerting them; and, in the case of New Zealand, it was with great reluctance that it was annexed to the Crown. This is not to say that the entry into the Pacific was not at all points conjoint with metropolitan preoccupations; but it tended to disturb domestic beliefs and to realize potent dreams in a contradictory and unconsoling way. If anything it magnified the contradictions at the heart of civil society; and instead of providing a convenient point of otherness from which to celebrate the consistency of national identity, it held up a distorting mirror to the certainties of the hearth. This is particularly evident in the nervous egoism of the accounts of voyages, as if the very category of selfhood is under threat—an unease that may be responsible for the many supplementary selves, in the form of compilers, editors, and ghostwriters, who were needed as conduits between the South Seas and the home audience. Certainly it is responsible for the appropriation of the format and style of voyages to the terra incognita by satirists such as Jonathan Swift,

G. F. Coyer, Denis Diderot, and the anonymous author of *Hildebrand Bowman* (1778).

If there was a point of origin to the history of the British in the Pacific, it would not be found in Drake's circumnavigation (1577) or in Narborough's reconnaissance of the western coast of South America (1669). These were peeps into the storehouse of the Spanish Empire that had no hope of establishing a foothold anywhere near it. The first real challenge to the Spanish hegemony in the New World and the Pacific under Pope Alexander VI's Bulls of Donation was mounted by Oliver Cromwell. In 1656 he organized the first deliberate attempt to seize Spain's possessions in the Caribbean and to establish an empire there. It was called the Western Design, and although it was regarded by Cromwell as a failure, it won Jamaica for the Commonwealth and consolidated there the English sugar industry, already thriving in the Leeward Islands of Barbados and St. Christopher. The buccaneers of the Caribbean, celebrated by Daniel Defoe and Guillaume Raynal as terrifying exemplars of democratic government and utopian idealists of surpassing cruelty, were the seaborne trash of the sugar trade, washing up on islands such as Catalina and Tortuga. Whether on land or sea, these strangely millenarian figures observed "Jamaica discipline," the rule of the majority that formed the basis of their self-government. Occasionally buccaneers were recruited by the state for attacks on enemy shipping or settlements. (Henry Morgan's destruction of Panama was a notorious example.) Then they were known as privateers, sailing under an authorization known as Letters of Marque and Reprisal. But it was a thin line dividing privateering from piracy.

It was as privateers that parties of Jamaica-based buccaneers followed Morgan's route into the South Sea. William Dampier and Lionel Wafer had arrived in the Caribbean as employees on sugar plantations, one as factor and the other as surgeon, and had taken the buccaneer option. The South Sea was the ocean on the other side of the Panama isthmus (known then as Darien), stretching away to the south and west, filled with the promise of treasure. When Dampier and Wafer crossed the isthmus they were looking for gold and silver, either in the settlements of coastal Peru and Chile or on board the fabulous galleons that carried the pillage of the New World from Lima and Manila to Acapulco. They were followed by other privateers such as Richard Simson, Woodes Rogers, John Clipperton, and George Shelvocke, some of whom were lucky enough to catch a treasure ship. They constituted the English presence in the Pacific between 1680 and 1720. After that it was largely a naval affair, although Anson's expedition in the 1740s was a privateering venture in all but name. The expeditions of the 1760s were of a different cast. Astronomical and cartographical investigations were the priority, and none of the vessels involved was engaged in hostilities. The link with the Caribbean sugar industry remained intact, however. Captain Bligh was twice dispatched to gather breadfruit seedlings, intended to provide cheap food for plantation slaves. Similarly, Hans Sloane, whose collection of natural and artificial curiosities was to be considerably enriched by the contributions of these scientific voyagers, had begun his career in Jamaica and made an important collection of manuscript buccaneer narratives of the South Seas, still known by his name.

Sugar production was by no means the sole link between the South Seas and British commerce. After his trip across the Darien isthmus Lionel Wafer was recruited as consultant by the Darien Company, a scheme for settling on the Panama coast financed by Scottish venture capital. Although the English ensured the scheme foundered, its successor was an English version of the same thing, the South Sea Company, set up by Robert Harley and Henry St. John in 1711. Unlike the East India Company or the Royal African Company, the South Sea Company had no solid prospect of trading in the Pacific. By the terms of the Treaty of Utrecht Britain was allowed to supply slaves to the Spanish colonies and to send an annual trading ship. But this arrangement was limited to the Atlantic side of South America. The spate of publications by privateers who had been in the Pacific, such as William Dampier, Bartholomew Sharp, John Strong, Woodes Rogers, William Funnell, and John Welbe, many of them appearing the year after the foundation of the company, were clearly intended as publicity for the scheme. A notable addition was Sir Richard Steele's interview with Alexander Selkirk in his periodical *The Englishman*, the story of whose stranding on the island of Juan Fernandez had already appeared in Rogers's *A Cruising Voyage round the World* (1712) and was soon to form the basis of one of the first true novels written in English.

No doubt the excesses that led to the South Sea Bubble of 1720 were partly provoked by the limitless possibilities of a large empty space. The privateers who dutifully reported prospects for gold mining, trade, anchorages, and staging posts—valiantly supported by Daniel Defoe, who, in his journalism and fiction (*An Essay on the South-Sea Trade* [1712] and *A New Voyage round the World* [1724], as well as *Robinson Crusoe* [1719])—argued for the solidity and reality of a future trade between the islands, the mainland, and China. But the case was put with brutal simplicity by James Burney in his great history of Pacific exploration: "In the year 1711 was erected in England, a South Sea Company, concerning which it is sufficient in this place to observe, that its formation had no relation to any scheme or plan for establishing a commercial intercourse between the British Nation and the Countries bordering on the South Sea, or to any maritime enterprise then carrying on, or in contemplation" (J. Burney 1816, 4:486). When the crash came, and England found its national credit ruined on a South Seas hypothesis, John Trenchard wrote bitterly, "Our highest Enjoyment is of that which is not: Our Pleasure is Deceit; and the only real Happiness that we have is derived from Non-Entities" (Trenchard 1725, 2:51). He and Swift saw crocodiles, cannibals, and castaways on the streets of London; Hogarth showed the same enormities in his print of 1721, *The South Sea Scheme*. The recriminations following the Bubble were joined by the privateers themselves. Dampier was in hot and public dispute with members of his crew, chiefly William Funnell and John Welbe; Shelvocke had a public row with his lieutenant, Willian Betagh; Woodes Rogers was pursued in Chancery many years after the end of his voyage, accused of secreting the profits of the cruise.

The South Sea Bubble blurred the difference between truth and falsehood, as well as between nothing and something. In this respect it promoted a confusion that had always belonged to speculations about the enigmas of the South Seas, particularly the vast landmass, the terra incognita, that was believed to extend from the eastern edge of the Indian Ocean all the way to the South Atlantic. In his *Cosmographie* Peter Heylyn supposes that the wildest fictions of romance might find a local habitation in the terra incognita: "the Isle of Adamants in Sir Huon of Bordeaux; the Firm Island in the History of Amadis de Gaul; the hidden island, and that of the Sage Aliart in Sir Palmerin of England." Moreover, he declares Spenser's *Faerie Queene* took place there. He knows for a fact it is where Hall's *Mundus alter et idem* and More's *Utopia* are situated; the location is undeniable, even if the fiction isn't (Heylyn 1667, 1094). The earliest maps of the world had purposely left an empty space as a coy gesture at the location of a terrestrial paradise. The possibility of finding in the South Seas a place that had previously been nothing but "a vain EU-TOPIA seated in the Brain," as Bernard Mandeville put it, had already been seized by Spanish mariners such as de Quiros, when he found New Jerusalem in Vanuatu. He was followed by Richard Walter, the chaplain on board Anson's flagship, who viewed Juan Fernandez with the same compromised delight as Satan views Eden. Bougainville and Commerson discovered New Cythera and Utopia respectively when they landed at Tahiti. Even Cook was tempted to think of the Society Islands as a terrestrial paradise, where the inhabitants went naked and bread grew upon trees.

George Keate fashioned a sentimental garden world out of the Palau Islands.

The blend of the literary and the historical arising from narratives of the terra incognita is strong in the early novel. Defoe's *Robinson Crusoe* is an influential example. Smollett's *Roderick Random* (1748), Coyer's *Supplement* (1752), and Rousseau's *La nouvelle Heloise* (1761) are partly based on Anson's voyage. Coyer's Patagonian fantasy in his *Letter to Dr. Maty* (1767) is based on Byron's voyage; and *The Adventures of Hildebrand Bowman* (1778) and Coleridge's *Ancient Mariner* rely directly on Cook's second voyage. Likewise Diderot's *Supplement* fictionalizes Bougainville's experience of Cytherean bliss. Despite the strongly "enlightenment" profile given to Cook's three voyages, there is an ulterior utopian logic to all of them, insofar as they concern the discovery of nonentities. The first and second proved that the Great Southern Continent (aka the terra incognita) did not exist; and the third put beyond a shadow of doubt the nonexistence of a Northwest Passage. All three were inspired by Alexander Dalrymple, for whom these geographical speculations had been, as he confessed, "the passion of his life." Dalrymple spent time with Benjamin Franklin planning a utopian settlement on the Atlantic portion of the Great Southern Continent once the Pacific segment had disappeared.

Delight always goes hand in hand with dismay in the Pacific. As Swift points out, once the imagination has risen up to a notion of what is highest and best, it is instantly intent upon furnishing its opposite. Is this the reason the Pacific, the great source of evidence concerning noble and ignoble savages, yokes ideas of perfection and putrescence, and of virtue and vileness, so violently and persistently together? An unstable and voluptuous mood is evident to some degree in the following extracts, often disguised as a judicious distinction between the good and the bad. In fact, it is either a blend of disgust and delight or a way of announcing the description of the one that will do quite as well for the other.

I

WILLIAM DAMPIER

The Discovery of New Holland

. . . .

WILLIAM DAMPIER (1652–1715) was a buccaneer, a colleague of Lionel Wafer on Bartholomew Sharp's first expedition into the South Seas in 1680. He was with Cowley four years later when he witnessed the reunion between William, the Miskito Indian left on Juan Fernandez in 1681, and his cousin Robin. He was with Captain Swan in the *Cygnet* when he first sighted the coast of New Holland in 1688, where he spent two months in an area he called Cygnet Bay on the northern coast, and in the *Roebuck* he visited the continent again in 1699. Although he was by no means the first European to land on the continent, Dampier's reports, contained in *A New Voyage Round the World* (1697–1703) and *A Voyage to New Holland* (1703), were eagerly read. They provided Swift with material for his *Gulliver's Travels*, especially the descriptions of the Yahoos in book 4, together with an archetypal voyager's style of narrative, "more particular than might be needful," as Dampier puts it in the preface to *A New Voyage*. His works also gave a huge boost to the interest in the South Seas that surrounded the formation of the South Seas Company in 1711. Some years before, John Locke had thought it "stupendous that so great a Part of the World should lie conceal'd so many Ages," and praised Dampier's part in its discovery, concluding, "The Empire of Europe is now extended to the utmost Bounds of the Earth . . . and the Relation of one Traveller is an Incentive to stir up another to imitate him" (Awnsham and Churchill 1704, lxxiii).

Dampier seems to have been a much better navigator than he was a buccaneer. His inglorious expedition in command of the *St. George* and the *Cinque Ports* in 1703–4 ended in a mutiny and a litany of accusations concerning Dampier's cowardice and incompetence. However, it was a voyage notable for the marooning of Alexander Selkirk, the master of the *Cinque Ports* left on Juan Fernandez by Captain Stradling, whose experiences supplied the outline of Defoe's *Robinson Crusoe* (1719) after Woodes Rogers picked him up in 1709, on a voyage where the inveterate Dampier was acting as pilot. In this extract from *A New Voyage* Dampier gives a remorselessly negative account of this strange new land, listing with great pertinacity the things it does not contain. His impressions were no more positive a decade later, when once again he was struck by what was lacking: "There were no Trees, Shrubs, or Grass to be seen . . . I saw there was no Harbour here . . . a place where there was no shelter . . . we searched for Water, but could find none, nor any Houses, nor People, for they were all gone" (Dampier 1697–1703, 118–44). It is a habit of negative notation that persists in the European discoveries in the South Seas. After his first landing in New Zealand, Cook reported, "We weigh'd, and stood out of the Bay which I have named Poverty Bay because it afforded us no one thing we wanted" (Cook 1955, 172). Swift gives it an odd twist in the fourth book of Gulliver, where the excellence of the Houyhnhnm commonwealth is defined by what it does not contain: "No ranting lewd expensive Wives: No stupid, proud Pedants: No importunate, over-bearing, quarrelsome, noisy, roaring, empty, conceited, swearing Companions: No Scountrels raised from the Dust upon the Merit of their Vices" (Swift 1971, 284). — JONATHAN LAMB

. . . .

William Dampier, *A New Voyage Round the World,* edited by N. M. Penzer, introduced by Sir Albert Gray (London: Argonaut Press, 1927). Originally published 1697–1703 (London: James Knapton).

« CHAPTER 16, PP. 312–14. »

New-Holland is a very large Tract of Land. It is not yet determined whether it is an Island or a main Continent; but I am certain that it joins neither to *Asia, Africa,* nor *America.* This part of it that we saw is all low even Land, with sandy Banks against the Sea, only the Points are rocky and so are some of the Islands in this Bay.

The Land is of a dry sandy Soil, destitute of Water, except you make Wells; yet producing divers sorts of Trees; but the Woods are not thick nor the Trees very big. Most of the Trees that we saw are Dragon-Trees as we supposed; and these too are the largest Trees of any there. They are about the bigness of our large Apple-trees, and about the same heighth; and the

FIG. 1. *Dampier trouve dans l'isle Fernandes un Moskite qu'on y avoit laissé depuis trios ans.* Engraved frontispiece to vol. 3 of Jean Pierre Berenger, *Collection de tous les voyages faits autour du monde par les differentes nations de l'Europe* (Paris: Chez Fr. Dufart, Imprimeur-Libraire, 1795). By permission of the National Library of Australia.

Rind is blackish, and somewhat rough. The Leaves are of a dark Colour; the Gum distils out of the Knots or Cracks that are in the Bodies of the Trees. We compared it with some Gum-Dragon or Dragon's Blood that was aboard, and it was of the same colour and taste. The other sort of Trees were not known by any of us. There was pretty long Grass growing under the Trees; but it was very thin. We saw no Trees that bore Fruit or Berries.

We saw no sort of Animal, nor any Track of Beast, but once; and that seemed to be the Tread of a Beast as big as a great Mastiff-Dog. Here are few small Land-birds, but none bigger than a Black-bird; and but few Sea-fowls. Neither is the Sea very plentifully stored with Fish, unless you reckon the Manatee and Turtle as such. Of these Creatures there is plenty; but they are extraordinary shy; though the Inhabitants cannot trouble them much having neither Boats nor Iron.

The Inhabitants of this Country are the miserablest People in the World. The *Hodmadods* of *Monomatapa*, though a nasty People, yet for Wealth are Gentlemen to these; who have no Houses, and skin Garments, Sheep, Poultry, and Fruits of the Earth, Ostrich Eggs, &c. as the *Hodmadods* have: And setting aside their Humane Shape, they differ but little from Brutes. They are tall, strait-bodied, and thin, with small long Limbs. They have great Heads, round Foreheads, and great Brows. Their Eyelids are always half closed, to keep the Flies out of their Eyes; they being so troublesome here, that no fanning will keep them from coming to one's Face; and without the Assistance of both Hands to keep them off, they will creep into ones Nostrils, and Mouth too, if the Lips are not shut very close; so that from their Infancy being thus annoyed with these Insects, they do never open their Eyes as other People: And therefore they cannot see far, unless they hold up their Heads, as if they were looking at somewhat over them.

They have great Bottle-Noses, pretty full Lips, and wide Mouths. The two Fore-teeth of their Upper-jaw are wanting in all of them, Men and Women, old and young; whether they draw them out, I know not: Neither have they any Beards. They are long-visaged, and of a very unpleasing Aspect, having no one graceful Feature in their Faces. Their Hair is black, short and curl'd, like that of the Negroes; and not long and lank like the common *Indians*. The Colour of their Skins, both of their Faces and the rest of their Body, is Coal-black, like that of the Negroes of *Guinea*.

They have no sort of Cloaths, but a piece of the Rind of a Tree tied like a Girdle about their Waists, and a handful of long Grass, or three or four small green Boughs full of Leaves, thrust under their Girdle, to cover their Nakedness.

They have no Houses, but lie in the open Air without any covering; the Earth being their Bed, and the Heaven their Canopy. Whether they cohabit one Man to one Woman, or promiscuously, I know not; but they do live in Companies, 20 or 30 Men, Women, and Children together. Their only Food is a small sort of Fish, which they get by making Wares of Stone across little Coves or Branches of the Sea; every Tide bringing in the small Fish, and there leaving them for a Prey to these People, who constantly attend there to search for them at Low-water. This small Fry I take to be the top of their Fishery: They have no Instruments to catch great Fish, should they come; and such seldom stay to be left behind at Low-water: Nor could we catch any Fish with our Hooks and Lines all the while we lay there. In other Places at Low-water they seek for Cockles, Muscles, and Periwincles: Of these Shell-fish there are fewer still; so that their chiefest dependance is upon what the Sea leaves in their Wares; which, be it much or little they gather up, and march to the Places of their Abode. There the old People that are not able to stir abroad by reason of their Age, and the tender Infants, wait their return; and what Providence has bestowed on them, they presently broil on the Coals, and eat it in common. Sometimes they get as many Fish as makes them a plentiful Banquet; and at other times they scarce get every one a taste: But be it little or much that they get, every one has his part, as well the young and tender, the old and feeble, who are not able to go abroad, as the strong and lusty. When they have eaten they lie down till the next Low-water, and then all that are able march out, be it Night or Day, rain or shine, 'tis all one; they must attend the Wares, or else they must fast: For the Earth affords them no Food at all. There is neither Herb, Root, Pulse nor any sort of Grain for them to eat, that we saw; nor any sort of Bird or Beast that they can catch, having no Instruments wherewithal to do so.

I did not perceive that they did worship any thing. These poor Creatures have a sort of Weapon to defend their Ware, or fight with their Enemies, if they have any that will interfere with their poor Fishery. They did at first endeavour with their Weapons to frighten us, who lying ashore deterr'd them from one of their Fishing-places. Some of them had wooden Swords, others had a sort of Lances. The Sword is a piece of Wood shaped somewhat like a Cutlass. The Lance is a long strait Pole sharp at one end, and hardened afterwards by heat. I saw no Iron, nor any other sort of Metal; therefore it is probable they use Stone-Hatchets, as some *Indians* in *America* do, described in Chap. IV.

How they get their Fire I know not; but probably as *Indians* do, out of Wood. I have seen the *Indians* of *Bon-Airy* do it, and have my self tried the

Experiment: They take a flat piece of Wood that is pretty soft, and make a small dent in one side of it, then they take another hard round Stick, about the bigness of one's little Finger, and sharpening it at one end like a Pencil, they put that sharp end in the hole or dent of the flat soft piece, and then rubbing or twirling the hard piece between the Palms of their Hands, they drill the soft piece till it smoaks, and at last takes Fire.

These People speak somewhat thro' the Throat; but we could not understand one word that they said. We anchored, as I said before, *January* the 5th, and seeing Men walking on the Shore, we presently sent a Canoa to get some Acquaintance with them: for we were in hopes to get some Provision among them. But the Inhabitants, seeing our Boat coming, run away and hid themselves. We searched afterwards three Days in hopes to find their Houses; but found none: yet we saw many places where they had made Fires. At last, being out of hopes to find their Habitations, we searched no farther; but left a great many Toys ashore, in such places where we thought that they would come. In all our search we found no Water, but old Wells on the sandy Bays.

Further Reading

For a good contemporary summary of Dampier's career, covering the buccaneering background and the rise of the South Sea Company, see James Burney, *A Chronological History of the Discoveries in the South Sea* (London: Luke Hansard, 1803–16). The recent most authoritative account is given in the fourth chapter of Glyndwr Williams, *The Great South Sea: English Voyages and Encounters, 1570–1750* (New Haven: Yale University Press, 1997). On the relationship between travel writing and fiction, see Michael McKeon, *The Origins of the English Novel* (Baltimore: Johns Hopkins University Press, 1987); and Percy Adams, *Travellers and Travel Liars* (New York: Dover, 1962).

2

———

LIONEL WAFER CROSSES DARIEN

. . . .

WITH WILLIAM DAMPIER, Lionel Wafer (1660–1705) joined the first big privateering venture into the South Seas in 1680, under the leadership of Bartholomew
Sharp. And like Dampier, Wafer is an acute observer of strange places and unprecedented events, writing of them in a finely paced, laconic style. In the following extract Wafer describes his adventures on the three-month trip back across the
Darien isthmus from the "South" into the "North" Seas, beginning with the injury
to his leg—which makes necessary his sojourn with the Cuna Indians—and ending with his eventual reunion with Dampier and their resumption of privateering.
He assembles a good deal of information about the natural history of the isthmus,
supplying fascinating details of the tribe he lived with, including an extraordinary
account of shamanism, or pawawing. It was owing to his knowledge of the region
(particularly a fine stand of Nicaragua wood) and his close links with the Cuna
that the Darien Company employed him as a consultant when it was planning its
settlement there in 1698.

As well as advising the Darien Company, Wafer's "Secret Report" to the British
government appears to be the first carefully considered estimate of England's options for planting a colony in the South Seas. Besides listing the major harbors on
the mainland coasts of Peru and Chile, Wafer recommends Juan Fernandez as a
tolerable anchorage and a fit place for settlement, having stopped there in 1680
(the scene of Sharp's usurpation by Watling), in 1684 (picking up Will, the Mos-
quito Indian), and again in 1687, when Davis lands the men that Simson will write
about. He catalogs its advantages:

> Part of the Hill[s] are covered with Woods and itt is well watered with small
> Rivalets; there I met with greatest Quantity of Fish I ever see . . . Here may

Black Cattle, Sheep and Goats be Easely Breed, and itt is a good place for a Look Out or to Sett Wounded or Sick Men on Shore, In order for their Recovery (Wafer 1934, 144).

His report of the customs and language of the Cuna people is a different order of information: "a precious document of ethnohistory" (Spate 1983, 2:157). Fletcher of Saltoun, Adam Ferguson, and Johann Gottfried Herder are all interested in Wafer's eyewitness accounts, not least for the connections they suggest between the structure of hunter-gatherer communities and the concept of political virtue in classical republican theory. — JONATHAN LAMB

. . . .

Lionel Wafer, *A New Voyage and Description of the Isthmus of America*, ed. L. E. Elliott Joyce (Oxford: Hakluyt Society, 1934).

« CHAPTER I, PP. 2–29. »

I had a Brother in Jamaica, who was imployed under Sir Thomas Muddiford, in his Plantation at the Angels: And my chief Inducement in undertaking this Voyage was to see him. I staid some time with him, and he settled me in a House at Port-Royal, where I followed my Business of Surgery for some Months. But in a while I met with Capt. Cook, and Capt. Linch, 2 Privateers who were going out from Port-Royal, toward the Coast of Cartagena, and took me along with them. We met other Privateers, on that Coast; but being parted from them by Stress of Weather about Golden-Island, in the Samballoe's, we stood away to the Bastimento's, where we met them again, and several others, who had been at the taking of Portobel, and were rendesvouzed there. Here I first met with Mr. Dampier, and was with him in the Expedition into the S. Seas. For in short, having muster'd up our Forces at Golden-Island, and landed on the Isthmus, we march'd over Land, and took Santa Maria; and made those Excursions into the S. Seas, which Mr. Ringrose relates in the 4th Part of the *History of the Buccaniers*.

Mr. Dampier has told, in his Introduction to his *Voyage Round the World*, in what Manner the Company divided with Reference to Capt. Sharp. I was of Mr. Dampier's Side in that Matter, and of the Number of those who chose rather to return in Boats to the Isthmus, and go back again a toilsome Journey over Land, than stay under a Captain in whom we experienc'd neither Courage nor Conduct. He hath given also an Account of what befel us in that Return, till such Time as by the Carelessness of our Company, my Knee was so scorch'd with gunpowder, that after a few Days further March, I was left behind among the Wild-Indians, in the Isthmus of Darien.

Being now forc'd to stay among them, and having no Means to alleviate the Anguish of my Wound, the Indians undertook to cure me; and apply'd to my Knee some Herbs, which they first chew'd in their Mouths to the Consistency of a Paste, and putting it on a Plantain-Leaf, laid it upon the Sore. This prov'd so effectual, that in about 20 Days Use of this Poultess, which they applied fresh every Day, I was perfectly cured; except only a Weakness in that Knee, which remain'd long after, and a Benummedness which I sometimes find in it to this Day. Yet they were not altogether so kind in other Respects; for some of them look'd on us very scurvily, throwing green Plantains to us, as we sat cringing and shivering, as you would Bones to a Dog. Not that they were naturally inclin'd to use us thus roughly, for they are generally a kind and free-hearted People; but they had taken some particular Offence, upon the Account of our Friends who left us, who had in a Manner awed the Indian Guides they took with them for the Remainder of their Journey, and made them go with them very much against their Wills; the Severity of the rainy Season being then so great, that even the Indians themselves had no Mind for travelling, tho' they are little curious either as to the Weather or Ways.

When Gopson, Hingson, and I had lived 3 or 4 Days in this Manner, the other 2, Spratlin and Bowman, whom we left behind at the River Congo, on the 6th Day of our Journey, found their way to us; being exceedingly fatigued with rambling so long among the wild Woods and Rivers without Guides, and having no other Sustenance but a few Plantains they found here and there. They told us of George Gainy's Disaster, whose drowning Mr. Dampier relates p. 17. They saw him lie dead on the Shore which the Floods were gone off from, with the Rope twisted about him, and his Money at his Neck; but they were so fatigued, they car'd not to meddle with it. These after their coming up to us, continued with us for about a Fortnight longer, at the same Plantation where the main Body of our Company had left us; and our Provision was still at the same Rate, and the Countenances of the Indians as stern towards us as ever, having yet no News of their Friends whom our Men had taken as their Guides. Yet notwithstanding their Disgust, they took care of my Wound; which by this Time was pretty well healed, and I was enabled to walk about. But at length not finding their Men return as they expected, they were out of Patience, and seem'd resolved to revenge on us the Injuries which they supposed our Friends had done to theirs. To this End they held frequent Consultations how they should dispose of us: Some were for killing us, others for keeping us among them, and others for carrying us to the Spaniards, thereby to ingratiate themselves with them. But the greatest Part of them mortally hating the Spaniards, this last Project was soon laid aside; and they came to this Resolution, to forbear doing any thing to us, till so much Time were expir'd as they thought might reasonably be allow'd for the Return of their Friends, whom our Men had taken with them as Guides to the North Sea-Coast; and this, as they computed would be 10 Days, reckoning it up to us on their Fingers.

The Time was now almost expir'd, and having no News of the Guides, the Indians began to suspect that our Men had either murther'd them, or carried them away with them; and seem'd resolv'd thereupon to destroy us. To this end they prepared a great Pile of Wood to burn us, on the 10th Day; and told us what we must trust to when the Sun went down; for they would not execute us till then. But it so happened that Lacenta, their Chief, passing that way, disswaded them from that Cruelty, and proposed to them to send us down towards the North-side, and 2 Indians with us, who might inform themselves from the Indians near the Coast, what was become of the Guides. They readily hearkn'd to this Proposal, and immediately chose 2 Men to conduct us to the North-side. One of these had been all along, an inveterate Enemy to us; but the other was the kind Indian, who was so much our Friend as to rise in the Night and get us ripe Plantains.

The next Day therefore we were dismissed with our 2 Guides, and marched joyfully for 3 Days; being well assured we should not find that our Men had done any Hurt to their Guides. The first 3 Days we march'd through nothing but Swamps, having great Rains, with much Thundering and Lightning; and lodg'd every Night under the dropping Trees, upon the cold Ground. The third Night we lodg'd on a small Hill, which by the next Morning was become an Island: For those great Rains had made such a Flood, that all the low Land about it was cover'd deep with Water. All this while we had no Provision, except a Handful of dry Maiz our Indian Guides gave us the first 2 Days: But this being spent, they return'd Home again, and left us to shift for our selves. . . .

[For two days they struggle to cross two swollen rivers, not sure of their direction, and short of food; out of bark they make canoes to float down-river.]

By that time we had finished our Bark-logs it was Night, and we took up our Lodging on a small Hill, where we gathered about a Cartload of Wood, and made a Fire, intending to set out with our Bark-logs the next Morning. But not long after Sun-set, it fell a Raining as if Heaven and Earth would meet; which Storm was accompanied with horrid Claps of Thunder, and such Flashes of Lightning, of a sulphurous Smell, that we were almost stifled in the open Air. Thus it continued till 12 a-Clock at Night; when to our great Terror, we could hear the Rivers roaring on both sides us; but 'twas so dark, that we could see nothing but the Fire we had made, except when a flash of Lightning came. Then we could see all over the Hill, and perceive the Water approaching us; which in less than half an Hour carried away our Fire. This drove us all to our shifts, every Man seeking some means to save himself from the threatning Deluge. We also sought for small Trees to climb: For the place abounded with great Cotton Trees, of a prodigious bigness from the Root upward, and at least 40 or 50 Foot clear without Branches, so that there was no climbing up them. For my own Part, I was in a great Consternation, and running to save my Life, I very opportunely met with a large Cotton Tree, which by some accident, or thro' Age, was become Rotten, and hollow on one Side; having a Hole in it at about the Height of 4 Foot from the Ground. I immediately got up it as well as I could: And in the Cavity I found a Knob, which serv'd me for a Stool; and there I sat down almost Head and Heels together, not having room enough to stand or sit upright. In this condition I sat wishing for Day: but being fatigued with Travel, though very hungry withal, and cold, I fell asleep: But was soon awaken'd by the Noise of great Trees which were brought down by the Flood; and came with such force against the Tree, that they made it shake.

When I awoke I found my Knees in the Water, though the lowest Part of my hollow Trunk was, as I said, 4 Foot above the Ground; and the Water was running as swift, as it 'twere in the middle of the River. The Night was still very Dark, but only when the flashes of Lightning came: which made it so dreadful and terrible, that I forgot my Hunger, and was wholly taken up with praying to God to spare my Life. While I was praying and meditating thus on my sad Condition, I saw the Morning-Star appear; by which I knew that Day was at hand: This cheared my drooping Spirits; and in less than half an Hour the Day began to dawn, the Rain and Lightning ceased, and the Waters abated, insomuch that by that time the Sun was up, the Water was gone off from my Tree. Then I ventur'd out of my cold Lodging; but being stiff and the Ground slippery, I could scarce stand: Yet I made a shift to ramble to the Place where we had made our fire, but found no Body there. Then I call'd out aloud, but was answer'd only with my own Eccho; which struck such Terror into me, that I fell down as dead, being oppress'd both with Grief and Hunger; this being the 7th Day of our Fast, save only the *Maccaw*-berries before related.

Being in this Condition, despairing of Comfort for want of my Consorts, I lay sometime on the wet Ground, till at last I heard a Voice hard by me which in some sort revived me; but especially when I saw Mr. Hingson one of my Companions, and the rest found us presently after; having all sav'd themselves by climbing small Trees. We greeted each other with Tears in our Eyes, and returned Thanks to God for our deliverance.

The first thing we did in the Morning was to look after our Bark-logs or Rafts which we had left tied to a Tree, in order to prosecute our Voyage down the River; but coming to the Place where we left them, we found them sunk and full of Water, which had got into the hollow of the Bamboes, contrary to our Expectation; for we thought they would not have admitted so much as Air, but have been like large Bladders full blown: But it seems there were Cracks in them which we did not perceive, and perhaps made in them by our Carelessness in working them; for the Vessels made of these hollow Bamboes are wont to hold Water very well. . . .

But to return to my Story: being thus frustrated of our Design of going down the Stream, or of crossing either of these Rivers, by Reason of the sinking of our Bark-logs, we were glad to think of returning back to the Indian-Settlement, and Coasted up the River-side in the same Track we came down by. As our Hunger was ready to carry our Eyes to any Object that might afford us some Relief, it hapned that we espied a Deer fast asleep: Which we design'd if possible to get, and in order to it we came so very near, that we might almost have thrown our selves on him: But one of our Men putting the Muzzle of his Gun close to him, and the shot not being wadded, tumbled out, just before the Gun went off, and did the Deer no hurt; but starting up at the Noise, he took the River and swam over. As long as our way lay by the River side, we made a shift to keep it well enough: But being now to take leave of the River, in order to seek for the Indians Habitation, we were much at a loss. This was the Eighth Day, and we had no Sustenence beside the *Maccaw*-Berries we had got, and the Pith of a *Bibby*-Tree we met with, which we split and eat very savourly. . . .

[They find an Indian settlement, and are conducted along the river to Lacenta's house.]

This House is situated on a fine little Hill, on which grows the stateliest Grove of Cotton Trees that ever I saw. The Bodies of these Trees were generally 6 Foot in Diameter, nay some 8, 9, 10, 11; for 4 Indians and my self took hand in hand round a Tree, and could not fathom it by 3 Foot. Here was likewise a stately Plantain-walk, and a Grove of other small Trees, that would make a Pleasant artificial Wilderness, if Industry and Art were bestowed on it.

The Circumference of this pleasant little Hill, contains at least 100 Acres of Land; and is a Peninsula of an oval Form, almost surrounded with 2 great Rivers, one coming from the East, the other from the West; which approaching within 40 Foot of each other, at the Front of the Peninsula, separate again, embracing the Hill, and meet on the other Side, making there one pretty large River which runs very swift. There is therefore but one Way to come in towards this Seat; which as I before observed is not above 40 Foot wide, between the Rivers on each Side; and 'tis fenced with hollow Bamboes, Popes-heads and Prickle-pears, so thick set from one Side the Neck of Land to the other, that 'tis impossible for an Enemy to approach it.

On this Hill live 50 principal Men of the Country, all under Lacenta's Command, who is a Prince over all the South-part of the Isthmus of Darien; the Indians both there and on the North-side also, paying him great Respect: But the South-side is his Country, and this Hill his Seat or Palace. There is only one Canoa belonging to it, which serves to ferry over Lacenta and the rest of them.

When we were arrived at this Place, Lacenta discharged our Guides, and sent them back again, telling us, that 'twas not possible for us to travel to the North-side at this Season; for the rainy Season was now in its height, and Travelling very bad; but told us we should stay with him, and he would take care of us: And we were forc'd to comply with him.

We had not been long here before an Occurrence happen'd, which tended much to the increasing the good Opinion Lacenta and his People had conceiv'd of us, and brought me into particular Esteem with them.

It so happen'd, that one of Lacenta's Wives being indisposed, was to be let Blood; which the Indians perform in this Manner: The Patient is seated on a Stone in the River, and one with a small Bow shoots little Arrows in the naked Body of the Patient, up and down; shooting them as fast as he can, and not missing any Part. But the Arrows are gaged, so that they penetrate no farther than we generally thrust our Lancets: And if by chance they hit a Vein which is full of Wind and the Blood spurts out a little they will leap and skip about, shewing many Antick Gestures, by way of Rejoycing and Triumph.

I was by while this was performing on Lacenta's Lady: And perceiving their Ignorance told Lacenta, that if he pleased, I would shew him a bet-

ter way, without putting the Patient to so much Torment. Let me see, says
he; and at his Command I bound up her Arm with a Piece of Bark, and
with my Lancet breathed a Vein: But this rash Attempt had like to have
cost me my Life. For Lacenta seeing the Blood issue out in a Stream,
which us'd to come Drop by Drop, got hold of his Lance and swore by his
Tooth, that if she did any otherwise than well, he would have my Heart's
Blood. I was not moved, but desired him to be patient, and I drew off
about 12 Ounces, and bound up her Arm, and desired she might rest till
the next Day: By which Means the Fever abated, and she had not another
Fit. This gain'd me so much Reputation, that Lacenta came to me, and before all his Attendants, bowed and kiss'd my Hand. Then the rest came
thick about me, and some kissed my Hand, others my Knee, and some my
Foot: After which I was taken up in a Hammock, and carried on Men's
Shoulders, Lacenta himself making a Speech in my Praise, and commending me as much superiour to any of their Doctors. Thus I was carried about from Plantation to Plantation, and lived in great Splendour and
Repute, administring both Physick and Phlebotomy to those that wanted.
For though I lost my Salves and Plaisters, when the Negro ran away with
my Knapsack, yet I preserv'd a Box of Instruments, and a few Medica-
ments wrapt up in an Oil Cloth, by having them in my Pocket, where I
generally carried them.

I lived thus some Months among the Indians, who in a Manner ador'd
me. Some of these Indians had been Slaves to the Spaniards, and had
made their Escapes; which I suppose was the Cause of their expressing a
Desire of Baptism: But more to have an European Name given them than
for any thing they know of Christianity.

During my Abode with Lacenta, I often accompanied him a Hunting,
wherein he took great Delight, here being good Game. I was one Time
about the Beginning of the dry Season, accompanying him toward the
South-East part of the Country, and we pass'd by a River where the
Spaniards were gathering Gold. I took this River to be one of those which
comes from the Gulph of St. Michael. When we came near the Place
where they wrought, we stole softly through the Woods, and placing our
selves behind the great Trees, looked on them a good while, they not seeing us. The Manner of their getting Gold is as follows. They have little
wooden Dishes which they dip softly into the Water, and take it up half
full of Sand, which they draw gently out of the Water; and every dipping
they take up Gold mix'd with the Sand Water, more or less. This they
shake, and the Sand riseth, and goes over the Brims of the Dish with the
Water; but the Gold settles to the Bottom. This done they bring it out and

FIG. 2. *The Indians' Maner of Bloodletting.* Published in Lionel Wafer, *A New Voyage and Description of the Isthmus of America* (London: James Knapton, 1699).

dry it in the Sun, and then pound it in a Mortar. Then they take it out and spread it on Paper, and having a Load-stone they move that over it, which draws all the Iron, &c. from it, and then leaves the Gold clean from Ore or Filth; and this they bottle up in Gourds or Calabashes. In this Manner they work during the dry Season, which is 3 Months; for in the wet Time the Gold is washed from the Mountains by violent Rains, and then commonly the Rivers are very deep; but now in the gathering Season, when they are fallen again, they are not above a Foot deep. Having spent the dry Season in gathering, they imbark in small Vessels for Santa Maria Town; and if they meet with good Success and a favourable Time, they carry with them, by Report (for I learnt these Particulars of a Spaniard whom we took at Santa Maria under Captain Sharp) 18 or 20 thousand Pound Weight of Gold: But whether they gather more or less, 'tis incredible to report the Store of Gold which is yearly wash'd down out of these Rivers.

During these Progresses I made with Lacenta, my 4 Companions staid behind at his Seat; but I had by this Time so far ingratiated my self with Lacenta, that he would never go any where without me, and I plainly perceiv'd he intended to keep me in this Country all the Days of my Life; which raised some anxious Thoughts in me, but I conceal'd them as well as I could.

Pursuing our Sport one Day, it hapned we started a Pecary, which held the Indians and their Dogs in Play the greatest Part of the Day; till Lacenta was almost spent for want of Victuals, and was so troubled at his ill Success that he impatiently wish'd for some better Way of managing this Sort of Game. I now understood their Language pretty well, and finding what troubled him, I took this Opportunity to attempt the getting my Liberty to depart, by commending to him our English Dogs, and making an Offer of bringing him a few of them from England, if he would suffer me to go thither for a short Time. He demurr'd at this Motion a-while; but at length he swore by his Tooth, laying his Fingers on it, that I should have my Liberty, and for my Sake the other 4 with me; provided I would promise and swear by my Tooth, that I would return and marry among them; for he had made me a Promise of his Daughter in Marriage, but she was not then marriageable. I accepted of the Conditions: And he further promised, that at my Return he would do for me beyond my Expectation.

I return'd him Thanks, and was the next Day dismiss'd under the Convoy of 7 lusty Fellows; and we had 4 Women to carry our Provisions, and my Cloaths, which were only a Linnen Frock and a pair of Breeches. These I saved to cover my Nakedness, if ever I should come among Christians again; for at this Time I went naked as the Salvages, and was painted by their Women; but I would not suffer them to prick my Skin, to rub the Paint in, as they use to do, but only to lay it on in little Specks.

Thus we departed from the Neighbourhood of the South Seas, where Lacenta was hunting, to his Seat or Palace, where I arrived in about 15

Days, to the great Joy of my Consorts; who had staid there during this hunting Expedition I made with Lacenta to the South-East.

After many Salutations on both Sides, and some joyful Tears, I told them how I got my Liberty of Lacenta, and what I promised at my Return; and they were very glad at the Hopes of getting away, after so long a Stay in a Savage Country.

I staid here some few Days till I was refreshed, and then with my Companions marched away for the North-Seas, having a strong Convoy of armed Indians for our Guides.

We travelled over many very high Mountains; at last we came to one surpassing the rest in Heighth, to which we were 4 Days gradually ascending, tho' now and then with some Descent between while. Being on the Top, I perceiv'd a strange Giddiness in my Head; and enquiring both of my Companions, and the Indians, they all assured me they were in the like Condition; which I can only impute to the Height of the Mountains, and the Clearness of the Air. I take this part of the Mountains to have been higher than either that which we cross'd with Captain Sharp, or that which Mr. Dampier and the rest of our Party cross'd in their Return: For from this Eminence, the Tops of the Mountains over which we passed before, seem'd very much below us, and sometimes we could not see them for the Clouds between; but when the Clouds flew over the Tops of the Hill, they would break, and then we could discern them, looking as it were thro' so many Loop-holes.

I desired two Men to lie on my Legs, while I laid my Head over that Side of the Mountain which was most perpendicular; but could see no Ground for the Clouds that were between. The *Indians* carried us over a Ridge so narrow that we were forced to straddle over on our Breeches; and the *Indians* took the same Care of themselves, handing their Bows, Arrows, and Luggage, from one to another. As we descended we were all cured of our Giddiness. . . .

The next Morning we set forward, and in 2 Days Time arrived at the Sea-side, and were met by 40 of the best Sort of Indians in the Country, who congratulated our coming and welcom'd us to their Houses. They were all in their finest Robes, which are long white Gowns, reaching to their Ancles, with Fringes at the Bottom, and in their Hands they had half Pikes. But of these Things, and such other Particulars as I observ'd during my Abode in this Country, I shall say more when I come to describe it.

We presently enquired of these *Indians* when they expected any Ships? They told us they knew not, but would enquire; and therefore they sent for one of their Conjurers, who immediately went to work to raise the Devil, to enquire of him at what Time a Ship would arrive here; for they are very expert and skilful in their Sort of Diabolical Conjurations. We were in the House with them, and they first began to work with making a Partition with Hammocks, that the *Pawawers*, for so they call these Conjurers, might be by themselves. They continued some time at their Exercise, and we could hear them make most hideous Yellings and Shrieks; imitating the Voices of all their kind of Birds and Beasts. With their own Noise, they joyn'd that of several Stones struck together, and of Conch-shells, and of a sorry Sort of Drums made of hollow Bamboes, which they beat upon; making a jarring Noise also with Strings fasten'd to the larger Bones of Beasts. And every now and then they would make a dreadful Exclamation, and clattering all of a sudden, would as suddenly make a Pause and a profound Silence. But finding that after a considerable Time no Answer was made them, they concluded that 'twas because we were in the House, and so turn'd us out, and went to work again. But still finding no Return, after an Hour or more, they made a new Search in our Apartment; and finding some of our Cloaths hanging up in a Basket against the Wall, they threw 'em out of Doors in great Disdain. Then they fell once more to their *Pawawing*; and after a little time they came out with their Answer, but all in a Muck-sweat; so that they first went down to the River and washed themselves, and then came and deliver'd the Oracle to us, which was to this Effect: That the 10th Day from that Time there would arrive two Ships; and that in the Morning of the 10th Day we should hear first one Gun, and sometime after that another; that one of us should die soon after; and that going aboard we should lose one of our Guns: All which fell out exactly according to the Prediction.

For on the 10th Day in the Morning we heard the Guns, first one, and then another, in the Manner that was told us; and one of our Guns or Fusees was lost in going aboard the Ships; For we 5, and 3 of the Indians went off to the Ships in a *Canoa*; but as we cross'd the Bar of the River it overset, where Mr. Gopson, one of my Consorts, was like to be drowned; and tho' we recover'd him out of the Water, yet he lost his Gun according to the Prediction. I know not how this happen'd as to his Gun; but ours were all lash'd down to the Side of the Canoa: And in the *West-Indies* we never go into a Canoa but a little Matter oversets, but we make fast our Guns to the Sides or Seats: And I suppose Mr. *Gopson*, who was a very careful and sensible Man, had lash'd down his also, tho' not fast enough.

Being over-set, and our Canoa turn'd upside down, we got to Shore as well as we could, and dragg'd Mr. Gopson with us, tho' with Difficulty.

Then we put off again, and kept more along the Shore, and at length stood over to La Sound's Key, where the 2 Ships lay, an English Sloop, and a Spanish Tartan, which the English had taken but 2 or 3 Days before. We knew by the Make of this last that it was a Spanish Vessel, before we came up with it: But seeing it in Company with an English one, we thought they must be Consorts; and whether the Spanish Vessel should prove to be under the English one, or the English under that, we were resolv'd to put it to the Venture, and get aboard, being quite tir'd with our Stay among the wild Indians. The Indians were more afraid of its being a Vessel of Spaniards, their Enemies as well as ours: For this was another Particular they told us 10 Days before, when they were *Pawawing*, that when their Oracle inform'd them that 2 Vessels would arrive at this Time, they understood by their Daemons Answer, that one of them would be an English one; but as to the other, he spake so dubiously, that they were much afraid it would be a Spanish one; and 'twas not without great Difficulty that we now perswaded them to go aboard with us; which was another remarkable Circumstance, since this Vessel was not only a Spanish one, but actually under the Command of the Spaniards at the Time of the *Pawawing*, and some Days after, till taken by the English.

We went aboard the English Sloop, and our *Indian* Friends with us, and were receiv'd with a very hearty Welcome. The 4 Englishmen with me were presently known and caress'd by the Ship's Crew; but I sat a while cringing upon my Hams among the Indians, after their Fashion, painted as they were, and all naked but only about the Waist, and with my Nose-piece (of which more hereafter) hanging over my Mouth. I was willing to try if they knew me in this Disguise; and 'twas the better Part of an Hour before one of the Crew, looking more narrowly upon me, cry'd out, *Here's our Doctor*; and immediately they all congratulated my Arrival among them. I did what I could presently to wash off my Paint; but 'twas near a Month before I could get tolerably rid of it, having had my Skin so long stain'd with it, and the Pigment dry'd on in the Sun: And when it did come off, 'twas usually with the peeling off of Skin and all. As for Mr. Gopson, we brought him alive to the Ship, yet he did not recover his Fatigues, and his drenching in the Water, but having languish'd aboard about 3 Days, he died there at La Sound's Key; and his Death verify'd another Part of the *Pawawer's* Prediction. Our Indians, having been kindly entertained aboard for about 6 or 7 Days; and many others of them, who went to and fro with their Wives and Children, and Lacenta among them, visiting us about a Fortnight or 3 Weeks, we at length took leave of them, except 2 or 3 of them who would needs go with us to Windward; and we set sail, with the

Tartan in our Company, first to the more Eastern Isles of the Samballoes, and then towards the Coast of *Cartagene*.

But I shall not enter into the Discourse of our Voyage after this, Mr. Dampier, who was in the same Vessel, having done it particularly. It may suffice just to intimate, That I was cruising with him up and down the West-India Coast and Islands, partly under Capt. Wright, and partly under Capt. Yanky; till such time as Capt. Yanky left Mr. Dampier and the rest under Capt. Wright, at the Isle of Salt Tortuga, as Mr. Dampier relates in the 3d Chapter of his *Voyage round the World*, p. 58. I went then away with Capt. Yanky first to the Isle of Ash where the French took us, as he relates occasionally, Chap. 4. p. 68. as also their turning us there ashore; our being taken in by Capt. Tristian another French Man; his carrying us with him almost to Petit-Guaves; our Men seizing the Ship when he was gone ashore, carrying it back to the Isle of Ash, and there taking in the rest of our Crew: The taking the French Ship with Wines, and the other in which Capt. Cook, who was then of our Crew, went afterwards to the South-Seas, after having first been at Virginia: So that we arrived in Virginia with these Prizes about 8 or 9 Months after Mr. Dampier came thither. I set out with him also in that new Expedition to the South-Seas under Capt. Cook, though he forgot to mention me in that Part of his Voyages. We went round Terra del Fuego, and so up the South-Sea Coast, along Chili, Peru, and Mexico, as he relates at large in his 4th, 5th, 6th, 7th, and 8th Chapters. There, p. 223, he tells how Capt. Davis, who had succeeded Capt. Cook at his Death, broke off Consortship with Capt. Swan, whom we had met with in the South-Seas. That himself being desirous to stand over to the East-Indies, went aboard Capt. Swan: But I remain'd aboard the same Ship, now under Capt. Davis, and return'd with him the way I came. Some few Particulars that I observ'd in that Return, I shall speak of at the Conclusion of the Book: In the mean while, having given this Summary account of the Course of my Travels, from my first parting with Mr. Dampier in the Isthmus, till my last leaving him in the South-Seas, I shall now go on with the particular Description of the Isthmus of America, which was the main Thing I intended publishing in these Relations.

Further Reading

L. E. Elliott Joyce's edition of Wafer's *New Voyage and Description of the Isthmus of America* has a detailed introduction and includes Wafer's "Secret Report," in which he recommends Juan Fernandez as a promising settlement (Oxford: Hakluyt Society, 1934). For the buccaneering background, see O. H. K. Spate, *The Pacific since Magellan*, vol. 2, *Monopolists and Free-booters* (Minneapolis: University of Minnesota Press, 1983). Wafer has always enjoyed the esteem of ethnographers. Herder quotes from *A New Voyage* to forge an ambitious link between the remote areas of America and the forests of Germany in terms of "that proud savage love of liberty and war": "A few centuries only have elapsed since the inhabitants of Germany were patagonians." *Outlines of a Philosophy of the History of Man*, trans. T. Churchill (New York: Bergman, 1800), 158–64. Adam Ferguson cites Wafer along with Charlevoix and Colden as an authority on property relations among Indian tribes in *An Essay on the History of Civil Society* (New Brunswick: Transaction, 1980), 84 n. More recently Michael Taussig cites him in a discussion of mimicry among the Cuna people in *Mimesis and Alterity: A Particular History of the Senses* (London and New York: Routledge, 1993), 7.

3

RICHARD SIMSON AT
JUAN FERNANDEZ

. . . .

RICHARD SIMSON sailed from Plymouth in 1689 as surgeon on the *Welfare*, under the command of Captain John Strong. The owners of the *Welfare* were trying to realize the dream of a trading base in the Pacific that was to exercise the commercial imagination of the English in the first quarter of the eighteenth century, when speculation in South Seas stock fed off the sort of fantasy found in Defoe's *New Voyage Round the World* (1724). However, the promised return of 1600 percent on the investment in the voyage resulted in a loss of £1200, which would have been worse had Strong not picked up a couple of prizes in the English Channel at the end of his voyage.

Simson's narrative is not only vivid and cleverly self-conscious (as when he compares his list of what was found in the abandoned Indian canoes with the curious inventories of "the Author of Garagantua"), but it culminates in an account of four Juan Fernandez castaways and their black slaves. Scarcely alluded to, save very briefly by John Campbell (1764, 1:133–37) and James Burney (who quotes bits of Simson, 1803–16, 4:137, 210, 335), this narrative of castaways on Juan Fernandez comes shortly after the celebrated account of William, the Miskito Indian left on the island by Sharp and Watling in 1681 and picked up three years later by Cowley and Dampier. And it predates Alexander Selkirk's famous solitude, which began when he was left on Juan Fernandez by Stradling in 1704 and ended when Rogers picked him up in 1709 (see Ayres 1694, 45; Hacke 1699, 7; Rogers 1712, 125–30; and Dampier 1729, 1:84). Simson's narrative throws into stark relief the questions of power and violence that Defoe only begins to explore in his fictionalization of Selkirk's marooning, *Robinson Crusoe* (1719). The men found by the

Welfare were four of the five sailors left there in 1687 by Captain Davis, commander of the *Batchelor's Delight*, each of whom was supplied with weapons, stores, and a black servant (J. Campbell 1764, 1:88; J. Burney 1803–16, 4:210, 335). Although it appears that they tried to establish a commonwealth, or a federation, where each was secured his own portion of the island and guaranteed sufficient privacy to begin the work of spiritual reformation, the story takes a more sinister turn when it comes to the slave rebellion and how it was put down. Suddenly the privacy and the piety of the castaways is exchanged for corporate violence pursued "in the Old Privateer stile," and no more is heard about the work of redemption. In some respects their story repeats the pattern of violence meditated by Crusoe against the cannibals, or by the Houyhnhnms against the Yahoos; for in all three narratives the utopian possibilities of desert-island life are introduced at first as the bulwark against the forces of savagery, only to demonstrate in the end a cruelty whose impulse belongs not to the state of unimproved nature but to the degeneration of an ambitious civility (Raynal 1783, 5:37–83; Pagden 1995a; G. Williams 1994).
— JONATHAN LAMB

. . . .

Richard Simson, *Observations Made During a South-Sea Voyage, 1689,* **Sloane MS 86 (672), British Library, London.**

The Design of our Voyage (of which afterwards) being part to make Discoveryes, Oblidged our Commander to stay some time at this place [Saint Iago]. The sound in several places was so full of Weeds, that the Ship could hardly make her way; and if one might Judge by appearance, there it was, we sayled rather through a Medow then an Arme of the Sea, and notwithstanding our Officers Courage in the Attempt and Skill in the Management we grazed (as they call it) the Ship drawing 3 fathoms water, we had just so much to carry us, and the Channell being hard gravel, gave a new but Melancholy diversion to the Ear, our sayling being for some time extreemly rugged and attended with a rattling, like that of hackney Coach in the streets of London . . . Before I proceed farther it will be convenient to speak something of the designe of the voyage; I have said, that to make discoveries was part of it. As to the rest; there was Information given of a rich wreak or two, at or near to St Helena, not farr from the Bay of Puna, about two Degrees South Latitude, and for Greater encouragement and our better reception, in those Spanish plantations, we had a Cargo of such goods as were thought most usefull amongst them, such as

Bayes, Stockins, Arms, & other Iron work as Hatchets, Hows &c. and withall, it was farther represented and alledged, that this Merchandize would bring a return of sixteen hundred p cent. Thus encouraged, and for the pursuance of such great and honourable purposes, we were armed with King William and Queen Maryes Comission.

[The crew of the *Welfare* have a difficult time going through the Straits of Magellan, where they are detained by bad weather for three months.]

Tis time now to give an Account of the Inhabitants of the Straits . . . They are a very barbarous people, they travell in small colonies, and pass from one side of the Straits to another in small canoes, made of the Bark of Trees, which they sew together ingeniously enough, considering their Tools . . . Their houses are in the forme of Bee-hives; and not above 16 or 18 times larger, made of branches of Trees, into which they creep on all foure. [When they eat seals' flesh] the raw and rank morsell is first received by the Matrone, or Mother of the black Clann . . . She chews the Morsel for some time, then delivers it to an other, she does the like, then hands it about to a third, and so it goes round, and is good teeth proof . . . But there is an other way of their subsisting which is circulatory and itinerant. They goe from Beach to Beach a Muscelling, and it is worth the observation, that amongst other ordinary sorts of this shell ffish, there is a very Extraordinary and rich sort both for size and quality, being larger then others and exceeding white and plump, with perfect bloud running in and from visible veines, their sweetness to the tast answers the rest of their description . . . those faire and large Mussells are not only very gratefull to the palate, but of a very kindly digestion, affording copious and speedy nourishment. . . . When they have pickt and chosen, from one bank, they pass to another, and so round till they come where they begun, and find them encreased and muliplyed a new . . . Once unfortunately they perceived our ships crew a ffishing with a seene or Nett about 80 ffathom long. The great number of ffishes they caught, raised first their amazement and then their indignation.

[In order to placate the inhabitants, they are invited on board.]

There were about 30 of the Indians; the oldest and most venerable person amongst them led up the rest, besides the precedency he had, there were other particuler marks of distinction about him being gross and brutal Badges of an Antient dignity that was altogether corrospondent; ffor wheras they meaner sort content themselves with one kinde of Oaker for colouring their ffaces the old sophester (as others of his quality) had many; and whilst they bind the head and Hair with a piece of Skin or perhaps a Clout, he and others of his ranke take the two wings of a large ffowle, and fasten them to their heads, with the Tipps uper most, which by reason of the sittuation are not unlike our Granadeer's Caps . . . The Old Gentleman who first accosted our men with such splended accouterments (as I have said) and habited in the richest furr's with a Bow & Arrow, Sling, Bone-Dagger &c; drew near & with hands and Eyes lift up to Heaven bow'd himself thrice before the Company, all this while muttering somewhat with a great deal of Affection and zeale. Then he pointed up to Heaven and offer'd to carress our companyes leader, by which obscure signes it was understood by some that the poor Creaturs imagined that the Gods had come or sent to deliver them; which disposition of mind in the Indians, during any great oppression they lay under is frequently observed in the History of that people translated by Sir Paul Rycaut.

[One Indian is particularly curious, dubbed John Englishman, who is amused with European goods until the time comes for him to go home.]

He went often to the poop, and looked down on the water with wet eyes, which he lift up sometimes to measure the distance he was to swim (being two Miles if he was so resolved). Then he calls out Squa (pointing to the Shoar) which word some of our men understood to signifie a Wife or Concubine, then he pointed to the Victuals he had gott in the Skirts of his Mantle, and then to the Shoar againe, which genourous and communicative Intention (as we understood it) of imparting with his shee what he had gott a board was the moving inducement to our people to despach the Boat with him a shoar. But John Englishman as aftwards appear'd liked no such doeings he drank deep of reveng. Ashor he goes, consults with his Country men,—was one of the forwardest that led them, and offered to molest our Ships company, which provoked them in their own defence, and by way of prevention, before the maine forces of the Indians were gathered together, to fire amongst them. There were some of them wounded, and the said John, tis thought was killed.

[The Indians flee and the Europeans rifle their canoes.]

The Author of Garagantua had a good hand at drawing up such Curious Inventories. For my part, because I would be concise, I but touch at the particulars, enumerating the various sorts of things so near as I can remember of which the odd collection did consist, which were stones, Marcassites, Bones, Calabashes, Baggs of Seal-Oyles, Baggs of Oaker, of divers sorts, Arrows, Shafts & heads, Javelins Shafts & heads; Bows, Bowstrings, fflintstones—Sulphur Mineral, Indented Daggers cut out of Bone, Seals flesh dryed, a Childs fflesh dryed, Beads, Braceletts, Slings, some few pieces of old Iron sharpned which they had taken up from some Shipwreck; Wings, ffeathers, ffurs, Netts. . . .

I shall not particularize the tossings we had the Night before [they enter the South Seas], and after we weather'd the Cape, We had reason to believe that then, and there all the powers of darkness were mett, whilst we expected every Minuit that the Ship should yeeld to ffate, and (with us all) as a Sacrafice to the Infernall Maclice be torn into a thousand pieces, so it was that often we were clear of the said Cape during the darkness of the next ensuing night, we were so Ignorant of our way, that we steered a direct contrary course, till by the help of the first appearance of day, we but very narrowly missed splitting on those tremendous Rocks that fright that Coast . . . It was our *welcome* in the South-Seas. If it was any signe, and if we may judge what we found, it was a signe of a very bad welcome . . . On the 29th of the month of May we reconed there had died one tenth part of our Company; and the Cloaths of him that died were sold at the Mast according to the Custom.

[They find it impossible to trade among the Spanish settlements on the Chilean and Peruvian coasts, nor can they locate the French privateers their commission gives them a license to plunder. The attempted salvage is a failure. They head for Juan Fernandez.]

On the 11th Day of September we discover'd a large Island, which we supposed to be the right fferdinando; The Pinnace was sent a shoare, about Eight of the Clock at night. The Company brought us back an account, That the Island was very fruitfull, & full of Goates, we observed abundance of red Mold which signified there were Iron Mines there, but wished heartily it had been better Mettall. Before daylight was spent we saw a fire on the higher place of the Island; we had a great Suspition that the Pinnace (then a shore) had mett with bad Company, upon its return, we concluded that it was kindled by the persons we were told lived in the Island.

September the 12th. The pinnace was sent a shore betimes and returned with Goate & two Kidds, and about 200 lusty Cavalloes, and brought aboard two of the English men that were resident there; The History of their Life and Adventures would be worth the while. They informed us, we might load the Shipp with Goates if we pleased. They had of tame Stock of that kinde the matter of 300, before the Spaniards robed them, which misfortune frequently befell them; on such occasions they betook themselves to the Mountains, thro which they had digged passages, and made Lines of Communication with ropes for the Convenient retreat upon any such danger. The Privateers that they came along with to the South-Seas lay before Panama, where they Joyning with more forces made up 900 Men. The two English men staid with us all Night, and a day or two after they brought their other two associates and their Boyes aboard of us.

Our Commander had come a great deal out of his road to carry them home, believing that his kindness therein would have been gratefully accepted; but they subtilly pretended that they lived as Kings in the Islands having no Law, or Superiour to Controule them, that they wanted for Nothing, Turnipp-topps supplying their want of Bread, their ffood being Venison, their drink Goates milk and excellent water, ffor several dayes they made show as they had been of all the Men in the world, the most Content with their Condition, thinking with themselves that our Captain would allow them wages, as he did other Seamen; but they pulld off this Vaisard before we sayled from thence, and declared themselves glad to have the oppertunity of seeing their owne Country once more, nay they plainly told us that they resolved to goe off the Island with the next Privateere that should happen to victualing there.

One of them spake to me in the Old Privateere stile that we had a Captain did not love himselfe, otherwise he would venture to make himselfe and Company, and by and by that the Captain must needs have an Estate that was so civill to Dons when it was in his power to gett vast riches; he thought it strang, that our Commander had not run the risque as he termed it; I answered him, if our Captain should have run it he must have run all his Life for it, as they were resolved to doe. . . .

The Island is woody, and bears an Excellent Herbage; Turnipps, Sorrill, and Cabbage trees (the last of a prodigious height) are very plentifull there . . . The late English *proprietours* had given names to the severall districts of the Island. They called one Scotland from one Cranston a Scotch Irishman who went over to the Spaniards. The said planters had led their life there for the most part at distance from one another upon this occasion; Considering, that according to the Custom of pirates, they had led an ill life, for the time past, and being sencible that their swearing and blaspheming which they still kept up, was provoking to Almighty God in whose hands they thought themselves then to be, as being deprived of al the society, they made an agreement in order to begin & perfect a through reformation and particulerly of that crime, to live severally and part every Man in a several Cave for some Months, or till they should deposite so bad a habite, which purpose and resolution of theirs being put in practice, had the desired Effect, so far that after that time, they could converse with one another, with all the moderation and gravity imaginable. We found them in very good plight. The Life they had led had them very sharp, they very well understood the condition and state of the Spanish plantations, and very well provided for their own substance, when they came upon the Island, carrying a shore all necessary utensills especially such as contribute to their defence. They never walk'd abroad, without their hands being on the Cocks of their Guns. Amongst other things they carryed a shore a Salt pan, and made their owne Salt by the Sea-Side. They had Hammers, Saw's & other Iron Tools for felling of Trees, & building of Hulls. One of the four told me that if he went home with us, he would Endeavour the like reformation amongst our Men, as was affected amongst them dureing their Hermitical life, but he found himselfe very farr mistaken, for instead of the good he proposed to doe; Hee againe learned to drink and swear of the Ships Company, so that reflecting on his relaps, he afterwards often wished himselfe on the Island againe.

[An expedition is sent to the island to catch goats, and returns with only three carcasses.]

The Lieutenant Old and Crazey as he was, went a shore with the Lowzy Crew, which consisted of your Lazy, Hungrey fellowes. They took up their quarters in a little Salt Hutt . . . The Captain was so offended, that he told them he would punch their Gutts for them, for they commonly expect punch after some hard Service . . . The English with their Negroes we brought off the Island were designed by the Captain, to be a mess by themselves, but the advantage of their Conversation and intelligence obliged him afterward to disperse them amongst the Shipps Company.

On the 27th Day [of September], the wind having come about Northerly, and no Shipp appearing, I seriously reflected on the almost unintelligible occasion of our Stay there . . . We were a little Israelitish in that Wilderness; then it was, I prayd God that we should not pay for it as they did afterwards. It was not the first time we were desirous to gett off the shore, and Divine Providence had often delivered us from such, and many other dangers.

[Ignoring the warnings of one of the Englishmen from Juan Fernandez, they try trading at Santa Maria, just south of Concepcion, where the better part of the crew are killed or taken prisoner in an ambush. Simson concludes his account with another story of the island, concerning the attempted revolution of the blacks and Indians—the "boys" referred to above—against the regime of the four Englishmen.]

They are a desperate sort of Creatur's we understood by an instance related to us by the fferdinando Men, we brought with us. Their four Boyes, whereof the Leader was a Negro, (now in the possession of my Lord ffaulkland) having been severall times chastised by their Masters, were at last resolved to cut their throats, they were very cautious in their Councells, and secrett in the managements, till, the time of the Execution drawing nigh, One Boy's heart failed him, and made a discovery of the rest.

These being sufficiently acquainted with the strongholds of the Islands, kept out a long time till their Patrons were glad to come to a Parley, and were willing to promis them honourable quarters; however when the Sparks had once surrendred themselves, they were severally hung up by the Thumbs, their Armes being brought backwards over their heads, and Chastis'd in the Customary Manner and Measure, that's usual amongst Privateers. They wanted by a Hoyse or two of getting the Strapado. They were then tyed a part and disciplin'd with fasting till some sattisfactory degree of reformation was read in their ffaces.

Further Reading

Simson's voyage is mentioned in James Burney, *A Chronological History of the Discoveries in the South Sea or Pacific Ocean*, 5 vols. (London: Luke Hansard, 1803–16); and John Campbell, ed., *Navigantium atque Itinerantium Bibliotheca; or, A Complete Collection of Voyages and Travels*, 2 vols. (London: T. Osborne, 1764). Background material on privateering ventures of the English in the latter part of the eighteenth century can be found in Philip Ayres, *The Voyages and Adventures of Captain Bartholomew Sharp* (London, 1694); and William Hacke, *A Collection of Voyages* (London: James Knapton, 1699). Defoe's fictional account of how trade was to be initiated in the region is presented in *A New Voyage Round the World* (London: A. Bettesworth, 1725); and his theory of how it might be accomplished is outlined in *An Essay on the South-Sea Trade by the Author of the Review* (London: J. Baker, 1712). Recent discussions of these plans for commerce in the South Seas include Robert Markley, "'So Inexhaustible a Treasure of Gold': Defoe, Capitalism, and the Romance of the South Seas,"; and Glyndwr Williams, "Buccaneers, Castaways, and Satirists: The South Seas in the English Consciousness before 1750," both in *The South Pacific in the Eighteenth Century: Narratives and Myths*, ed. Jonathan Lamb, Robert Maccubbin, and David Morrill, (special edition of *Eighteenth-Century Life* 18, no. 3: 148–67, 114–281. For the degeneration of civil subjects in distant places, see Guillaume Thomas Raynal, *A History of the East and West Indies*, trans. J. O. Justamond, 8 vols. (London: W. Strahan and T. Cadell, 1783); and Anthony Pagden, "The Effacement of Difference: Colonialism and the Origins of Nationalism in Diderot and Herder," in *After Colonialism: Imperial Histories and Postcolonial Displacements*, ed. Gyan Prakash (Princeton: Princeton University Press, 1995), 129–52.

4

COMMODORE ANSON LANDS AT JUAN FERNANDEZ

. . . .

GEORGE ANSON's (1697–1762) voyage around the world, 1740–44, was in every respect an amphibian affair, with feet in both worlds. Although it was a naval expedition, sent to "annoy and distress" Spanish shipping on the Pacific coast of South America, it was also conceived as a land campaign, shipping 260 marines. Unlike the naval expeditions of the 1760s, which were advertised as a means of acquiring scientific knowledge, Anson's was firmly anchored in earlier traditions of navigation. His marines were intended to weigh the feasibility of British political influence, and possibly a British base, on the mainland; and his squadron hoped to capture the Spanish treasure ship that plied between Manila and Acapulco. The notion of a trading base in the South Seas belonged to the web of fantasies surrounding the flotation of the South Sea Company in 1711, and Anson's voyage was the last attempt to give those dreams some substance, via advice given the Admiralty by Hubert Tassell, an agent of the company. The Acapulco ship was the *ne plus ultra* of every buccaneering enterprise in these seas, ever since Bartholomew Sharp and his Jamaica colleagues (including William Dampier) crossed into them from Panama in 1680. And Anson was to take his place with Shelvocke, Rogers, Narborough, and Drake as one of those who laid his hands on vast amounts of Spanish treasure.

Despite these old-fashioned auspices, however, Anson's experiences supplied modern Europe with a good deal to think about. Smollett rewrote the wreck of the *Wager*, Anson's storeship, in his first novel *Roderick Random*; and Cowper used a description of a man lost overboard round the Horn for his poem "The Castaway." Rousseau assigns the descriptions of Juan Fernandez and Tinian to St.

Preux, the hero of his novel *Julie, ou, la nouvelle Heloise* (1761), who reports that he accompanied Anson through the Pacific. The terrible losses to scurvy (two-thirds of the total complement of two thousand men died from it) became a point of reference for many of the treatises written on the disease in the latter half of the century, such as James Lind's influential *Treatise of the Scurvy* (1757), republished many times. Those who survived this grueling test went on to forge the navy that fought so successfully in the Seven Years' War (1757–63). Finally, the story of the voyage itself became a classic of maritime literature, thanks to the skill of Richard Walter, who wrote up the original account from the journals of the crews, and Benjamin Robins, who was responsible for the finished copy. — JONATHAN LAMB

. . . .

George Anson, *Voyage Round the World, 1740–44*, comp. Richard Walter (London: W. Bowyer et al., 1776).

« PP. 101–20. »

Soon after our passing Streights Le Maire, the scurvy began to make its appearance amongst us; and our long continuance at sea, the fatigue we underwent, and the various disappointments we met with, had occasioned its spreading to such a degree, that, at the latter end of April, there were but few on board who were not in some degree afflicted with it; and that month no less than forty-three died of it on board the Centurion. But though we thought that the distemper had then risen to an extraordinary height, and were willing to hope, that as we advanced to the northward, its malignity would abate: yet we found, on the contrary, that in the month of May we lost near double that number: and, as we did not get to land till the middle of June, the mortality went on increasing; and the disease extended itself so prodigiously, that, after the loss of above two hundred men, we could not, at last, muster more than six fore-mast men in a watch capable of duty.

This disease, so frequently attending long voyages, and so particularly destructive to us, is surely the most singular and unaccountable of any that affects the human body: its symptoms are inconstant and innumerable, and its progress and effects extremely irregular; for scarcely any two persons have complaints exactly resembling each other; and where there hath been found some conformity in the symptoms, the order of their appearance has been totally different. However, though it frequently puts on the form of many other diseases, and is therefore not to be described by any exclusive and infallible criterions; yet there are some symptoms which are more general than the rest, and, occurring the oftenest, deserve a more particular enumeration. These common appearances are large discoloured spots, dispersed over the whole surface of the body, swelled legs, putrid gums, and, above all, an extraordinary lassitude of the whole body, especially after any exercise, however inconsiderable; and this lassitude at last degenerates into a proneness to swoon, and even die, on the least exertion of strength, or even on the least motion.

This disease is likewise usually attended with a strange dejection of the spirits, and with shiverings, tremblings, and a disposition to be seized with the most dreadful terrors on the slightest accident. Indeed it was most remarkable, in all our reiterated experience of this malady, that whatever discouraged our people, or at any time damped their hopes, never failed to add new vigour to the distemper; for it usually killed those who were before capable of some kind of duty; so that it seemed as if alacrity of mind, and sanguine thoughts, were no contemptible preservative from its fatal malignity.

But it is not easy to compleat the long roll of the various concomitants of this disease; for it often produced putrid fevers, pleurisies, the jaundice, and violent rheumatick pains, and sometimes it occasioned an obstinate costiveness, which was generally attended with a difficulty of breathing; and this was esteemed the most deadly of all the scorbutick symptoms: at other times the whole body, but more especially the legs, were subject to ulcers of the worst kind, attended with rotten bones, and such a luxuriancy of fungous flesh, as yielded to no remedy. But a most extraordinary circumstance, and what would be scarcely credible upon any single evidence, is, that the fears of wounds, which had been for many years healed, were forced open again by this virulent distemper. Of this, there was a remarkable instance in one of the invalids on board the Centurion, who had been wounded above fifty years before at the battle of the Boyne; for though he was cured soon after, and had continued well for a great number of years past, yet, on his being attacked by the scurvy, his wounds, in the progress of his disease, broke out afresh, and appeared as if they had never been healed: nay, what is still more astonishing, the callous of a broken bone, which had been compleatly formed for a long time, was found to be hereby dissolved, and the fracture seemed as if it had never been consolidated. Indeed, the effects of this disease were in almost every instance wonderful; for many of our people, though confined to their hammocks, appeared to have no inconsiderable share of health; for they eat and drank heartily, were chearful, and talked with much seeming vigour, and with a loud strong tone of voice; and yet, on their being the least moved, though it was only from one part of the ship to the other, and that too in their hammocks, they have immediately expired; and others, who have confided in their seeming strength, and have resolved to get out of their hammocks, have died before they could well reach the deck; nor was it an uncommon thing for those who were able to walk the deck, and to do some kind of duty, to drop down dead in an instant, on any endeavours to act with their utmost effort, many of our people having perished in this manner, during the course of this voyage.

Our deplorable situation, then, allowing no room for deliberation, we stood for the Island of Juan Fernandes. On the 9th of June, at day-break, we first descried the Island of Juan Fernandes, bearing N. by E. 1/2 E., at eleven or twelve leagues distance. And though, on this first view, it appeared to be a very mountainous place, extremely ragged and irregular; yet, as it was land, and the land we fought for, it was to us a most-agreeable sight: because at this place only we could hope to put a period to those terrible calamities we had so long struggled with, which had already swept away above half our crew; and which, had we continued a few days longer at sea, would inevitably have completed our destruction. For we were, by this time, reduced to so helpless a condition, that, out of two hundred and odd men which remained alive, we could not, taking all our watches together, muster hands enough to work the ship on an emergency, though we included the officers, their servants, and the boys.

The wind being northerly when we first made the Island, we kept plying all that day, and the next night, in order to get in with the land; and, wearing the ship in the middle watch, we had a melancholy instance of the almost incredible debility of our people; for the Lieutenant could muster no more than two Quarter-masters, and six Fore-mast-men, capable of working; so that, without the assistance of the officers servants and the boys, it might have proved impossible for us to have reached the Island, after we had got sight of it; and, even with this asistance, they were two hours in trimming the sails: to so wretched a condition was a sixty-gun ship reduced, which had passed Streights Le Maire but three months before with between four and five hundred men, almost all of them in health and vigour.

However, on the 10th in the afternoon, we got under the lee of the Island, and kept ranging along it, about two miles distance, in order to look out for the proper anchorage, which was described to be in a bay on the North-side. Being now nearer in with the shore, we could discover that the broken craggy precipices, which had appeared so unpromising at a distance, were far more barren, being in most places covered with woods; and that between them there were every where interspersed the finest vallies, clothed with a most beautiful verdure, and watered with numerous streams and cascades; no valleys, of any extent, being unprovided of its proper rill. The water too, as we afterwards found, was not inferior to any we had ever tasted, and was constantly clear. The aspect of this country, thus diversified, would, at all times, have been extremely delightful; but, in our distressed situation, languishing as we were for the land and its vegetable productions (an inclination constantly attending every stage of the sea-scurvy), it is scarcely credible with what eagerness and transport we viewed the shore, and with how much impatience we longed for the greens, and other refreshments, which were then in sight, and particularly the water; for this we had been confined to a very sparing allowance a considerable time, and had then but five ton remaining onboard. Those only who have endured a long series of thirst, and who can readily recal the desire and agitation which the ideas alone of springs and brooks have at that time raised in them, can judge of the emotion with which we eyed a large cascade of the most transparent water, which poured itself from a rock near a hundred feet high into the sea, at a small distance from the ship. Even those amongst the diseased, who were not in the very last stages of the distemper, though they had been long confined to their hammocks, exerted the small remains of strength that were left them, and crawled up to the deck, to feast themselves with this reviving prospect. Thus we coasted the shore, fully employed in the contemplation of this enchanting landskip, which still improved upon us the farther we advanced. But at last the night closed upon us, before we had satisfied ourselves which was the proper bay to anchor in; and, therefore, we resolved to keep in soundings all night (we having then from sixty-four to seventy fathom), and to send our boat next morning to discover the road: however, the current shifted in the night, and set us so near the land, that we were obliged to let go the best bower in fifty-six fathom, not half a mile from the shore. At four in the morning, the Cutter was dispatched, with our third Lieutenant, to find out the bay we were in search of, who returned again at noon, with the boat laden with seals and grass; for though the Island abounded with better vegetables, yet the boat's crew, in their short stay, had not met with them; and they well knew that even grass would prove a dainty, as, indeed, it was all soon and eagerly devoured. The seals, too, were considered as fresh provision; but as yet were not much admired, though they grew afterwards into more repute: for what rendered them less valuable, at this juncture, was the prodigious quantity of excellent fish, which the people on board had taken, during the absence of the boat.

The excellence of the climate, and the looseness of the soil, render this place extremely proper for all kinds of vegetation; for if the ground be any where accidentally turned up; it is immediately overgrown with turnips and Sicilian radishes: Mr. Anson, therefore, having him garden seeds of all kinds, and stones of different sorts of fruits, he, for the better accomodation of his countrymen who should hereafter touch here, sowed both lettuces, carrots, and other garden plants; and set in the woods a great variety of plumb, apricot, and peach stones: and these last, he has been informed, have since thriven to a very remarkable degree; for some Gentleman, who, in their passage from Lima to Old Spain, were taken and brought to England, having procured leave to wait upon Mr. Anson to thank him for his generosity and humanity to his prisoners, some of whom were their relations, they, in casual discourse with him about his transactions in the South-Seas, particularly asked him, if he had not planted a great number of fruit-stones on the Island of Juan Fernandes; for they told him, their late Navigators had discovered there numbers of peach-trees and apricot-trees, which being fruits before unobserved in that place, they concluded them to have been produced from kernels set by him.

This may in general suffice, as to the soil and vegetable productions of this place: but the face of the country, at least of the North part of the Island, is so extremely singular, that I cannot avoid giving it a particular consideration. I have already taken notice of the wild, inhospitable air with which it first appeared to us, and the gradual improvement of this uncouth landskip as we drew nearer, till we were at last captivated by the numerous beauties we discovered on the shores. And I must now add, that we found, during the time of our residence there, that the inland parts of the Island did no ways fall short of the sanguine prepossessions which we first entertained in their favour: for the woods, which covered most of the steepest hills, were free from all bushes and underwood, and afforded an easy passage through every part of them; and the irregularities of the hills and precipices, in the northern part of the Island, necessarily traced out, by their various combinations, a great number of romantic vallies; most of which had a stream of the clearest water running through them, that tumbled in cascades from rock to rock, as the bottom of the valley, by the course of the neighbouring hills, was at any time broken into a sudden sharp descent: some particular spots occurred in these vallies, where the shade and fragrance of the contiguous woods, the loftiness of the overhanging rocks, and the transparency and frequent falls of the neighbouring streams, presented scenes of such elegance and dignity, as would with difficulty be rivalled in any other part of the globe. It is in this place, perhaps, that the simple productions of unassisted nature may be said to excel all the fictitious descriptions of the most animated imagination. I shall finish this article with a short account of the spot where the Commodore pitched his tent, and which he made choice of for his own residence, though I despair of conveying an adequate idea of its beauty. The piece of ground which he chose was a small lawn, that lay on a little ascent, at the distance of about half a mile from the sea. In the front of his tent there was a large avenue cut through the woods to the sea-side, which, sloping to the water with a gentle descent, opened a prospect of the bay and the ships at anchor. This lawn was screened behind by a tall wood of myrtle sweeping round it, in the form of a theatre, the slope on which the wood stood rising with a much sharper ascent than the lawn itself; though not so much, but that the hills and precipices within land towered up considerably above the tops of the trees, and added to the grandeur of the view. There were, besides, two streams of crystal water, which ran on the right and left of the tent, within an hundred yards distance, and were shaded by the trees which skirted the lawn on either side, and compleated the symmetry of the whole. Some faint conceptions of the elegance of this situation may perhaps be better deduced from the draught of it, inserted in the adjoining plate.

It remains now only that we speak of the animals and provisions which we met with at this place. Former writers have related, that this Island abounded with vast numbers of goats; and their accounts are not to be questioned, this place being the usual haunt of the buccaneers and privateers, who formerly frequented those seas. And there are two instances; one of a Musquito Indian, and the other of Alexander Selkirk, a Scotchman, who were left here by their respective ships, and lived alone upon this Island for some years, and consequently were no strangers to its produce. Selkirk, who was the last, after a stay of between four and five years, was taken off the place by the Duke and Duchess Privateers of Bristol, as may be seen at large in the journal of their voyage: his manner of life, during his solitude, was, in most particulars, very remarkable; but there is one circumstance he relates, which was so strangely verified by our own observation, that I cannot help reciting it. He tells us, amongst other things, that, as he often caught more goats than he wanted, he sometimes marked their ears, and let them go. This was about thirty-two years before our arrivall at that Island. Now it happened, that the first goat that was killed by out people, at their landing, had his ears slit; whence we concluded, that he had doubtless been formerly under the power of Selkirk. This was, indeed,

FIG. 3. *A View of the Commodore's Tent at the Island of Juan Fernandes.* Engraved by J. Mason and published in Richard Walter, *A voyage 'round the world, in the years* MDCCXL, *I, II, III, IV by George Anson* (London: A. Merryman, 1776, plate XVIII). Department of Rare Books and Special Collections, Princeton University Library.

an animal of a most venerable aspect, dignified with an exceeding majestic beard, and with many other symptoms of antiquity. During our stay on the Island, we met with others marked in the same manner; all the males being distinguished by an exuberance of beard, and every other characteristick of extreme age.

Further Reading

A valuable collection of original material relating to the voyage is to be found in Glyndwr Williams, *Documents Relating to Anson's Voyage Round the World, 1740–44* (London: Navy Records Society, 1967); and the chapter on Anson in Williams' *The Great South Sea* (New Haven: Yale University Press, 1997) should also be consulted. A good contemporary account of the voyage is given by Pascoe Thomas, *A True and Impartial Journal of a Voyage to the South Seas* (London: S. Birt, J. Newbery, J. Collyer, 1745). For scurvy, see Eleanora Gordon, "Scurvy and Anson's Voyage," *American Neptune* 44, no. 3 (1984): 155–66. The connection with Rousseau is handled by Christopher Thacker, "'O Tinian! O Juan Fernandez!': Rousseau's 'Elysee' and Anson's Desert Islands," *Garden History* 5, no. 9 (1977): 41–47.

5

BYRON AND THE
PATAGONIAN GIANTS

. . . .

WHEN COMMODORE BYRON (1723–86), leader of the first of the four expeditions mounted by the British in the 1760s to explore the Pacific Ocean, reported that he had landed at the Rio Gallego (near Cape Fairweather on the southern tip of South America) and discovered people of an enormous size, he put fresh life into a controversy as old the Magellanic navigations. Magellan claimed to have found giants on the coast of Patagonia (literally the place of big feet), an achievement sung in prophetic vein in the tenth of Camoens's *Lusiads:*

> Rather more than half-way from equator to South Pole he will come on a land, Patagonia, where the inhabitants are of almost gigantic stature; then, farther on, he will discover the strait that now bears his name, which leads to another sea and another land, that Terra Incognita. (Camoens 1952, 246)

Drake's experiences in the same place, as reported by John Winter and then published by Hakluyt, failed to authenticate Magellan, being limited to meetings with people "of a mean stature" (Hakluyt 1600, 3:751). But Purchas restored giants to Patagonia in order, James Boon suggests, to preserve lurid associations of giantism, sodomy, and devil worship with the Spanish imperium (Boon 1982, 37–38). Despite Narborough's decisive rejection of the evidence for Patagonian giants after his expedition in 1670, there were surprising recurrences to Magellan's opinion. Among the buccaneers Amedee Frezier, highly respected as a navigator, mentions a tribe of Indians in southern Chile called Caucabues, said to stand "near four

Yards high, that is about nine or ten Foot," and who frequently migrate to the east coast (Frezier 1717, 84). He cites French and Dutch accounts, and concludes:

What I have here deliver'd upon the Testimony of Persons of Credit, is so agreeable to what we read in the Relations of the most famous Travelers, that I am of Opinion, it may be believ'd, without the Guilt of an Over-Credulity, that there is in that Part of America, a Nation of Men much exceeding us in Stature. (85)

After the 1740s, when the South Seas ceased to be the exclusive domain of free-booters and privateers and became the object of British and French naval ambitions and scientific research, it might be expected that no more would be heard of giants in Patagonia. However, John Bulkeley, who sailed with Anson into the South Seas, reports Indians in southern Chile "of a gigantick Stature," despite the elaborate sarcasms heaped by his colleague Pascoe Thomas on lurid tales of "wild and gigantick Cannibals" who are in fact "a harmless, civil, inoffensive People; of a middling Stature, well-shap'd, and of a tawny olive Complexion" (P. Thomas 1745, 125–26). It was on the same expedition that John Byron sailed as a midshipman, sharing the hideous privations that descended on the crew of the *Wager* when she was wrecked on the South Chilean coast. His account includes detailed descriptions of Indians of the common size, but no mention of giants. His second entry into these seas, twenty years later, is notorious for his report of people "of a gigantic stature, [that] seemed to realize the tales of monsters in a human shape" (Hawkesworth 1773, 1:28). Whether it was owing to the bulky cloaks of the inhabitants, or the fact that they were chiefly seen while sitting down, or, as Bougainville speculated when he saw no Patagonian standing above five feet and ten inches, their immensely broad shoulders and their large heads that caused them to appear like Titans (Bougainville 1772, 146–47), Byron was convinced that the Indians of Patagonia were of a preternatural size. The debate about these giants sputtered on until the end of the century. James King, who had the responsibility of editing and publishing the journal of Cook's final voyage, is equally positive that the fact of Patagonian giants, "whose stature considerably exceeds that of the bulk of mankind, will no longer be doubted or disbelieved" (Cook and King 1784, 1:lxxi).

The extract that follows is taken from an unnumbered insertion, twenty-six pages long, placed between pages twenty-five and twenty-six of the British Library's copy of the anonymous *Journal of a Voyage Round the World in the* Dolphin (London: M. Cooper, 1767). The insertion is from G. F. Coyer's *Letter to Dr Maty* (London: T. Beckett and P. A. de Hondt, 1767), in which the French philosopher amuses himself with the extravagant claims made by Byron and the credulity of

the Royal Society when it received Maty's endorsement of them. It was a species of ridicule first developed by Coyer in *A Supplement to Lord Anson's Voyage Round the World* (1752), where he transformed Richard Walter's lyrical description of Juan Fernandez into a mock-utopia, Frivoland, inhabited by creatures of the most exquisite taste who dwell in a world of artificial curiosities. In both satires Coyer resituates a "factual" account inside the utopian framework that had shaped the first European images of the South Seas, a satirical technique perfected by Swift.
— JONATHAN LAMB

. . . .

John Byron, *Journal of a Voyage Round the World in the* Dolphin (London: M. Cooper, 1767).

« G. F. COYER, *A Letter to Dr Maty* (LONDON, 1767). »

A Patagonian is not fabricated as a man of London or Paris, of five feet high; he does not approach his mistress with corrupted manners, a weakened constitution, and a body hurt by excess and debauchery, but with a virtuous behaviour, a good constitution, and noble sentiments.

The Patagonian approaches nearest to the man of nature of all men that live in a state of society; ignorant of the arts of luxury, he finds water, and satisfies his thirst; wine is only sold by apothecaries as a medicine, as well as other fermented liquors; he finds milk refreshing, and the most simple foods nourishing, and at the same time pleasing to his taste; he thinks the skins of animals a sufficient covering, and finds his horse relieves him when he is tired with walking; he thinks himself very fine when he is dressed with a metal collar, and a few feathers; these are almost all the Patagonian desires. He is passionately fond of a domestic life, and every thing is pleasing and interesting to him in the midst of his family, his wife, his children, their education, even their noise, his servants, agreeable repasts with his family sometimes in a grove, sheltered from the heat of the sun, and other times in a valley, by the side of a murmuring brook, at other, on the top of a rock, from when he may observe an extensive horizon. He is unacquainted with cold ceremonious visits, and makes none but those of freindship, humanity, or business. He is happiest in his own house, for there he governs, loves, and is beloved. He is not shut up in his house, as we are in ours, a garden, a part, and a live stock are all necessary to his happiness. He is only susceptible of the milder passions, has no ambition, but

FIG. 4. *Entrevue de Biron avec les Patagons.* Engraved frontispiece to vol. 5 of Jean Pierre Berenger, *Collection de tous les voyages faits autour du monde par les differentes nations de l'Europe* (Paris: Chez Fr. Dufart, Imprimeur-Libraire, 1795). By permission of the National Library of Australia.

that of an happiness easily obtained, by treading the steps of nature. If he is called upon to attend publick affairs, and leave this state of tranquillity, he makes that sacrifice for the cause and good of his country, for the offices of state are only burthensome: he returns as soon as possible to his own former private station, his family being to him a most agreeable and lasting amusement.

The Patagonians have also their publick diversions, they have their circus and their amphitheatres, where their youth dispute the prize of leaping, wrestling, running, the management of the bow, the sling, at carrying weights, and fighting with beasts. The young females also display their charms there in the most ingenious and forcible manner; they are finely shaped, without having been squeezed in a box of whalebone, or cramped with bars of iron. Such a publick day is the most agreeable of their whole lives; on this occasion they distribute the prizes, and make choice of their husbands, who must be twenty-eight years of age at least: the inequality of condition between families is no objection to any match, the only lawful obstacle is difference of age; they say nature hath for ever separated summer from winter. As to fortune, each individual finds a competency in labour and industry.

Their opera is without action, and consists intirely in recital and description. They sing of the beauty of the sun, the succession of the seasons, the fruitfulness of the earth, conjugal affection, the annual increase of population, friendship, brotherly love, patriotism, the inventors of the plough, the mill, the art of building, language, writing, navigation, etc.

In their tragedies the persons of the drama consist of ancient giants, who wanted to tyrannize over others, because they were stronger and taller. The catastrophe being always consistent with poetical justice, and ending with the punishment of the guilty.

By their comedies it would seem, that the Patagonians don't like to be diverted at the expence of each other, but they keep some little men as we do dwarfs in Europe, and take pleasure in introducing these on the stage by way of contrast; for example, they represent a Patagonian beauty as setting a man of five feet upon her knee, treating him with great kindness, and desiring him to reach her some fruit from the top of an high tree. The little creature, who has neither the nimbleness nor strength of the country, looks up at it, but despairs; she gives him an ax to break down the tree, but he is not able to lift it. A wild beast approaches them; A my dear lover! cries the fair Patagonian, protect me: He seizes a bow, but alas! finds himself so weak, he cannot bend it, which obliges his mistress to fly with her brave defender under arm. In another scene there is a prize depending upon a leave over a little ditch of water, only thirty feet broad; our little man jumps, and falls in the middle. He is offered revenge in a fight with a petty Patagonian, not seven feet and a half high, who knocks him down the first blow; his antagonist is enraged, and the spectators diverted at his impotent resentment.

The Patagonians generally despise men of our size, on account of their own majestick stature, but behave kindly to them, even while they divert themselves with them. These people hope to have comedies soon in a better taste, for the Beaux-esprits, that have succeeded already in the tragedy and opera, are improving the comic theatre at present, but as they are whimsical and quarrelsome, it is feared it will delay the work, but their quarrels furnish the publick with very high entertainment.

The Patagonian theatre is very singular, for without having read either Vitruvius or Palladio, or seen any models from them, their houses are build in the elliptical form, so well proportioned to the eye and ear, that the beholders may see and hear from the most distant parts of the theatre. There are seats in the pit as well as the boxes for the company; the Patagonians say they should not make a toil of a pleasure. Their theatres in general are larger than ours; that of the capital is of an extraordinary size, and so it should be, to hold thirty thousand giants: their inhabitants are about that number, including the common people, who partake of all publick diversions. Their magistrates say, the more people labour, they have the more need for relaxation, and it cannot be a publick diversion which the populace do not share in. There is not the least disturbance either at coming in, or going out of the theatre, notwithstanding the great multitude, because the doors are large, and it is situated in the middle of an extensive square, the avenues spacious and wide in proportion. The building is rustic, but from its height and grandeur, has a majestic appearance.

The Patagonians are ignorant of every thing but what is necessary, and that they find where ever they want it. They have no foreign trade, nor have they any notion of the usefulness of commerce, notwithstanding that they have cut a number of artifical rivers a-cross their country, which has the appearance of a trading nation, but they are only canals, which serve to water the country, and afford an easy conveyance from one city to another, and a communication with the capital. The sides of these canals are planted with trees, which adds, greatly to the beauty of the country.

The Patagonians are unacquainted with civil strife; they are not courteous enough to cut each others' throats, and being sensible, and being sensible that foreign wars had brought a train of evils on their country, it was determined they should enter into no wars for the future, but such as were in their own defence.

Every Patagonian being bred up to arms and hard labour, he is of course a soldier, and able to defend the land he cultivates; they therefore keep no standing army in time of peace, as they are fearful that soldiers well armed, and well paid, may be converted into slaves ready to obey the call of ambition, and crush their countrymen.

Among the Patagonians, all persons who have behaved well to their country, by obtaining a victory, cultivating a desart, draining a morass, improving the useful arts, or [who] discover remedies against diseases, are maintained by the state, look'd upon as people of consequence, and have places of pre-eminence appointed them in all publick meetings. This honour is only personal, and their children enjoy no benefit from it, but are obliged to labour, and strive to raise themselves by their own industry, that they become as noble as their ancestors.

If any of the nobility among them, by his superior virtues, or fine talents, engages the particular esteem of his nation, he is presented with some valuable possessions, and a collar of topaz. As the noblemen must do the honours of the capital, by preparing entertainments, they are generally good oeconomists, to enable them to be just, magnificent, and generous.

They don't pay their court to their prince in person, unless to give him an opportunity of doing some good; so that he is certain his subjects are happy, when he is alone: he therefore enjoys the pleasures of private life as much as individuals do.

By the laws he is obliged to spend three months every year in making a tour thro' Patagonia, to see whether any part of the government be deficient; and his successor accompanies him in this tour, which instructs him in the nature of the country, the inhabitants, and their employments.

Since the Patagonians have been capable of thinking seriously, they have always paid respect to the laws, which are made at general meetings, and remain in force till grow out of use, and are no longer suited to the times.

The Patagonians were neither unjust nor cruel originally, but had a pride in their humanity and justice. They had however adapted barbarous laws, without knowing them to be so; the people who demanded justice, were ruined by the forms of justice: they punished before conviction, tortured, broke on the wheel, burnt, and impaled all, because it was the custom; till an old Patagonian, a professor in the law, who had distinguished himself in the magistracy, published a new book, intitled, *The Good Sense of the Laws*, which was agreeably received. I shall give you a few of its articles.

There had been many degrees of jurisdiction before this reformation, that it was necessary to gain the same cause three or four times over, which occasioned great uneasiness to the clients, and hindrance of business to carry on their suits. The reformer said, the expedition of justice was as necessary as justice itself, and that the judge cannot be too near the matter to be decided: he was attended to, and heard. Every inhabited town and village had a tribunal of its own, from which there was no appeal; and, by this means, more disputes were determined by arbitration, than by the courts, and that was what was mostly desired by the judges.

The costs were so great before this reformation, that those who gained their cause, said, they had better have given up their point in dispute: it was of no consequence to the client, whether he was ruined by justice or injustice, if he must be ruined at all events. The officers and attendants of the court should be properly provided for, at the expence of the publick, because they cannot improve their land. It was therefore determined, that justice should be had at no expence, and consequently pure and undefiled.

Before the reformation, local customs took place of the laws, and it frequently happened, that a person in doing the same thing, might be right in one place, and wrong in another. The reformer said, reason was every where the same, the same troops ought to have the same discipline. Then the laws were made universal, as the same weights and measures were before, which prevented the unjust trader from imposing upon the honest purchaser; and if any party commenced an unjust suit, he was obliged to pay a certain penalty.

The laws concerning criminal affairs had been very cruel; the person accused of a crime was thrown into a dungeon, without the necessaries of life, infectious, unwholesome, and dark. The reformer said, you are not certain that he is guilty, he should not be punished till he is convicted, imprisonment ought not to be severe but secure: so now the prisoner is as much at ease, except freedom, as in his own house, having the choice of any two friends to be with him in the prison.

Before the reformation they found an hundred trifling excuses for delaying the tryal of prisoners; it was sometimes a year or more before his fate was determined. Says the author of the new code, if he should be innocent, a long imprisonment must be hurtful to justice, and the humanity of the Patagonians: it was therefore decreed, that the accused should be tried within a month, a space of time too long, says the law, for the ordinary course of things.

Every thing was done privately before the reformation, the examination, deposition of the witnesses, confrontation. and judgment, as if justice was afraid of the light. The new code addresses the judges in these terms: If the accused is justifiable, you should afford him every means of defence, and to reap the honour of your own integrity; but as all men are subject to pre-possession, you don't know but the publick may give you some light into the affair; a person who might witness falsly in private, may be, possibly, struck with remorse in the face of whole nation: a man that is innocent, may appear guilty by his timidity, therefore needs a council to plead for him. When a Patagonian's life is at stake, if his crime is not quite clear, it should at least appear so clear, that all the judges agree in their sentence. This prejudice was laid aside, and according to the new method of pro-ceeding, the judges hear causes, and pass sentence in publick.

Before the reformation, when proofs against the person accused were insufficient, the judges made use of the torture, to see if they could force them to a confession. The reformer says, how cruel and shocking to nature and humanity is such proceeding, if the person is innocent, to be dislo-cated, broil'd, and torn to pieces; the law cannot torture before judgment. It was with difficulty the courts were prevailed on to give up this point, least it might give room for criminals to escape; but while they were dis-cussing this matter, it happened, that a hardy criminal, by denying the fact obstinately, was saved, and a poor innocent creature of a weak constitution, who could no longer bear the tortures, made confessions to be released, and was executed. This truth was engraved on brass, as was also the law that destroyed the torture.

Before the reformation was the punishment of all trifling crimes. A number of servants were put to death for pilfering trinkets from their mas-ters, which prevented masters from prosecuting their servants, least they should be universally disliked, and agreed to give them up to justice if they would punish them moderately, to prevent their robbing elsewhere.

Nobody ever proposed saving common robbers, or house breakers from the gallows, yet there were not fewer robberies committed. Punishments were invented for the good of society: a hundred robbers, under proper order, might break up a common drain, a morass, dig a canal, make high-ways, and so be serviceable to the state, even in their punishments, and these lasting examples of justice might have more effect, than the sight of an execution, which is immediately over.

Another abuse very hurtful to publick safety was, that there was no dif-ference made between the punishment for a robber and murderer, and a robber on the highway. The reformer, who always consulted the first law of good sense, observed on this occasion, that there should be degrees of punishment, as well as degrees in crimes, and that it was by degrees that mankind were led to have such impressions made on their minds, as might deter them from crimes: it was therefore resolved, that the mere robber should be condemned to work on the publick highways.

They referred the punishment of death for murder, but it was difficult to determine the manner of inflicting it. The courts were inclined to the most severe punishment, imagining that the horror of them would deter men from crimes; and they were confirmed in that opinion by a Patagonian, who had talked with a Spaniard among the Chanos' he was informed by him, that the enlightened people on the continent of Europe were extremely severe on these occasions. Heaven protect us from beings so enlightened! replied the reformer; men are not to be worked upon by extremes, let us try to affect their minds by moderate punishments, as much as they now are by these severe ones, which I am certain leave a stain of barbarity on the nation who uses them: having shewed his good sense on all other subjects, the publick depended on him in this also. From that time they have only drowned murders, and don't find, since that time, that crimes have increased, and therefore are convinced, that tormenting punishments have no effect towards reforming. The people shut themselves up in their houses on the day of an execution, so great is their terror to see the death of a Patagonian.

What the new code is mostly admired for, is, its laws are sensible, clear, precise, simple, and not arbitrary. The former laws were scarce known to the publick, and were often wrong interpreted: a sure proof that they were captious, and hard to be understood. Interpretation of the present laws is not allowed, and they are so plain, that they are taught to you in the very words of the text.

Further Reading

The original version is contained in G. F. Coyer, *A Letter to Dr Maty* (London: T. Becket and P. A. de Hondt, 1767), and pasted into the anonymous *Journal of a Voyage round the World in the* Dolphin (London: M. Cooper, 1767). For the Patagonians, see Luis Vaz de Camoens, *The Lusiads*, trans. William C. Atkinson (Harmondsworth: Penguin, 1952); Richard Hakluyt, *Voyages of the English Nation*, 3 vols. (London: George Bishop, 1600); Horace Walpole, "An Account of the Giants Lately Discovered: In a Letter to a Friend in the Country (1766)," appendix 3, 200–9, in *Byron's Journal of His Circumnavigation, 1764–66*, ed. Robert E. Gallagher (Cambridge: Hakluyt Society, 1964); and James A. Boon, *Other Tribes, Other Scribes* (Cambridge: Cambridge University Press, 1982). For utopias, see

Gregory Claeys, *Utopias of the British Enlightenment* (Cambridge: Cambridge University Press, 1994); J. C. Davis, *Utopia and the Ideal Society* (Cambridge: Cambridge University Press, 1981); and David Fausett, *Writing the New World: Imaginary Voyages and Utopias of the Great Southern Land* (Syracuse: University of Syracuse Press, 1993). A general background for the improbable tales of voyagers can be found in Percy Adams, *Travellers and Travel Liars* (New York: Dover, 1962), 19–43; and a good account of this specific tall-story is given (together with Walpole's satire) in Helen Wallis, "The Patagonian Giants," appendix 1, 185–96, in *Byron's Journal,* ed. Robert E. Gallagher.

6

SAMUEL WALLIS

The Discovery of Tahiti

. . . .

ALEXANDER DALRYMPLE, the formidable doyen of the history of Pacific navigation, was adamant that in the South Seas "no new Lands . . . have been discovered
under his Majesty's auspices" (*Letter to Hawkesworth* 1773, 31). Yet Wallis (1728–95)
is credited with the first official landfall at Tahiti in 1767, which he called King
George the Third's Island, in honor of the royal endorsement of the four voyages
of discovery launched in the 1760s under Byron, Carteret, Wallis, and Cook. The
name didn't stick, but the delicious island paradise known as Otaheite to the
British, and Taiti to the French, was to be widely celebrated in the journals of
Bougainville, Commerson, Cook, and Banks as a place where voluptuous pleasure
was the only law and bread grew plentifully upon trees. Whether it was owing to
his being the first to land there, or to his being badly afflicted with scurvy, Wallis's
encounter with the natives was marred by violence that Bougainville and Cook
avoided. In this respect he takes up his place in a long line of discoverers of Pacific
islands, going back to de Quiros and Mendana and forward to Cook himself in
New Zealand, who signalized their arrival at paradise with acts of bloodshed.

Venereal disease was soon contracted by the Tahitians from visiting crews,
causing mutual accusations between the French and the English. Wallis himself
seems uneasily divided between suspicion of the natives and a scurvy victim's respect for the various products of the soil. His journal was used by Hawkesworth
in his *Account of the Voyages and Discoveries in the Southern Hemisphere* with relatively little addition; and since then it has remained unpublished, probably owing
to the more racy and vivid descriptions supplied by George Robertson in his *Journal of the Second Voyage of the Dolphin*. Robertson details how the traffic in sex and

nails began to thrive, and completely banished thoughts of war ("our Liberty men and the Natives is now turnd so friendly that they walk Arm in Arm" [Robertson 1948, 183]) until the *Dolphin* began to loosen, so many nails and cleats had been taken from her timbers. Robertson was also the first to encounter Oberea, or Purea, who was later to play the part of Dido to Banks's Aeneas: she felt the muscles in his legs, "and calld out with Admiration Oh, Oh, Oh, and desired the Chief feel my legs" (211).

Wallis, Robertson, and the balladeer Richardson all mention the *Dolphin's* pennant, which was set up as a token of possession by the English and immediately removed by the Tahitians. Although such gestures were intended not as a sign of annexation, but of priority of claim with respect to the French, the Spanish, and later the Americans, the *Dolphin's* ensign played a part in island history, being woven into the *maro ura*, the red feather girdle that was the sign of a premier chief. Bligh saw the ensign in the girdle when he arrived in Tahiti in 1792, on his second attempt to collect breadfruit seedlings. By this time the *maro ura* contained the hair of Richard Skinner, one of his mutineers, and it was playing an important part in the consolidation of Pomare I's dynasty. The ballad provides another commentary on the events at Tahiti, together with a tour of the important sites of these navigations, such as Patagonia and its giants and the island of Tinian, already made famous by Byron and Anson. — JONATHAN LAMB

. . . .

Samuel Wallis, log-book in 3 vols., safe 1/98, Mitchell Library, State Library of New South Wales, Sydney

Wednesday, 24 June 1767

Moderate [wind] and fine Weather. PM we warped the Ship up the Harbour & anchord in 15 fathom; & moord with the Stream [anchor] the Boats deployed in Sounding in order to warp the Ship up to the Head of the Bay. Many Canoes about the Ship, from whom we purchasd fruits, Hogs & fowles which is given to the Sick and other people. Put the Ships Company at four watches. Loaded all the Guns & small arms & kept thirty Men Constantly armed. The rest of the People had Arms ready at a Moments warning—At six there came of about three Hundred Canoes & before Nine they were near Double the Number with Multitudes of People on each. Some few had Sixteen or Eighteen. They brought of plenty of Hogs fowles & fruit, which we got in exchange for Nails, Beads &c. At 1/2 past Nine a Boat with a large Canopy over the Middle brought a large Plantain Tree with a Bunch of various Coloured feathers and a Pig. & a Man who sat on the Top of the Canopy made Motions of peace & pointed to himself & then to the Ship in sho[w] twas to be given to the superior. I being very ill came & lookd out of the Gallery window, & was preparing some presents to give him in Lieu & he seemd to be very attentive to all the Boats that were round the Ship, in many of which they had placed three or four well looking Girls in a Row on board severall large Canoes who were making all the Lascivious Motions, & playing all the wanton tricks imaginable. During this time like wise the Boats drew nearer the Ship, & I perceived they had vast Quantities of Pebble Stones of a Pound or two or three weight which we supposed they had for Ballast. However kept the People constantly on their Guard. Just as I had prepard [ ] present, there was a Silence amongst the Canoes and two More Covered Canoes came off who were mounted with a Man on the Top of Each, and in an Instant after he that was on the first Canoe lifted up a Plantain Leaf & threw a stained Red Cloth over his Shoulders, on which every Canoe set up a Halloo, & threw such a Shower of Stones at all parts of the Ship that was astonishing, on which I ordered the people to fire on them. They persisted some time but some of our Great Guns breaking a few of their Large Canoes & the two Quarter Deck Guns fird, loaded with Musquett Shot made them sheer off. However they kept hovering at a Distance & throwing Stones with slings which they did with great Judgment, and hurt many of our People. They on our ceasing fire after a Pause made a second Effort and came on with great resolution. But on their coming on & slinging Stones we fired a few Great Guns Load with Roundshot and Grape at them, and they all pulled for the shore so that at Noon there was not a Canoe to be seen. Got up the Six Guns that were in the Hold and Mounted them, put two of them out of the Sterne & two forward.

25 July 1767

Sent Mr Gore, Mate of the Dolphin, with Two Midship men, Serjeant & all the Marines, & Twenty Seamen Armed, with four less armed to carry Provisions up the River to search for Minerals and Explore the Hills, Valleys & bring me an account of what he had seen or found. Who at his return said as is follows—

When we Landed we went up to the Queen's Great House to get the
the [*sic*] Old Man to go with us, which he did. We then marched in two
Partys one on each side of the River. But the Mountains were too steep
that we were frequently obliged to join again & the river winding so much
from the foot of one mountain & the other that it made it very difficult
travelling. The first two Miles was well inhabited the soil seemed very rich,
but in many Places Stoney[. T]hey had many Gardens fenced in with
Stonewalls, & canalls to turn the water into the gardens from the River[.
T]he chief things that were in their gardens, were Rows of Apple, Bread
fruit &, Plantain Trees, and between them a Plant with a Broad dark
coloured leaf, which they eat of and tastes like Coliloo [?] in the West Indies. After we left, this valley still grew Narrower & only a house was to be
seen in a Quarter of a Mile. About three Miles up they sat down to breakfast but had not sat long before they heard a Number of People hallooing
and making a great Noise. Sent the Old Man to them, who soon made
them quiet, and soon after they brought green Boughs, with a Pig ready
Roasted, Bread fruit, Cocoa Nutts & Apples,—made them presents in return. We then proceeded up the vally about five Miles; in our way saw on
each side of the Hills many Plantations. Several of the Peoples followed
us,—they gathered some Red Berrys of a tree & squeezed them and expressed a yellow Juice with which they stained their Clothes. We gathered
several of them but they were so watery they would not keep. They likewise cut of the Rind of a tree & painted themselves red with it. This tree
had no fruit on it. We saw severall large Canoes building & Plank preparing both sides of the River. [Traveling] five Miles up the Valley, here we
found a very large fall of Water and having searched the River all the way
up without finding any thing, hoped that here we might meet with something, but were disappointed having only found two Mineral Stones which
we brought to the Captain. Here we were obliged to Climb the Hills or
rather the Mountains. The Old Man made signs to the Natives and they
cleared away a Path and carried the Peoples Baggage, helped them in the
Difficult places, & supplyed them with Cocoanutts, Apples, & Water all
the way up which was near a Mile and very fateaguing. When they came
to the Top they seated themselves and it being very high they overlook'd
many Valleys which they say were delightfully Pleasant, full of Houses &
Plantations and Gardens well fenced in. They Judged themselves to be
about six Miles from the Watering place. The Tops of the Hills are very
Rocky & full of fern, above them I call Mountains which are full of Trees,
what sort I cannot tell but many very large. The[y] gathered the fruit of
severall on the Sides of the Hills, but none were ripe & they all rotted.

FIG. 5. *Otaheite or King Georges Island.* Pen and wash by Samuel Wallis (c. 1767, 28.7 x 44 cm). By permission of the National Library of Australia.

The[y] met with a Tree or Weed that was about 4 inches Diameter and fifteen or 16 feet High, exactly like a fern. They cut it down & found it striped black & white—they would have brought it with them but the Roads they had to pass made it Impossible.

After resting sometime on the Top of the Hill we walked round and observed the Country which we found had much the same appearance as before mentioned. Vis.—the Valleys very fertile and the sides of the Hills if not too steep were full of Bread fruit, Apple & Cocoa Nutt Trees & good Plantations. The Plain or easyest ascent of the Hill [has] very rich good soil but not cultivated, the Inhabitants choosing to live in Valleys or on the side of the Hills above the Rivers—high up the hill very Rocky & full of Ferns—the mountains clothed with large Trees to the very Top. They saw no kind of wild animal—except Rats which are plenty in the Valleys, but none in the hills—here were an abundance of Wild duck in the River and on the Hills, numbers of Parretts and Paraquetts of different kinds—and green Doves & a sort of Heron—white & white & black—at the Plantations they had only Hogs & Cocks, for they scarce saw a Hen and never saw an Egg or young Chicken. The Inhabitants all the way the[y] went behaved with great kindness to them and gave them to eat & drink what they had & followed them with more in case they wanted. At Night they returned to the Ship. I gave the Queen & Old Man—a Cock & Hen Turkey, Three Guinea Fowles, a Cock & Two Hens, a Goose & Gander;— some Iron Potts, Bottles, Glasses, Hatchetts, Saws, Chizzels, Nails, with a Number of other things, besides all kinds of Garden seeds, & showed them how to plant them. I planted Lime, Lemon, Orange, Cherry, Peach, Plum & Apricot in a great Number of Places, some of which I hope will come to perfection—I had two Shee Goats, but had lost the Hee Goat in the Straights of Magillan, which I was very sorry for, as from their being left amongst them in a few years the whole Country would be stocked. I gave them a Cat big with kitten, of which they were vere fond,—and surprized to see her attack the Rats so eagerly. They have a sort of Cur dog amongs them which they keep by way of pet, for they all-ways carry them in their arms, especially if they came to a brook. We had three Dogs which used to go on shoar with Sick and the Natives were so much afraid of them, that one of them would make five hundred run away, they having vast dread of them, as the Dogs had at first bit several of them who had come too near the Tent.

Given me on the Passage from St Helena to England: A Poetical Essay on the Dolphin Sailing Round the Globe in the Years 1766–1768—by B. Richardson, Barber of the said Ship.

> Let Holland, France or Haughty Spain
> Boast their Discoveries o'er the Main
> And Sing their Heroes Mighty Frame
> Which now with time Decays.
> Brittania's Isle at length hath found
> A Man who sail'd the Globe around
> Discovering Isles till now Unfound
> And well deserves the Bays.
>
> Wallis I sing the Hero Brave
> Who to his Country like a Slave
> Undaunted Plough'd the Southern Wave
> In search of Land Unfound:
> His Ship the Dolphin, and his Crew
> All Young and healthy, tho' but few
> Yet with him Dauntless, Bold and True
>   They sailed the Globe around.
>
> A wellcome Breeze fills every Sail
> No more the Maidens tears travail
> For Honour o'er their Fears prevail

Adieu to Plymouth Sound
Ye Virgins fair forbear to Weep
For you, sincere our hearts we'll keep
For you we'll plough th' extensive Deep
And sail the Globe around—

Madeira first supply'd our need
St Jago next; from thence with speed
Whilst Oxen for us daily Bleed
  So West, our Course we Steer.
The well known Streight we Enter then
So famed for its Gigantic Men
Whose Height from six feet reach'd to Ten
  And safely Anchor'd there

As farther tho' the Streights we go
Where lofty Clifts are tip't with Snow
And rapid Cataracts swiftly flow
  A down their Craggy Sides
Where Winter too incessant Reigns
And Aeolus mighty God, disdains
To curb the Wind, who free from Chains
  Our utmost [skills] derides

Some Natives here, the few we find
A Savage Race of human Kind
Scarce blest with Senses, to reason Blind
  In Ignornace rudely bred
Nought to defend their swarthy sides
But Beasts, or Fishes skins and hides
More nauseous Food, and nought besides
  Morassy Ground their Bed.

Into the Wide Pacific Sea
From such unpleasing sights as these
Waft us some fair auspicious Breeze
  And be our constant Guides
The Mighty God the Prayer received
Our Sails we loos'd, our Ship relieved

The Streight we clear, & undeceived
   Our Toils he well rewards

No longer now our greif he mocks
No more Our ship in Streights he locks
From Dangers freed we see those Rocks
   At distance far behind
Pleased with the Change those Dangers o'er
With Joy we View the Distant Shore
And Bless the God whose awfull Pow'r
   Is ever unconfin'd.

Now fraught with Wind our Canvass swells
Tho' some rude Squalls our Ship assail
Yet all in Vain, they nought avail
   Wide from the Dangerous Coast
For Neptune kind with Pleasant Gales
For some few Weeks repleats our Sails
And on his Son such Fame intails
   As Europe ne'er could boast.

Swiftly he wafts us o'er his Waves
Grants every Boon our Hero craves
Scarce in the Southern Seas he leaves
   An Isle to him unknown
Respecting every Son of Fame
Great Wallis gives to each a Name
With Titles free from others Claim
   But trusts to Fate his Own.

On Whitsun day the first was seen
Which bore the Name with due esteem
The next to Brittains Royall Queen
   Charlotte's Name he fixed.
Some few we pass'd in Number Four
Whose names are still reserved in Store
The next the Royal Bishop Bore
   And George great George the next.

Here wait my muse awhile to View
A Beauteous scene to Brittains New
Whose Climate equalled is by few
  The British Monarch's Isle
And as my Muse, thou Heavenly Maid
An Artless Bard Invokes your Aid
Let all his skill be here display'd
  And o'er this Essay smile.

Our Anchors well secured in Ground
Sails furled, Yards, Topmasts Lower'd down
Well pleased we View the Fertile Ground
  Well worth a Monarchs care
Safe in Port Royal Bay we Ride
Where's no rude Wind, no rapide Tide
Or Rugged Rocks unseen abide
  But all's Serene and fair.

The Swarthy Indians round us flock
With each a pittance from their Stock
Which they for various trifles truck
  Content with what we spare
Oft on our Ship they fix their Eyes
As oft on us with Deep Surprize
And deem our Floating world a prize
  For them next Morn to share.

Prepar'd next Morn with Stones they came
Which well they Hurled with Dextrous Aim
But soon were all repulsed with Shame
  And some Canoes unmann'd
Fatal Attempt, Ambitious thought:
Poor Simple men, to[o] late you're taught
That Brittons ne'er are easy Caught
  With Schemes so badly plann'd.

No safe Retreat they now can finde
For dire distraction unrestrain'd
With Balls swift Whistling thro' the Wind

O'ertakes the Insulting Bid
But O! to paint their Vast Surprize
The Terror sparkling in their Eyes
Or their confused & hideous Cries
   Requires an abler Hand.

Then cease my Muse the Cannons Roar
Is ceased: the Vanquish'd make for Shore
Their Comrades Fate with Tears deplore
   And seek a speedy flight
A gentler Theme demands your care
To paint the Beauteous Isle prepare
Whilst we fatigued tho' void of fear
   In Slumbers pass the Night.

The Morning Dawns the well known Call
From gentle Sleep awakes us all
Our Boats well mann'd and Arm'd withal
   The Conquer'd Isle we claim
Soon as the Sea Beach side we make
The Indians all their Hutts forsake
And we in form Possession take
   In George's Royal Name.

Now free to Range we find with Fruits
Pigs, Fowles and most salubrious Roots
Refreshment such as aptly suits
   The Seamen's Briny food
Than all of these an Iron Bar
Or Rusty Nail's more precious far
To them, e'en Gold or Diamonds are
   Less Valued, less aproved.

The Natives yet more polished are
Than other Savage Indians are
The Girls well featur'd, passing fair
   And kind in all respects,
The Men well made, Robust and Tall,
Subject to none, by none enthrall'd

Thoughtless of every future call
  They live as life directs.

In Tillage quite a useless Band
But Nature kindly tills their Land
When fertile Soil at her Command
  Yeilds all the Sweets of Life
At least such necessary Store
That pleased with it they seek no more
Nor Covet Gold or Silver Oar
  The common Source of Strife.

The slender Garb their Bodies hide
Is far too Curious to Discribe
In this Invention's well supply'd
  With Nicest Art their Wants
Attend ye Criticks of the Trade
Whom here I seek not to degrade
It's neither Wove, nor Spun, but made
  From Wild & simple plants.

I scorn with Lyes your thoughts to Bilk
But know it's neither Flax nor Silk
Cotton nor Wool tho' white as Milk
  And wrought with Matchless pains
Some Coarse, some fine, and Painted O'er
Some Plain, In Breadth two yards or more
And Oft in lengths full seven Score
  Each Curious piece Contains.

Thro' every Grove a Silver Stream
Clear as the Brightest Christal Gem
Which Banks of Beauteous flowers Limn
  Unnumber'd Vales Adorn
Whilst unmolested Birds unite
To form the Rural Sweet Delight
Closing with Various Notes each Night
  And ushering in the Morn—

A Thousand Beauties more's too few
To give this Royall [Isle] its due
But here I cease, least these tho' true
   Should seem Romantic talk
Yet let me not in Silence pass
What well in this deserves a Place
An Island Sacred to his Grace
   The Royal Duke of York—
Which here in View with grandeur Rears
Proud of the Royal Name it Bears
High as the lofty glittering Stars
   Its ever verdant Head.
Beneath whose Shadey Pleasant Lawn
Which Various fragrant shrubs adorn
And Beauteous flowers daily born
   Around the borders spread.

But hark! The Boatswain's call, how shrill
Up Anchor Boys your Topsails fill
And Staysails hoist with free good Will
   Each jovial Tar Obeys.
And now we dare the wave once more
Ne'er Plow'd by Europe['s] Keels before
Discovering still a long hid Store
   Of Isles within those Seas.

For daily now fresh Land we make
And all in course their titles take
Saunders & How[e] the first partake
   Next Scilly's dangerous Isles we Spy
A Beauteous Island then we made
Be that Boscawen's, Wallis said,
Tho' low in Dust the Hero's laid
   His Name shall never Dye.

The next we made was Keppel's Isle
Where Nature kindly seem'd to smile
Fertile in fruits as Rich in Soill
   Inferior to none
Then several Days (with Gentle Gales

Smooth Seas, nor more than half-fill'd Sails
Elapsed) But Neptune scorn'd to fail
  A work so well begun.
Pleased with his Noble Generous Soul
Who rather chose the fame t'unroll
Of Absent friends, than keep the whole
  T'immortalize his own.

An Island soon the God prepared
Which just att Dawn of Day appear'd
And thus the friendly Monarch's heard
  T'address his Darling Son
Wallis! Be this your own, he said
Rearing above the Waves his head
Whilst Nereids round the Godhead spread
  And all approved the same.

From me Your Sire my Son receive
With Laurells such as I shall give
This Isle, which time shall ne'er outlive
  But ever Crown your Fame.

Pursue your Voyage with utmost Speed
May every future Wish succeed
Long may you Wear what Fate's decreed
  Should only Crown your Breed
My self will o'er the Dangerous Seas
Escort you safe where e'er you please
Then disappear'd. A gentle Breeze
  Confirm'd the Monarch's Vow.

The Breeze Increas'd, and fresh'ning Gales
Repleat the Bosoms of our Sails
Swift o'er the Boundless deep she steals
  Our Course for Tinian steers
But nothing Notice worth Occurs
No Isles except the Piccadores
We make, and those described before
  Need no discription here.

Of Wind or Weather Good or Bad
Or weather calm or Storm we had
Or whereabouts these Lands were made
   Some may conjecture well
Let homeward Travellers as they Please
Whose Book's their Helm, their Ship & Seas
Perplex their thoughts. To such as these
   O! Muse forbid to tell.
Why starts my muse, what sudden Cry
Proclaims the wish'd for Island Nigh
From Topmast head Tinian the spy
   At least some Neighbouring Cliffs
Wellcome thrice Wellcome happy Isle
Whose much reputed fertile Soil
So well rewards the Seaman's Toil
   With Nature's Bounteous Gifts.

With Crowded Sails we make the Shore
Our Anchors Drop, not long before
Our Boats we Man & ply each Oar
   The friendly beach to gain
With some few Spanish Huts we found
Our Tents we Pitch and form a Town
And Groves with Various fruits around
   Compleat a Rural scene.

Domestic Fowles around us fly
Wild as the Birds that Climb the sky
Of these each Day a Number Dye
   Each Day as many hatch'd.
Reptiles of many Various forms
Tho' few from which fear much harm
Yet Flyes innumerable swarm
   Unmiss'd the millions catch'd.

And now O'er Hills with swiftest pace
Young Steers or fairer Bulls we Chace
Who stranger to all human Race
   Gaze at th'unusual form
In numerous Herds they daily feed

Undaunted all, yet Fate's decreeed
One of their Milk white Herd shall bleed
  For us each coming Morn.

And once in Chace we kill'd a Boar
Thick as the sheild Great Ajax wore
His Brisley Hide, with hideous Roar
  The dread Monster falls
His Burnished Tusks of Wondrous Size
Ploughs up the Ground the Savage Dies
Tryumphant home we bear the Prize
  Astonishing to all.

Minute details I here forbear
In Anson's Voyage they're better far
Described in Prose than here I dare
  Attempt to Write in Verse
May it suffice that whilst we staid
Refreshment Various ways we had
Our ship repair'd our Anchors Weigh'd
  And steer'd our Destin'd Course.

In Java's famous Belgick Isle
The Pride of Holland Seamans Toil
Batavia's ever fertile soil
  Which all their States Obey
Here Grandeur Luxury and Pride
And all the Pomp of Wealth beside
O'er all their Indian States Preside
  With Arbitrary Sway.

Hither in some few weeks we came
But all remarks I cease to Name
The Indian Seas so well has Fame
  Described in every Realm
Let Infant Bards such Themes decline
At least an artless pen like mine
Wholly unformed for such design
  Shall ne'er attempt the Helm

.   .   .   .

Be kind ye Gales & waft us O'er
The Briny Waves to Brittains Shore
Let us with joy behold once more
  Our much loved Native Land
Then shall our Voyage in lists of Fame
Immortalize the Dolphins Name
Wrote in a more aspiring Strain
  By some more able Hand—

Further Reading

Hawkesworth's *Account of the Voyages* (London: Strahan and Cadell, 1773) has the fullest available narrative of Wallis's voyage from Wallis's point of view. George Robertson's journal is detailed and entertaining, and the Hakluyt Society edition, *The Discovery of Tahiti: Journal of the Second Voyage of the Dolphin*, ed. Hugh Carrington (London: Hakluyt Society, 1948), provides a good background to the voyage. On the *maro ura*, consult the chapter "Possessing Tahiti" in Greg Dening's *Performances* (Melbourne: Melbourne University Press 1996); see also Douglas Oliver, *Ancient Tahitian Society* (Honolulu: University of Hawaii Press, 1974). Bougainville's *Voyage Round the World*, trans. Johann Reinhold Forster (London: J. Nourse and T. Davies, 1772); and Diderot's "Supplement au voyage de Bougainville," in *Political Writings*, ed. John Hope Mason and Robert Wokler (Cambridge: Cambridge University Press, 1992), offer a more enthusiastic view of Tahitian culture than Wallis supplies; Banks's and Cook's journals are somewhere in between.

7

JOHN HAWKESWORTH
The Unfortunate Compiler

· ·

JOHN HAWKESWORTH (1715–73), friend and associate of Samuel Johnson, must have felt a worthy career in belles lettres had been crowned with public recognition when he was appointed by Lord Sandwich, first lord of the Admiralty, to prepare for publication the journals of the commanders and scientists recently involved in the naval explorations of the Pacific Ocean. Besides the fame, there was the addition of a considerable sum of money (£6000), the amount agreed between him and William Strahan for the copy. But even before the volumes were ready for sale, Hawkesworth was involved in litigation with Stanfield Parkinson, who was trying surreptitiously to publish the journal of his brother Sydney, Joseph Banks's artist on the first voyage. Once the public had an opportunity to digest Hawkesworth's achievement, his peace of mind was at an end. He was widely criticized, sometimes abusively, for the scandalous scenes of public sexuality Wallis, Cook, and Banks had witnessed in Tahiti; and he was taken to task for his heterodox views of providence, which he had outlined in his preface. Many readers found his narrative overloaded with particulars, while others thought him too sententious and generalizing. Alexander Dalrymple blamed him for the bad cartography that had contributed, in his opinion, to Cook's failure to find the Great Southern Continent; and went on with great asperity to reprobate the shooting down of native people, as if Hawkesworth were implicated. Elizabeth Carter wrote to Elizabeth Montagu, "It gives one pleasure to find that this nation has still virtue enough left to be shocked and disgusted by an attack upon religion, and an outrage against decency" (Carter 1817, 2:209). Whether it was virtue or humbug that was being defended was a question Hawkesworth was beyond resolving six months later, when he died of a broken heart, according to Fanny Burney (F. Burney 1907, 1:271). Mrs. Piozzi lamented: "Hawkesworth, the pious, the virtuous, and the wise" who fell a "sacrifice to wanton malice and cruelty" (Piozzi [1786] 1984, 85).

Hawkesworth's problems with his public arose to some extent from an ambiguous relationship to his journalists, particularly Cook and Banks; and from the definite and unflattering views he took of human behavior. He adopted a convention already common among French compilers of delivering voyages in the first person, as if he were Cook or Byron, and resorting to the third person only when he was in doubt about the accuracy of the original observation. This, he believed, would leave the same vivid impressions on the reader's mind as an epistolary fiction (indeed he compares his work to Richardson's novels), "by bringing the Adventurer and the Reader nearer together, without the intervention of a stranger" (Hawkesworth 1773, 1:iv). Seemingly, all the bad things that Cook saw, and all the equivocal situations into which Banks inserted himself, were laid at Hawkesworth's door, while all the heroism of discovery and scientific curiosity was reserved to the originals. This unfair distribution of praise was owing to Hawkesworth's other narrative proviso, namely of interspersing "such sentiments and observations as my subject should suggest" (1773, 1:v). Although it is often assumed that this resulted in an overwrought literary burlesque, with Hawkesworth making a maladroit display of his learning in the face of primitive material that was handled more concisely in the original journals, he is not often guilty of pointless parallels or sentimentalizing ornaments, as the following extracts indicate. It is true that Hawkesworth expands a scene he thinks important, but it is seldom with the intention of palliating European reactions or of idealizing indigenous ones. Instead he suggests that there is no limit to what human beings are capable of, either in the spheres of sexual desire or violence. He has a very unconsoling view of the degree to which any action can be moralized. Of Cook's (and Banks's and Solander's) shooting down of four unarmed Maori, he simply observes, "When the command to fire has been given, no man can restrain its excess, or prescribe its effect" (1773, 2:290). Similarly, the Timorodee dance suggests that even in paradise, "there is a scale in dissolute sensuality, which these people have ascended" (1773, 2: 206). The fight for the boats that he imagines would have taken place if the *Endeavour* had foundered off the Australian coast, a hypothesis all his own and without any authority from Cook and Banks, is consonant with those uncharitable judgments of the instinct for self-preservation common earlier in the century among thinkers such as John Trenchard and Bernard Mandeville. Indeed, the tendency to underestimate Hawkesworth's skill at probing the abyss opening up between facts and values in an increasingly commercial culture derives from a similar tendency to assume that Johnson, his friend and collaborator, was largely and imprecisely sententious; whereas Johnson told Mrs. Thrale that "he had been a great reader of Mandeville, and was ever on the watch to spy out those stains of original corruption, so easily discovered by a penetrating observer even in the purest minds" (Piozzi [1786] 1984, 40). — JONATHAN LAMB

. . . .

James Cook, The *Endeavour* Journal, 1768–71, MS 1, National Library of Australia, Canberra; Joseph Banks, Journal on *HMS Endeavour*, Mitchell Library, State Library of NSW, Sydney, Safe 1/12–13; John Hawkesworth, *An Account of the Voyages Undertaken by the Order of His Present Majesty for Making Discoveries in the Southern Hemisphere*, 3 vols. (London: W. Strahan and T. Cadell, 1773).

Massacre at Poverty Bay

« JAMES COOK, THE ENDEAVOUR JOURNAL. »

Monday 10th [October 1769]. PM I rowed round the head of the Bay but could not find no place to land, on account of the great surff which beat every where upon the shore; seeing two boats or Canoes coming in from Sea, I rowed to one of them in order to seize upon the people and came so near before they took notice of us that Tupia called to them to come a long side and we would not hurt them, but instead of doing that they endeavoured to get away, upon which I order'd a Musquet to be fire'd over their heads thinking that this would either make them surrender or jump over board, but here I was misstaken for they immidiately took thier arms or whatever they had in the boat and began to attack us, this obliged us to fire upon them and unfortunatly either two or three were kill'd, and one wounded, and three jumped over board, these last we took up and brought on board, where they were clothed and treated with all immaginable kindness and to the surprise of every body became at once as cheerful and as merry as if they had been with their own friends; they were all three young, the eldest not above 20 years of age and the youngest about 10 or 12—

I am aware that most humane men who have not experienced things of this nature will cencure my conduct in fireing upon the people in this boat nor do I my self think that the reason I had for seizing upon her will att all justify me, and had I thought that they would have made the least resistance I would not have come near them, but as they did I was not to stand still and suffer either my self or those that with me to be knocked on the head.

« JOSEPH BANKS, JOURNAL ON *HMS Endeavour.* »

[9 October 1769] The Indians retird gently carrying with them their wounded and we reembarked in our boats intending to row round the bay, see if there might be any shelter for the ship on the other side, and attempt to land there where the countrey appeared to be much more fruitfull than where we now were. The bottom of the bay provd to be a low and sandy beach on which the sea broke most prodigiously so that we could not come near it; within was flat, a long way inland over this water might be seen from the mast head probably a lagoon but in the boat we could see no entrance into it. We had almost arrivd at the farthest part of the bay when a fresh breze came in from the seaward and we saw a Canoe sailing in standing right towards [us], soon after another padling. The Captn now resolvd to take one of these which in all probablility might be done without the least resistance as we had three boats full of men and the canoes seemd to be fishermen, who probably were without arms. The boats were drawn up in such a manner that they could not well escape us: the padling canoe first saw us and made immediately for the nearest land, the other saild on till she was in the midst of us before she saw us, as soon as she did she struck her sail and began to paddle so briskly that she outran our boat; on a musquet being fird over her she however immediately ceasd padling and the people in her, 7 in all, made all possible haste to strip as we thought to leap into the water, but no sooner did our boat come up with her than they began with stones, paddles &c. to make so brisk a resistance that we were obligd to fire into her by which 4 were killd. The other three who were boys leapd overboard, one of them swam with great agility and when taken made every effort in his power to prevent being taken into the boat, the other two were more easily prevaild upon. As soon as they were in they squatted down expecting no doubt instant death, but on finding themselves well usd and that Cloaths were given them they recoverd their spirits in a very short time and before we got to the ship appeard almost totaly insensible of the loss of their fellows. As soon as they came onboard we offerd them bread to eat of which they almost devourd a large quantity, in the mean time they had Cloaths given them; this good usage had such an

effect that they seemd to have intirely forgot every thing that had happ-
ned, put on chearfull and lively countenances and askd and answerd questions with a great deal of curiosity. Our dinner came, they expressd a curiosity to taste whatever they saw us eat, and did; salt pork seemd to please
them better than any thing else, of this they eat a good deal. At sunset they
eat again an enormous quantity of Bread and drank above a quart of water
each; we then made them beds upon the lockers and they laid down to
sleep with all seeming content imaginable. After dark loud voices were
heard ashore as last night. Thus ended the most disagreable day My life
has yet seen, black be the mark for it and heaven send that such may never
return to embitter future reflection. I forgot to mention in its proper place
that we pickd up a large pumice stone floating in the bay in returning to
the ship today, a sure sign that there either is or has been a Volcano in this
neighbourhood.

   10 [October]. In the middle of the last night one of our boys seemd to
shew more reflection than he had before done sighing often and loud;
Tupia who was always upon the watch to comfort them got up and soon
made them easy. They then sung a song of their own, it was not without
some taste, like a Psalm tune and containd many notes and semitones; they
sung it in parts which gives us no indifferent Idea of their taste as well as
skill in musick. The oldest of them is about 18, the middlemos[t] 15, the
youngest 10; the midlemost especialy has a most open contenance and
agreable manner; their names are *Taáhourange, Koikerange,* and *Maragooete,*
the first two brothers. In the morning they were all very chearfull and eat
an enormous quantity, after that they were dressd and ornamented with
bracelets, ancklets and necklaces after their own fashion.

« JOHN HAWKESWORTH, *An Account of the Voyages.* »
VOL. 2, BOOK 2, CHAPTER I, PP. 289–90.

[Monday 9 October 1769] To my great regret I found no place where I
could land, a dangerous surf every [w]here beating upon the shore; but I
saw two canoes coming in from the sea, one under sail, and the other
worked with paddles. I thought this a favourable opportunity to get some
of the people into my possession without mischief as those in the canoe
were probably fishermen, and without arms, and I had three boats full of
men. I therefore disposed the boats so far as most effectually to intercept
with the[m] in their way to the shore; the people in the canoe that was
paddled perceived us so soon, that by making to the nearest land with their

utmost strength, they escaped us; the other sailed on till she was in the midst of us, without discerning what we were; but the moment she discovered, the people on board struck their sail and took to their paddles, which they plied so briskly that the[y] out-ran the boat. They were within hearing, and Tupia called out to then to come along side, and promised for us that they should come to no hurt: they chose, however, rather to trust to their paddles than our promises, and continued to make from us with all their power. I then ordered a musquet to be fired over their heads, as the least exceptionable expedient to accomplish my design, hoping it would either make them surrender or leap into the water. Upon the discharge of the piece, they ceased paddling; and all of them, being seven in number, began to strip, as we imagine to jump overboard; but it happened otherwise. They immediately formed a resolution not to fly, but to fight; and when the boat came up, they began to attack with their paddles, and with stones and with other offensive weapons that were in the boat, so vigorously, that we were obliged to fire upon them in our own defence: four were unhappily killed, and the other three who were boys, the eldest about nineteen, and the youngest about eleven, instantly leaped into the water; the eldest swam with great vigour, and resisted the attempts of our people to take him into the boat by every effort that he could make: he was however at last overpowered, and the other two were taken up with less difficulty. I am conscious that the feeling of every reader of humanity will censure me for having fired upon these unhappy people, and it is impossible that, upon a calm review, I should approve it myself. They certainly did not deserve death for not chusing to confide in my promises; or not consenting to come on board my boat, even if they had apprehended no danger; but the nature of my service required me to obtain a knowledge of their country, which I could no otherwise effect than by forcing my way into it in a hostile manner, or gaining admission through the confidence and good-will of the people. I had already tried the power of presents without effect; and I was now prompted, by my desire to avoid further hostilities, to get some of them on board, as the only method left of convincing them that we intended them no harm, and had it in our power to contribute to their gratification and convenience. Thus far my intentions were certainly not criminal; and though in the contest, which I had not the least reason to expect, our victory might have been complete with out so great and expense of life; yet in such situations, when the command to fire has been given, no man can restrain its excess, or prescribe its effect.

The Timorodee Dance

« JAMES COOK, THE *Endeavour* JOURNAL. »

[July 1769] The young girls when ever they can collect 8 or 10 together dance a very indecent dance which they call *Timorodee* singing most indecent songs and useing most indecent actions in the pratice of which they are brought up from their earlyest Childhood, in doing this they keep time to a great nicety; this exercise is however generaly left of as soon as they arrive at years of maturity for as soon as they have form'd a connection with man they are expected to leave of dancing *Timorodee*. One amusement or Custom more I must mention tho I must confess I do not expect to be believed as it is founded upon a Custom so inhuman and contrary to the first principals of human nature: it is this, that more than one half of the better sort of the inhabitants have enter'd into a resolution of injoying free liberty in love without being troubled or disturbed by its concequences; these mix and cohabit together with the utmost freedom and the Children who are so unfortunate as to be thus begot are smother'd at the moment of their birth; many of these people contract intimacies and live together as man and wife for years in the Course of which the Children that are born are destroy'd. They are so far from concealing it that they rather look upon it as a branch of freedom upon which they value themselves. They are call'd *Arreoy's* and have meetings among themselves where the men amuse themselves with wristling &ca and the women in dancing the indecent dance before mentioned, in the Course of which they give full liberty to their desires but I believe keep up to the appearence of decency. I never saw one of these meetings. Dr Munkhouse saw part of one enough to make him give credit to what we had been told.

Both sexes express the most indecent ideas in conversation without the least emotion and they delight in such conversation behond any other. Chastity indeed is but little Valued especialy a mong the middle people, if a wife is found guilty of a breach of it her only punishment is a beating from her husband; the men will very readily offer the young women to strangers even their own daughters and think it very strange if you refuse them but this is done meerly for the lucre of gain—

« JOSEPH BANKS, JOURNAL ON *HMS Endeavour.* »

[August 1769] Besides this they dance especialy the young girls whenever they can collect 8 or 10 together, singing most indecent words using most indecent actions and setting their mouths askew in a most extrordinary manner, in the practise of which they are brought up from their earlyest childhood; in doing this they keep time to a surprizing nicety, I might almost say as true as any dancers I have seen in Europe tho their time is certainly much more simple. This excercise is however left off as soon as they arrive at Years of maturity for as soon as ever they have formd a connection with a man they are expected to leave of Dancing *Timorodee* as it is calld.

One amusement more I must mention tho I confess I hardly dare touch upon it as it is founded upon a custom so devilish, inhuman, and contrary to the first principles of human nature that tho the natives have repeatedly told it to me, far from concealing it rather looking upon it as a branch of freedom upon which they valued themselves, I can hardly bring myself to beleive it much less expect that any body Else shall. It is this that more than half of the better sort of the inhabitants of the Island have like Comus in Milton enterd into a resolution of enjoying free liberty in love without a possibility of being troubled or disturbd by its consequences; these mix together with the utmost freedom seldom cohabiting together more than one or two days by which means they have fewer children than they would otherwise have, but those who are so unfortunate as to be thus begot are smotherd at the moment of their birth. Some of these people have been pointed out to me by name and on being askd have not denyd the fact, who have contracted intimacies and livd together for years and even now continue to do so, in the course of which 2, 3 or more children have been born and destroyd.

They are calld *Arreoy* and have meetings among themselves where the men amuse themselves with wrestling &c. and the women with dancing the indecent dances before mentiond, in the course of which they give full liberty to their desires but I beleive keep strictly up to the appearances of decency. I never was admitted to see them, one of our gentlemen saw part of one but I beleive very little of their real behavior tho he saw enough to make him give credit to what we had been told.

This custom as indeed it is natural to suppose Owes as we were told its existence cheifly to the men. A Woman howsoever fond she may be of the name of Arreoy and the liberty attending it before she conceives, generaly desires much to forfeit that title for the preservation of her child: in this she has not the smallest influence; if she cannot find a man who will own it she must of course destroy it; and if she can, with him alone it lies whether or not it shall be preserv'd: sometimes it is, but in that case both the man and woman forfeit their title of Arreoy and the privelege annext thereunto, and must for the future be known by the term *Whannownow*, or bearer of children: a title as disgracefull among these people as it ought to be honourable in every good and well governd society. In this case the man and woman generaly live together as man and wife for the remainder of their lives.

« JOHN HAWKESWORTH, *An Account of the Voyages.* »
VOL. 2, BOOK I, CHAPTER 18, PP. 206–9.

1769. Among other diversions there is a dance they called the *Timorodee*, which is performed by the young girls whenever eight or ten of them can be collected together, consisting of motions and gestures beyond the imagination wanton, in the practice of which they are brought up from their earliest childhood, accompanied by words, which, if it were possible, would more explicitly convey the same ideas. In there dances they keep time with an exactness which is scarcely excelled by the best performers upon the stages of Europe. But the practice which is allowed to the virgin, is prohibited to the woman from the moment that she has put the hopeful lessons in practice, and realized the symbols of the dance.

It cannot be supposed that, among these people, chastity is held in much estimation. It might be expected that the sisters and daughters would be offered to strangers, either as a courtesy, or for reward; and that breaches of conjugal fidelity, even in the wife, should not be otherwise punished than by a few hard words, or perhaps a slight beating, as indeed is the case: but there is a scale in dissolute sensuality, which these people have ascended, wholly unknown to every other nation whose manners have been recorded from the beginning of the world to the present hour, and which no imagination could possibly conceive. A very considerable number of the principal people of Otaheite, of both sexes, have formed themselves into a society, in which every woman is common to every man; thus securing a perpetual variety as often as their inclination prompts them to seek it, which is so frequent that the same man and woman seldom cohabit together more than two or three days.

These societies are distinguished by the name of *Arreoy*; and the members have meetings, at which no other is present, where the men amuse themselves by wrestling, and the women, notwithstanding their occasional connection with different men, dance the Timorodee in all its latitude, as an incitement to desires which it is said are frequently gratified upon the spot. This however is comparatively nothing. If any of the women happen to be with child, which in this manner of life happens less frequently than if they were to cohabit with only one man, the poor infant is smothered the moment it is born, that it may be no incumbrance to the father, nor interrupt the mother in the pleasures of her diabolical prostitution. It sometimes indeed happens, that the passion which prompts a woman to enter into this society, is surmounted when she becomes a mother, by that instinctive affection which Nature has given to all creatures for the preservation of their offspring; but even in this case, she is not permitted to spare the life of her infant, except that she can find a man who will patronise it as his child: if this can be done the murder is prevented; but both the man and woman being deemed by this act too have appropriated each other are ejected from the community, and forfeit all claim to the privileges and pleasures of Arreoy for the future; the woman from that time being distinguished by the term *Whannownow*, "bearer of children," which is here a term of reproach; though none can be more honourable in the estimation of wisdom and humanity, of right reason, and every passion that distinguishes the man from the brute.

It is not fit that a practice so horrid and so strange should be imputed to human beings upon slight evidence, but I have such as abundantly justifies me in the account I have given. The people themselves are so far from concealing their connection with such a society as a disgrace, that they boast of it as a privilege; and both myself and Mr. Banks, when particular persons have been pointed out to us as members of the Arreoy, have questioned them about it, and received the account that has been given from their own lips. They have acknowledged, that they have long been of this accursed society, that they belonged to it at that time, and that several of their children had been put to death.

On and Off the Reef

« JAMES COOK, THE *Endeavour* JOURNAL. »

[11 June 1770] Before 10 oClock we had 20 and 21 fathom and continued in that depth untill a few Minutes before a 11 when we had 17 and before the Man at the lead could heave another cast the Ship Struck and stuck fast. Emmidiatly upon this we took in all our sails hoisted out the boats and sounded round the Ship, and found that we had got upon the SE edge of a reef of Coral rocks having in some places round the Ship 3 and 4 fathom water and in other places not quite as many feet, and about a Ships length from us on our starboard side (the ship laying with her head to the NE) were 8, 10 and 12 fathom. As soon as the long boat was out we struck yards and Topmts and carried out the stream anchor upon the starboard bow, got the Casting anchor and cable into the boat and were going to carry it out the same way; but upon my sounding the second time round the Ship I found the most water a stern, and therefore had this anchor carried out upon the Starboard quarter and hove upon it a very great strean which was to no purpose the Ship being quite fast, upon which we went to work to lighten her as fast as possible which seem'd to be the only means we had left to get her off as we went a Shore about the top of high-water. We not only started water but throw'd over board our guns Iron and stone ballast Casks, Hoops staves oyle Jars, decay'd stores &ca, many of these last articles lay in the way at coming at heavyer. All this time the Ship made little or no water. At a 11 oClock in the AM being high-water as we thought we try'd to heave her off without success, she not being a float by a foot or more notwithstanding by this time we had thrown over board 40 or 50 Tun weight; as this was not found sufficient we continued to Lighten her by every method we could think off. As the Tide fell the Ship began to make water as much as two Pumps could free. At Noon she lay with 3 or 4 Strakes heel to Starboard. Latitude Observed I5°45' South—

Tuesday 12th. Fortunatly we had little wind fine weather and a smooth Sea all these 24 hours which in the PM gave us an oppertunity to carry out the two bower Anchors, the one on the Starboard quarter and the other right astern. Got blocks and tackles upon the Cables brought the falls in abaft and hove taught. By this time it was 5 oClock in the pm, the tide we observed now begun to rise and the leak increased upon us which obliged us to set the 3rd Pump to work as we should have done the 4th also, but could not make it work. At 9 oClock the Ship righted and the leak gaind upon the Pumps considerably. This was an alarming and I may say terrible Circumstance and threatend immidiate destruction to us as soon as the Ship was afloat. However I resolved to resk all and heave her off in case it was practical and accordingly turnd as many hands to the Capstan & windlass as could be spared from the Pumps and about 20' past 10 oClock the Ship floated and we hove her off into deep water having at this time 3 feet 9 Inches water in the hold. This done I sent the Long boat to take up the stream anchor—got the anchor but lost the Cable among the rocks, after this turn'd all hands to the Pumps the leak increasing upon us. A Mistake soon after happened, which for the first time caused fear to operate upon every man in the Ship. The man which attend the well took ye depth of water above the ceiling, he being relieved by another who did not know in what manner the former had sounded, took the depth of water from the out side plank, the difference being 16 or 18 Inches and made it appear that the leak had gain'd this upon the pumps in a short time; this mistake taken was no sooner clear'd up than acted upon every man like a charm; they redoubled their Vigour in so much that before 8 oClock in the Morning they gain'd considerably upon the leak. We now hove up the best bower but found it impossible to save the small bower so cut it away at a whole Cable. Got up the fore topmast and fore yard, warped the Ship to the SE and at a 11 got under Sail and Stood in for the land with a light breeze at ESE, some hands employ'd sowing ockam wool &ca into a lower Studding sail to fother the Ship, others emplo'd at the Pumps which still gain'd upon the leak—

Wednesday 13th. In the PM had light airs at ESE with which we kept edgeing in for the land, got up the Main topmast and Main yard and having got the sail ready for fothering the Ship we put it over under the Starboard fore chains where we suspected the Ship had sufferd most and soon after the leak decreased so as to be kept clear with one Pump with ease, this fortunate circumstance gave new life to every one on board. It is much easier to conceive then to discribe the satisfaction felt by every body on this occation, but a few minutes before our utmost wishes were to get hold of some place upon the Main or an Island to run the Ship ashore where out of her Materials we might build a vessel to carry us to the East Indias; no sooner were we made sensible that the outward application to the Ships bottom had taken effect than the feild of every mans hopes inlarged so that we now thought of nothing but rainging along shore in search of a harbour where we could repair the damages we had susstaind. In justice to the Ships Company I must say that no men ever behaved better than they have done on this occasion, animated by the beheavour of every gentleman on board, every man seem'd to have a just sence of the danger we were in and exerted himself to the very utmost—

« JOSEPH BANKS, JOURNAL ON *HMS Endeavour.* »

[10 June 1770] While we were at supper she went over a bank of 7 or 8 fathom water which she came upon very suddenly; this we concluded to be the tail of the Sholes we had seen at sunset and therefore went to bed in perfect security, but scarce were we warm in our beds when we were calld up with the alarming news of the ship being fast ashore upon a rock, which she in a few moments convincd us of by beating very violently against the rocks. Our situation became now greatly alarming: we had stood off shore 3 hours and a half with a pleasant breeze so knew we could not be very near it: we were little less than certain that we were upon sunken coral rocks, the most dreadfull of all others on account of their sharp points and grinding quality which cut through a ships bottom almost immediately. The officers however behavd with inimitable coolness void of all hurry and confusion; a boat was got out in which the master went and after sounding round the ship found that she had ran over a rock and consequently had Shole water all round her. All this time she continued to beat very much so that we could hardly keep our legs upon the Quarter deck; by the light of the moon we could see her sheathing boards &c. floating thick round her; about 12 her false keel came away.

11. In the mean time all kind of Preparations were making for carrying out anchors, but by reason of the time it took to hoist out boats &c. the tide ebbd so much that we found it impossible to attempt to get her off till next high water, if she would hold together so long; and we now found to add to our misfortune that we had got ashore nearly at the top of high water and as night tides generaly rise higher than day ones we had little hopes of getting off even then. For our Comfort however the ship as the tide ebbd settled to the rocks and did not beat near so much as she had done; a rock however under her starboard bow kept grating her bottom making a noise very plainly to be heard in the fore store rooms; this we doubted not would make a hole in her bottom, we only hopd that it might not let in more water than we could clear with our pumps.

In this situation day broke upon us and showd us the land about 8 Leagues off as we judgd; nearer than that was no Island or place on which we could set foot. It however brought with it a decrease of wind and soon after that a flat calm, the most fortunate circumstance that could Possibly attend people in our circumstances. The tide we found had falln 2 feet and still continued to fall; Anchors were however got out and laid ready for heaving as soon as the tide should rise but to our great surprize we could not observe it to rise in the least.

Orders were now given for lightning the ship which was began by starting our water and pumping it up; the ballast was then got up and thrown over board, as well as 6 of our guns (all that we had upon deck). All this time the Seamen workd with surprizing chearfullness and alacrity; no grumbling or growling was to be heard throughout the ship, no not even an oath (tho the ship in general was as well furnishd with them as most in his majesties service). About one the water was faln so low that the Pinnace touchd ground as he lay under the ships bows ready to take in an anchor, after this the tide began to rise and as it rose the ship workd violently upon the rocks so that by 2 she began to make water and increasd very fast. At night the tide almost floated her but she made water so fast that three pumps hard workd could but just keep her clear and the 4th absolutely refusd to deliver a drop of water. Now in my own opinion I intirely gave up the ship and packing up what I thought I might save prepard myself for the worst.

The most critical part of our distress now aproachd: the ship was almost afloat and every thing ready to get her into deep water but she leakd so fast that with all our pumps we could just keep her free: if (as was probable) she should make more water when hauld off she must sink and we well knew that our boats were not capable of carrying us all ashore, so that some, probably the most of us, must be drownd: a better fate maybe than those would have who should get ashore without arms to defend themselves from the Indians or provide themselves with food, on a countrey where we had not the least reason to hope for subsistance had they even every convenence to take it as netts &c, so barren had we always found it; and had they even met with good usage from the natives and food to support them, debarrd from a hope of ever again seing their native countrey or conversing with any but the most uncivilizd savages perhaps in the world.

The dreadfull time now aproachd and the anziety in every bodys countenance was visible enough: the Capstan and Windlace were mannd and they began to heave: fear of Death now stard us in the face; hopes we had none but of being able to keep the ship afloat till we could run her ashore on some part of the main where out of her materials we might build a vessel large enough to carry us to the East Indies. At 10 O'Clock she floated and was in a few minutes hawld into deep water where to our great satisfaction she made no more water than she had done, which was indeed full as much as we could manage tho no one there was in the ship but who willingly exerted his utmost strengh.

12. The people who had been 24 hours at exceeding hard work now began to flag; myself unusd to labour was much fatigued and had laid down to take a little rest, was awakd about 12 with the alarming news of the ships having gaind so much upon the Pumps that she had four feet water in her hold: add to this that the wind blew off the land a regular land breeze so that all hopes of running her ashore were totaly cut off. This however acted upon every body like a charm: rest was no more thought of but the pumps went with unwearied vigour till the water was all out which

was done in a much shorter time than was expected, and upon examination it was found that she never had half so much water in her as was thought, the Carpenter having made a mistake in sounding the pumps.

We now began again to have some hopes and to talk of getting the ship into some harbour as we could spare hands from the pumps to get up our anchors; one Bower however we cut away but got the other and three small anchors far more valuable to us than the Bowers, as we were obligd immediately to warp her to windward that we might take advantage of the sea breeze to run in shore.

One of our midshipmen now proposd an expedient which no one else in the ship had seen practisd, tho all had heard of it by the name of fothering a ship, by the means of which he said he had come home from America in a ship which made more water than we did; nay so sure was the master of that ship of his expedient that he took her out of harbour knowing how much water she made and trusting intirely to it. He was immediately set to work with 4 or 5 assistants to prepare his fother which he did thus. He took a lower studding sail and having mixd together a large quantity of Oakum chopd fine and wool he stickd it down upon the sail as loosely as possible in small bundles each about as big as his fist, these were rangd in rows 3 or 4 inches from each other: this was to be sunk under the ship and the theory of it was this, where ever the leak was must be a great suction which would probably catch hold of one or other of these lumps of Oakum and wool and drawing it in either partly or intirely stop up the hole. While this work was going on the water rather gaind on those who were pumping which made all hands impatient for the tryal. In the afternoon the ship was got under way with a gentle breeze of wind and stood in for the land; soon after the fother was finishd and applyd by fastning ropes to each Corner, then sinking the sail under the ship and with these ropes drawing it as far backwards as we could; in about 1/2 an hour to our great surprize the ship was pumpd dry and upon letting the pumps stand she was found to make very little water, so much beyond our most sanguine Expectations had this singular expedient succeeded. At night came to an anchor, the fother still keeping her almost clear so that we were in an instant raisd from almost despondency to the greatest hopes: we were now almost too sanguine talking of nothing but getting her into some harbour where we might lay her ashore and repair her, or if we could not find such a place we little doubted to the East indies.

During the whole time of this distress I must say for the credit of our people that I beleive every man exerted his utmost for the preservation of the ship, contrary to what I have universaly heard to be the behavior of sea men who have commonly as soon as a ship is in a desperate situation began to plunder and refuse all command. This was no doubt owing intirely to the cool and steady conduct of the officers, who during the whole time never gave an order which did not shew them to be perfectly composd and unmovd by the circumstances howsoever dreadfull they might appear.

« JOHN HAWKESWORTH, *An Account of the Voyages.* »
VOL. 3, BOOK 3, CHAPTER 5, PP. 545–49.

[Sunday, 10 June 1770] We had the advantage of a fine breeze, and a clear moonlight night, we deepened our water from fourteen to twenty-one fathom, but while we were at supper it suddenly shoaled, and we fell into twelve, ten, and eight fathom, within the space of a few minutes; I immediately ordered every body to their station, and all was ready to put about and come to an anchor, but meeting at the next cast of the lead with deep water again, we concluded that we had gone over the tail of the shoals which we had seen at sun-set, and that all danger was past: before ten, we had twenty and one and twenty fathom, and this depth continuing, the gentlemen left the deck in great tranquillity, and went back to bed; but a few minutes before eleven, the water shallowed at once from twenty to seventeen fathom, and before the lead could be cast again, the ship struck, and remained immoveable, except by the heaving of the surge, that beat her against the crags of the rock upon which she lay. In a few moments every body was upon the deck, with countenances which sufficiently expressed the horrors of our situation. We had stood off the shore three hours and a half, with a pleasant breeze, and therefore knew that we could not be very near it, and we had too much reason to conclude that we were upon the rock of coral, which is more fatal that any other, because the points of it are sharp, and every part of the surface so rough as to grind away whatever is rubbed against it, even with the gentlest motion. In this situation all the sails were immediately taken in, and the boats hoisted out to examine the depth of the water around our ship: we soon discovered that our fears had not aggravated our misfortune, and that the vessel had been lifted over a ledge of the rock, and lay in a hollow within it: in some places there was from three to four fathom, and in others not so many feet. The ship lay with her head to the N.E.; and at the distance of about thirty yards on the starboard side the water deepened to eight, ten, and twelve fathom. As soon as the long-boat was out, we struck our yards and topmasts, and carried out the stream anchor on the starboard bow, got the coasting anchor and cable into the boat, and we were going to carry it out the same way; but upon founding a second time round the ship, the water was found to be deepest astern: the anchor therefore was carried out from the starboard quarter instead of the starboard bow, that is, from the stern instead of the head, and having taken ground, our utmost force was applied to the capstern, hoping that if the anchor did not come home, the ship would be got off, but to our great misfortune and disappointment we could not move her: during all this time she continued to beat with great violence against the rock, so that it was with the utmost difficulty that we kept upon our legs; and to complete the scene of distress, we saw by the light of the moon the sheathing boards from the bottom of the vessel floating away all round her, and at last her false keel, so that every moment was making way for the sea to rush in which was to swallow us up. We had now no chance but to lighten her, and we had lost the opportunity of doing that to the greatest advantage, for unhappily we went on shore just at high water, and by this time it had considerably fallen, so that after she should be lightened so as to draw as much less water as the water had sunk, we should be but in the same situation as at first; and the only alleviation of this circumstance was, that as the tide ebbed the ship settled to the rocks, and was not beaten against them with so much violence. We had indeed some hope from the next tide, but it was doubtful whether she would hold together so long, especially as the rock kept scraping her bottom under the starboard bow with such force as to be heard in the fore store-room. This however was no time to indulge conjecture, nor was any effort remitted in despair of success: that no time might be lost, the water was immediately started in the hold, and pumped up; six of our guns, being all we had upon the deck, our iron and stone ballast, casks, hoop staves, oil jars, decayed stores, and many other things that lay in the way of heavier materials, were thrown overboard with the utmost expedition, every one exerting himself with an alacrity almost approaching to cheerfulness, without the least repining or discontent; yet the men were so far imprest with a sense of their situation, that not an oath was heard among them, the habit of profaneness, however strong, being instantly subdued, by the dread of incurring guilt when death seemed to be so near.

[Monday, 11 June] While we were thus employed, day broke upon us, and we saw the land at about eight leagues distance, without any island in the intermediate space, upon which, if the ship should have gone to pieces, we might have been set ashore by the boats, and from which they might have taken us by different turns to the main: the wind however gradually died away, and early in the forenoon it was a dead calm; if it had blown hard, the ship must inevitably have been destroyed. At eleven in the forenoon we expected high water, and anchors were got out, and every thing made ready for another effort to heave her off if she should float, but to our inexpressible surprize and concern she did not float by a foot and an half, though we had lightened her near fifty ton, so much did the day-tide fall short of that in the night. We now proceeded to lighten her still more, and threw overboard every thing that it was possible for us to spare: hitherto she had not admitted much water, but as the tide fell, it rushed in so fast, that two pumps, incessantly worked, could scarcely keep her free. At two o'clock, she lay heeling two or three streaks to starboard, and the pinnace, which lay under her bows, touched the ground: we had now no hope but from the tide at midnight, and to prepare for it we carried out our two bower anchors, one on the starboard quarter, and the other right a-stern, got the blocks and tackle which were to give us a purchase upon the cables in order, and brought the falls, or ends of them, in abaft, straining them tight, that the next effort might operate upon the ship, and by shortening the length of the cable between that and the anchors, draw her off the ledge upon which she rested, towards the deeper water. About five o'clock in the afternoon, we observed the tide begin to rise, but we observed at the same time that the leak increased to a most alarming degree, so that two more pumps were manned, but unhappily only one of them would work: three of the pumps however were kept going, and at nine o'clock the ship righted, but the leak had gained upon us so considerably, that it was imagined she must go to the bottom as soon as she ceased to be supported by the rock: this was a dreadful circumstance, so that we anticipated the floating of the ship not as an earnest of deliverance, but as an event that would probably precipitate our destruction. We well knew that our boats were not capable of carrying us all on shore, and that when the dreadful crisis should arrive, as all command and subordination would be at an end, a contest for preference would probably ensue, that would increase the horrors even of shipwreck, and terminate in the destruction of us all by the hands of each other; yet we knew that if any should be left board to perish in the waves, they would probably suffer less upon the whole that those who should get upon shore, without any lasting or effectual defence against the natives, in a country, where even nets and fire-arms would scarcely furnish them with food; and where, if they should find the means of subsistence, they must be condemned to languish out the remainder of life in a desolate wilderness, without the possession, or even hope, of any domestic comfort, and cut off from all commerce with mankind, except the naked savages who prowled the desert, and who perhaps were some of the most rude and uncivilized upon the earth.

To those only who have waited in a state of such suspense, death has approached in all its terrors; and as the dreadful moment that was to determine our fate came on, every one saw his own sensations pictured in the countenances of his companions: however, the capstan and windlace were manned with as many hands as could be spared from the pumps, and the ship floating about twenty minutes after ten o'clock, the effort was made, and she was heaved into deep water.

Further Reading

The most informed assessments of Hawkesworth's failure as a compiler are to be found in W. H. Pearson, "Hawkesworth's Alterations," *Journal of Pacific History* 7 (1972): 45–71; P. J. Marshall and Glyndwr Williams, *The Great Map of Mankind: British Perceptions of the World in the Age of Enlightenment* (London: Dent, 1982), especially pp. 270–74; the introduction to Robert E. Gallagher, ed., *Byron's Journal of His Circumnavigation, 1764–66* (Cambridge: Hakluyt Society, 1964); and J. C. Beaglehole, ed., *The Voyage of the Endeavour* (Cambridge: Hakluyt Society, 1955), ccxlii–liii. For the most lucid of the contemporary onslaughts, read Alexander Dalrymple, *A Letter to Dr Hawkesworth* (London: Printed for J. Nourse, T. Payne, Brotherton and Sewell, B. White, J. Robson, P. Elmsly, T. Davies and S. Leacroft, 1773); and *Mr Dalrymple's Observations on Dr Hawkesworth's Preface to the Second Edition* (London: 1773). A sympathetic biography is to be found in John Lawrence Abbott, *John Hawkesworth: Eighteenth-Century Man of Letters* (Madison: University of Wisconsin Press, 1982); and a defense of Hawkesworth's editorial procedure is mounted in Jonathan Lamb, "Circumstances Surrounding the Death of John Hawkesworth," *Eighteenth-Century Life* 18, no. 3 (1994): 97–113.

8

JOHANN REINHOLD FORSTER

Providential Cannibalism

. . . .

BY THE MID–NINETEENTH CENTURY, South-Sea islanders were to become stereotypically notorious for their anthropophagy. Over the last quarter of the eighteenth century, however, Pacific peoples were not generally assumed to be cannibals, and the causes and character of the practice occasioned debate. Until reports of cannibal feasts from Fiji were exploited in sensational literature early in the nineteenth century (see Patterson, chapter 15 below), the consumption of slain enemies was attested almost exclusively from New Zealand. Participants in Cook's first voyage seem to have been unprepared for the discovery of the practice in Queen Charlotte's Sound, and there is some evidence that Maori responded to the peculiar horror that it elicited among the Europeans by insisting on the appetizing character of human flesh.

Shocking as intra-Maori cannibalism may have been, the massacre of a boat's crew from the *Adventure*, some of whom were dismembered and partially consumed, is reported as having occasioned pure horror. The incident took place in Grass Cove, Queen Charlotte's Sound, after the *Adventure* and *Resolution* had been separated. The response is unsurprising, given that Cook's crews had enjoyed generally pacific relations with the Tahitians, and that the occasional violence of Europeans against Polynesians had yet to be dramatically reciprocated (though the killing of Marion du Fresne and members of his crew preceded the Grass Cove incident, participants in Cook's second voyage were unaware of it until those on the *Resolution* met Crozet at the Cape, on their route back to Britain). It appears, moreover, to have been presumed that Marion and his men were simply killed rather than eaten. The Grass Cove incident differed from this and lesser skirmishes in the sense that it moved beyond the exchange of injury and death that might have been anticipated, given the propensity of any people to defend their land against apparent invaders. According to James Burney's log, those discovering parts of their shipmates' bodies "remained almost stupified on the spot" until their attention was drawn to an apparent Maori attack: "Such a shocking scene of Carnage & Barbarity as can never be mentioned or thought of, but with horror" (J. Burney 1975, 97–98).

Yet the "horror" of the event was not immediately conducive to a verdict upon Maori character. Even before Cook inquired into the incident during a further visit to Queen Charlotte's Sound on his third voyage, it was conjectured that the fault lay at least in part on the European side; Burney's view that the boat's crew had been "very incautious" was elaborated upon by George Forster, probably on the basis of conversation with Burney. In his *Voyage*, it is suggested that a contemptuous attitude toward the Maori, and a fatal impetuosity, permitted an excessive response to some trifling act of theft, which in turn provoked an all-out Maori assault (Forster 1777, 2:458–59).

Despite the confusion that this event occasioned, it is striking that Johann Reinhold Forster (1729–98) evades any location of Maori cannibalism in the particular circumstances of the voyage and instead insists upon contextualizing in an essentially theoretical way, placing Maori at a particular stage in the history of civil society. While Cook and Hawkesworth implied some relativization by describing cannibalism as a "custom," Forster rejected Hawkesworth's claim that it was motivated by hunger. He begins from the paradox that the New Zealanders are more advanced than peoples such as the Tierra del Fuegians, in multiple respects, yet acknowledges that such adjudications must pause at the "one circumstance" that "seems to degrade them." He argues that cannibalism was formerly in use among other more civilized nations in the Pacific, and suggests (speculatively, but as it happens correctly), that it was still practised by one people whom he took to be at a similar level of development, namely the Tannese of the southern New Hebrides, now Vanuatu. He suggests that cannibalism has a logic in the "whole oeconomy of their societies," that is, it manifests a martial and patriotic sociality that happens to be carried to excess. "Odious" as the custom may be, these propensities are intimately connected in a global dynamic of the development of human society; the Maori merely possess, in a more extreme form, the warrior virtues of early European populations such as the Germans. He goes further toward excusing cannibalism, in suggesting that it is part of an evolution toward a happier polity, since war occasions conquest, larger political unions, and ultimately a form of government in which enemies are more likely to be enslaved than eaten.

Forster therefore insists not only that a purely horrifying practice has a logic, but that its rationality is intimately connected with forces general to the history of human society, and specifically the antinomy between martial and commercial values that was conventionally central to accounts of political evolution in Europe. He was extending the vocabulary of the political and historical essay to encompass phenomena that had transfixed other participants in the second voyage, that confronted them with a sublime excess. If Forster's was not the commonest response to reports of Maori cannibalism, it may be seen to mark the ambitions of his "natural history" and "ethic philosophy." — NICHOLAS THOMAS

. . . .

Johann Reinhold Forster, *Observations Made During a Voyage Round the World* (London: G. Robinson, 1778).

« CHAPTER 6, SECTION 5, PP. 324–32. »

It seems likewise equally obvious, that the more improved state of the New-Zeelanders, is owing to several causes, viz. the mildness of the climate, the greater population, and also that they are more immediately descended from such tribes as had more remains of the general principles of education. In the extremities of the Southern isle of New-Zeeland, perhaps the numbers may be only equal to those of the Pesserais, but being more happy in regard to the mildness of their climate, and the preservation of such ideas and improvements as were handed down to them, by their more happy and less degenerated ancestors; even these straggling families are, in my opinion, to be ranked higher in the scale of human beings.

There is however one circumstance already alluded to, which seems to degrade them, viz. the odious and cruel custom of eating those, who are killed in their frequent feuds and petty wars. This has been represented by a late ingenious writer, as originally introduced among the New-Zeelanders, by distress and hunger; but I cannot help dissenting from his opinion: for I did not find that these nations ever are so much distressed; they have prudence enough to provide in the proper season, stores of all kinds: when they catch more fish than they can eat, they carefully dry, and lay them up; their women go frequently up the hills, which are covered to an immense extent with fern, and dig up the roots, which they likewise dry, and preserve as a food to which they may have recourse, when neither fish nor any other kind of eatables are to be procured. We saw great quantities of these provisions in their huts, and frequently found them employed in preparing both fish and fern-roots, for the bad season. We were likewise told by Capt. Crozet, the friend and companion of the brave but unfortunate Capt. Marion; that when he got possession of the hippah or fortress of the New-Zeelanders, in the Bay of Islands, he found immense stores of dry fish, fern-roots, and other roots, in houses filled solely with these provisions. It seems therefore, to me, by no means probable, that a nation perfectly convinced of the necessity of providing against the season of distress, and so very careful and active in collecting stores of eatables, should nevertheless have been induced by necessity and hunger, to eat the corses of those slain in battle. Nay, we heard from the natives, that they never eat those, who die a natural death, but either sink them in the sea, or bury them under ground: were necessity the true cause of this custom, why should they not feast upon the dead who formed the same community with them? But it will be objected, that hunger may be allowed so far to stifle all sentimental feelings of humanity, that they might suffer themselves to satisfy its cravings upon the corse of a slain foe, but that it will never carry them so far as to feed upon the flesh of those who lived in the same society with them. How specious soever this objection may be, it never can persuade me that hunger will make these nice distinctions, in a people, who have not those tender, humane feelings and emotions, of which we are capable, in so highly civilized a state, with a refined education, and principles infinitely superior to theirs.

But I had reason to believe, that all the nations of the South seas were formerly cannibals, even in the most happy and fertile climates, where they still live upon the almost spontaneous fruits, though their population be extremely great. The natives of Tanna gave us more than once to understand, that if we penetrated far into the country against their will, and without their permission, they would kill us, cut our bodies up, and eat them: when we purposely affected to misunderstand this last part of their story, and interpreted it, as if they were going to give us something good to eat, they convinced us by signs which could not be misinterpreted, that they would tear with their teeth the flesh from our arms and legs.

In Mallicollo, we had likewise some intimation that they were cannibals. The Taheiteans frequently enumerated to us isles inhabited by men-eaters: for instance, they said, that beyond Tabuamanoo is a high island called Manua, whose inhabitants "have but very few canoes, are ferocious, have wild and furious eyes, and eat men:" nay, we were at last told, that they themselves had formerly been *Tahéäi*, i.e. men-eaters. As the inhabitants of New-Zeeland certainly belong to the same race of people with the Taheiteans, it is evident that this custom has been common to the whole tribe. What is still more remarkable, it seems from thence to follow, that the want of a sufficiency of food in this isle, which is less fertile than the tropical countries, cannot have occasioned their cannibalism, since even the inhabitants of the happy and fertile tropical isles were men-eaters, without being forced to it by distress and hunger, and we must therefore certainly be convinced that there must be some other cause, which originally introduced this unnatural custom.

If we examine the whole oeconomy of their societies, we find that their education is the chief cause of all these enormities. The men train up the boys in a kind of liberty, which at last degenerates into licentiousness: they suffer not the mothers to strike their petulant, unruly, and wicked sons, for fear of breaking that spirit of independency, which they seem to value above all things, and as the most necessary qualification for their societies; this naturally brings on an irascibility, which, in the men, cannot brook any controul, action or word, that can be construed according to their manners and principles into an affront, or injury; inflamed by passion, they are impatient to wreak their vengeance: wild fancy paints the injury so atrocious, that it must be washed in blood; they know not where to stop, and being more and more incensed by the power of imagination, they go to battle with a loud and barbarous song, each feature is distorted, each limb is set in a cadenced motion; they brandish their destructive weapons, and stamp upon the ground with their feet, while the whole band join in an awful, tremendous groan; the song begins a new, and at last the whole troop is lost in frenzy and rage; they fall to, and every one fights as if animated by furies; and destruction and carnage await the routed party: whosoever falls, is murdered without mercy, and the corses of the slain immediately serve to glut the inhuman appetites of the conquerors. When the bounds of humanity are once passed, and the reverence due to the bright image of divinity, is conquered by frenzy, the practice soon becomes habitual, especially as it is reckoned among the honours due to the conqueror, to feast upon the wretched victims of savage victory; add to this, that a nation which has no other animal food, than a few stupid dogs and fish, will soon reconcile themselves to human flesh, which, according to several known instances, is reputed to be one of the most palatable dishes.

To us, indeed, who are used to live in better regulated societies, where for many years backwards, anthropophagy has been in disuse, it is always a horrid idea, that men should eat men. But I cannot help observing, that this barbarism is one of the steps, by which debased humanity, is gradually prepared for a better state of happiness; in the savage state, where man is just one remove from animality, wherein he has no other impulse for action, than want, he soon sinks into stupid indolence, which more and more debases all his powers and faculties: but scarce have the passions begun to act as the main springs of human actions, when man is carried from the first excentric action to a second, from one enormity to another, and from this or that shocking scene of cruelty, barbarism and unhumanity to others of a higher degree: these would grow to an outrageous height, were it not for certain circumstances, which at last naturally put a total stop to those inhuman practices. If therefore barbarians, who still preserve the shocking custom of eating men, meet with other tribes that have the same barbarous custom, and are strong or active enough, either by chance or bravery, to check their neighbours in their inhuman wrongs, they will soon be sensible, that their own numbers must decrease by these losses; they will therefore grow more cautious in provoking their anger or vengeance by new outrages, and will gradually become sober enough to be convinced, that it is more reasonable to lay aside the custom of eating men, and that a living man is more useful than one that is dead or roasted; they in consequence change their unnatural cruelty into a more humane behaviour; though it be not quite free from injustice and interest, it is however, less destructive to mankind, and prepares the way to a more humane and benevolent scene. Or let us on the other hand suppose, these barbarians meet with unmerited success, and always rout their neighbours, as often as they take the field; these humiliated foes, in order to avoid their utter ruin and destruction, will at last offer terms of accommodation; and though their condition should become as abject as possible, they will prefer it to a greater and unavoidable evil, involving the whole ruin of their tribe; the conquerors will soon discover, that by preserving the lives of their subjected foes, they may reap considerable advantages from their labour and united force, which will gradually improve their condition, and render them more and more happy.

This idea might be deemed imaginary; but upon examination, it will appear to be established in truth. In the Northern Isle of New-Zeeland, in a district of more than 90 miles, Captain Cook, found in his former voyage, the name of a great chief, called TEIRATOO, to be generally acknowledged; and it should seem from thence, that the small tribes under his dominion, were either subdued by him and his adherents; or that they found it their interest, upon their own account, to acknowledge his authority, to become his subjects upon certain conditions, and thus to form one large political body, for greater security and defence; the better regulations, a security both of person and property, and a more impartial administration of justice, mentioned in the same account, prove beyond dispute, that from the violent state of cannibalism, the New-Zeelanders will soon arrive in their most populous districts, to a more settled and more happy state. For though the subjects for TEIRATOO still eat men, this custom is rather kept up on account of the vicinity of such tribes as still retain the same custom, otherwise their more improved situation would hardly admit of it.

Further Reading

For the full text of Forster's *Observations*, and a set of contextualizing and interpretive essays, see the recent republication, Johann Reinhold Forster, *Observations Made During a Voyage Round the World*, ed. Nicholas Thomas, Harriet Guest, and Michael Dettelbach (Honolulu: University of Hawaii Press, 1996). For early contacts between voyagers and Maori, see Anne Salmond, *Two Worlds* (Auckland: Viking, 1991) and *Between Worlds* (Auckland: Viking, 1997). For varying interpretations of anthropophagy in its Maori contexts and in European discourse, see Marshall Sahlins, "Hierarchy and Humanity in Polynesia," in *Transformations of Polynesian Culture*, ed. Antony Hooper and Judith Huntsman (Auckland: The Polynesian Society, 1985); and Gananath Obeyesekere, "'British Cannibals': Contemplation of an Event in the Death and Resurrection of James Cook, Explorer," *Critical Inquiry* 18, no. 4 (1992): 630–54.

9

WILLIAM WALES
MAKES OBSERVATIONS

. . . .

WILLIAM WALES (1734–97), an astronomer and mathematician, was a member of Cook's second expedition. He was charged with a second calculation of the transit of Venus from the Antipodes, and with testing two chronometers, Kendall's and Arnold's, as part of the series of experiments designed to solve the problem of the longitude. After George and Johann Reinhold Forster, the two naturalists on the second voyage, blamed him for forgetting to wind the chronometers and for damaging one of their cases with a screwdriver, Wales published an exasperated account of the trials he had suffered as their shipmate, *Remarks on Mr Forster's Account of Captain Cook's Last Voyage* (1778). It is ironic, therefore, that Barbara Stafford, in her paean to the experimental rigor of these Enlightenment scientists, should fancy such a close collaboration between Wales and the elder Forster that she imagines them rowing out to the icebergs of the Antarctic to make companionable observations: "Two scientists sat in a tiny boat on an immense ocean encircled by ice" (Stafford 1984, 367). Wales had a very poor opinion of J. R. Forster's observational accuracy: "Dr Forster gives us his account of the water-spouts, which we saw in Cook's Straits, in which there are several extraordinary circumstances. In the first place, he says, that 'the bases of these spouts, on the sea, looked bright and yellowish when illuminated by the sun' . . . we never saw any of them illuminated by it, not even the least glimpse of the sun, any where, all the time that they lasted . . . as all that part of the heavens where the sun was situated, was covered with one black, dense, impenetrable cloud, as everyone on board can testify" (Wales 1778, 23).

After his travels, Wales settled down to a life of school-mastering at Christ's Hospital, where he taught Coleridge mathematics. Bernard Smith supposes that in the wider circuits of their conversation, Wales would have supplied the young poet with the data he would later refashion into *The Rime of the Ancient Mariner*: "the most vivid descriptions of waterspouts, phosphorescent seas and the perils of navigating the polar ice" (Smith 1992, 140).

Wales's journal provides a useful checkpoint for well-known descriptions and pictures, such as those of Dusky Bay provided by the Forsters, Anders Sparrman, and William Hodges. His skepticism is most resolutely directed at reports of cannibalism in New Zealand until he witnesses the scene of anthropophagy in Queen Charlotte Sound that impelled Forster's meditations in the previous extract. However, once convinced of the fact he makes some original observations, concluding that it is not, as Hawkesworth thought, a shortage of protein that causes Maori to eat one another, nor, as Forster held, their warrior propensities, but "from Choice, and the liking which they have for this food." Likewise Wales takes a restrained view of Bougainville's "Nouvelle Cythere" when he gets to Tahiti, where he makes some sober estimates of sexual and gender roles in the South Seas, befitting the future author of *An Inquiry into the Present State of Population* (1781).
— JONATHAN LAMB

. . . .

William Wales, Journal of William Wales, Board of Longitude Papers, vol. 46, Royal Greenwich Observatory, Hurstmonceux, Surrey.

Dusky Sound, New Zealand, April 1773.

11th. About Noon the Natives who had been seen by the Capt and Officers as abovementioned were discovered coming towards the Ship in their Canoe. They now came within about 100 yards of the Ship and there went on Shore, hauled up their boat, left it & came over the point & sat down on the Rocks opposite the Ship, and about 20, or 30 yards from it but no perswasion could get them on board. They stayed there all the Afternoon the night & untill noon the next day: they then left us and went we know not whither, for they did not go to the place they came from.

The Man seemed to me to be near 50, was of a midling hight and very broad set; of a pleasing, open Countenance, and not the least ferosity in his looks. His hair was black of a moderate length & curled at the ends. His lips inclining to be thick, his Nose rather flat—it seemed as if the end had been pressed down to his face. His two wives were something younger than himself, and were small sized; their features not disagreeable nor in the least masculine; but one of them was rendered barely not frightfull by a large Wen which grew on her left Cheek & hung down below her Mouth. The Girl's Person was on the whole very agreeable, but rather masculine, exceeding like the old man, and I dare say a very great Pet. She soon singled out a young Fellow, one of the Ship's Company for whom she expressed great fondness & seemed very unhappy whenever he was away from her: but on his offering at some familiarities, to which I suppose he was emboldened by her apparent fondness, she left him, went and sat down between her father & mother, & I never saw her take the least notice of him afterwards except when one of the Officers offered to shoot him for the insult offered to her, and then she seemed much affected and even shed Tears. We afterwards thought she had mistaken him for one of her own sex as his features were rather femnine.

The Man seemed almost continually lost in wonder at the construction of the ship & boats and whenever any of them came near him he examined them in the strictest manner particularly how they were put together and seemed particularly pleased with the motion & effects of the Rudder which he examined & tried over & over.

The Cloathing of the Men and Women, were not that I could perceive in the least different. It consisted of a sort of mat made of the hemp-plant and feathers intermixed: this was hung over their Shoulders, and tied down before; it reached about the middle of their Thighs; below which they had no covering. The hinder part of this Ahou, as they call it, passed between their legs & was made fast to the part before. On very cold days they had over ye Ahou a very thick rug-like Garment, made of Rushes, or the very course parts of the hemp plant, which they called Buggy-Buggy [*pakepake*]. Every one had a bunch of feathers, Grass &c tied under their chins by a String which went round their necks, & the Women's hair was tied in a bunch on the Crowns of their heads & adorned with the feathers of Parrots & other birds.

A Corporal of Marines who had learned something of the New-Zeeland language last Voyage asked the Man to let him have his Daughter for a Wife; but was told that it was a matter of too great moment for him to determine on before he had consulted his God. Almost all the Night, and very often in the Day while they stayed near the ship, they Sung and made many strange Gestures, which as far as we could understand, was a conversation which they held with some Being above the Clouds.

To what I have before said of their Boats, I may now add that one is considerably larger than the other, I think that on the starboard side is about 1/4th part longer than the larboard one: Those which I have seen being 18 feet & 14 ft respectively. They are fixed so as to approach nearer to each other at the head than at the Stern, which is an useful precaution. The Cross pieces are made fast to the two Canoes with lashings made of the hemp Plant, and they have wash boards above the solid part of the boats fastened in the same manner, so well, that very little water can come in between them. The Tools which they have to perform this work with are made of a green stone which is very hard and bears working to an indifferent good edge, and are used by them either as Chissells, Axes or Adzes, according as they are without or lashed in different positions to a handle. They had variety of fish-hooks in their Canoes some made all of wood, others all of bone & others again part of wood & part of bone, join'd by tying them together, their lines are made of the hemp Plant some twisted as our Cordage is with two, three & four strands or twists, and other platted like the lash of a whip. The former part of this Day, fine Weather; the latter cloudy with Showers. . . .

Queen Charlotte Sound, New Zealand, May 1773.

22d. Moderate Wind northerly, and Cloudy weather. Several of the Natives came on board us without any ceremony. I had conceived vast things from report of the New-Zeelanders to the Northward of Dusky Bay But must confess my self much disappointed.

23d. Light Breezes south-westerly, and fine Weather for the most Part: More of the Natives on board: I cannot help again making a comparison between these and our late friends at Dusky Bay. These are importunate for every thing they see, and are as great theives as the Eskimaux; but want much of their ingenuity in concealing it: whereas those at dusky Bay scarce ever asked for any thing, or ever received any considerable Present without making one in return, and that in Articles which to them must be very valuable. As to stealing, for aught that I saw to the contrary, their Creator had utterly deprived them of the Idea. . . .

Being going to leave this land of Canibals, as it is now generally thought to be, it may be expected that I should record what bloody Massacres I have been a witness of; how many human Carcases I have seen roasted and eaten; or at least relate such Facts as have fallen within the Compass of my Observations tending to confirm the Opinion, now almost universally believed, that the New Zeelanders are guilty of this most detestable Practice. Truth, notwithstanding, obliges me to declare, however unpopular it may be, that I have not seen the least signs of any such custom being amongst them, either in Dusky Bay or Charlotte sound; although the latter place is that where the only Instance of it was seen in the Endeavour's Voyage. I know it is urged as a proof positive against them, that in the representation of their War-Exercise, which they were very fond of shewing us, they confessed the Fact. The real state of the Case is this. They first began with shewing us how they handled their Weapons, how they defyed the Enemy to Battle, how they killed him: they then proceeded to cut of his head, legs & arms; they afterwards took out his Bowels & threw them away, and lastly shewed us that they went to eating. But it ought by all means to be remarked that all this was shewn by signs which every one will allow are easily misunderstood, and for any thing that I know to the contrary they might mean they Eat the Man they had just killed; but is it not as likely that after the Engagement they refreshed themselves with some other Victuals which they might have with them? It ought farther to be remarked that I did not see one out of the many who went through those Massacres, who did not stop before he made the sign of eating; or that did it before some of us made the sign, as if to remind him that he had forgot that part of the Ceremony. This circumstance is brought as a proof both that they are, and that they are not Caniballs. One says, it is plain they Eat their Enemy after they have killed him, but are ashamed to acknowledge it, because they know we disapprove of it. The others say no; it is plain they looked on the Action as complete & stoped untill you reminded them that it was necessary to take some refreshment after their Labour.

No stronger proofs, than the above have been seen by any person on board the Resolution this Voyage: but more substantial ones are said to have been seen on board the Adventure. One of the Gentlemen found amongst the Baggage in a Canoe, a raw human head, cut off close to the shoulders. This discovery is said to have produced much consternation amongst the People in the Canoe, who put it out of sight again with all possible expedition, nor could it be found afterwards. But hard as this circumstance is made to bear against them, it does by no means follow with certainty that this Head was preserved to be eaten: Saul, had he been a stranger to the Affair, might with equal justice have concluded that David was a Caniball when he was brought before him with the Head of Goliath in his hand. On the other side it must be admitted that after what is reported to have been seen here in the Endeavour's Voyage it was most natural to conclude that this head was intended for a very different purpose than that which David carried his up to Jerusalem for.

I cannot help relating a circumstance or two before I quit the subject entirely, as they tend to shew how far we are liable to be misled by Signs, report, & prejudice. Two Canoes of Natives came alongside one of the Ships & after they had traded such little matters as they had, went away out of the sound. Sometime after One Canoe only returned & the people of the ship enquired ernestly what was become of the other. They made the same sign they do at the conclusion of their Exercise and it was immediately concluded that they had met with Enemies who had killed & eaten them; and it would certainly have passed so, had not the other Canoe returned a day or two after with every soul in it alive & well. Another circumstance is the following. A person on board the Adventure not only asserted that he saw one Indian killed by the others, but also related the particulars and manner in which it was done: nay it had gone so far on board our Ship with some as to suppose that a fire which we saw on shore, had been kindled to dress him at, & it was expected that Capt Cook who was gone on shore at the place would surprize them in the very fact & probably bring on board some part of the unhappy Victim, to silence all unbelievers of this Custom for the future. The Capt notwithstanding returned without having seen any thing of the sort; & it was afterwards certainly known that the man was not only un-roasted, but even alive and well. . . .

Tahiti and the Society Islands, August–September 1773.

The face of the Country, making some allowance for a warm imagination, is not badly described by Mr Bougainville; but some allowances must be made by every Person, who has not seen the Place, and would not be deceived. That Gentleman seems to have been almost lost in admiration of its Beauties, and those of its Inhabitants all the time he was here. His colouring is indeed so high, that one cannot help suspecting a false glace; for his description suits much better with Mahomet's Paradise, than any terrestial Region: It must notwithstanding be allowed to be a very beautiful Island, and appears, no doubt, to great advantage after a long Voyage. I remember well that England does so, and run no risk in asserting that Otahitee would make but an indifferent appearance if placed beside it.

The Lands here do not seem to be considered as private property, any farther than as they are planted with fruit Trees, Yams, &c all which are manifestly so: and it appeared to me that the property of the land was rather determined by the Trees which were Planted on it than that of the

Trees by the Land whereon they were planted, as in England. I conceive that it is lawfull for any person to raise a Plantation on Ground not already occupied by another.

With regard to the Personal Beauties of the Otahitean Ladies, I believe it would be most prudent to remain entirely silent; since by a contrary pre-ceedure I must expose in the grossest manner my own want of tast, or that of those Gentlemen who have asserted that 'they may vie with the great-est beauties of Europe', and that 'the English Women appeared Verry or-dinery on their first arrival there' from this celebrated Cythera: but it is no new thing for the itch of writing to get the better of prudence; it will not therefore be wondered at if I run all risks of this kind to have the pleasure of describing their persons; at least, so far as there appears to be any na-tional characteristic in it. In the first place then their stature is very small, and their features although rather regular have a masculine turn. Their Complexion is a light Olive, or rather a deadish Yellow; their hair is of a glossy black and cut short in the bowl-dish fasion of the Country People in England; but had here, I think, a pretty effect, as it corresponded more with the simplicity of their Dress than any other form would. Their Eyes are exceeding black and lively but rather too prominent for my liking. Their noses are flat especially towards the lower end and their nostrils in consequence wide, as are also their mouths. Their lips are rather thick than otherwise; but their teeth are remarkable close, white, and even. The Breasts of the young ones before they have had Children are very round and beautifull, but those of the old ones hang down to their Navals. I have no occasion to call in the Aids of Imagination to describe every part of them, down to their very toes, as there were plenty of them who were not solicitous to hide any of their beauties from our Eyes; but it may be best to stop here, and proceed to say a little in defence of their Characters, which have, in my opinion, been as much depreciated as their beauties have been Magnifyed.

All our Voyagers both French and English have represented them with-out exception as ready to grant the last favor to any man who will pay for it. But this is by no means the Case; the favours of Maried Women are not to be purchased, except of their Husbands, to whose commands they seem to pay implicit obediance, and therefore it is possible a thing of this kind may sometimes be done, where a woman happens to be married to a man who is mean enough to do it; but these instances are undoubtedly very rare, & cannot be charged to the woman's Account. Neither can the Charge be understood indescriminately of the unMarried ones. I have great reason to believe that much the greater part of these admit of no such familiarities, or at least are very carefull to whom they grant them. That there are Prostitutes here as well as in London is true, perhaps more in proportion, and such no doubt were those who came on board the ship to our People. These seem not less skilfull in their profession than Ladies of the same stamp in England, nor does a person run less risk of injuring his health and Constitution in their Embraces. On the whole I am firmly of opinion that a stranger who visits England might with equal justice draw the Characters of the Ladies there, from those which he might meet with on board the Ships in Plymouth Sound, at Spithead, or in the Thames; on the Point at Portsmouth, or in the Purlieus of Wapping.—I am not altogether of opinion that the Natives of Otahitee are indebted to any of our *late* Voyagers either French or English for the Disorder above hinted at: there is not the least doubt but that they can cure it; and it seems difficult to conceive how they should so soon find out a remedy for a disease, which baffled the most skilful Physitions of Europe for so many Years. But be this as it may, the English have certainly got the credit of it, as the natives have no other name for it, that we know of, than Opay-no-Britannia so that if the French had realy the honour of introducing it, as some suspect, they are now even with us for calling it the French-Disease. . . .

On my first going on shore I was much charmed with the friendliness & seeming hospitality of these People: every one almost invited me to his house to eat Fruit &c. I could not resist their kind Invitations and had not sooner sat down amongst them but one beged Beads another nails, a third a Knife & a fourth My Handkerchief, Neckcloth, Coat, Shirt &c. I had stocked my self pretty well with some of the former Articles and thought it incumbent on me to give to every one of my kind Entertainers whilst they lasted, but was not well pleased to find many things gone which I had not the satisfaction of giving; but my chagrin was much greater on finding that I quitted no house without leaving more Persons unsatisfied than otherwise with what I thought generosity. I pursued this Plan the two or three first days: at the end of which I found my stock in Trade considerably decreased, & scarce any thing in return for it but Tyo! Tyo! As this way of proceeding seemed to give so little satisfaction to either Party, I resolved to alter my conduct for the future, and neither give or receive any thing by way of Friendship; but proceed by the less noble & generous, though perhaps more just and equitable way of Barter & Trade, and have the utmost reason to be satisfied with having done so; as none left me without being pleased with his bargain, and I was generally pleased with mine, I walked where ever my bussiness or pleasure called me in company or alone, armed or otherwise as it might happen, and never had the least quarrel with, or received incivillity from one of them, whilst very few of those who acted on the score of friendship escaped without. . . .

[September] 11th. The former Part Moderate Wind; the latter more brisk, at South and SE, with Showers.—This Afternoon went with some of the Officers to the House of the Aree of the district where the Ships lay, and who is Brother to the Principal King, or Aree of the Whole Island; where we were entertained with what they call a *Heava*; that is an entertainment of Music and Dancing. The Music was performed on three Drums of different Tones, arrising from their different magnitudes & form. The Base, or deepest toned one, was about 12 or 14 Inches high, and perhaps as much in diameter: The Middle one was about 2 1/2 feet high and about 10 Inches diameter; and that which had the highest tone, might be near 3 1/2 feet high and about 7 or 8 Inches Diameter. Their Heads were made of Shark's Skin and braced much in the same Manner as ours are, only without the slides which ours have for bracing and unbracing; and they beat them with their fingers. The Dancing, as we called it, was performed by two girls, one of whom is the daughter of the Aree, and accounted a capital Performer, under the direction of an old Man, who travills from place to place for that purpose, and is said to have made great improvement to this divirsion, on which account he is held in great Esteem. The Dress of the Performers is extraordinary and very grand on these Occasions. It consists of a great quanity of their cloth of different Colours bound very tight around the Waist with Cords, and disposed so as to stand off sideways from the Hips in a vast number of plaits or folds, to the extent of a fine Lady's Hoop-Peticoat when in a full Dress. To this is attached a parcel of Coats below, and a sort of Waist coat without sleeves above. Round the Head is wound a great quantity of plaited Hair in such Manner as to stand up like a Coronet, and this is stuck full of small floures of various colours which renders the Head-Dress, in My opinion, truly elegant. The Dexterity of the Performers does not lie in the Motion of the feet; but in that of the Hips, Arms, Fingers and Mouth: all which they keep in motion together, and ye principal skill of the performer seems to lie in contriving to have these several motions as opposite & contrary to one another as possible. These Motions they perform in all attitudes viz standing sitting kneeling Lying, as also with their face in all directions as East, west &c. all which is directed by the above mentioned old Man who not only gives the word, but sets the example also. In this part of the *Heava*, although the principal with them, there is little very entertaining to an European Eye. The wriggling of their Hips, especially as set off with such a quanity of Furbeloes, is too Ludricrous to be pleasing, and the distortion of their mouths is realy disagreeable, although it is for this the young Princess is chiefly admired. Her face is naturally one of the most beautiful on the Island; but in these performances she twists it in such a manner that a stranger would some times realy question whether her right Eye, Mouth & left Ear did not form one great Gash passing in an oblique direction across her face.

It may be supposed this Exercise is too violent to last long at a time, especially in this climate and under such a load of dress: accordingly the dancing seldom lasts longer than about 5 or 6 Minutes at a time, and in the intervals we were entertained with the performances of 5 or 6 men which sometimes consisted in a sort of figure Dance, wherein they were very carefull that their feet kept exact time to the Drums; at others in the action of short Interludes, which were in my opinion by far the best parts of the Performance, and realy diverting. The subjects of these were sometimes tricks which they are supposed to put on one another either through cunning, or under cover of a dark night; but oftener turn on intimacies between the Sexes, which at times they carry great lengths. These Parts were performed exceeding well, the command which they have over their Features and Countinance is extraordinary, and I am not certain that I ever saw Mr Garrick perform with more propriety than one Man did most of his parts. Their Stage, if I may be allowed the Expression, is under a Shed, open in the Front, and at one end is their dressing Room; into, and out of which they make their *exits*, and enterances as occasion requires; & the floor is spread with very curious Mats: In short, it may be said without exaggeration, that the Drama is advanced in these Islands, very far beyond the Age of Thespis. . . .

Queen Charlotte Sound, New Zealand, November 1773.

23d. I have this day been convinced beyond the possibility of a doubt that the New-Zeelanders are Cannibals; but as it is possible others may be as unbelieving, as I have been in this matter, I will, to give all the satisfaction I possibly can, relate the whole affair just as it happened. After dinner some of the Officers went on shore at a place where many of the Natives generally dwelt to purchase Curiosities, and found them just risen from feasting on the Carcase of one of their own species. It was not immediately perceived what they had been about; but one of the Boats Crew happening to see the head of a Man lying near one of their Canoes, they began to look round them more narrowly, and in another place found the Intestines Liver Lungs &c lying on the ground, as fresh as if but just taken out of the Body, and the Heart stuck on the points of a two pronged spear & tied to the Head of their largest Canoe. One of the Natives with great gayety struck his spear into one lobe of the Lungs, and holding it close to the Mouth of one of the Officers made signs for him to eat it; but he beged to be excused, at the same time taking up ye Head & making signs that he would Accept of that which was given to him, and he presented them with two Nails in return. These Gentlemen saw no part of the Carcase nor even any of the Bones; but understood that the unhappy Victim had been brought from Admiralty Bay, where these natives had lately been on a *hunting Party*; and one of them took great pains to inform them that he was the person who killed him.

When the Head was brought on board, there happened to be there several of the Natives who resided in another part of the sound, and who although in friendship with were not of the Party of whom the Head was purchased. These were, it seems very desirous of it; but that could not be granted: However one of them who was a great favorite was indulged with a piece of the flesh, which was cut off carried forward to the Gally, broiled and eaten, by him before all the Officers & ships Company then on board. Thus far I speak from report: the Witnesses are however too credible & numerous to be disputed if I had had no better authority; but coming just now on board with the Capt and Mr Forster, to convince us also, another Steake was cut off from the lower part of the head, behind, which I saw carried forward, broiled, and eaten by one of them with an avidity which amazed me, licking his lips and fingers after it as if affraid to lose the least part, either grease or gravy, of so delicious a morsel.

The Head as well as I could judge had been that of a Youth under twenty, and he appeared to have been killed by two blows on the Temple, with one of their Pattoos, one crossing the other; but some were of opinion that the whole might have been done at one blow, and that what appeared to have been caused by the other, was only a cross fracture of the Scull arising from the first.

My Account of this matter would be very defective, was I to omitt taking notice of the Behavior of the young Man whom we brought with us from Uliateah & who came on board with the Captain, &c. in the Pinnace. Terror took possession of him the moment he saw the Head standing on the Tafferal of the Ship; but when he saw the piece cut off, and the Man eat it, he became perfectly motionless, and seemed as if metamorphosed into the Statue of Horror: it is, I believe, utterly impossible for Art to depict that passion with half the force that it appeared in his Countenance. He continued in this situation untill some of us roused him out of it by talking to him, and then burst into Tears nor could refrain himslf the whole Evening afterwards.

From this Transaction the following Corollaries are evidently deducible, viz—

1st) They do not, as I supposed might be the Case, eat them only on the spot whilst under the Impulse of that wild Frenzy into which they have shewn us they can & do work themselves in their Engagements; but in cool Blood: For it was now many Days since the Battle could have happened.

2d) That it is not their Enemies only whom they may chance to kill in War; but even any whom they meet with who are not known Friends: since those who eat the part of the head on board, could not know whether it belonged to a friend or Enemy.

3d) It cannot be through want of Annimal food; because they every day caught as much Fish as served both themselves and us: they have moreover plenty of fine Dogs which they were at the same time selling us for mere trifles; nor is there any want of various sorts of fowl, which they can readily kill if they please.

4th) It seems therefore to follow of course, that their practice of this horrid Action is from Choice, and the liking which they have for this kind of Food; and this was but too visibly shewn in their eagerness for, and the satisfaction which they testified in eating, those inconsiderable scrapts, of the worst part on board the Ship: It is farther evident what esteem they have for it by the risks which they run to obtain it; for although our neighbours feasted so luxuriously, we had abundant reasons to conclude that they came off no gainers in the Action, since almost all of them had their foreheads & Arms scarrified, which is, it seems, their usual custom, when they lose any near Relation in War.

Further Reading

For other opinions of cannibalism, see John Hawkesworth, *An Account of the Voyages and Discoveries in the Southern Hemisphere* (London: W. Strahan and T. Cadell, 1773), 3:447–49; Anders Sparrman, *A Voyage Round the World with Captain James Cook in HMS* Resolution (London: Golden Cockerel, 1944), 45–46; and Johann Reinhold Forster, *Observations Made During a Voyage Round the World* (previous extract). Wales's relationship with Coleridge is discussed in Bernard Smith, *Imagining the Pacific* (Melbourne: Melbourne University Press, 1992), and a context for his scientific achievements is provided by Dava Sobell, *Longitude* (New York: Walker, 1995). Barbara Stafford paints a larger and more dramatic backdrop for his experiments in *Voyage into Substance* (Cambridge: MIT Press, 1984). Wales's irritation with the Forsters is expressed in *Remarks on Mr Forster's Account of Captain Cook's Last Voyage* (London: J. Nourse, 1778). For another skeptical handling of Tahiti as terrestrial paradise, see Denis Diderot, "Supplement au voyage de Bougainville," in *Political Writings*, ed. John Hope Mason and Robert Wokler (Cambridge: Cambridge University Press, 1992). A background for Pacific paradises can be found in O. H. K. Spate, *The Pacific Since Magellan*, vol. 3, *Paradise Found and Lost* (Minneapolis: University of Minnesota Press, 1988).

GEORGE KEATE

Benevolence on the Beach

. . . .

GEORGE KEATE'S (1729–97) *Account of the Pelew Islands* described the 1783 wreck of the East India Company packet, the *Antelope*, on Ulong (here called Oroolong) in the Palau archipelago. Captain Henry Wilson's crew enjoyed generally good relations with the people of Koror over the three months it took them to build a new vessel, which they sailed to Macao. Keate was a literary gentleman, not a participant in the adventure, and prepared the book on the basis of information provided by Wilson and other members of his crew. The *Account* ran into four editions within two years of publication and was subsequently widely abridged, pirated, translated, and otherwise reprinted; it was one of the most popular voyage works of the late eighteenth century.

Though the book's appeal arose in part from the story of "Prince" Le Boo, the young Palauan aristocrat who traveled back to England with Wilson, it may be more broadly attributed to the text's presentation of cross-cultural relationships in resolutely optimistic and sentimental terms. In contrast, a number of the Cook voyage narratives had proceeded from broadly anthropological premises, in the sense that they explored and emphasized the differences between the manners and customs of various peoples encountered and those of Europeans. It was appreciated that these differences, and the defective mutual understandings that followed from them, were likely to occasion the conflict that led to unjustifiable killings of indigenous people and the death of Cook himself. Readers might have drawn the conclusion that contacts between peoples were unlikely to be mutually improving, and that there was real doubt as to whether voyages ought to be undertaken.

Keate's *Account* could be seen to address and resolve such ambivalences. The people of Palau are presented as novel, but not as exotic; they do not bear strange and untranslatable dispositions. Although misunderstandings take place, they are swiftly resolved; an underlying mutual benevolence is postulated, which is manifest in the honorable protection given to the Europeans by Ibedul (Keate's Abba Thule) and by his son Le Boo's effort to acquire knowledge of real utility to his people. Though Le Boo's English education is poignantly cut short by smallpox, the larger imputation is that the Palauans are highly deserving recipients of British gratitude. An exchange is described and projected that can be based in true friendship and that will result in true benefit. This beach is a very different one to that described by Cook, George Forster, and others in Queen Charlotte Sound, where novel appetites for European goods prompt Maori men to coercively prostitute their women.

The situation in which fleeting confusions provoke alarm, but are succeeded by good-humored mutual understanding, becomes something of a motif in Keate's *Account*. In the first extract, Ibedul's troubling "coolness" is deftly employed to evoke the absolute vulnerability of the English, but is shown rather to stem from his "delicacy" in enlisting the foreigners' military assistance. In the second, Arthur Devis's sketching provokes the anxiety of his unknowing subjects, but is then recognized for what it is—a pleasing art—and appreciated in those terms.

Or so Keate would have us understand. Yet his presentation of friendly equality between the British and the people of Koror is likely to have been quite inconsistent with the Palauan view. All the evidence suggests that Ibedul and his people regarded Wilson and his crew as Ibedul's subordinates; the chief protected them and feasted them, but the English in turn were required to surrender their valuables and to provide their armed service. Equally, when Ibedul emulates Devis's sketching, he does so not out of some pure appreciation characteristic of urbane nobility, but in part because art and decoration are part of the work of the high chief, who paints potent hereditary insignia onto houses and vessels: here again, precedence was being asserted. — NICHOLAS THOMAS

. . . .

George Keate, *An Account of the Pelew Islands, situated in the western part of the Pacific Ocean* (London: G. Nicol, 1879).

« CHAPTER 12, PP. 71–74. »

In the afternoon the *Malay* informed Captain WILSON, that the King was come round into the bay, being on his return to Pelew, and if he wanted to take leave of him he must go off to his canoe. The Captain accordingly went in the jolly-boat, having with him TOM ROSE his linguist, and four other men. The meeting was, to his great surprise, very cool on the King's part, of course reserved on that of his own: far unlike, indeed, that undisguised openness which marked the interview of the preceding day.—And I doubt not but by this time the reader will have shared a portion of that concern, for his unfortunate countrymen, which was awakened in their bosoms by this unexpected alteration in the behaviour of the natives. What will he think of the hearts of these *yet unknown* inhabitants of PELEW?—He will have already loaded them with reproach, and judged, too hardly judged them to be an inconsistent, faithless people, on whom no reliance could be placed, whom no profession could bind.—His imagination may have started a multitude of conjectures, yet at last will probably suppose any thing sooner than the real cause which spread this visible dejection over their true character.—Never perhaps was exhibited a nobler struggle of native delicacy; their hearts burnt within them to ask a favour, which the generosity of their feelings would not allow them to mention.— The *English* had been and still were in their power; they had sought their protection as unfortunate strangers.—The natives had already shewn them, and still meant to shew them, every mark of hospitality which their naked, unproductive country could afford.—They conceived that what they wished to ask, as it might prove a temporary inconvenience, would look ungenerous; and that which most checked their speaking was, that, circumstanced as the *English* were with respect to them, a request would have the appearance of a command; an idea this, which shocked their sensibility.—The matter they laboured with was, in their opinions, of the highest imaginable consequence to them. The King had probably talked it over with his brothers the preceding day, had deliberated on it in the evening at the back of the island, and came to the cove this day determined to propose it, but when there, wanted resolution to make it known; yet the object being so important, he felt unwilling to leave it in silence, and perhaps conceived that he could better disclose it from his canoe, than when surrounded by so many *English*.—After much apparent struggle in the King's mind, the request with great difficulty was at last made, and proved to be this:—that the King being in a few days going to battle against an island that had done him an injury, he wished Captain WILSON would permit four or five of his men to accompany him to war with their musquets. Captain WILSON instantly replied, that the *English* were as his own people, and that the enemies of the King were their enemies. The interpreter certainly very well translated this declaration, for in an instant every countenance, which was before overshadowed, became brightened and gay. The King said he should want the men in five days, by which time his own

FIG. 6. *View of Part of the Town of Pelew, and the Place of Council.* Engraved by T. Malton after Robert White and published opposite page 105 in George Keate, *An Account of the Pelew Islands* (London: G. Nicol, 1789).

people would be prepared for battle, and that he would take them down to PELEW with him the next day. Thus was harmony restored between our people and the natives; interrupted only for a few hours, from no other cause than that extreme delicacy of sentiment which no one would have expected to have found in regions so disjoined from the rest of the world.

« CHAPTER 10, PP. 102–4. »

After the repast was ended, MR. DEVIS, who was a draughtsman, being struck with the appearance of a woman who was present, took out a piece of paper, and was making a sketch of her figure; which, before he had completed, the lady noticing that he had repeatedly looked her earnestly in the face, and marked something down, was distressed at it, and rose up to go away, in appearance very much agitated; nor could she be persuaded to stay, although some of the *Rupacks* present laughed heartily at her alarm; which led our people to conceive that she was the wife of one of them. A *Rupack* looking over MR. DEVIS's shoulder, seemed pleased at the representation, or likeness, and wished to hand it up to the King; who so readily entered into a true idea of the art, that he immediately sent a messenger to order two of his women to come down to the house where he was: they arrived very soon, and placed themselves at the window fronting where MR. DEVIS was seated, at which these ladies could stand without being seen lower than the waist;—perceiving, as they looked into the house, a smile on every countenance, they at first appeared pleased themselves, and the King told them the reason why he had sent for them; but soon noticing MR. DEVIS fixing his eyes earnestly on them, they did not know what to make of the business, and began to look exceedingly grave. The King then seemed to chide them, on which they stood quiet, and rather assumed an easier air. MR. DEVIS having finished his sketches, presented them to the King, he shewed them immediately to his women, who seemed pleased in viewing on paper a fancied likeness of themselves, and appeared as if a little ashamed at having been so foolishly and unnecessarily distressed.

The King then desired MR. DEVIS to lend him a piece of paper, and his pencil, on which be attempted to delineate three or four figures, very rudely, without the least proportion; their heads, instead of an oval, being in a pointed form, like a sugar-loaf. Nor let any one conclude from this circumstance, that the King was ostentatious to exhibit the little knowledge he possessed of the art; I rather mention it as a proof of his openness of temper, to let MR. DEVIS see that he was not totally ignorant of what was meant by it; nor was it less a mark of his condescension, in shewing he could very imperfectly trace what the artist was able more happily to delineate. He approved in the stranger those talents he would himself have been ambitious to possess, and in his manner of testifying his approbation, exhibited in captivating colours that which no pencil could display—the urbanity of a noble mind.

Further Reading

For the full text of Keate and interpretive commentary, see the recent re-publication, George Keate, *An Account of the Pelew Islands*, ed. Karen L. Nero and Nicholas Thomas (London: Leicester University Press, 2001); for ethnohistorical and anthropological interpretations of Palau (also now called Belau), see Richard J. Parmentier, *The Sacred Remains* (Chicago: University of Chicago Press, 1987); and Karen Nero, "A Cherecha a Lokelii: Beads of History of Krakor, Palau 1783–1983," Ph.D. diss., University of California, Berkeley, 1987.

part two

Beachcombers & Missionaries

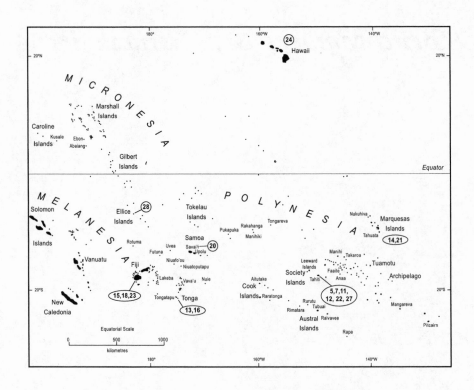

MAP 2. Pacific Islands (circled numbers indicate chapters in which corresponding islands are discussed).

Introduction

Beachcombers and missionaries are commonly regarded as representing the two main forces of European settlement in the Pacific in the period immediately after exploration. This teleological coupling unites beachcomber nativization and missionary endeavor within an overarching imperial project, eliding the degree of contestation that existed between the two groups. Beachcombers and missionaries represented a split, rather than unified, European identity, and it is clear that contradictions between their self-representations were apparent to the islanders among whom they resided. Early settlement among the Pacific islands was as much an exercise in self-fashioning, fraught by barriers of language and by the potential for violence, as it was one of cultural self-affirmation.

"Beachcomber" is itself a term of Pacific coinage. As H. E. Maude pointed out in his seminal essay on beachcombers and castaways, the beachcomber was a figure of the same vintage in Pacific history as the explorer (Maude 1968, 134–38). From the first European voyages, survivors of shipwrecks or individuals deserting or deserted by their ships adopted novel statuses within, or at the margins of, Pacific communities. Beachcombing became a more recurrent phenomenon after the settlement of Port Jackson and with the opening up of whaling and trade routes in the Pacific in the early nineteenth century. Escaped convicts and crew members of ships trafficking between New South Wales and England joined ranks with deserting whalemen and itinerant traders to establish, for a brief period, an active and interactive beachcombing presence among the islands. While some of these figures made only a brief sojourn, taking the first available passage home, others remained in the islands, sometimes to the ends of their lives. Beachcombers acted as interpreters and go-betweens with European ships, including those bringing early missionary groups to Tahiti and Tonga. Those skilled in the use and maintenance of firearms often became head warriors and privileged chiefly attendants, adopting tattoos to camouflage physical difference and marrying into their communities. With the arrival of missions and more regular contacts, the stereotypically wild and disreputable beachcomber was subsequently displaced by the more domesticated types of the settler or resident trader.

That beachcombing could be construed as a comment on "civilized" society rather than a merely circumstantial phenomenon became apparent to the British public following the events of the mutiny on the *Bounty*. The *Bounty*, commanded by Lieutenant William Bligh, was commissioned to transport breadfruit seedlings from the South Pacific to the West Indies, where it was hoped that the trees would become established and that breadfruit would come to provide a cheap alternative to imported grain in the diet of plantation slaves. The project had the patronage of Joseph Banks, who acted as agent and lobbyist at court for West Indian slave owners. The *Bounty* arrived in Tahiti in October 1788 and remained there for five months while the breadfruit was collected and stored: almost twice as long as the *Endeavour* during the recording of the transit of Venus and a couple of months longer than Wilson's sojourn in Paelau. It was the most extended period of authorized cross-cultural contact yet experienced between Europeans and Pacific islanders, offering the opportunity for an unprecedented depth of communication between the two societies. Retrospectively, the duration of the stay was held responsible for the breakdown of shipboard order that resulted in the mutiny. Bligh claimed that the formation of new social and sexual allegiances by members of the crew undermined the authority of his command.

The ship departed Tahiti on April 4, 1789, and the mutiny occurred on April 28. It was an event that produced a set of circumscribed choices for the crew members. Eighteen opted to venture with Bligh in an open launch (which made a harrowing journey that eventually brought them to Coupang in Timor suffering from starvation and exhaustion). The mutineers meanwhile attempted to set up a fortified colony at Tubuai but, deterred by the hostility of the local population, they returned to Tahiti in September 1789. A group of nine mutineers, twelve Tahitian women, and six Polynesian men (four from the Society Islands and two from Tubuai) immediately departed in the *Bounty* with Fletcher Christian and were not heard of again until 1808, when Captain Mayhew Folger of the *Topaz* discovered the survivors and descendants of this party on Pitcairn Island. The remaining sixteen mutineers stayed at Tahiti for eighteen months before they were captured by Captain Edwards of the *Pandora*, a ship sent out from England with the specific goal of recovering the *Bounty*'s crew. The three options seized upon by *Bounty* crew members—to share the fortunes of the captain and endorse the ship's order that he continued to represent; to reintegrate into the now familiar community of the Tahitian beach and risk recapture by visiting British ships; or to seek an island space outside the course of shipping and turn their backs upon European society—encapsulate the alternative degrees of nativization open to sailors in the Pacific and foreground an element of political choice that is present in even the most apparently fortuitous of beachcomber narratives.

It is this rejection of the values represented by the home culture that most immediately distinguishes the beachcomber from the missionary. It accounts for the concern evident in missionary texts to maintain a distinction between the two groups: a distinction that is initially blurred and complicated as beachcombers share the task of representing Euro-American subjectivity to Pacific islanders. The slight but significant precedence of beachcombers in the islands gave them advantages of linguistic and local knowledge, forcing the missionaries to acknowledge an initial dependence upon men whose moral code and local influence they were ultimately determined to oppose. The first missionary party sent out by the London Missionary Society in the *Duff* in 1796 was equipped with a Tahitian vocabulary given to Samuel Greatheed, one of the society's directors, by *Bounty* mutineer Peter Heywood. Both the missionary groups that landed in Tahiti and in Tonga were met by established beachcombers, who first appeared to be providential informants and translators, but gradually revealed their competitive treachery. Initially there was little significant class difference between beachcomber and missionary: missionaries tended to be men of practical rather than literary attainments, known as "godly mechanics" (Gunson 1978, 11–28), and brought with them no great wealth of trade with which to win over local populations. They met with little success, and it was not until 1811, when the London Missionary Society received the support of Pomare II in Tahiti, that missionaries could be said to have gained a foothold in Polynesia. However, from this period onward the balance of power between beachcomber and missionary quickly shifted. Islanders were able to recognize the endorsement given to missionary enterprises by the captains of visiting ships, while the vaunted advantages of literacy offered missionaries a valuable bargaining tool for obtaining the allegiance and support of local chiefs. The American Board of Commissioners for Foreign Missions established a mission in Hawaii in 1820; Wesleyan missionary activity began in Tonga in 1822 and spread to the Lau islands and Samoa, where it encountered rivalry with the London Missionary Society; Roman Catholic missionaries were working in Hawaii in 1827 and in Tahiti by 1841; and the Mormon Church began evangelizing in Tahiti in 1844. Each of these groups initially aligned itself with the interests of influential chiefs, in relationships of mutual strategy.

Both beachcombers and missionaries were uniquely positioned to observe Pacific cultures in the earliest phases of European contact. They played a role akin to that of the later anthropological fieldworker, of ongoing participant observation, whereas earlier explorers and the captains of trading ships obtained a briefer, potentially comparativist glimpse of Pacific societies. (The trader perspective is encapsulated here in selections from books by Abby Jane Morrell and Mary Wallis, two traders' wives whose writings are representative of a limited corpus of women's texts from the Pacific during this period.) Yet beachcomber and missionary texts cannot simply be seen as direct routes into early contact Pacific societies. Beachcomber narratives rarely made their way into print. In the instances where this did happen, often through the intervention of a mediating editor or author, beachcombers ran the risk of being perceived as unreliable narrators, whose rejection of civilized values and frequently disreputable pasts added savor to their forays into that notoriously untrustworthy genre, the traveler's tale. Missionaries, on the other hand, went to the Pacific with an agenda of transformation rather than observation of local cultures, which seemed to preclude any proto-ethnographic understanding. Yet although their accounts expressed, to varying degrees, an overweening cultural confidence, the events and occasionally the insights of their narratives reflected the precariousness of their situation. Missionary references to the interventions of providence can be read as shorthand acknowledgment of their real dependence upon the goodwill of the communities among which they resided. And paradoxically, their interventionist policy could result in an active dialogue with local people on issues of belief and ethical practice, producing commentary that was relativizing rather than condemnatory.

II

JAMES MORRISON
Resident Observer

JAMES MORRISON (1761–1807) first entered the navy in 1779 and joined the crew of the *Bounty* as boatswain's mate on September 9, 1787. Morrison's journal details the voyage of the *Bounty* to Tahiti, the vessel's five-month stay at the island, the mutiny, and the mutineers' attempt to establish a settlement at Tubuai. He documents in detail the lives of those mutineers who returned to Tahiti in September 1789 and remained there until their arrest by the crew of the *Pandora* in March 1791, describing the treatment they met with on board that vessel, the wreck of the *Pandora*, and the journey of the survivors in open boats to Timor. His narrative closes with the commencement of the mutineers' trial in Portsmouth harbor upon their return to Britain, supplemented by a detailed "account of the island of Tahiti and the customs of the islanders."

Morrison's journal is too structured and retrospective a work to represent simply a daily record of shipboard and island life, yet, as Owen Rutter points out, the detailed observation and accuracy of dating suggests that it was composed with the aid of notes taken on the spot. Rutter conjectures that the final text was reworked from "some form of diary," possibly impounded by Captain Edwards when Morrison was taken on board the *Pandora* at Tahiti, saved from the wreck among the ship's papers, and returned to Morrison when he reached England. He suggests that Morrison composed the journal on the basis of this earlier record while he awaited trial and that he presented it to fellow mutineer Peter Heywood after they both received King's Pardon in September 1792 (Rutter, introduction to Morrison 1935, 6). Greg Dening has further argued that the text was itself instrumental in the outcome of Morrison's trial: that the existence of the manuscript was public knowledge, and that his supporters bargained for lenient treatment on the assurance that it would remain unpublished (Dening 1992, 41). Morrison's account emerges in Dening's interpretation as an agent, not just a record, of history: its status as a private document—withholding its capacity to refute public charges laid down in Bligh's hastily published account of the mutiny—influences the subsequent career of its author while serving as a continuing silent reproach to official history. Morrison went on to serve as a gunner in the British navy and perished among the crew of the flagship *Blenheim*, which sank on February 1, 1807, in a gale off Madagascar.

If Morrison's journal is comprised of both retrospective narrative and day-to-day account, its formal composition foregrounds this double structure. The text is divided into the compelling diachronic narrative of the *Bounty* voyage and mutiny, and a synchronic ethnography of Tahitian culture. Although this implies a superficial division between a story of European historical agency and a synthesizing description of timeless Tahitian culture, the relationship between the two texts is more complex. The story of the mutiny is a quintessential emplotted narrative: the story of a plot. Yet Morrison's task in telling it is to deny his culpability, so that the tale has the paradoxical effect of appearing to be motivated not by the characters' actions, but by sleight of hand and disclaimer: by what individuals didn't do, as instruments of a desperate fatality. In fact, it is in the ethnographic passages that Morrison effectively recuperates his own agency, reinventing himself as the first South Seas ethnographer, a Joseph Banks figure with the additional authority of a resident observer, whose classifying eye and linguistic experience contribute more significantly to the Enlightenment project of extending knowledge than to mutiny's disruption of the advancement of empire. In the final pages of his account, he addresses some of the misunderstandings and generalizations that have been promulgated "by former voyagers" who lacked the benefit of an extended period of cultural investigation in Tahiti. The London Missionary Society (an organization that claimed Banks as patron) subsequently used Morrison's ethnography, along with a Tahitian vocabulary that he (or possibly Peter Heywood) collected during his stay in Tahiti, in preparing the first missionaries for their reception at Tahiti (see chapter 12), thereby signaling the rehabilitation of the mutineer's text.

A number of reciprocities link the narrative and ethnographic sections of the work, indicating that Morrison views Tahitian society through the lens of his experiences on the *Bounty*. Discussing the semiotics of Morrison's journal, Greg Dening isolates two of the most recurrent motifs or "yarns" of the narrative section: food and bad language (Dening 1992, 74, 76). The obsessive quantification of food in the early pages of the journal, and the sense of affront that is registered when weights appear to be short or inadequate substitutes are made to serve for the staples of bread and meat: "pumpions" (pumpkins) in place of loaves, oil and sugar in place of butter and cheese, is contrasted, but not in any simple way, with the plenty that greets the sailors when they reach Tahiti. The depiction of Tahiti in the second part of the account as a place of natural bounty is also a reflection of the earlier deprivation represented by Bligh's *Bounty*. Tahiti is in Morrison's ethnography a land of natural bread substitutes: many of the trees and root vegetables he describes produce fruits or dishes that are compared to bread or promoted as interesting equivalents for diverse foodstuffs such as potatoes, pancakes, and asparagus. Yet these substitutes represent value rather than scarcity precisely because they belong to an order that Morrison perceives to be one of good government. Whereas in the journal what goes into the mouth (food) and what comes out of it (language) are linked by an abusive relationship of power, Morrison's ethnography links a fruitful land with beneficent rule. Tahitian chiefs, he claims, are not ashamed to labor side-by-side with their subjects: "Their only pride is Cleanlyness and Generosity for which they are remarkable." When it is necessary to impose restrictions upon their people, or "Rahooe," they do so with grace and forethought; their subjects "always have timely Notice before it takes place, and know the Reason why it is to take place," and the period of restriction is followed by one of feasting where "every thing is carried on with the Greatest Harmony, no quarrels ever ensuing" (Morrison 1935, 169, 194–95). This emphasis on egalitarian aspects of chiefly rule—one certainly not typical of early accounts of Tahiti and vehemently contradicted in initial missionary reports that advertised a different political agenda—is thrown into sharp relief by the earlier portrait of the autocratic and inflexible regime instituted by Lieutenant Bligh on board the *Bounty*. And while Morrison's ethnography continues to tell the tale of the *Bounty*, the Tahitians of the *Bounty* narrative are in turn fleshed out in testimony to the duration and depth of Morrison's observation of their culture and lifeways.

The journal narrative historicizes the potentially static cultural account of Tahiti. Tahitians of different ranks are depicted as active participants in the events surrounding the mutiny, exploiting the presence of Europeans for often opaque and sometimes transparent political purposes. They are also shown developing their own historical and ethnographic understanding of the European visitors. Having been apprised by a visiting ship of the death of Captain Cook, they express disgust at Bligh's strategy of keeping the news a secret: his apotheosizing mentality has locked them into a static relationship with a history of contact that they had perceived as interpersonal and evolving. The mutineers introduce them to numerous aspects of British "Country fashion," which are incorporated selectively within Tahitian ceremony. Yet Morrison is not simply a cultural relativist. His concluding remarks draw attention to the failure of more transient voyagers not only to accurately observe but also transform Tahitian society. The animals left behind by Cook were "intended for the Good of Mankind" but "for want of Europeans to take care of them they were soon destroyed." Earlier, he describes the mutineers' efforts to convey the principles of Christianity, in a manner preemptive of early missionary activity. In such passages Morrison attempts to justify his party's rebellion against the order represented by Bligh's command, and its sojourn outside civil society, as a form of protocolonialism, enabling the establishment of productive husbandry and the transmission of religious values. — VANESSA SMITH

. . . .

James Morrison, *The Journal of James Morrison, Boatswain's Mate of the Bounty, describing the Mutiny and subsequent Misfortunes of the Mutineers together with an account of the Island of Tahiti,* introduction by Owen Rutter (Great Britain: The Golden Cockerel Press, 1935).

« PART I, PP. 18–19, 28–29. »

[The *Bounty* departs England on December 23, 1787, and reaches Tenerife on January 5, 1788.]

Four quarters of Miserable Beef a few pumpions & a Goat & Kid (which died soon after) were all the refreshments this Island afforded, the Beef was for the most part thrown overboard as soon as it was served out by the People who were not yet sufficiently come to their Stomacks to eat what they supposed to be either an Ass or Mule. Evry necessary except Wine was here both scarce & dear, nor Could the loss of the Topsail Yard & Sweeps be here repaird.

The Water being Compleated & the Hold Stowd the boats were got in on the 10th and the 11th We Weighd and Stood to the SW with a fine breeze and pleasant weather, the Ships Company were now put in three Watches and Mr. F. Christian appointed to act as leutenant by Order of Lieut. Bligh which order was read to the Ships Company—Mr. Bligh then informd them that as the length of the Voyage was uncertain (till He should get into the South Sea, and that He was not certain whether or no He should be able to get round Cape Horn as the Season was so far spent but at all events was determined to try,) it became Necessary to be Careful of the Provisions (particularly Bread) to Make them Hold out for which reason He orderd the Allowance of Bread to be reduced to two thirds, but let evry thing else remain at full, this was cheerfully received, and the Beer being out Grog was served. The Weather still Continuing fine a few days after, the Cheese was got up to Air, when on opening the Casks two Cheeses were Missed by Mr. Bligh who declared that they were stolen, the Cooper declared that the Cask had been opend before, while the Ship was in the River by Mr. Samuel's order and the Cheeses sent to Mr. Bligh's house—Mr. Bligh without making any further inquiry into the Matter, ordered the Allowance of Cheese to be stoppd from Officers and Men till the deficiency should be made good, and told the Cooper He would give him a dam'd good flogging If He said any More about it.

These orders were strictly obey'd by Mr. Samuel, who was both Clerk and Steward; and on the next Banyan day butter only was Issued, this the seamen refused, alledging that their acceptance of the Butter without Cheese would be tacitly acknowledging the supposed theft, and Jno. Williams declared that He had carried the Cheeses to Mr. Blighs house with a Cask of Vinager & some other things which went up in the Boat from Long Reach—as they persisted in their denial of the Butter, it was kept also for two Banyan days and no more notice taken.

As the Ship approachd the Equator the pumpions began to spoil, and being in general too large for the Cabbin Use, they were issued to the Ships Company in lieu of bread. The People being desirous to know at what rate the exchange was to be, enquired of Mr. Samuel who informd them that they were to have one pound of Pumpion in lieu of two pounds of bread, this they refused, and on Mr. Blighs being informd of it He Came up in a violent passion, and Calld all hands telling Mr. Samuel to Call the first Man of every Mess and let him see Who would dare to refuse it, or any thing else that He should order to be Served, saying 'You dam'd Infernal scoundrels, I'll make you eat Grass or any thing you can catch before I have done with you.'

This speech enforced his orders, and evry one took the pumpion as Calld, Officers not excepted, who tho it was in their eyes an imposition said nothing against it, tho it was plain to be seen that they felt it more severely than the Men, who having yet a Good Stock of Potatoes which they had laid in at Spitbead did not Immediately feel the effects of such a reduction of their Bread—as the pumpion was always served at one pound a Man it was frequently thrown together by the seamen and the Cooks of the diffrent Messes drew lots for the Whole. The pumpion was Issued evry other day, till they were all expended, and in all probability the grievance would have ended with them, but private stock began to decreace and the Beef and Pork to appear very light, and there had never yet been any

Weighd when Opend, it was supposed that the Casks ran short of their Weight, for which reason the people applyd to the Master, and beggd that he would examine the business and procure them redress. . . .

[After attempting unsuccessfully to round Cape Horn, the *Bounty* pursued its course to the Pacific around the Cape of Good Hope, and reached Tahiti in October 1788.]

[October 1788] at 4 in the Morning of the 25th made sail and anchord at 10 In Port Royal (or Ma'taavye) Bay.

We were presently surrounded by the Natives in their Canoes, who brought off Hogs, Bread fruit & Cocoa Nuts, in abundance, and a trade for Nails hatchets &ca. soon commenced; of the Cocoa Nuts the sick were desired to drink plentifully and these contributed so much to their recovery, that in a few days there was no appearance of sickness or disorder in the ship, and the Great Plenty of Provisions with [which] the Natives supply'd us soon renewd their Strength.

Imediatly on anchoring, an order signd by Mr. Bligh was stuck up on the Mizen Mast, Prohibiting the Purchase of Curiosities or any thing except Provisions—there were few or no instances of the order being disobeyd, as no curiosity struck the seamen so forcibly as a roasted pig & some bread fruit, and these Came in abundance evry species of Ships Provision except grog being stop'd.

November, 1788. As soon as the Ship was moord, a tent was pitchd on Point Venus, and Mr. Nelson & his Assistant went on Shore to Collect Plants, the Gunner also went to the Tent to trade for Hogs for the Ships Use; it being found more convenient then trading alongside, as the Canoes came so thick as to put a stop to all Work. Mr. F. Christian Mr. Heywood & Mr. Peckover the Gunner & four men were also sent on shore as a guard in case the natives should behave amiss.

A shed was built for the reception of the Plants and the Pots Carried on shore as Mr. Nelson filld them. Mean time the Carpenter and his Mates fitted the Cabbin for their reception. Some hands were employd Cutting Wood & filling Water for present Use, the Forge was set up and the Armourer set to work to make trade and all the Salt in the ship was soon expended in curing pork for sea store and evry thing seemd to go on in a prosperous manner.

While the salting time lasted, provisions were in great Plenty, as each Man was allowd two Pounds of the Bones and such parts as were not fit for salting, Pr. day which with what they could get by purchace themselves was always sufficient to enable them to live well.

December, 1788. . . . The Market for Hogs beginning now to slacken
Mr. Bligh seized on all that came to the ship big & small Dead or alive,
taking them as his property, and serving them as the ship's allowance at
one pound pr. Man pr. Day. He also seized on those belonging to the Master, & killd them for the ships use, tho He had more then 40 of different
sizes on board of his own, and there was then plenty to be purchaced: nor
was the price much risen from the first, and when the Master spoke to
him, telling him the Hogs were his property, he told him that 'He Mr.
Bligh would convince him that evry thing was *his*, as soon as it was on
board, and that He would take nine tenths of any mans property and let
him see who dared say any thing to the contrary', those of the seamen were
seized without ceremony, and it became a favour for a man to get a Pound
extra of His own hog.

The Natives observing that the Hogs were seized as soon as they Came
on board, and not knowing but they would be seized from them, as well as
the People, became very shy of bringing a hog in sight of Lieut. Bligh either on board or on shore, and watchd all opportunitys when he was on
shore to bring provisions to their friends but as Mr. Bligh observed this,
and saw that His diligence was like to be evaded, he ordered a Book to be
kept in the Binnacle wherein the Mate of the Watch was to insert the
Number of Hogs or Pigs with the Weight of each that came into the Ship
to remedy this, the Natives took another Method which was Cutting the
Pigs up, and wraping them in leaves and covering the Meat with Bread
fruit in the Baskets, and sometimes with peeld Cocoa Nuts, by which
means, as the Bread was never seized, they were a Match for all his industry; and he never suspected their artifice. By this means provisions were
still plenty. . . .

« PP. 51–53. »

[After five months in Tahiti gathering breadfruit plants, the crew of the
Bounty set sail for Jamaica. They touched at the Friendly Islands (Tonga).
In the early hours of the April 28, 1789, the mutineers under Fletcher
Christian took the ship. Morrison claims to have been asleep at the time.
Bligh and his supporters were put to sea in the longboat. The *Bounty* made
for Tubuai, where Christian formed a plan of settling. The ship returned
to Tahiti to procure supplies.]

June, 1789. On the Passage He [Christian] Gave orders that no man
should tell the name of the Island, or mention It to the Natives and if any

person was found to mention the real name he would punish Him severely and declared if any Man diserted he would shoot him as soon he was brought back, which promise evry one knew he had in his power to perform and having appointed his own Party to keep Constant Guard, he distributed the trade amongst all Hands disiring them to make the Best Market they Could, as it was to be the last they would ever have the Opportunity of making. He also made several distributions of the Cloaths &c which had been left by the Officers & Men who went in the Boat, these were made out in lotts by Churchill & were drawn for by ticketts, but it always happend that Mr. Christian's party Were always better served then these who were thought to be disaffected, however as they had different views No Notice was taken of it at present.

On the 6th of June we anchord in Mataavye Bay when the Natives flockd on board in great Numbers; they were glad to see us and Enquired where the rest were, and what had brought us back so soon, where we had left the Plants as they knew our stay had been too Short to have reachd home from the account we had formerly given them of the distance. To all these Questions Mr. Christian answerd them that We had met Captain Cook who had taken Mr. Bligh and the others with the Plants & the Longboat and had sent us for Hogs Goats &c for a New Settlement which the King had sent him to make which he described to be on New Holland. This being made known to the People none dared to Contradict what he said, knowing if they said any thing Contrary it would soon reach his ears, as the Taheiteans are not remarkable for keeping secrets. But if this had not been the Case there were few who Could explain the Matter properly as they were not so well versed in the language.

While we lay here the Armourer was set to work to make trade, and Churchill & Myself were sent on Shore to purchace Hogs Goats &c. Meanwhile Mr. Christian entertaind the Chiefs on board plying them with Wine & Arrack of which they became very fond—and evry one on board was busey purchacing Stock and Provisions for them and altho the general oppinion when we saild before was that we had impovrishd the Island we were now Convinced that they Had not Missd what we got as we now found the Country full of Hogs and they which before had been kept out of sight & they appeard now better able to supply a Fleet then they seemd before to supply our single Ship and the demand for Iron Work increased so fast, that the Armourer Could not supply them tho Constantly employd and there was a tolerable good stock ready made found in the Ship which had not been expended during our former Stay.

On the 10th Willm. McCoy, being Centinal, fired upon a number of the natives who throngd the Ganway and did not get so fast out of His way as he thought proper, but as no damage was done no notice was taken of it, and on the night of the 14th Churchill observing a Canoe ahead of the Ship haild her but getting no answer he fired at them and they paddled off.

It may here be observed that Mr. Christians account of Himself passd very well with the Natives, who had not yet been informd of Captain Cooks Death, Mr. Bligh having given orders that no person should mention his death, but tell the Natives that He was yet alive in England and that He would probably Come again to Taheite, and as Mr. Christian informd them that He would Come to Taheite as soon as he had settled the Country which he Calld Wytootacke, they were perfectly satisfied, and as they were more intent on trading then any thing else they made but few enquiries, and thought little about it.

We remained here till the 16th during which time we were plentifully supplyd with evry necessary by the Natives our old friends nor do I think they would have thought any worse of us had they known the truth of the Story or been any way shy of supplying us as Mr. Christian was beloved by the whole of them but on the Contrary none liked Mr. Bligh tho they flatterd him for His Riches, which is the Case among polishd Nations those in power being always Courted.

The grand object of these people is Iron and like us with Gold it matters not by what means they get it or where it comes from if they can but get it.

By the 16th we had Mustered about 460 Hogs, Mostly breeders, 50 Goats and a quantity of Fowles, a few dogs & Cats; and for a Few red feathers we got the Bull and Cow on which they set little store. With these and a quantity of Provisions for present Use we prepared for Sea Having on board 9 Men 8 Boys 10 Weomen & one female Child, some of which hid themselves below till we were at sea, when having shortend in the Cable the Ship drove and droping near the Dolphin Bank we were forced to Cut away the Anchor and Make sail. When we were out a number made their appearance, among which was Heteeheete & Several of our old friends, and Mr. Christian finding it too late to put them on Shore, at the request of some of His party he Consented to proceed to sea with them but told them they would Never See Taheite again—at which they seemd perfectly easey and satisfied never betraying the least sign of Sorrow for leaving their friends nor did I observe that they ever repined afterwards. . . .

« PP. 76–79, 83–84. »

[The attempt to settle at Tubuai proves unsuccessful, due to the resistance of the local population. The mutineers resolve to return to Tahiti, where some will remain, while Christian and his supporters sail on in search of another island to settle. They return to Matavai Bay.]

Immediately on landing they informd us that a Vessel had been there lately, and had left a man who they Call'd Browne who was then at Tyarrabboo with Matte settling some business with Vayheeadooa, Chief of that Pininsula, and as we heard they told strange storys of him We wishd to know what had been the true Cause of his Stay, and therefore appointed Churchill & Millward to go to Tyarrabboo & take presents to Matte and at the same time See who this Man was. . . . They also informd us that the Captain had told Matte of Captain Cook's death and had left them the Picture of it and on which Score they were angry that we had not told them before, and accused Mr. Bligh of imposing on them by saying that he was alive in England, that He was Capt. Cooks Son which they were informd to the Contrary of by Captain Cox, who told [them] that Captain Cooks son was then in England. . . .

On the 27th, having appointed that We should meet at Opparee, and make out presents to the Young King, We marchd in a body under Arms to Oparee, taking with us the Toobouai Images and several other presents of red Feathers, Friendly Island & Toobouai Cloth, Matting and War Weapons Iron Work &c.—and were Joined by those who were at Oparre and after being Welcom'd to the District by the Priest Making a long Oration and presenting each of us with a young Plantain tree with a Sucking Pig or a Fowle. Having made known our business to Areepaeea—who told us that we must not approach the Young king as he was yet Sacred, unless we Strip'd the Clothing off from our Head & Shoulders, which we refused telling him that it was not Customary to remove any part of our Dress except our hats and if we were under arms it was not our Country Manner to remove our hat even to the King. However that we might not seem to be deficient in point of Good Manners each was provided with a piece of Tahteite Cloth to put over their Shoulders and take off in the Young Kings Presence, when we March'd to his House in procession each attended by a friend to remove the Taheite Cloth which we had on, all of Whom Stripd as they entered the Sacred Ground, the Men to the Waist, and the Weomen uncovering their Shoulders and tucking their Cloths up under their arm, and our Taheite Cloaths were removed. We were followed by a Multitude of both Sexes, all of whom observed the Same rules in their

Homage; having got to the opposite bank of the River facing the Farre Raa or Sacred House, the Young King Appeard, sitting on the Shoulders of a Man; and having a large piece of White Cloth round his Shoulders and his Head almost Hid with a Garland of Black & red Feathers. As He approachd the Bank, he Saluted us with the Word Manoa (Welcome) which he repeated to each, calling us by the Name of our Taheite Friends; and having placed himself over against us, Heete-heete Strip'd himself Naked to Carry the presents, and the Party drew up on the Bank for the Purpose. The Toobouai Images were first sent in the Name of the whole, with which Heete-heete told a long Story and which from the Number of red feathers were thought a Valuable present, and produced a general exclamation of wonder when they were held up to publick View on the opposite bank of the river.

After these were delivered, evry one sent his present seperatly, which Consisted of Red feathers Cloth &c.—and the whole being finishd, the Party formd three divisions & dischargd their arms, at which the Young Chief was so much pleased that He told us to follow our own Country fashion in evry thing, and take no heed of their Ceremonies, when we retired.—we were Now Conducted to Areepaeeas house where a Feast was provided for us of a Baked Hog, Fish, Bread, Tarro & Cocoa Nuts, Plantains &c.—after which a Proportion of land was pointed out for the Use of the Whole when in this district, and in the Evening we returned to Maatavye, and Next day the 28th a Messenger arrived from Matte with a Hog and a Piece of Cloth for each of us and pointed out two pieces of land for the use of the Whole; the One (Point Venus) for Cocoa Nuts and the other well stockd with Bread fruit Trees near the Spot where Poenos House stood; these were ordered for our present use, tho we stood in no need of His Care, having abundance of evry thing supplied by our Friends. . . .

We kept the Hollidays in the best manner that we could, killing a Hog for Christmas Dinner, and reading Prayers which we never Omitted on Sundays, and having wet weather we were not able to do any thing out of doors for the remainder of the Year.

We informd the Natives of the reason of our Observing these Hollidays, and especially Christmas Day; all of which seemd to regard with attention, and readily believed all that we could inform them of, never doubting that the Son of God was born of a Woman, and they always behooved with much decency when present at our worship; tho they Could not understand one word; yet several were desirous to have it explaind to them, and some of them wishd to learn our prayers which they all allowed to be better then their own; those who were constantly about us knew when our Sunday came, and were always prepared accordingly. Seeing that we rested on that day they did so likewise and never made any diversions on it. One of them was always ready to hoist the Ensign on Sunday Morning and if a stranger happened to pass, and enquire the meaning, they were told that it was Mahana'Atooa (Gods Day) and tho they were intent on their Journey, would stop to see our manner of keeping it, and would proceed next day, well pleased with their Information. . . .

« PART 2, PP. 235–39. »

[From the second section of Morrison's text, "An Account of the Island of Tahiti and the Customs of the Islanders."]

And here it May not be improper to remark that the Idea formd of this Society and of the Inhabitants of this Island in general by former Voyagers could not possible extend much further then their own Oppinion, None having remaind a sufficient length of time to know the Manner in which they live and as their whole system was overturned by the arrival of a ship, their Manners were then as much altered from their Common Course, as those of our own Country are at a Fair, which might as well be given for a specimen of the Method of living in England—and such was always their situation as soon as a ship Arrived their whole thought being turnd toward their Visitors, & all Method tryd to win their Friendship. Mean time they were forced to live in a different way of life that they might the better please their new friends.

Their general Notion of delicacy is undoubtedly different from Ours, perhaps from their want of refinement, without which many of our own Countrymen would be as bad if not worse then them, many of whom would not keep within bounds but for fear of the law.

A woman is not ashamed to shew her limbs at a dance, or when bathing, if they are perfect; if they are not, she will avoid being seen as much as possible, and tho the Men and Weomen frequently bathe together they are more remarkable for their decency then levity at such a time.

They have no Walls to their houses nor do they require any, Notwithstanding which they cannot be charged with holding Carnal Conversation in Publick and like privacy in such cases as much as we do, nor did I see any thing of the kind during our stay in the islands tho they are not remarkable for their vertue. Yet this is not the General Charracter and the large Familys of some shew that there are some of that stamp.

Their Actions might possibly be for the sake of Gain—brought to a stile of what we call indecency, but where are the Countrys that do not produce Weomen of the Same discription—Iron is to them More Valuable then Gold to us, for the posession of which some of our own Country weomen would not stick at acts of indecency nor even horrid Crimes which these People would tremble to think of. Nay, they Challenge us with the Verry Crime and say we are ashamed of Nothing, using these things which we knew they were fond of to perswade them to commit such acts as their innocence had taught them to be ashamed of. If they can purchase Iron at the expence of their Beauty, or are able to get it by theft, they will. Neither of which Methods I hold to be a Crime in them. They know its Value and think no price to[o] great for it.

Gold is preferd in Other Countrys and some, as fine Weomen as any in Europe, are said to prefer it to Virtue yet we upbraid these untaught and uncontrould people with such actions as we ourselves help them to Commit.

They lay no restraint on their Children because they are the Head of the Family and therefore do as they please; having no law nor Custom to prevent them they have a Number of Amusements which would not suit the Idea of Europeans, which however are dropd as they Grow up, when they become ashamed of these Childish sports but are not Compelld unless they think proper themselves—and as there are always sufficient in all Countrys to promote evil practices they who do not like them can only reform themselves, having no power over others; for which reason they are sufferd to proceed in their own way.

Those who Make a Trade of Beauty know how to value it, and when they come on board bring with them their Pimps or Procurers under the denomination of relations to receive and secure the Price and these ladys are as well qualified to Act their part as any of their profession in other Countrys and are no ways bashful in making their Demands—but if a Man Makes a friend that Friend can never have any Connection with any female of the Family except His friends Wife, evry other becoming His relations which they hold an abomination to have any Conexion with, nor can they be perswaded to alter that Custom on any Consideration, detesting as much as we do to have their own relations as wives.

The Weomen of rank are Most remarkable for their licentious practices and Many of them have a Number of Favourites, in which they pride themselves, tho many of the lower Class are what may honestly be Calld Virtuous, never admitting a Second to share in their favours.

The Famous Queen Obooraya being herself an Areeuoy, it is not to be wondered at that evry licentious practice was carried on by her followers and Attendants, her Court being filld with such as preferd the Rites of

Venus to those of Mars and as she saw that they were also more agreeable to her Visitors (the general Case with Sailors after a long Voyage) they were no doubt practised and carried to the utmost verge of their lattitude, it being in all Countrys the Case that those in power always lead the fashions, let them be good or evil.

However the ladys who act these parts are not to be taken as a standard for the Whole no more then the Nymphs of the Thames or Syrens of Spithead are to be taken as Samples of our own fair Country Weomen.

Their Ceremonies have also been misunderstood by Former Voyagers— The Flys being Numerous they are forced to use fly flaps and when they have none they use branches of the first tree, and with these they are ever ready to supply evry stranger, especially if any Food is at hand; as they cannot bear to see a Fly toutch what they Eat, and have a number of Hands always employd to drive them away with these branches.

The other branches used in Ceremonies are the Rou avva and are Commissions borne by substitutes for Chiefs and evry person bearing one of them is treated in the same Manner as the Chief would be if he were present; these Commissions or Emblems of truth are Never Assumed by any unless on such occasions as they would suffer death for such fraud, the Plantain as before mentioned being the only Emblem of Peace—When any person is sent with such a Commission he gives a leaf to each of the party to whom he is sent, on the receipt of which, and being informd who sent him, his word is never doubted.

Besides the different Classes & Societys already discribed they have a Set of Men Calld Mahoo. These Men are in some respects like the Eunuchs in India but are Not Casterated. They Never Cohabit with weomen but live as they do; they pick their Beards out & dress as weomen, dance and sing with them & are as effeminate in their Voice; they are generally excellent hands at Making and painting of Cloth, Making Matts and evry other Womans employment. They are esteemd Valuable friends in that way and it is said, tho I never saw an instance of it, that they Converse with Men as familiar as weomen do—this however I do not aver as a fact as I never found any who did not detest the thought.

The Manners and Customs of the other Islands are as Near the same as those of Different Countys in the Same Kingdom, and their produce nearly the Same & the Inhabitants of all the Society Isles are one and the same people—Taheite is by Much the largest and most powerful when the Strength of the Island is united, and is therefore acknowledged Mistress Paramount of the whole. They all distinguish their Language, Customs

&c. by the Name of Taheite as well at home as when they are at Taheite and there are but few Men of Property who do not visit Taheite once in their lifetime and many visit it frequently.

It must be acknowledged that Captain Cook, when he first thought of stocking these Islands with Cattle, Poultry and the Fruits and Roots of Europe, intended it for the Good of Mankind, but these people knew not the Value of them and for want of Europeans to take Care of them they were soon distroyd, the Curiosity of the Natives to see such Strange Animals made each wish to have one by which means they were seperated and their Increase prevented; the Poultry soon became extinct—the Sheep, who did not as in Other Warm Climes lose their Wool, died for want of Sheering—the Black Cattle alone thriving tho kept Mostly seperate, the Seeds & Plants were destroyd by being removed as soon as they made their Appearance, evry one Wishing to posess some part of the Curiositys which they esteemd the whole and would part with the best Cow for a Good Axe, setting No Value on them for food tho they Killd several and eat part of them in the Wars, but having No Method of taking of the Hides they Cleand them as hogs but could not fancy they were good therefore took No pains to save a Breed.

The Rams & He Goats they could Not abide from their disagreeable Smell and Many of the Goats were banishd to the Mountains as their Flesh was not a Compensation for the Mischief they did to the Cloth plantations, those they keep now are always tyed if they are near one of these Plantations and at best are not esteemd equal to a Dog—this Method of treating them prevents the Island from being over run with them which it soon would be if they were suffered to range at large.

Notwithstanding their having lost all these Valuable Curiositys they still remember Captain Cook for bringing them and take More Care of his Picture then all the rest. They Made frequent enquiry after him & Sir Joseph Banks, both of whom will never be forgotten at Taheite—they were exceeding sorry when they heard of Captain Cooks death and Wishd that His Son might come and take possession of His fathers land, He being acknowledged Chief of Maatavye and will be as long as his Picture lasts.

They were also very inquisitive about all their friends and were happy when we entertaind them with an Account of their Welfare. Their Language is Soft and Melodious, abounding in vowels; they have only seventeen letters yet they can express any thing with ease, tho for want of the others which Compose our Alphabet they never could pronounce any English word which Contains them.

Further Reading

Bligh's version of events was published in 1790 as *A Narrative of the Mutiny on Board His Majesty's Ship the* Bounty *and subsequent voyage of part of the crew in the ship's boat from Tofoa, one of the Friendly Islands, to Timor, a Dutch settlement in the East Indies* (London: G. Nicol) and in 1792 as *A Voyage to the South Seas, undertaken by command of His Majesty, for the purpose of conveying the breadfruit tree to the West Indies in His Majesty's Ship the* Bounty (London: G. Nicol). His comments on Morrison's journal are reproduced in *Bligh's Voyage in the* Resource *from Coupang to Batavia, together with the Log of his Subsequent passage to England in the Dutch packet* Vlydt *and his remarks on Morrison's Journal* (Great Britain: Golden Cockerel Press, 1937). Bligh's second breadfruit voyage is documented in Douglas Oliver, *Return to Tahiti: Bligh's Second Breadfruit Voyage* (Melbourne: Melbourne University Press, 1988). Greg Dening's *Mr Bligh's Bad Language: Passion, Power and Theatre on The* Bounty (Cambridge: Cambridge University Press, 1992) is a virtuoso meditation on the literature and theater of the *Bounty* mutiny. Jocelyn Dunphy, "Insurrection and Repression: Bligh's 1790 *Narrative of the Mutiny on Board H.M. Ship Bounty*," in *1789: Reading Writing Revolution: Proceedings of the Essex Conference on the Sociology of Literature, July 1981*, ed. Francis Barker et al., 281–301 (Colchester: University of Essex, 1982), looks at parallels between the *Bounty* mutiny and French Revolutionary politics. Neil Rennie, *Far-Fetched Facts: The Literature of Travel and the Idea of the South Seas* (Oxford: Clarendon Press, 1995); and Rod Edmond, *Representing the South Pacific: Colonial Discourse from Cook to Gauguin* (Cambridge: Cambridge University Press, 1997), both examine the literary impact of the *Bounty* story.

12

WILLIAM WILSON

The Brethren and the "Tayos"

. . . .

THE LONDON MISSIONARY SOCIETY, founded in 1795, chose the South Sea islands as the site of its first evangelical mission for reasons that were always paradoxical. On the one hand, director Thomas Haweis represented the Tahiti he
knew from Cook's *Voyages* as an Edenic site, free from the curse of labor that
would distract potential converts (Cathcart et al. 1990, 14). On the other, the islands were necessarily perceived as a paradise given over to heathenism and corruption. The idea of the mission was enthusiastically greeted in Britain, and thousands of pounds worth of donations had been received by the time the society
directors purchased the ship *Duff* in April 1796 and projected an expanded missionary voyage that would also include Tonga and the Marquesas in its trajectory.
The vessel was to be commanded by James Wilson (1769–1814), a retired captain
who had served in India and whose miraculous escape from death some years before his conversion seemed to indicate a special providential dispensation. Wilson
was effectively placed in charge of the mission and equipped with a set of special
instructions from the directors of the Missionary Society. The *Duff* departed England on August 10, 1796, to convey twenty-nine missionaries and settlers, a surgeon, six women, and three children to the islands. Only four missionaries were at
that stage ordained ministers. The rest had been selected for practical rather than
literary skills, since, as Haweis later explained, the directors were "not . . . persuaded that deep attainments in literary pursuits in all Missionaries will be so essential to the great object we have in view" (letter, January 19, 1798, Haweis papers
vol. 1). They made efforts on the journey to master "a manuscript vocabulary of the
Otaheitean language . . . providentially . . . preserved from the mutineers who were

seized by the Pandora, and brought to Portsmouth for their trial, which was of unspeakable service to the missionaries" (Wilson 1799, 13–14), but they made poor
progress, the words proving more literally "unspeakable" than anticipated.

The *Duff* eventually arrived off Tahiti on March 5, 1797. It was greeted by a
large party of islanders including Ha'amanemane ("Mānne Manne"), an elderly
priest who was keen to "make tayo"—that is, to form a customary friendship—
with Wilson. Over the ensuing days, the missionaries met Tu ("Otoo"), who had
recently been handed power by his father Pomare I, formerly Otoo, a figure familiar to the missionaries from the literature of Cook's voyages. Following Cook
and Bligh, the missionaries believed the Pomare family, powerful chiefs of the
Matavai region, to be kings of Tahiti (Cathcart et al. 1990, 143–44). They only
gradually became aware that Pomare and Tu were rivals locked in a struggle for
power that may have had echoes for the English missionaries of their own monar-
chy's regency crisis of 1788. The politics of these early encounters were further
complicated by the missionaries' reliance on the mediations of two Swedish beachcombers: Peter Haggerstein, who had deserted from the ship *Daedalus*, and Andrew Lind, formerly of the *Matilda*. These disreputable interpreters were regarded
initially as instruments of providence, and then with increasing suspicion as mis-
informants and troublemakers. Their difference from the missionary party is heavily signaled in the following extract, where tattooed, swarthy, and blasphemous but
fluent beachcombers are implicitly aligned with scarified, dark-skinned, and incomprehensible natives in a community of savagery. The two Swedes were
"dressed in the teboōta and māro as the natives, and tattowed also about the legs
and arms": their nativized appearance allowed the missionaries to act out, in dumb
show, a fantasy of primacy they might have expected to forgo as relative latecom-
ers to Tahiti. Tu's wife is represented as marveling at the white skin of one missionary, which contrasts with "the dark complexions of the naked shipwrecked
sailors who had lately taken refuge amongst them."

The missionaries' initial hesitancy about forming *taio* relationships—where the
obligations of friendship were instituted by the exchange of names—was less in-
dicative of their awareness of local political tensions than of their faith that significant relationships must be reserved for the perceived "king," Pomare. Their re-
serve is evident in the entry from the manuscript of their communal diary for
Wednesday, March 8, which records:

> In a short time almost all the Missionaries were Clothed in Otaheitean Cloth
> and had pigs made them presents of by several Chiefs, who expressed their
> friendship and requested to change names: the Missionaries complying so far
> as prudence and reciprocal friendship would permit. It was not long before
> Mannemanne made his appearance, and requested to Change Names with Bro

Cover, observing that as the Captn bore the name of Mannemanne, he (Bro C.) must take that of Moe, ore another of his names, he then brought us a present of Taheitean Cloth and 3 Pigs ready dressed for dinner. (Haweis papers, vol. 2)

The missionaries responded to the pressures of Tahitian generosity with their own clumsy gift-giving, including the presentation of clothing recorded in the extract. However, by the time the Duff made its return visit to Matavai Bay the significance of the taio bond seems to have been diminished in their eyes. In one manuscript a missionary is described as working "with the help of his Tyos": the word "friends," which appeared afterwards as a definition, has been deleted and replaced by the term "Servants" (Haweis papers, vol. 1).

The missionaries also made a policy of refusing to engage in a variety of other well-established forms of exchange, thus asserting a distinction between themselves and previous visitors to Tahiti. The London Missionary Society directors' instructions to Captain Wilson (reprinted at the beginning of the *Missionary Voyage*) suggested that any land "should not be purchased, but required, as the condition of our remaining with them; and that the presents we make should not be considered as payments, but as gratuities, the expressions and pledges of our good will" (Wilson 1799, xcviii). These new rules of exchange devalued preexisting practices of reciprocity, advertising instead the value of the Christian message as a bargaining tool within the cross-cultural economy. The missionaries refused to trade for food on their Sabbath or to condone any form of sexual transaction. They also confessed to a lack of facility with that most immediate form of exchange, spoken language, which, although in no way condoned by missionary policy—Samuel Harper's shipboard journal records that "The President reproved sundry of the Brethn for neglecting the Otaheitean Manuscript, & desired each of us to bring before the Committee an account of the Progress made therein" (Haweis papers, vol. 2)—seemed equally to reflect a moral agenda. Spoken communication, as the shared domain of the fluent beachcomber and the unredeemed native, was tainted, just as other forms of exchange from which the missionaries wished to exempt themselves were tainted with lucre, or with the threat of sexual contamination, or, in the case of performance, by the moral values of those consummate "strolling players," the Arioi. The concern to reject any sense of complicity with the ethical framework represented by established forms of cross-cultural transaction rendered language potentially duplicitous, to be haltingly and tentatively acquired. The missionaries confessed to slow progress and difficulty in picking up Tahitian, and admitted to having failed the test of performance established by earlier visitors: "the chief thought it was time to inquire after entertainments: and first sky-rockets, next the violin and dancing, and lastly the bagpipe, which he humorously described by putting a bundle of cloth under his arm, and twisting his body like a Highland piper. When we told them that we had none of these, they seemed rather dejected" (Wilson 1799, 73).

A party of twenty-five was left at Tahiti. The *Duff* sailed on to Tongatabu, arriving on April 10, where it deposited ten missionaries (one of whom was George Vason, whose story is detailed in chapter 13). On June 5 the ship anchored in Resolution Bay, Tahuata, in the Marquesas, intending to deposit two missionaries, though only one, William Pascoe Crook, remained. The *Duff* returned to Matavai Bay on July 6, where to all appearances settlement was progressing well. Wilson made a tour of the island, and finally departed on August 4, visiting the missionaries at Tonga before sailing home via Macao and arriving in London on July 11, 1798. The missionaries at Matavai Bay remained isolated as a community. The arrival of the ship *Nautilus* in March 1798 led to altercations with the Tahitians, and the majority of the missionary party eventually departed aboard this ship for Port Jackson, leaving a core group of eight to continue evangelical work in Tahiti. This group made a more rigorous attempt to acquire the language, but their number was further reduced by crises of faith and declension among the members. The arrival of the *Royal Admiral* in July 1801, commanded by William Wilson, nephew of the *Duff*'s commander, brought reinforcements from England.

William Wilson had served as first mate aboard the *Duff* and was the author of the official account of the first missionary voyage. However, *A Missionary Voyage to the Southern Pacific Ocean* is effectively a composite text, "compiled from journals of the officers and the missionaries" and comprising a "preliminary discourse" giving historical and ethnographic information concerning each of the island groups at which missionaries were deposited. The letter of instructions to Captain James Wilson was also published in the volume. *A Missionary Voyage* advertises in its opening pages the lunges of comprehension required of the reader to accommodate the modulations of a unified but disparate writing subject:

> The body of the journal is the composition of Mr. William Wilson, from the Captain's papers, his own, and the Missionaries' reports. As there was a necessity of filling up some chapters from the journals of the Missionaries themselves, there will sometimes be observed a change of persons, according as individuals, or the body, are introduced speaking. It is hoped that our readers will pardon this defect, and that whatever perplexity it may occasion will be removed by referring to the list of *Errata*.

"A change of persons" here implies more than just a shift in the personal pronoun: it involves a complete reconstitution of the narrating self, with attendant possibilities of misconstruction and misrepresentation. In this sense, the text of *A Mis-*

sionary Voyage becomes an analogue of the missionary project itself: disparate voices united within a single overarching narrative, yet each retaining the individual potential to disrupt its unified progression or to render contradictory its motivation. — VANESSA SMITH

. . . .

William Wilson, *A Missionary Voyage to the Southern Pacific Ocean, performed in the years 1796, 1797, 1798 in the ship* Duff, *commanded by Captain James Wilson, compiled from journals of the officers and the missionaries* (London: T. Chapman, 1799).

« CHAPTER 6, PP. 56–73. »

[Sunday, March 5, 1797.] The morning was pleasant, and with a gentle breeze we had by seven o'clock got abreast of the district of Atahoorōo, whence we saw several canoes putting off and paddling towards us with great speed; at the same time it fell calm, which being in their favour, we soon counted seventy-four canoes around us, many of them double ones, containing about twenty persons each. Being so numerous, we endeavoured to keep them from crowding on board; but in spite of all our efforts to prevent it, there were soon not less than one hundred of them dancing and capering like frantic persons about our decks, crying, "Tayo! tayo!" and a few broken sentences of English were often repeated. They had no weapons of any kind among them; however, to keep them in awe, some of the great guns were ordered to be hoisted out of the hold, whilst they, as free from the apprehension as the intention of mischief, cheerfully assisted to put them their carriages. When the first ceremonies were over, we began to view our new friends with an eye of inquiry: their wild disorderly behaviour, strong smell of the cocoanut oil, together with the tricks of the arreoies, lessened the favourable opinion we had formed of them; neither could we see aught of that elegance and beauty in their women for which they have been so greatly celebrated. This at first seemed to depreciate them in the estimation of our brethren; but the cheerfulness, good-nature, and generosity of these kind people soon removed the momentary prejudices. One very old man, Mānne Manne, who called himself a priest of the Eatooa, was very importunate to be tayo with the captain; others, pretending to be chiefs, singled out such as had the appearance of officers for their tayos; but as they neither exercised authority over the unruly, nor bore the smallest mark of distinction, we thought proper to decline their pro-

FIG. 7. *The Cession of the District of Matavai in the Island of Otaheite to Captain James Wilson for the use of the Missionaries.* Hand-colored aquatint by Francesco Bartolozzi after R. A. Smirke (60 x 78 cm). By permission of the National Library of Australia.

posals till we knew them and the nature of the engagement better. At this they seemed astonished, but still more when they saw our indifference about the hogs, fowls, and fruit, which they had brought in abundance. We endeavoured to make them understand, but I think in vain, that this was the day of the Eatooa, and that in it we durst not trade: but their women repulsed, occasioned greater wonder. They continued to go about the decks till the transports of their joy gradually subsided, when many of them left us of their own accord, and others were driven away by the old man, and one named Maurōa, who now exercised a little authority. Those who remained were chiefly arreoies from Ulietēa, in number about forty; and being brought to order, the brethren proposed having divine service upon the quarterdeck. Mr. Cover officiated; he perhaps was the first that ever mentioned with reverence the Saviour's name to these poor heathens. Such hymns were selected as had the most harmonious tunes; first, "O'er the gloomy hills of darkness;" then, "Blow ye the trumpet, blow;" and at the conclusion, "Praise God from whom all blessings flow." The text was from the first epistle general of John, chap. iii. ver. 23. "God is love." The whole service lasted about an hour and a quarter. During sermon and prayer the natives were quiet and thoughtful; but when the singing struck up, they seemed charmed and filled with amazement; sometimes they would talk and laugh, but a nod of the head brought them to order. Upon the whole, their unweariedness and quietness were astonishing; and, indeed, all who heard observed a peculiar solemnity and excellence in Mr. Cover's address on that day.

We had hitherto received very unsatisfactory answers to our inquiries after the Matilda's crew; but at last saw two of them coming in a canoe: these were Swedes, dressed in the teboōta and māro as the natives, and tattowed also about the legs and arms: having got on board they were called into the cabin, and gave the following account of themselves:—The youngest, named Andrew Cornelius Lind, about thirty years of age, a native of Stockholm, said, that after the loss of the Matilda they took to the boats, and bearing down towards Otaheite, landed on the 6th of March 1792, on the south side of the island; they were immediately plundered of all they had, but afterwards treated kindly by the natives. Since that, the captain and most of the crew had gone homeward by different methods: six of them decked one of their boats, and set off towards New Holland; but it was improbable they would ever reach thither. The other, whose name is Peter Haggerstein, aged forty, a native of Elsinfors in Swedish Finland, was left here by Captain New of the Daedalus. They both spoke tolerably good English, and being well acquainted with the Otaheitean tongue, we entertained a hope that they would prove of great service.

From them we learnt, that the old man who was so solicitous to have the captain for a tayo, had formerly been king of Ulietēa, was a near relation of the royal family, and of considerable consequence in the islands, being chief priest over Otaheite and Eimēo. Upon this, Mānne Manne was invited into the cabin and treated kindly. He now redoubled his importunities to gain the captain for his friend, who desired him to wait till tomorrow, when he would consider of it. The Swedes further informed us, that the former Otoo had transferred his name and title of Eāree rāhie (or king) to his son, and had now assumed the name of Pomārre: that in a contest about twenty months ago with Temārre, the chief of all the south side of the greater peninsula, Pomārre's party prevailed, and subjected his adversary to a state of dependance, and soon after Tiarabōo was conquered; and thus the whole island became subject to him, or rather to his son Otoo, and has remained so ever since. Motuāra, the chief of Eimēo, being dead, Pomārre laid claim to the government of that island; and having only the widow of the deceased to contend with, was, after a few skirmishes, acknowledged as chief, or king. Thus was the power of Pomārre and his son Otoo so greatly increased, that none dared any longer to dispute their authority.

6th. About thirty of the natives, chiefly arreoies, intending to go to Matavāi, remained on board all the night, and part of the following day, till we anchored in the bay; as did the two Swedes; and slept on the deck. The missionaries watched; all perfectly quiet. At daybreak the old priest awoke, and being impatient to secure the tayoship with the captain, awoke him also. There was now no refusing him any longer, as even good policy was on his side; therefore they exchanged names, and Mānne Manne, wrapping a long piece of cloth around the captain, and putting a tebōota over his head, requested for himself a musket, some shot and gunpowder: but being told that none of these were to spare, and that he should be amply repaid for what friendly offices he might do us, he seemed satisfied. All the forenoon was employed in working up without the reefs of Opārre; but gaining little ground, at one P.M. we came to anchor in Matavāi bay, Point Venus bearing N.E. by E. and One Tree hill S. ½ W. distant from the beach about three quarters of a mile. We had not been long at anchor, when all the arreoies, both men and women, sprung into the water and swam to the shore: their place, however, was soon supplied by others, who surrounded the ship with hogs, fruit, and other articles: of these we took a little for present use; but the old priest having promised to supply all our wants by next morning, consequently little was done in the trading way.

Almost the whole afternoon it rained hard till near four o'clock, when we had some intervals of fair weather; then the captain, Mānne Manne, the two Swedes, with brother Cover, Henry, and a few more of the missionaries, went on shore in order to examine a large house standing on the extremity of Point Venus. They called it E Fwhārre no Prītane (the British House), and said it had been built by Pomārre for Captain Bligh, who had said he should come back and reside there. . . . —Thus hath the Lord appeared to set before us an open door, which we trust none shall henceforth be able to shut.

The chief of the district (an old man named Pytēah) welcomed them to the island, said that the house was theirs, and should be cleared for their reception the next day. He then shewed them the picture of Captain Cook, upon the back of which were written the names of his Majesty's ships and their commanders who had visited Matavāi since that great navigator's time. The natives on shore seemed transported with the idea of men coming purposely from Prētane to settle among them: this set those missionaries off who were to fix here, in very high spirits.

7th. Mānne Manne was as good as his word, coming early alongside with three hogs, some fowls, bread-fruit, cocoa-nuts, and a quantity of their cloth; the whole intended as a present for his tayo, the captain. He made a long oration, descriptive of all the ships and captains which had touched at Otaheite, with the names of the gods of Ulietēa; but said, that Otaheite had none but from him, acknowledging the British God to be the best, and that he should request Otoo to worship him, and to order the people to do the same.

Soon after Peter the Swede arrived from a distant part of the island with more fruit, and a remarkably large hog, the two sides of which, exclusive of the head and entrails, weighed three hundred and forty pounds; it had on each side of its mouth two large tusks; for use it was far too fat for us, and as many small pigs were brought in the course of the day, but little of it was eaten.

Mānne Manne, the aged high-priest, had brought five of his wives with him on board, not one of which exceeded fifteen years old, and desired he might sleep in the cabin; and, according to the custom of the country, very cordially desired Captain Wilson, his tayo, to take his choice, and could hardly persuade himself he was serious in declining the offer; nor failed the next morning to inquire of them which he had chosen. This brought on a conversation on the nature of their customs; the captain explained to the old priest, how little such a state of polygamy was suited to happiness; that no woman could be either so attached, faithful, affectionate, or careful to promote domestic felicity, as where the heart was fixed on one object without a rival. The old priest did not at all relish this doctrine, and said, such was not the custom of Otaheite; but the ladies highly approved, and said the Pritāne custom was my ty, my ty, very good.

Mānne Manne was now very desirous for us to go to Eimēo with the ship, and there land the missionaries under his protection, making use of all his rhetoric to persuade the captain, and bringing the two Swedes, whom he seems to have much under his command, to prove that Pomārre never acted honourably by the English, or any other, after he had done with their services; that themselves had assisted him in his wars, had been the principal instruments of his success; but, since his turn was served, he would hardly give them a small hog. This, and all they urged, might have gained credit with us, as all the late voyagers have related incidents which mark this chief's character with selfishness; but, on the other side, it might be inferred, that these Swedes, after they had lent their assistance, might be unreasonable, and even insolent in their demands, and by such conduct render it necessary for Pomārre to treat them with bare civility only. Therefore, concluding them prejudiced, and the old priest only arguing from views of interest, it was resolved, that as Otaheite was the most eligible island, the settlement should first be made there; and the friendship and protection of Pomārre and his son Otoo be courted by kindness and attachment to his interest, to be expressed and shewn on every occasion; but never to take any part in their wars, except as mediators.—In the interval of fair weather, betwixt daybreak and eight o'clock, we purchased a few things from the canoes alongside, merely to please them; for the liberality of our friends had left us no other plea.

The rain beginning again as violent as before, prevented the missionaries landing till near eleven in the forenoon; when the captain, Mr. Jefferson (president), with a few more of the missionaries, went on shore, accompanied by Mānne Manne and Peter. The natives had assembled upon the beach to the number of four or five hundred, and as the boat approached some ran into the water, and laying hold of her hauled her aground; then took the captain and missionaries on their backs, and carried them dry on shore. They were received by the young king (Otoo) and his wife Tētua, both carried on men's shoulders; each took the captain by the hand, and in dumb silence surveyed him attentively, looking in his face and minutely examining every part of his dress: they beheld the brethren also with much the same curiosity. The queen opened Mr. Cover's shirt at the breast and sleeves, and seemed astonished at so clear a sight of the blue veins. That this should be the case now, after so many visits from Europeans, may surprise some; but let such consider, that though the oldest and the middle-aged have been fully gratified in these respects, the young ones have as yet seen very little; for there could be but small difference between themselves and the dark complexions of the naked shipwrecked sailors who had lately taken refuge amongst them.

The captain now informed the king, through Peter as interpreter, that our only inducement for leaving Prētane to come and visit them was to do them good, by instructing them in the best and most useful things; and for this end, some good men of our number intended to settle among them; requiring, on their part, the free gift of a piece of land sufficiently stocked with breadfruit and cocoa-nut trees, and so large as to contain a garden and admit of houses being built upon it; that this land should be their own; that they would not, on any account, intermeddle in their wars, nor employ their arms but for self-defence; and at all times should live free and unmolested among them: to which if he consented, they would stay on the island; if not, they would go elsewhere. Much pains were taken to make this plain; but as Otoo appears to be a vacant-looking person, I doubt whether he understood the half of it, though he signified the large house was our own, and we might take what land we pleased.

After this, Mānne Manne stood up in the middle of the ring, and made a long speech, passing many encomiums on Prētane. When all was over, the king, still holding the captain by the hand, led him to the house, thence to the beach, and so on; till, tired, he requested to return on board. When arrived at the boat, Otoo desired to hear the muskets fired, and, to gratify him, the four they had were discharged twice; with which compliment he seemed highly pleased.

After dinner Otoo and his wife came off, each in a small canoe, with only one man paddling: whilst they went several times round the ship, the queen was frequently baling her canoe with a cocoa-nut shell. This may help to form an idea of what a queen is in Otaheite. They would not venture on board, because wheresoever they come is deemed sacred, none daring to enter there afterwards except their proper domestics.

He appears tall and well made, about seventeen; his queen handsome and finely proportioned, about the same age, and always carried about, on shore, on men's shoulders. The king appears thoughtful, speaks little, but surveys things with attention. The missionaries supposed something majestic in his appearance, but the captain thought him stupid, and to discover little capacity. As he paddled round the ship he was offered the compliment of firing the great guns, but he begged us not, as he was afraid, and the noise would hurt his ears. . . .

8th. It rained hard all the morning till about nine o'clock, when it cleared up, and the missionaries went on shore with their chests and beds, and took possession of their house. By the captain's desire, "I," says Mr. Wm. Wilson, "followed to assist them in planning their separate apartments. A vast concourse of the natives had gathered on the beach, watching who should land in the pinnace; among them were Otoo and his wife, carried upon men's shoulders, as on the preceding day. This, I understand, is always the custom when they go beyond the precincts of their dwelling. The queen used the same freedoms with me as she had done the day before with Mr. Cover, and, when gratified, put my shirt neck and sleeves again in order. With one holding each hand, I was led about for a considerable time, and might perhaps have been so most of the day, had I not intimated that I had business to do within the house. He immediately walked with me to the door, but would not enter, because the house would then become sacred to himself.

"However, before he let me go, he introduced a woman named Whyerīdde, the sister of Iddeah, and also wife of Pomārre: her Otoo wished me to take as a tayo. And considering that I was but a transient visitor, who knew not how far a refusal might disoblige him, I consented to exchange names, and was immediately wrapped in cloth; besides, in the course of the day, several hogs, both alive and ready dressed, were sent me as presents."

The first thing we set about with the house was to close it quite round with the thicker sort of bamboo, fixing a door on each side, and by this means to keep the natives from crowding so much upon us. The several births or apartments were next planned, and partitions of smaller bamboo begun; but in consequence of the great distance the natives had to go up the valley for these bamboos, the work went but slowly on; though one man stripped his own house to supply us. In the arrangement, the married people had a part of one side to themselves, and the single men the other side: all these apartments were at one end, and chosen by lot. Next to them were marked out a store-room, library, and a place for the doctor and his medicines. To enclose the whole, a partition went from side to side, with two lock doors. The remaining space was left for a chapel, and into it the outer doors opened.

Several of the arreoies of Ulietēa having arrived here about the same time as we did with the ship, they with their hēivas made much the same stir in Matavāi as a company of strolling players often do in the small villages of our own country. Probably the hopes of pleasing the English strangers was also a spur to their exertion, for either in our sight or our hearing they were engaged the whole day in some sport or other. In the afternoon they collected in great numbers before the door of our house, and began a kind of box-fighting or wrestling. First forming a ring, within it stood about a dozen of the stoutest fellows, with their backs to the crowd and faces towards each other. Then the game began with an act of defiance or challenge, made by beating heavy strokes with the flat hand upon the left arm above the elbow, where this part was quite black with the repeated strokes it had received. At last one steps forward to the centre of the circle; another, who thinks himself an equal match, advances to meet him; sometimes only a smart blow or two ensues before they fall back again into their places. At another time, after advancing and gazing at each other for a while, one will suddenly plump the top of his head into the face of his opponent, and this causing him to retire in the dumps, sets all the crowd a-laughing. The worst of the game is, when one gets an advantageous hold of his adversary: a severe wrestling then takes place, and it is only at the expense of strength, and blood, and hair, that they will submit to be parted.

Mānne Manne sent us in three hogs ready dressed for dinner, with baked bread-fruit, cocoa-nuts, &c. He laid them on a large piece of cloth, and invited us to fall to, but not before we had called upon God to bless it. We found it very good, though we had yet neither dish, spoon, knife, fork, table, nor chair. Innumerable presents came in from the various chiefs who were courting our friendship; and we were all dressed in Otaheite cloth. . . .

[9th.] The business of the house did not go on to-day with much alacrity, owing to the natives slackening in their officiousness, so that we got but few bamboos; however, in the afternoon some were dispatched, taking my word, as an eāree of the pāhie (an officer of the ship), that they should be rewarded for their trouble; accordingly in the evening we had as many brought to the house as would keep us employed all the following day. As on board, so at the house, numberless presents were brought, consisting of live hogs, cocoa-nuts, bread-fruit, and cloth, which are their staple articles; and besides these, more ready-dressed meat was brought than the brethren and the natives employed could consume. But in the midst of this profusion, some were apprehensive of its being followed with inconvenience and embarrassments, and therefore wholly disapproved of making tayos so soon.

Whilst the business was going on ashore, the crew were employed in weighing the anchor, warping farther up the bay, and mooring the ship with the two bowers. Peter, the Swede, also brought his canoe, and such things as the missionaries first wanted were dispatched on shore. Thermometer 76½°.

10th. The wind easterly, moderate and pleasant weather. The people employed hoisting out of the hold and sending sundries ashore on account of the mission.

To-day the captain landed for the purpose of presenting some shewy dresses to the young king and his wife. They met him at the beach as usual. Peter informed him of what was intended, and, shewing him the box which contained the treasure, desired Otoo to walk towards his house, a temporary shed they had erected for the purpose of being near our people. This was complied with; and when they came near, the captain, stopping under a tree, ordered them to form a ring, and placing the box in the midst, Otoo was requested to alight, that the brethren might dress him; he replied, By and by, and gazed sullenly for a considerable time, till the patience of the captain was pretty well exhausted; repeating the request and receiving no answer, they opened the box, and on taking out the dress for the queen, she instantly alighted from the man's shoulder, and Otoo followed her example. The fancy cap fitted her exceedingly well, and she seemed very proud of it, but it was only by unripping that the other articles could be put upon her or Otoo. The captain told him that the eārees of Prētane thought he was not yet so stout a man. Dressed complete in this gaudy attire, the surrounding crowd gazed upon them with admiration. She, true to the foibles of her sex, appeared delighted, but Otoo thought little of them, saying an ax, a musket, a knife, or pair of scissars were more valuable: which was saying more for himself than we expected, or that he had even sense to do.

Just as the ceremony was ended, Mānne Manne appeared before the house, and calling the captain to him, clothed him in a 'Taheitean dress, putting an elegant breast-plate over all. They then walked towards the British house, where they found the work going on very well; and it being past noon, the old priest accompanied the captain on board to dinner.

11th. The crew employed in sending sundries on shore on account of the mission. At the house they were very busy fitting up the apartments for the women, whom it was intended to land in the afternoon. The brethren had informed the natives, that next day being the day of the Eātooa, no work would be done, nor any thing received; therefore, on this account, they brought what provisions might serve till Monday, but were in reality sufficient to last a week.

After dinner the pinnace was manned for the women and children, and by the captain's desire I accompanied them on shore. Vast numbers of the natives crowded to the beach to gratify their curiosity, all behaving with great respect and very peaceable. Otoo and his wife kept for a while at a little distance, seemingly in doubt whether he should approach the women; but thinking it proper to salute him, he was a little encouraged: however, he still kept silence, and all the way as we walked to the house, gazed stupidly, like another Cymon. The house was surrounded all the afternoon by the natives, who were much delighted with the two children, and sent often for them and the women to shew themselves at the door. In the dusk of the evening they all retired; and this, the brethren remark, they have uniformly done since they first landed. Orders being likewise given at the ship for none of their canoes to come near on the Sunday, they supplied us in the same plentiful manner as they had done the missionaries.

As Mānne Manne had already distinguished himself as a very useful man, besides bringing several hogs, fruit, &c. the captain, to recompense him in part, made him a handsome present, leaving it to himself to enumerate the articles which he most needed; to do this he was at no loss, having great presence of mind on such occasions; therefore he run off a long list of things which he wanted for a small schooner which he was building at Eimēo; of these such as we had to spare were given to him.

As yet we have had no reason to complain of any improper behaviour in the Otaheiteans, men or women. Neither have we lost a single article to our knowledge, though many have unavoidably been much exposed.

The goodness and love of God to us should be graven on the tables of our hearts. After prayer the brethren retired to rest.

Before the Otaheiteans departed they were informed no work would be done the next day, and they asked if it would be more devoted to prayer than the other days, and were told it would.

The Sunday passed very quietly, not one canoe coming near the ship; and on shore no interruption was attempted, the natives, with the king and queen, attending, and conducting themselves in peace and good order. A discussion took place among the brethren concerning the propriety of speaking to the natives upon the important subject of their mission, when it was agreed that the president (Mr. Jefferson) should address them through the medium of Andrew the Swede as interpreter. Accordingly, at three o'clock in the afternoon, they met for this purpose, several of the natives being present both within and without the house; and as soon as Andrew interpreted the first sentence, finding the discourse directed to them, they placed themselves in attentive postures. When they understood a little of what was said, they put very pertinent questions; among others, doubting whether we would bestow aught that could be esteemed a benefit equally on all. They asked, whether the message of the British God was to the toūtous as well as to the king and chiefs? They were answered in the affirmative; and further, Mr. Jefferson, pointing to his brethren, told them that they were the messengers of the only true God; and that though all men had offended him, he was, notwithstanding, a merciful God; conferring on those who believed his word great blessings in this life, and after death took them to a state of eternal happiness. Otoo was present, but, according to human judgment, his stubborn, unteachable nature seems to be the last that any impression can be made upon. We retired to rest, thankful for the occurrences of the day, and for the promising prospects before us through the providence of our God.

13th. Wind easterly, and pleasant weather. The crew employed in hoisting up goods, and sending various articles on shore on account of the mission; two of the brethren from each party dividing a large chest of books.

The natives had perfectly understood that the prohibition was but for yesterday, for early in the morning several canoes were alongside, and in one of them, with our constant friend Mānne Manne, came several chiefs and their wives; but the principal person to be introduced at this time was the father of Pomārre, Otēw, formerly Whāppai, who is a very venerable looking man, aged about seventy, his head covered with gray hairs, and his chin with a remarkable white beard: his name had once been Otoo; but, on the birth of his son, in compliance with the general custom, he changed it to Otēw. As usual, he presented the captain with a piece of cloth and a pig, receiving in return, and on account of his rank, two axes, four pair of scissars, and four knives, two looking-glasses and two old shirts, which was all he asked for; and it appears that their requests always include the utmost bounds of their expectation; so that to add aught more is quite superfluous and unnecessary. When breakfast was ready, most of our visitors went upon deck, seemingly through a sense of good manners and a fear of offending, which we may suppose them to have learnt from former visitors, who, for their own sakes, might have taught them thus much; for it certainly would be very uncomfortable to have them crowding at meals continually: but Mānne Manne had no scruples, and, as if conscious of a right, placed himself next his tayo at table, and being exceedingly fond of the tea and our bread and butter, played rather an epicurean part. In the forenoon Otoo and the queen sent off to beg leave of the captain to send him their presents; to which ceremonial an answer was made in the affirmative; and in consequence thereof we had them presently alongside: the king's consisted of thirteen live hogs, and three ready dressed; the queen's was one dressed, six alive, and a bale of cloth; themselves followed in a large double canoe, accompanied by Otoo's younger brother, now prince of Tiaraboo. They would not come on board, but expressed a wish for a great gun to be fired; and, to gratify them, two were cast loose: Mānne Manne took the match, and though almost blind with age, he boldly fired them off; with which act of his own courage he was highly transported. Their stay was short; for after they had paddled twice or thrice round the ship, they returned to the shore.

About four in the afternoon Pomārre and his wife Iddeah, having just arrived from Tiaraboo, paid their first visit at the ship; besides his usual attendants a number of others had put themselves in his train. When alongside he refused to come farther till the captain shewed himself; this being done, he immediately ascended the side, and coming on to the quarterdeck, wrapped four pieces of cloth round the captain as his own present; then taking that off, repeated the operation with the like quantity in the name of Iddeah. While he was doing this, I thought joy evident in his countenance, and was glad to find in him a picture of good-nature very different from the morose figure which represents him in some editions of Cook's voyages; and could not help thinking that his presence, which we now enjoyed, would afford pleasure to thousands in refined Europe, who have heard so much of the hospitality and favour this prince of savages has always shewn to his visitors.

Further Reading

Transactions of the Missionary Society, 2nd edition, vol. 1 (London: Bye and Law, 1804), reported on the fate of the missions at Tahiti and Tonga up until the arrival of the *Royal Admiral* at Tahiti in 1801. Michael Cathcart et al., *Mission to the South Seas: The Voyage of the Duff 1796–1799* (Melbourne: Department of History, University of Melbourne, 1990), offers a detailed discussion and analysis of the first missionary voyage, based on examination of manuscript sources held in the Mitchell Library, Sydney. Histories of missionary activity, such as Thomas Smith, *The History and Origin of the Missionary Societies*, 2 vols. (London: Thomas Kelly, 1838); Richard Lovett, *The History of the London Missionary Society, 1795–1895* (London: Henry Frowde, 1899); Niel Gunson, *Messengers of Grace: Evangelical Missionaries in the South Seas, 1797–1860* (Melbourne: Oxford University Press, 1978); and John Garrett, *To Live Among the Stars: Christian Origins in Oceania* (Geneva: World Council of Churches, 1982), detail the background to the formation of the London Missionary Society in 1795, discuss the voyage of the *Duff*, and unfold the subsequent history of Pacific missions in the nineteenth century.

13

George Vason

Falling from Grace

· ·

GEORGE VASON (1772–1838) was landed on Tongatapu in 1797, among the group of missionaries sent by the London Missionary Society in the *Duff*. He was born in the English midlands and had apprenticed as a bricklayer before being baptized in Nottingham in 1794. His trade as well as his faith had qualified him for a position among the first missionaries, who—because they were selected in part for the skills they would be able to pass on to Pacific islanders—were known as "godly mechanics" (Gunson 1978, 32). Upon arriving in Tonga, the missionaries established themselves at Hihifo ("Aheefo") under the protection of the principal chief (Tu'i Kanokupolu), Tuku'aho ("Toogahowe"). Finding they made little progress in the language when grouped together, they separated and went to reside with different chiefs, typically in pairs. Vason, however, went to live alone with the chief Mulikiha'amea ("Mulkaamair"), the second most powerful chief of Tongatabu.

Instead of succeeding in converting the Tongans by word and example to the Christian faith, Vason became a convert to their lifestyle. He adopted Tongan dress and had his body tattooed, became the proprietor of a prosperous estate, and participated in the civil wars that commenced in Tonga in 1799. The fighting was instigated by Fīnau 'Ulukālala-'i-Feletoa, the chief who later became William Mariner's mentor. Fīnau led a party that assassinated Tuku'aho in order to instate Mulikiha'amea, his relative, as Tu'i Kanokupolu in his place. However, Mulikiha'amea was killed in battle, and Fīnau was eventually driven from Tongatabu. Three of the missionary party were killed early in the fighting. Early in 1800 an English vessel, the *Betsy*, stopped at Tonga and picked up all the remaining missionaries except Vason. Realizing that he had been abandoned, Vason was struck by despair: "[I] endeavoured to summon up all my fortitude to meet my unavoidable lot, and to reconcile my mind to the prospect of settling as a native, and spending my future days at Tongataboo" (Orange 1840, 184–85). He experienced renewed political upheaval and widespread famine before being appointed to a chieftainship of one of the Vava'u islands, and he claimed to have been living in fear of his life when he was picked up by the *Royal Admiral* in August 1801. Vason traveled to China, where he embarked on the life of a sailor. Eventually he returned to England, experienced a reconversion, and attained a respectable position as the governor of the Nottingham Town jail.

Vason began his time in Tonga as a missionary and became a beachcomber. His text hinges on the problem of his split identity, as degenerate beachcomber and as exemplary Christian, and always threatens in fact to become an exemplary tale of declension. By "going native," Vason manifested the instability of those "civilized" values that missionary parties were endeavoring to inculcate throughout the Pacific islands. The extract illustrates a tension between an evident ethnographic exuberance when describing the lives and customs of the Tongans among whom he resided, and a more conventional reiteration of the rhetoric of providentiality and remorse, which relies on interpolated biblical quotation for substantiation. Vason stresses that it is as a narrative of declension and redemption that his text can hope to serve his society, in particular as a guide to future missionaries, but his decision to structure a section of the extract as "A Day and Night at Tongataboo" indicates a consciousness that his experience is exemplary as a cultural account, and not simply as a spiritual journey. Although he reiterates certain broad cultural and sexual stereotypes (such as the "lazy native" or the titillating female dancer) and submits to the moral imperatives of retrospective evangelism (which lead him to hint at, rather than name, "alluring scenes" and "amusements that tend to pollute the heart"), recent historical accounts of Tonga have accepted Vason's authority in describing such varied cultural practices as dancing, warfare, cooking, and house construction (Ferdon 1987; Lātūkefu 1974).

A very real, and unconventional, aspect of Vason's enjoyment of the ethnographic experience is its reciprocity. In the nighttime communion of the male aristocrats of Tonga, he finds himself rendered the object of speculation. He is as interested in the ways in which his own cultural difference is perceived—in which he is rendered "Other" by the Tongans—as he is in reporting their differences. When he becomes fluent in the Tongan language, he develops the role of cross-cultural informant as a social skill: "They much respected me, and esteemed me as a very entertaining companion; as I could now, with a ready familiarity of language, amuse them with tales and descriptions of European customs, inventions and events" (Orange 1840, 159). The observations he makes upon Tongan culture reflect his class status within his home society. The "godly mechanic" is acutely aware of the ways in which rank functions to differentiate between Tongan subjects and comments freely on the injustices that he perceives to operate within Tongan society. Vason's life of declension in Tonga allows him temporarily to transcend the class position to which he was consigned as missionary tradesman; as a landowner and therefore a member of Tonga's aristocracy, Vason takes pride in developing the potential of his estate.

The *Duff* party had re-encountered the distinctions of European class during its first days in Tongatabu. The missionaries were met on their arrival by three beachcombers, Benjamin Ambler, John Connelly, and Morgan Bryan, who had been landed in a group of one seaman and five convict stowaways from the American ship *Otter* in 1796 (Maude 1968, 142). By Wilson's account, their class status was written on their faces: "in their countenance, one of them especially, there was so much of the villain marked, that in England a well-disposed person would shun them as he would a swindler or a pickpocket" (Wilson 1799, 97). The missionaries threatened the hitherto unique status of the beachcombers as representatives of European culture. Equally, the beachcombers threatened the lapsed missionary Vason with an uneasy reflection of his own adaptability to a secular Tongan lifestyle. Within the framework of his narrative, therefore, a heavy distinction is drawn between the circumscribed lapse of the missionary and the criminal behavior of the unrepentant beachcomber.

The beachcombers' linguistic fluency enabled them to invent fictions of home that served then abroad, and they proved to be unreliable intermediaries. Faced with competition from the missionaries, they attempted a kind of reversal of social status: "they gave it out, that they were persons of the greatest consequence, that one was the king's son, the other a duke, or a great chief; that we were only of the lower class, and servants to them in our own country" (Orange 1840, 116; Wilson 1799, 254). Their words, however, lacked the material substantiation that bolstered missionary discourse, however flawed, so that "Whatever pretensions they made of being dukes or princes, the natives had sense enough to conclude, that if they were really men of rank, they would have received presents from their country, as well as ourselves. But, as they had none to bestow, they were treated with little respect" (Orange 1840, 118). Vason emphasizes the missionaries' commitment to learning the Tongan language and describes the performances they were initially required to go through in attempting to communicate Christian practice. A footnote in Martin's *Account of the Tonga Islands* illustrates the fate of their efforts to convey the evangelical message; the editor claims that, "The king and several other chiefs at the Tonga islands appeared quite surprised when Mr Mariner informed them that the object of the missionaries had been to instruct them in the religion of the white people: they had thought that the latter came to live among them merely from choice, as liking the climate better than their own" (Martin 1818,

1:xxx–xxxi). In fact Vason reports that the concept that best served the missionaries in conveying the prohibitions of their religion was one that the English language adopted from Polynesian vocabularies: the word "taboo." In his role as cultural convert, Vason ultimately acquired a proficiency in the language that he lacked as evangelist, demonstrated in this extract in his discussion of social nuances that stratify the Tongan language. His linguistic fluency and moral reprehensibility were in this sense mutually implicated: both reflected his complete absorption in Tongan society.

Vason observes that one of the basic tenets of English civil government, the law of private property, does not apply to Tongan society. He argues that the evangelical project would have been more successful had missionaries traveled to the Pacific with families: it became apparent "that before we had introduced among our neighbours some of the arts of civilization, we should have little opportunity of instructing them in the knowledge of divine truth" (Orange 1840, 134). Such observations reinforce the example of his own declension to suggest the vulnerability of the missionary endeavor, dependent on the commitment of individuals who were liable, once absorbed within Pacific societies, to act not as emissaries of "civilization" but as litmus for the practices of their adopted societies. Yet in describing the secular estate he built up in Tongatabu (a farm, initially of fifteen acres, eventually expanded to fifty, where workers came to labor by choice, and bounty existed even in times of famine), Vason represents an ideal of civility and ordered community, enshrined at the very center of his narrative. He writes, "My little farm was a garden throughout. Many came to offer themselves for workmen," describing the Edenic site, with echoes of Milton, in terms of a harmonious interweaving: "sheltered on the outside with a skilful intertexture of the branches of the plantain tree"; "the rows of sugar canes . . . embowered and entwined themselves so as to form a shady walk." So perfectly balanced are the elements of this tapestry that they create a form of natural law: a thief is at one point "detected by some other natives, who with great dexterity, discovered that he was the person who had stolen some pines and plantains from my abbee, by bringing the fruits to the trees, from which they had been robbed, and fitting them to the branches where they had been broken off" (Orange 1840, 153). He expresses regret that he failed to make this garden the text or the site of a sermon. The pleasure he takes in its description becomes tinged in hindsight with shame.

The account of his life on his estate, a story without a moral, stands out within the defensively textual framework of Vason's confessional narrative. In fact Vason's testimony is a book he was never trusted to write, a tale that constantly risks slipping the control of its tellers. It appeared in two editions, in 1810 and 1840. In the earlier version his experiences were formulated by Solomon Pigott, the curate of Vason's church in Nottingham, who describes his discreet interposition in the text's production as an act of editorial ventriloquism: "By letting the Author relate his own life, while the writer only arranges the thoughts, and clothes them with language, the varying sentiments, sensations and motives, that actuated him in every changing circumstance and event, will be more exactly delineated" ([Vason] 1810, vii). The notion that authorship is contingent serves to reaffirm the unity of evangelical discourse, but the desire expressed here to "clothe" the autobiography of the fallen missionary is a post-lapsarian impulse, not just a sign of his renewed civility. The second edition throws into question the authority of the first. It is encased within the commentary of the Reverend James Orange, "Author of the History of the Town and People of Nottingham," who claims that "Every circumstance subsequently detailed, was taken down from Mr Vason's mouth and repeatedly revised in concurrence with himself, who had no intention that the facts should be made public during his life, and though by some means a *part* of the present work was published thirty years ago, it was crowded with gross mistakes &c., and in many respects incomplete" (Orange 1840, vi). Vason clearly did not relish being made into an example during his lifetime. He was uneasy with his recovered Christian identity, and Orange notes that he "never again ventured to make a *public profession* of his faith in Christ, after his lamented fall" (Orange 1840, 219). A potted biography appended to this later text describes Vason as a man who ended up finding social interaction difficult and who eventually succumbed to dementia. The period of easy communion he achieved in Tonga thus retrospectively figures, despite the aims of his confessional project, as a state of innocence before his lapse into redemptive shame. — VANESSA SMITH

. . . .

James Orange, *Narrative of the late George Vason, of Nottingham* (Derby: Henry Mozley, 1840).

« CHAPTER 8, PP. 118–19. »

Here, therefore, I am approaching a period of my life, in which I little regarded the pure heavenly design on which I set out, and disgraced my character as a christian. The remembrance of this has caused me bitter remorse, and often fills me, still, with deep contrition, shame, and self-abhorrence. But I trust, by the grace of God, I have now truly repented. I hope in the mercy of God through that gracious Redeemer who "came to seek and save the lost" and "call sinners to repentance." I am cheered by the belief that "he is able to save all that come to God by him, seeing he ever liveth to make intercession for them;" and I endeavour, by the aids of his blessed Spirit, which, I daily need, and therefore daily implore, to walk again in the paths of righteousness.

From the period that I returned to live with Mulkaamair; when the ship left the island, and I bade adieu to my companions, I had little or no connexion with them. The remainder of this Narrative will, therefore, relate principally to myself, and the circumstances in the island, in which I took a part, until my merciful escape from it. In this I shall not disguise my conduct, but declare everything with that scrupulous attention to truth, without exaggeration or palliation, to which I have endeavoured, uniformly, to adhere, in all that I have related. If the circumstances that perverted me from the paths of righteousness and purity, and the unhappy influence which they had on my mind, should serve as a caution to future missionaries, or deter any from those omissions of duty, and those indulgences of depraved inclination, which lead to declension and destruction, the narration of my disgrace will not be useless nor unprofitable.

« CHAPTER 9, PP. 120–29. »

A DAY AND NIGHT AT TONGABOO. The house of Mulkaamair, with whom I resided, was very spacious; its length was fifty feet. It was of an oval form. One large and lofty post was fixed in the centre; and round it, in an oval circle, were placed less posts, at equal distances, which formed the sides of the habitation. Upon these posts layers were fixed, to which rafters were fastened, that extended to the pillar in the middle, and united the whole building with it. The inside of the roof was ornamented with warm beautiful matting, which was sheltered on the outside with a skilful intertexture of the branches of the plantain tree. In rainy weather, screens of matting, called Takkabou, made of the branches of the cocoa-nut-tree, were fastened to the side posts, which almost reached the eaves, and left only the door-way open, which was never closed, night nor day.

Such spacious habitations are necessary for the chiefs, whose household, in general, is large, as composed of many attendants. But there are generally small apartments contiguous to the house, in which his wives and children lodge. One of his wives, however, for the most part, slept with him in the same room, in a space, separated from the rest by inclosures of Takkabou, or matting, three feet high, fitted up to the beams, that went across to the centre post, to keep it upright.

The household of Mulkaamair was considerable. He had at different times from four to eight wives, eight sons and five daughters, besides many attendants. The children were all in great subjection, and of different rank and dignity, according to the rank of their respective mothers. For family dignity, in Tongataboo, descends not from the fathers, but the mother, owing, it is probable, to the frequency of divorce, and of illicit intercourse. When the day declined, about seven o'clock, if they were not disposed to dance, they would retire to bed, or, more properly, to recline on their matting.

But when they had retired, the most social employment of the day took place. As they lay reclining at their ease, Mulkaamair and his numerous household that lay round him, would commence conversations, that amused them till they all fell asleep.

I have been delighted, for hours, in listening to these nocturnal confabulations, and often very much surprised and improved, by the shrewdness of their observations, and the good sense of their reasonings. When they were all lain down, the chief would say, "Tou tellanoa." "Let us have some conversation." Another would answer, Tou tellanoa gee aha, i.e. "what shall we talk about." A third would reply, "Tou tellanoa ge papa langee." "Let us talk of the men of the sky." They call us "the men of the sky," because, observing that the sky appeared to touch the ocean, in the distant horizon, and knowing that we came from an immense distance, they concluded that we must have come through the sky to arrive at Tongataboo.

I have heard them for hours talking of us, our articles, dress, and customs, and entertaining each other with conjectures respecting the distance of the country whence we came, the nature of it, its productions, &c. &c.

Their patriarchal mode of life, in which the younger and inferior part always surround the chief, as the father of one large family, is calculated much to refine and improve their mental faculties, and to polish their language and behaviour.

The social intercourse and the ceremonious carriage, which were constantly kept up in the families of the chiefs, produced a refinement of ideas, a polish of language and expression, and an elegant gracefulness of manner, in a degree, as superior and distinct from those of the lower and laborious classes, as the man of letters, or the polished courtier differs from the clown. The lower orders used terms of a much meaner and coarser import: the higher orders were so much refined, as often, for amusement, to take off the vulgar by imitating their expressions and pronunciations. The family of Duatonga, if they spoke to any of the domestics, or visitors, would always be answered, "Ahee," "Yes, Sire," but most others were answered with, "Cohou," Yes, Sir; this latter term, if pronounced as it is spelt, would be a polite reply, but if spoken as if it was spelt Cohaa, it would be very vulgar, and signify our broad expression "What," and if spoken to a chief, the man would be struck down for his rudeness.

Their nocturnal conversations would continue till ten or eleven in the evening, till they all fell asleep. Their conversations and comparisons were sometimes so very droll and ludicrous, that I occasionally burst out in to a fit of laughter which would make then say, "Coe Kata gee aha Balo." What are you laughing at, Balo? "Mannogge abai eyette ge mou touloo." "he is making a game of us, I suppose." They called me by the name of Balo.

If one chanced, during the night, to awake, he would renew the conversation with some neighbour that might happen to rouse, and then they would call to each other till they all awakened, and enjoy another hour's chat.

As soon as the morning dawned, they arose; and then took place the important ceremony of drinking Kava, and eating yams, &c. which formed their breakfast; in which as much order and exactness were observed, as in the forming and exercising a regiment of soldiers. The Kava is a root planted principally for the use of the chiefs: and too scarce for the lower orders.

It is made into a spirit of an intoxicating nature. The top and branches of this plant are thrown away. The root alone is used, and this is of a soft nature, that may be beaten to pieces. The root is first scraped with a shell, and rubbed clean with the rough husk of the cocoa-nut, and then divided among the company to be prepared for making the liquor.

During the preparation of the Kava, the Tomaagee, or principal servants of the chief, are busily employed in an out-house built for the purpose, in baking yams. These, as soon as ready, they bring in baskets, made of en-twined leaves, and lay them before the chief and the circle of guests as far as they go. They eat these yams after drinking the Kava; and during their meal talk with each other, as they please, on different subjects.

Whenever the lower orders can procure the Kava, they always drink it in companies in this festive manner; in which they often spend the two or three first hours of the morning. They have this pleasure, however, but sel-dom, as the chiefs generally exact it of them, to drink it with their brother chiefs and their attendants. They exercise an arbitrary power over the lower orders, and have every thing belonging to them in their power, which their sub-officers take from them, without ceremony, as the chief may need. Though the provision they have by them be ever so scanty, they are re-quired to cook a part of it for the chief; so that they are frequently obliged to eat the root of the plantain-tree, for a wretched subsistance, or to resort to the chief, and beg some food. The chief will send his attendants round

FIG. 8. *A Chieftain of Tongataboo.* Engraved by H. Wilkins and published as the frontispiece to James Orange, *Narrative of the Late George Vason of Nottingham* (Derby: Henry Mozley, 1840). By permission of the National Library of Australia.

the districts, in a time of scarcity, and order the people to dress a certain quantity of provisions for him by a limited time; with which he lays up a store for himself, and his wives and household; and leaves others to get what they can.

They often drink the Kava from break of day to eleven or twelve o'clock at noon, till their attendants are completely tired of waiting on them. They then go and lie down, and sleep for two or three hours; when they rise, they bathe, walk among the plantations, or amuse themselves in wrestling, boxing, or any other way that pleases their fancy; but particularly in bathing, playing in the water, and shooting of arrows. . . .

They are very active people, yet they often spend whole days, when they have no particular employment, in luxurious indolence. These days they generally close in dancing and singing; of which they are peculiarly fond.

The chief will send round the district, and collect together thirty, forty, or even fifty young people of both sexes, to dance with his attendants by the light of tomais, or torches, formed . . . from the unctuous bark of the cocoa-tree.

These dances are very beautiful. Young women of the most graceful figure and comely features assemble on these occasions, their dark ringlets bespangled with aromatic flowers of a peculiar whiteness, their necks and shoulders encircled with wreaths of variegated flowers, tastefully strung together like beads, their graceful limbs covered only with a thin drapery, and in some cases, only shaded with an entwined garland of gee-leaves.

Their dances are very much diversified, and performed with admirable grace and uniformity, by companies of eighty or a hundred, who all move together with the greatest exactness. I never saw soldiers go through their evolutions with more prompt regularity than these companies time the diversified motions that compose their dances.

They seem in their element when dancing; such is the ease, pleasure, grace and activity, which they exhibit, in every intricate part of this favourite amusement.

So fond are they of this amusement that they dance almost on all occasions. However extravagantly they have mourned for the dead, they generally terminate their grief with this ceremony of joy; in which I have seen the women so eager, that they have forgotten all sense of decorum and thrown off all encumbrance of dress for greater freedom and diversion.

This is the general mode of life at Tongataboo. They never rise, but the Kava is prepared, and distributed; and immediately the tackhangers call for the cooks in the badoo, or kitchen, who bring the baked yams, and present them to the guests. If there is no serious business for the chiefs, indolent slumbers, or the amusements of conversation and choice, fill up the middle part of the day, which is however sometimes diversified with boxing, or other athletic exercises; and luxurious festivities close the evening.

Such an indulgent life, however, is only in the power of the chiefs. The lower classes, as will be shown, are obliged to labour, not only for themselves, but for their superiors; and, after all, their little stock is not secured to them by that inviolable right of private property, which, in our unequalled land of liberty and law, renders the poorest peasant as secure and independent as the senate that guards, or the sovereign that rules it.

« CHAPTER 10, 130–33. »

. . . My evil inclinations, now unchecked by law, and by the reverential sense of the Divine Being, gradually gained the dominion. As my sense of the turpitude and guilt of sin was weakened, the vices of the natives appeared less odious and criminal. After a time, I was induced to yield to their allurements, to imitate their manners, and to join them in their sins.

Modesty, by degrees, lost with me its moralizing charm; and it was not long ere I disencumbered myself of my European garment, and contented myself with the native dress. . . .

At this time Shelly, one of my former companions, came to see me; he was struck with grief and surprise at my appearance; and seriously reproved me for it. My conscience seconded his reproofs. I acknowledged my error, but excused myself by a variety of empty pretexts; such as the warmth of the climate, the general custom of the natives, its convenience in a country where, when clothes were wet, it was difficult to dry them again, and when worn out, impossible to renew them. Shelly heard my excuses with pity, but did not see into the long train of evils connected with this violation of propriety: nor knew that my conscience, while I spoke, condemned the excuses with which I had softened his severity.

Unhappily, as the companion of the chiefs, I was constantly exposed to temptation, being present at every alluring scene.

He that indulges an evil imagination with amusements that tend to pollute the heart, will soon be seduced into criminality. No wonder, then, that the voluptuous attractions of several objects, thus daily presented to me, should in time allure me into the paths of vice.

It was not long after I had begun to imitate the dress and manners of the natives, and join their amusements, before Mulkaamair, the chief with whom I lodged, persuaded me to take a wife, a near relation of his. My conscience loudly cautioned me, not to be guilty of the sin of cohabiting with a woman without the sanction of marriage, and of taking a wife who was a heathen, and perfectly destitute of every mental, as well as religious endowment; who would most probably lead me still farther from the right way. But all these reasonings my evil inclinations soon taught me to refute or silence. "Mulkaamair was my chief friend, and regarded me with parental affection. I should gratify, honour, and in some measure, repay him for his kindnesses, by taking a relation of his for my wife; and thus also strengthen my interests with the rest of the natives, by forming an alliance with them." Pleased with these considerations, I consented. He sent for her: she agreed, and came, modestly dressed in her best apparel, at the head of a number of women; one of whom took her by the hand, and, leading her to me, seated her by my side. She was a handsome girl of the age of eighteen. Mulkaamair entertained the large company assembled on the occasion, with a plenteous feast, and they danced and sung till a late hour.

My marriage, which for a time rendered me very happy, threw down every barrier of restraint, which hitherto conscience had opposed to my inclinations, and opened the door to every indulgence. I lament to say, that I now entered, with the utmost eagerness, into every pleasure and entertainment of the natives, and endeavoured to forget that I was once called a christian, and had left a christian land to evangelize the heathen. Into such excesses is man ready to run when once he has violated his conscience, and given way to temptation.

« CHAPTER II, 133–35. »

This was the melancholy close of my conduct as a Missionary. In looking back on this lamentable frustration of the endeavours of the religious world, as far as it regarded me, I see that the guilt of it all attaches to myself.

Considering all obstacles, it must be a great satisfaction to the promoters of the South-Sea Mission, to be assured from one who has to condemn himself, and who remained at Tongataboo after all the brethren left it, that no other of the Missionaries whom he accompanied thither, acted unbecoming their sacred character. Living in companies, in a habitation of their own, or residing with a brother Missionary, in the Fallee, or mansion of a chief, they were a mutual help to each other against the influence of temptation.

Nevertheless, the great purpose of our Mission, the conversion of the natives, would, I am persuaded, have been far more successfully attained, had we settled there with families of our own.

It was very clear to us, soon after we landed in the island, that before we had introduced among our neighbours some of the arts of civilization, we should have little opportunity of instructing them in the knowledge of divine truth.

Our first resolution was to learn the native tongue, and meanwhile to take care, on every occasion, to show that mildness and humanity, that benevolence and attention to their interests and wants, which might impress them with favourable ideas of our character and religion. We also availed ourselves of every suitable opportunity to perform our daily worship, to sing and pray, when they were present. We endeavoured to impress them with sacred ideas of our sabbath, and invited them to attend our religious services; but informed them we were restrained from showing them our goods, and from doing any work on that day, because it was "taboo," or sacred; during which time we were "tabooed," or prohibited from all kinds of business.

They behaved with decorum and sobriety while the ordained ministers among us preached. But so firmly rooted were their superstitious prejudices, so contracted their notions of abstract and spiritual truths, and so confined in expressions the native language, that their attention was attracted by nothing but our singing.

From this circumstance, we took occasion to make them comprehend that we sang hymns and praises to the Deity, because of his great mercy and goodness, and because of his compassion in suffering and dying for us, to deliver us from the greatest misery in the world beyond death, and to bring us to a state of the greatest happiness. We so far succeeded as to excite their curiosity, by informing them we had come so far over the sea, to tell them of Him, that they might love and fear him, and attain to his region of happiness. But we found it impossible to interest them in such a manner, as to produce any good effect, till we became familiar in the native tongue.

Further Reading

The earlier version of Vason's account is *An authentic narrative of four years' residence at Tongataboo, one of the Friendly Islands, in the South Sea, by ——— — who went there in the "Duff," under Captain Wilson, in 1796* (London: Longman, Hurst, Rees, and Orme, 1810). *Transactions of the Missionary Society*, 2nd edition, vol. 1 (London: 1804), published the report of the missionaries left at Tonga, from the time of the departure of the *Duff* until their own departure under threat in January 1800. Histories that discuss Vason's period of residence in Tonga and employ his account as source material include Sione Lātūkefu, *Church and State in Tonga: The Wesleyan Methodist Missionaries and Political Development, 1822–1875* (Canberra: Australian National University Press, 1974); Edwin N. Ferdon, *Early Tonga, As the Explorers Saw It, 1616–1810* (Tucson: University of Arizona Press, 1987); and I. C. Campbell, *Island Kingdom: Tonga Ancient and Modern* (Christchurch: Canterbury University Press, 1992). Vason's declension and its impact upon the Tongan party of the *Duff* mission is discussed in Vivian Anceschi's chapter of Michael Cathcart et al., *Mission to the South Seas: The Voyage of the* Duff, *1796–1799* (Melbourne: University of Melbourne, 1990); and in Vanessa Smith, *Literary Culture and the Pacific: Nineteenth-Century Textual Encounters* (Cambridge: Cambridge University Press, 1998).

14

EDWARD ROBARTS

A Stranger in a Strange Country

· ·

EDWARD ROBARTS (1797–1824) was neither a professional nor an elegant writer, yet, perhaps accustomed to relating his life verbally, he was in no sense an unaccomplished storyteller. The very naivety of his prose, his direct exposure of his feelings and anxieties, and the particular immediacy of his narrative of events render his autobiographical memoir vivid and authentic. The text, which deals most extensively with his period of residence in the Marquesas Islands, is certainly, however, self-justifying. Robarts abandons his ship not in dereliction of duty because of the appeal or the illusion of the voluptuousness of the beach, but in order to exempt himself from the desperate evil of mutiny. His initially pathetic isolation is quickly succeeded by the warmth of his inclusion in Tahuatan society, which is marked at once by its sincerity and its excess.

On the one hand, these "benighted" people, who treat him as kindly as though he were a kinsman, are more genuinely hospitable than many civilized and professed Christians. This was a pretty conventional observation, though Robarts enunciates it feelingly, and it is not hard to believe that it was true to his experience. Its effect is to sentimentalize his situation, to draw the reader's sympathy into the terrain of the beach, which is presented not as a space of frightful savagery but as one of humane interaction, if nevertheless often also one of tension and conflict. Polynesian hospitality is, on the other hand, immediately also shown to be excessive: it extends, at least putatively, to sexual favors, for which Robarts must apologize in advance for mentioning ("I must here beg leave of my fair reader to permit me to relate such matters of fact as are within bounds"). Though it is not in fact clear that his friend's "consort" was doing any more than sharing her large barkcloth wrap, as was apparently customary (Robarts 1974, 54 n.11), the evocation of promiscuity, Robarts's acquiescence and his exhausted sleep, suggest at once the strangeness of the behavioral order that he is just beginning to encounter, his adaptation and inclusion, and yet his ability to refrain from those practices that were morally problematic.

These themes pervade Robarts's account and are manifest in different ways in his report of a sequence of events that took place after he had left Tahuata, first for Hiva Oa and then Nukuhiva. These involved the appropriation of an adoptive relative's land that, on his account, he went to some lengths to have restored. It is possible that dimensions of the story are omitted, and that Robarts personally had some stake in the dispute that he does not disclose. What at any rate is striking is the depth of his savoir-faire, his grasp of indigenous political strategy—which, however, is deployed in ways that are presumably modified, and perhaps unprecedented, in Marquesan practice. If this is correct, it would index the degree to which those beachcombers who succeeded in producing and maintaining some local standing (and many failed) had to do so by implicating themselves in indigenous values and relations, in a positive sense. If it took Robarts some time to grasp how this could be done, by the time of the incidents described (when he had been in the Marquesas for three years, if not somewhat longer), he had a sense of who he could call upon and how much he could ask of them. He must have known also what they expected in return. His narrative bespeaks these calculations, at the same time as it places the beach within a moral economy rather than a theater of indigenous political tactics. Yet even as the grave dangers that threaten the peace and welfare of Robarts's relatives are rendered tangible through his sleeplessness and gloom, the vulnerability of the islands to famine and Robarts's own departure make it plain that exchanges of sentiment could neither encompass nor reconcile the interplay of indigenous and exogenous conflict in the Marquesas. And this is the sense in which his moralization was quite unlike that of missionary ethnography and narrative: he was concerned to legitimize his own part, not to project a history. Marquesan society was what it was, not a present "before" that could play darkness to the light of a future "after." — NICHOLAS THOMAS

. . . .

Edward Robarts, *The Marquesan Journal of Edward Robarts, 1797–1824*, ed. Greg Dening (Canberra: Australian National University Press, 1974).

« CHAPTER 2, PP. 50–55. »

In the course of our stay at this place our Chief Officer began his former manner of behaviour towards the ships crew. The minds of the men was so agitated they consulted among themselves what to do. Some was for going on shore—others for a more desperate act. At lenght they formd a plan to take no notice of anything till the ship was at sea. Every thing was Keept secret.

I one eveng was siting alone on the forecastle as was my usual custom, passing away my time with the pleasing hopes that in a few days to be once more makeing my way towards the white cliffts of Briton, there to renew my tender tale to my favourite fair. But alas, how was my pleasing thoughts frustrated, when one of the crew came to me. He askd me if I could Keep a secret. I was greatly surprizd at this question [and] could not make any reply. He said it was of no use for me to make any objection, as all the foremast men had consented to take the Ship when at sea and make the best of their way to some spanish port on the coast of Peru. The Idea of so dark a deed filld me with the most heartfelt grief. I here at once saw the danger I was surrounded with. I could never consent to have anything to do with so atrocious crime. He bound me over never to devulge the affair to any one during my stay with them.

I became very unhappy. My appetite faild me. I was once on shore on liberty. I viewd every thing with a prying eye, but evry thing seemd to give but poor encouragement, tho the natives was remarkable Kind. However I returnd on board in the eveng and endevourd to compose my mind. I at times conversed with the Interpreter concearning the treatment among the natives towards him. He gave me a distant flattering idea of them.

Every thing was compleated on board; the two ships was ready for sea; We expected our stay would be short. Xmas day was come. We had plenty of roast and boild pork; Our Capt gave plenty of liquor for all hands to make merry. For my part my heart was too full to partake of mirth. I did not go to dinner. The Capt came to me when dinner was on table. I told him I was unwell and begd to be excused.

In the course of the afternoon I told the Interpreter, whose name was Tom, that I wised to go on shore to live. He seemd very happy and told one of the chiefs then on board of my intention. He came to me and clasped [me] in his arms with so much unaffected joy and made me understand I was wellcome to his house and should have his protection. But ah, how was my mind torturd! The thoughts of my native country, my friends and all that was dear to me, each was present to my view, but I found no other rescourse but to quit the ship.

I, with the help of my friend Tom, made the chief understand how I wished to carry on my Design. He accordingly obeyd my instructions, which was to come off from the shore just after the Evng gun was fired at 5 PM, Decr 25, 1798. The chief left me about 4 PM and paddled on shore. I was very unhappy, not yet firmly determined. Sometimes I thought to take my chance. Othertimes I shuddered to think of the horrid crime of Piracy. At all events I foresaw the remainder part of the voyage was a raged road and nothing to be expected that might tend to a peace of mind. I was doubtfull of the ships crews conduct lest they should committ some hot braind act that might bring them to an untimely end.

The evening drew near. Every one was below makeing merry. Capt. Fraser spent this day on board our Ship, also some of his men. The song and grog was moveing round cheirly. It was dark. I packed up a few Cloaths, not wishing to take much on deck for fear of discovery. The steward came on the forecastle, askd me what I was doing. I answerd I was makeing up my bed to sleep on deck, the weather being hot. He suspected my design, beg'd I would take him on shore with me, said he was weary of his brother in law the Chief Officer continually treating [him] in an unkind manner. He said he required no favour from him only common humanity. But I could not consent to take him with me on account of his sister, for she was on board some time with her husband before we left England, and I observd she [was] very tender over her brother. She was a fine woman and something so Kind in manner that gaind the love and esteem of those who became acquainted with her. I frequently had the pleashure of conversing with her. She was very fond of reading. I sometimes would amuse her with a few pages of some good novels I had. Whatever became of myself, I would not lead another into my missfortune.

I baffled him some time. At lenght the gun fired. Every one was below but Tom. He I had stationd in the fore stay sail nett to watch when the canoe came for me. As I had refused all day to drink any grog, I said to him if he was determined to leave the ship to go below and get some cloaths and bring up some grog for him and me to drink. Away he goes. The canoe was under the ships bow. I sliped down the cable in a Moment and my friend Tom handed my cloaths down to me.

Away we pulld towards the shore. The land being high, no one could see the canoe from the ship. The night was very dark. We arrived on the beach. The chief got out on shore. We Kept the canoe afloat. His friend the chief of this bay came and made me to understand if I stopt here some of the natives would see me and that would lead to a discovery. My new friend lived in another bay some distance from this place. We paddled along shore under cover of the shade of the land till we was out of the bay. I lookd at the ships as I left the Bay, biding them a silent adieu. On going round a point of land that opend to the wind and sea our canoe upset. My friend and his two men jumpt out. I Kept fast my few cloaths. They soon bailed the water out and got into the canoe again. It began to rain heavy and the wind blew very hard. We haveing the wind in our faces, what with the rain and the spra of the sea, we could not see our way.

However about midnight we arrivd at my friends house, which was on the beach. As soon as he was landed he hollowed for some time. This was giveing notice a stranger was come. It was still raining very hard. He led me to his house and introduced me to his royal consort who receivd me with every mark of friendship. I was greatly surprizd at the figure of this lady. I did not expect to have found so handsome a woman in this remote part of the globe. Her skin was white and delicate, her countenance open and mild, commanding respect, her brows finely archd. Her tresses flowd in natural ringlets on her shoulders, which gave her an agreeable appearance. Here was beauty in its native charms, no help from paint, french chalk, or poisonous washes, which is used in Some parts of globe much to the hurt of them that make use of this destroyer of beauty. It being late, nothing could be got that I could eat except some cocoa nutts. They brought me this. I eat with a good appetite and content of mind, a thing I had not enjoyd for some time before.

By this time, as is customary in that country night or day when a stranger comes to a King or chiefs house, the other natives comes to pay their respects. They are remarkable fond of strangers, several came round me to feel whether I was flesh and bone as they was. My cloaths being Wett they brought me a large cloth that I might pull of my cloaths. My new neighbours began to disperse except some few.

I must here beg leave of my fair reader to permit me to relate such matters of fact as are within bounds. My friend took me by the hand and led me to the side of his consort who was sitting on a fine matt. I was a little surpriz'd at this part of the cerimony when he told me I must sleep on the same matt with her. I must confess the ladys artillery was powerfull enough for any man to surrender, but I could not accept of this unrivaled peice of friendship. I ashurd him by sighns that I was perfectly satisfied of his sincear friendship towards me and begd leave to retire at a becomeing distance from his consort, which was granted. I told him it was against the laws of my country to sleep with other mens wives. He then insisted I should have a companion that was not married. He call'd a female by name, a relation of his, a very handsome young lady. She was extreamely fair. She might be 17 or 18 years of age. To oblige my friend I submitted. She cover'd me with her mantle and drew the one I had from under. It being now very early in the morng, I suppose about 2 O'Clock, our light was put out. We composed ourselves to sleep. For my part I was asleep in a few minutes.

At sun rise great numbers of our neibours came. The place was crouded. Their numbers became troublesome for a stranger in my situation. I retired along the rocks to bathe. Finding several large basons form'd by nature in the rocks and supply'd with water by the sea dashing against them, in one of these basons I bathed secure from the shark.

After spending some time in reflection I return'd, and set myself down on a bank at the back of the house in a grove of cocoa nutt trees, viewing the handy works of nature around me. I heard a sudden outcry among the inhabitants. I could not think what was the matter. I look'd towards the part I came from the night before. I saw the two ships comeing out of the harbour, standing for sea. There being but light winds all day, the ships was in sight till sun down. I view'd them with a heart full of grief, often uttering a prayer for their safety and prosperity. I had the satisfaction to hear some years after that they got safe to London.

Being now left alone I composed my mind and endeavour to be cheerfull. Two or three days after, Tom paid me a visit. I enquired of him how he left matters on board the ship. He inform'd me I had not long left the ship before I was missing. They on board thinking that I was drownded, Tom said he did not undeceive them. He stopt here some days and then return'd to Wiaetohoo.

I accompany'd him on my first visit to the chief of that place who received me in a very friendly manner. The inhabitants all seem'd to try to outdo each other in Kindness to me. My not being able to form any idea of their language, and their numbers so pressing round me made their company a burden, every one asking a number of questions. I could only answer with a smile or a nod. At times I was obligated to secret myself till they was gone, which sometimes would be sun sett. I would then return to the house. My friend and his consort very kindly receives me—more like a parent, a brother or some near Kinsman then an entire stranger, and that [from] an uncivilized race of people quite different from enlightened nations! These poor benighted people shews that hospitality not to be meet with among a number of people who call themselves christians. I speak as I have found, and deem it the duty of every one to greatfully acknowledge the worth of the friendly hut that screens him from want and misery; for this ceartenly was my situation, a stranger in a strange country, among a race of people I could not converse with. At times my heart was over-whelm'd with gratitude. I grievd I could not express my sentiments, only by dumb shew.

« CHAPTER 5, PP. 152–57. »

Now during my abscence a plot was pland among my relations against the King. When it came to my ears, I opposed it strongly. Thinking to gain my point without going to war, I plainly pointed out to them the danger of a family war; for, if a family is divided, they most ashuredly would be scatterd like sheep without a shepherd, and then become a prey to their enemies. And they never could recover their lands again out of the hands of the warriers. You may as well attempt to take a Kid from a tyger; for, when a war of this Kind happens, the conquering warriers divides the Land among themselves. If the Chieftaint happens to be on a large lott of land at the time of surrendering, he secures that lott. He gets no more. I plainly saw it was policy for me not to involve myself in a war among my relations. This would be makeing my friends my foes, and after my decease one or other Party would be enemies to my children. Their land would be taken from them, and they fall from royalty to be outcasts. These things I weighd in my mind and came to a determination to leave the country the first oppertunity, much against my real inclination.

I was well situated. My family lived on their own plantation, and I had a large one of my own that I had purchased. My servants took care of it and one that I took possession of, as the family that it belonged to was all dead. I had a right to it, as I took possession first after the decease of the family. No one dare dispute my right. I was their head in war. I headed them in war against their enemies and was at every battle in the heat of it. But to lift my hand against my relations I could never consent to.

When I first came to *New ka heava*, the warriers a short time before had drawn the King into a war against his eldest sister. This was a plot among the warriers to get hold of the Land. A short war commenced. The Sister & her family with her party was drove of their heritage and took shelter in another part of the Island. The warriers shared the land among them. Only a small lott fell to the Kings son. Some time after, the sister came with some of her family to visit the Old Queen, her mother. The King happend to come at the time. When I saw the sister fall prostrate at the Brothers feet, the whole of them began to weep bitterly. I sat at a short distance, a silent spectator to view this truly piteouse and sorrowfull interview.

At lenght I askd what was the reason of their weeping. They informd me of the whole, and from that moment I become interested in their behalf. As I observd the King weep much over his sister, I had a gleam of hope of recovering the lott for her again that fell into the young princes hand. She staid a few days and then returnd to her exile abode. One day the old Queen and I was alone. The conversation turnd about her eldest daughters miserable condition. I answered her: was there no means to bring the King round to give up the Land that fell to his son? She answerd, no one as yet had mentiond it to him for fear of offending him. I answerd that I would bring it about in the course of a few days.

Accordingly I did, and so far gaind his consent that the Old Queen was to take his sister and lead her on to the spot of ground and set her down on the spot where formerly the family had a house, and, if any one came with a branch, Another with some material for building a temporary house, others would follow the example. No one offerd to build a shelter for the unfortunate princess. The King was at a distance viewing the motions. Some warriers came and said, so that she might hear, that there was no land for her: she had her time; it was theirs now, and they would Keep it. I turn about and sternly told them it would be but for a short time, and then I walkd to the stone wall and pushd the stones down and made gaps in the enclosure. This was the token that a war would commence.

I then went to conduct the Old Queen and her daughter Back to the beach. The King returnd to his house. Some time passd, when a thought came in my mind that the Kings eldest daughter was married to a powerfull chieftain, and I was her adopted son. Her husbands tribe lived in the highland. When she came to *Tio foie*, she livd at her Grandmothers. This gave me an oppertunity of putting in motion the subject of her aunt being in possessions of the whole of her lands. My mother says: "You see how it was when you went before. No one offerd to build a shelter for her." My father was present. I address them in the presence of numbers of people who was come to pay their respects to her in such a manner that my mother says to my father: "Grant your son his request." She then burst into tears, at which my father got up and took his spear and brandishd it for war and set out to his tribe. My mother staid behind. When he got to the lower pass, he sett up the war whoop. This put the inhabitants into the greatest consternation.

Some time escaped. When my fathers tribe picked a Quarrell with the people which refusd to give up the land to the Kings Sister, this darling moment I embracd to make a second motion to the Old Queen to get all her party with her grand daughters tenents. The King would follow to accompany her on an appointed day with her daughter to seat her again on the ruins of her house. She with my mother thankd me for the part I so ardently undertook. It was resolvd and the day fixed on that she would again conduct her daughter to her land and my fathers tribe was to take possession of the pass to come down by.

No one of the warriers party Knew any thing of what was going on till the day the Old Queen with her daughter & most of the royal family had enterd the upper play ground with their parties from all parts of the lower valley. The Dolefull Drum beat the signal for war. My fathers tribe appeard on the mountains. They set up the war whoop in answer and came part of the way down to the pass to wait the second drum beat.

The Old Queen [and] her daughter was first. I accompanyd them to assist them in bad stoney places. The royal family followd behind. We arrivd. The Old Queen placed her daughter on the ruins of her house and waved her mantle saying: "Who is on my side?" All was silent. At lenght a respectable man came to me and put my leg on his shoulder, saying: "What is this war about?" I answerd: "Your Queen is come to see that you one and all consent to restore the land to her daughter, which you so cruelly and unjustly have taken possession of. If you refuse this day, the war commences and none will be spared." Others drew near to hear what was said. I waved to bring the signal drum.

When they saw that I would not be put of, they consulted a short time. When a large hog was brought and a distant house roof and utensils to erect the house, I then bid them to return the land in a proper manner and solemnize the same before their diety, or, on a future day, they would have a plea to say that the land taken in war was not restord with a general consent.

Their prophet came and the usual ceremony [was] performd, untill they came to the part which mentions and particularizes the names of such & such lotts of lands. They only mentiond the lott on which we stood. The King sat at a small distance from the spot. I sent him a Broken stick. This denoted that only a part of the land would be restord. He sent me in return a whole stick. This denoted that all must be restord, or else a war. I then refused the single lott and told them in plain & clear terms that all the land—with the springs of water, with the sea beach belonging thereto—which they had unjustly taken, must be restord. One thing I would grant, that what food they had in store they might take away, not any to remain in any part of the Princesses land, and that the trees should remain as they was, not a bread fruit or coco nutt that was on the trees should be broken. If they consented one and all, it was all I wanted. If not, the war would momently commence. The Drum stood before me, ready to the alarm. My fathers tribe on the mountain side [was] waiting the result of our meeting. They then proceeded with the cerimony to give up the whole.

I then sent a coco nutt Bunch with a white flag—this denoted peace. A second flag followd. This invited the Chieftain. A third flag with ten Knots on it—this invited some of the principal men to come down to bear whitness that the land taken from the Kings Sister was restord by general consent and the Cerimony performd according to the custom of the tribes. As soon as they came down, some hogs was brought to make a feast. The cerimony was finished and the people shouted with one voice, saying: "We return the Land we have taken and have no further claim."

The dancing drums beat a retreat. The Hogs was taken away alive by my fathers party and every one prepared to remove their store of food. I gave them three days to remove every thing belonging to them of the land. Every thing being adjusted in an amicable manner, we returnd to the Beach. Every countenance was cheerfull, and the family returnd me their greatfull thanks for haveing recoverd the land without blood shed, which they acknowledged they never could have done.

The tribe now lulls in slumber, nothing to disturb them for several years, except thier war with their avowd enemy. And now they draw in another tribe to war against the King. I used every means I could think of to persuade them against a war so unjust and cruel. Cato was a man slow to anger, was humane and liberal in time of need to his tribe and allways shewd the greatest affection to his Wife & family, but he was no warrier, nor had he the least Idea of forming his men to advantage in time of war. Things wearing such a gloomy aspect, my time hangs heavy, my nights restless.

Further Reading

The dynamics of cross-cultural interaction in the Marquesas, and Robarts's particular part in them, are discussed by Greg Dening in *Islands and Beaches: Discourse on a Silent Land* (Melbourne: Melbourne University Press, and Honolulu: University of Hawaii Press, 1980). For a discussion of Marquesan political practice, and the specific conflict described by Robarts, see also Nicholas Thomas, *Marquesan Societies* (Oxford: Oxford University Press, 1990).

15

SAMUEL PATTERSON AND RICHARD SIDDONS

The Violence of the Beach

. . . .

EVEN WHEN NOT obviously embellished, beachcomber narratives are typically highly dramatic. This to some extent reflects the realities of the phase of contact they emerged from, which really did entail extraordinary peril at sea (especially in poorly charted waters such as those around Fiji) and bloody confrontations between mariners and islanders. The more violent features of indigenous life that conversion to Christianity had generally put an end to by the second half of the nineteenth century (if not earlier) were still very much in evidence.

Although beachcombers were notoriously lawless, their published narratives were sometimes evangelically framed, and hence emphasize moral calculus and shifts between waywardness and salvation. Moral contests over the propriety of particular customs also dramatize relations between beachcombers and their hosts. Practices such as widow-strangling seem very early to become emblematic of indigenous Fijian sociality, and to be insisted upon and perhaps even elaborated in defiance of outsiders' interventions. An early struggle of this kind is manifest in Richard Siddons's account of his experiences in Fiji, which anticipates evangelical discourse in gendering heathenism. Native men, and priests in particular, are the agents; while women are victims of superstition and bearers of a universal human sensibility of which savage men are devoid. The active compliance of local women was subsequently to complicate the demonization of customs of this kind (see Mary Wallis and James Calvert in chapter 21).

If what was actually witnessed must often have been extraordinary and shocking, even for Europeans who were themselves violent, neither these writers nor their editors refrained from exaggerating the savagery of the peoples described. Patterson, below, for example, insists that human flesh was a routine article of diet among Fijians, evoking the specter of a cannibal race; its consumption was in fact restricted to feasts in the aftermath of battle, to a moment of exchange between chiefs and their warriors (Sahlins 1985). Less obvious is the particular inflection given to his pathetic situation. While the editors of the 1925 republication of Patterson's account treat it simply as an essentially factual description of the wrecked sailor's desperate predicament, omitting its evangelical framing and the homilies in verse that appear before each chapter, the prefatory material by one Ezekiel Terry draws attention to the exemplary significance of Patterson's trials (Patterson 1817; Im Thurn and Wharton 1925). The spectacle of a naked European without support among capricious and violent natives is reminiscent of Mungo Park's misfortune in west Africa. As in Park, desperate circumstances are ameliorated by the kindness of local women, who nevertheless seek to satisfy their curiosity in establishing whether the foreigner is circumcised (Park 1983, 100–101).

Perhaps unexpectedly, also, the writer points out that however evil Fijian religious customs may be, they are at least rigorously observed; on this point the heathens suggest an example to more civilized communities. There is surely therefore some confusion of arguments here: Fijians provide both negative and positive counterexamples to European manners; they are horrifying in their difference, yet recognizable in their charity, and seem to possess an interest in exotic customs not unlike that of the European inquirer. — NICHOLAS THOMAS

. . . .

Samuel Patterson, *Narrative of the Adventures,*
Sufferings of Samuel Patterson (Palmer, Mass.: The Press in Palmer, 1817).

« EZEKIEL TERRY, PREFACE, P. IV. »

Here the Reader may see the vanity of childhood and youth; and the transitions of riper years. We find before us the surprising sufferings of one of our fellow beings, and behold what God is able to uphold a worm of the dust to endure. We also see a poor distressed mortal, in the midst of his anguish, made happy in the God of his salvation . . .

« CHAPTER 16, PP. 82–86. »

[The shipwreck] On the 20th of June 1808, being in S. lat. 17, 40; E. long 179, at about eleven o'clock P.M. the man who had the lookout on the forecastle, seeing breakers but just ahead, cried out with the greatest vehemence, and gave us the alarm; I then was sick in my bunk below, but with the others I jumped out; but before we could get on deck the vessel struck on the rocks. We catched the axe and cut away the rigging, and the masts went over the side; and as they fell broke our whale boat in pieces; but we got the long boat out and put the money in it, to the amount of 34000 dollars; the navigating implements, muskets, a cask of powder and balls, cutlasses and some of our clothes: we also lashed two canoes together, and John Husk and Wm. Brown went on board of them to keep them astern of the long boat and heading the seas, while the rest of us went into the long boat. Our fears were great that, if the vessel went to pieces, we should be killed by the timbers. The violence of the swell and the sea running high, set the canoes a surging, which parted the line they were made fast with, and they went adrift, and Husk, being an excellent swimmer, said to Brown, I must bid you good bye and swim to the wreck, and he was seen no more; but Brown stayed on the canoes and drifted with them, and fortunately, three days after was drove on the shore of the island of Booyer, and six months after met us at Nirie. We lay by the wreck all night in the long boat, and when day light appeared in the morning, we saw the island of Nirie, one of the Feegees, about nine miles distant from us, and we took our two remaining boats and steered for it. The natives seeing us coming, came down in great numbers with their implements of war, such as bows and arrows, spears and war clubs, and gave us to understand that they would not injure us if we would give them what we had in our boats; and on the condition of our lives being spared, we let them take the whole. While the natives were carrying their spoil up to the village, I being sick was lagging along behind, when one of them came up to me, and took off my hat, in which was my pocket book, which contained my protection and other papers; but I gave them to understand that if they would let me retain my papers, they might freely have my hat and pocket book; but they took the papers and rolled them up and put them thro' the holes in the rims of their ears and wore them off. They then took from me my jacket, trowsers, and shirt, but I could not see what they wanted them for, for they were all naked, and never wore any clothes of consequence. I now was left naked, but was not much ashamed, for all around us were in the same condition. As I drew nigh the village where the officers and the rest of the crew were gone, and were eating of the produce of the island, I saw a great awkward savage have the captain's silk coat, trying to put it on for a pair of breeches or trowsers; I went up to him and took and put it on myself, and then took it off and handed it to him, and he put it on and wore it off; and not withstanding my situation I could not but smile for a moment at his ignorance. I found all my shipmates in the same naked situation with my-self. The captain endeavoured to encourage us, and told us he would try to prevail on the chief to let us have the long boat; and after about one week he procured it and started off with his two mates, and two others, having first collected as much of the money from the savages as they could, in all about 6000 dollars.

When they set off, the captain called us down to the boat, gave us our charge, and shook hands with us. He told us that he was going to the is-land of Booyer in hopes of finding a ship lying there; and if he did he would be back in the course of a week and take us off; he ordered us to col-lect what money we could from the savages, and take care of it, which we endeavored to do, though it was attended with considerable difficulty, for it was scattered extensively among the ignorant natives.

On parting with the captain, no tongue can tell my feelings; I then re-flected on my past conduct, especially in disregarding my mother, and leav-ing her as I had done. I retired to a cocoanut tree, and sat down under it and gave vent to a flood of tears.

Those who went with the captain were, Billy Ellekin chief mate, Seth Barton second mate, Charles Bowen a son of judge Bowen on the Mo-hawk river and nephew of Dr Bowen of Providence, and John Holden.

The captain found an American ship at Booyer, but did not return as soon as was expected, and not until after I was gone from Nirie. He, how-ever, at length came back, but succeeded only to bring off his boy. The sav-ages opposed him, and two of those with him were killed, and several wounded. He sailed for Canton, but before he arrived he put into port in distress, took charge of a Spanish ship, was cast away and died.

Charles Savage, who was with us when we landed in this melancholly place, could speak the language of this people, and was of great use to us as an interpreter.

« CHAPTER 17, PP. 86–88. »

A VISIT TO BETEGER, ANOTHER OF THE FEEGEE ISLANDS, WITH AN ACCOUNT OF THE RELIGION AND CUSTOMS OF THE PEOPLE OF FEEGEE. After we had been a while on the island of Nirie, a chief from another of the Feegee islands called Beteger, came to us, and being much pleased with us, persuaded myself and one of my shipmates, Noah Steere by name, to go home with him. We took all the money we had collected and went. Beteger lies not far from Nirie, and we arrived there in a few hours. The people of this place were very fond of us, and the chief used to take us over his plantations and shew us his cane, and the produce he had growing.

While on these islands, some of our company having some pumpkin and watermelon seeds and some corn, we planted them; but before they were ripe, or half grown, the ignorant savages picked them, and came to us to know what they should do with them. We told them that if they had let them alone till they had come to maturity, they would have been a good substitute for bread; but they said *sicingi*, that is, no.

The food of this country is, yams, potatoes, plantains, cocoanuts, bananas, taros, breadfruit, human flesh, an inferior kind of swine which they raise, &c. The breadfruit grows on trees fifteen or twenty feet high, and is as large as our middling sized pumpkins, and when ripe is yellow. They pluck it and boil it in pots made of clay, and then take out the core, and place it in a kind of vat fixed in the earth for the purpose; the women then, intirely naked, tread it down with their feet; and after putting on some plantain leaves, cover it with earth. After it is fermented, they take it out and make it into a kind of dumplings, called by them *munries*.

When cultivating their lands, and in their other labours, about noon they generally have a hole dug in the ground, heated by a fire made in it; and after they clean out the coal and ashes, they lay in their dead bodies, human, if they have any for eating, if not hogs, and also potatoes and yams. On these they place a covering of straw, and then bring on the hot ashes and earth. After a few hours they take out the flesh, &c., and each one receives his share.

Their method of tilling the ground, is by hand to dig up the earth with sticks sharpened, or levers; and then with their hands plant yams and potatoes. Plantains, and bananas are raised by separating and transplanting the sions each season; but about all the other fruits of these islands are naturally produced by the soil.

These savages are cannibals, and eat the bodies of their own malefactors, and all those of their prisoners: and as they were continually at war with some of the tribes around them, and the breach of their own laws, in nearly every case was punishable with death, they generally had a supply of human flesh.

« CHAPTER 18, PP. 94–97. »

I continued growing weaker till my feeble limbs could no longer support me, and one day in walking out I fell and could not get up; at which the savages called Steere to my assistance, and he carried me into the chief's hut. Here I stayed a few days and fared as they did: but one day they smelling a noisome scent, laid it to a man in the hut, but he denying it, they charged it to me. The chief then ordered me to be carried out, and placed in a hut they had built for the purpose of putting in yams, but it had stood so long as to be much decayed.

For about five weeks I was unable a considerable part of the time, to go out of this hut, or even to turn myself, and endured more than can possibly be expressed. All my bedding was only a hard brab map spread on the ground, on which, naked and without any cover I lay. When it rained the water would pour upon me in streams, and the ground under me became mud, and the water around me half deep enough to cover me. In this situation I was often obliged to lie, being unable to move or help myself. Night after night without any human being near me I have spent thus lying in the water and mud; while peals and peals of thunder, seemingly shook the very foundations of the earth, and unremitting streams of lightnings would seem as though volcanoes were bursting in every direction around me. When the storms ceased, and the water dried away from my bed, by day my naked emaciated body was bitten and stung with numerous insects, which constantly, on all days, never ceased to devour me. I was nearly blind with soreness of eyes, the use of one leg entirely gone, and distressingly afflicted with the gravel; which were my principal complaints, together with a general weakness through the whole system.

While lying in this situation these cannibals would often come and feel of my legs and tell me, *peppa longa sar percolor en deeni*, that is, white man you are good to eat. We had bullock's hides on board with their horns on, which the savages had taken, and I used to tell them if they would leave off eating their own flesh or human beings, God would send them such cattle as those hides were taken from; but they said they did not want them, for they should be afraid of them.

The women would also come and ask me when I was going to die, and I used to tell them, when the Lord should see fit to take me out of the world; and they would say if they were half so sick they should die right off. They asked me where I came from; and I told them from America, a land away out of sight; they then asked me if we had any women among us, I said yes, but they replied *sicingi*, that is, no; I then asked them where they thought we came from; and they pointed up to the sun, and said, *peppa longa tooronga martinasinger*, that is, white men are chiefs from the sun; I told them, no, we had women in our country and came into the world as they did, and that their God was our God, and that one God was God over all; but they said our God was a greater God than their's. After we found that they believed that our God was greater than theirs, we endeavored to make them afraid; and told them if they killed us our God would be angry with them, and they would not conquer their enemies, nor raise anything on their lands.

While confined in my hut the women would come and examine me, to see if I was circumcised, and when they found that I was not, they would point their fingers at me and say I was unclean. They used to bring calabashes of water, roll me over, and wash the mud from my body, and by my request stream breast-milk into my eyes, to cure them.

Joseph Arnold, "Captain Richard Siddons' experiences in Fiji 1809–15," *Gentleman's Magazine* 90 (1820): 184f., 211–13, and 297–300. Republished in *The journal of William Lockerby*, ed. Everard Im Thurn and Leonard C. Wharton (London: Hakluyt Society, 1925).

« PP. 166–70. »

When a man dies (said Mr Siddons), if he be a chief or man of importance, one or more of his wives are strangled at his funeral; some have but one wife, but I have known several with five or six. I myself was present at one of these ceremonies. The defunct was an old chief who had died of some lingering disease, and his body was wasted to skin and bone. A native friend, who was a chief, came on board my brig, and invited me on shore to see the ceremony, as I had formerly expressed a wish to that effect. The corpse was rolled up in large folds of a kind of cloth that is made in these islands, similar to, but coarser than that which is made at Taheite. They conveyed the body to the door of the house of the *caloo* or priest; who are men having great influence in the country, and who are supposed to foretell future events. The corpse was placed on the ground with the feet towards the door of the priest's house, and many hundreds of the natives were surrounding it. A woman was sitting at the head, which was uncovered, for the cloth was principally rolled across the belly. She had in her hand something like a powder-puff, and she continually puffed the face of the corpse with a black powder. I was anxious to get near the body, but my friend continually exhorted me to keep at a distance. I nevertheless persisted, and advanced to within a few yards of it. The women continued to sprinkle the face with the black powder; and when I had waited about an hour, a murmur among the multitude and a sort of shout attracted my attention. My native friend, who kept beside me, informed me that it was occasioned by the approach of the principal wife of the defunct chief, who lived some miles off, and who had just arrived in a canoe. In a few minutes she had made her appearance, accompanied by her female friends. I did not observe any mark of extreme dejection about her, but she appeared serious and thoughtful; she advanced to the body, kissed it, and then retreated backwards about twenty steps, keeping her face towards it. A woman well known to me was sitting there, and the widow placed herself upon her lap, when the females who had accompanied her to the place approached her and attempted to kiss her: but she repelled them scornfully with her arms. The woman upon whose lap she sat, then put one of her hands at the back part of the head of the widow, and the other on her mouth; a man suddenly placed a cord round her neck; six men, who were ready, took hold of it, three at each end, and pulled with all their force. I did not observe that the widow made the least struggle, although after the manner of the country she was only covered about the middle; not even her legs moved. I was anxious to know what would be done with the bodies, and had recourse to my friend for that purpose. He told me, however, that that was not permitted to be known, but that I might see all that they themselves knew; the final part of the ceremony being known only to the *caloo*. I accordingly went to the priest's house in the evening. The dead chief and his strangled widow were placed near the door. I had brought one of my boat's crew with me, and as the few natives that were present had some difficulty in forcing the chief's body through the door-way, in consequence of the many folds of cloth that were about it, this man assisted them in this part of the rite; and while this was doing I went into the apartment, anxious to discover whether there was any grave dug. It was dark, and I felt about the house cautiously with my feet, lest there should be a cavern beneath it, but I found none; and as they had then placed the two bodies beside each other in the house, my friend told me that I could not be permitted to see more, and we retired.

Another instance of the same ceremony I was more intimately acquainted with, and indeed was in some measure a party concerned. I had been on a cruise, and at my return I found my friend Riceammong dead. He was a fine young man, and a chief; I had formerly entered into an agreement with him for a cargo of sandal wood, which was not yet fulfilled. I greatly regretted the death of this man, not only because I had a friendship for him, but because I feared it would be a means of losing my cargo of sandal wood. I called immediately upon his mother, who had also been a great friend to me. As soon as she saw me she embraced me; and not knowing I had been informed of her loss, with tears told me, that Riceammong was dead; and what can I do, said she, how shall I be able to procure you the sandal wood? I told her I was much grieved at the loss of her son, and requested to pay my respect to the body. I knew very well before that it was customary to visit and speak to the dead as if they were living, and that there was always some person present to give answers for them. I therefore went with the mother to the apartment where the body was laid, and taking hold of the dead chief's hand, I said to him, "I see, Riceammong, what has happened to you; you are dead, and have left us; you know, Riceammong, the agreement that existed between us, that you were to procure me a freight of sandal wood, which I have already paid you for, and which I have not received; what is to be done in the business, Riceammong?" The mother, who stood by, answered, "Yes, I recollect the agreement, and I will take care that it shall be fulfilled." Much more conversation passed between us which it is needless to repeat, when we retired from the body. I was by this time intimate with many of the natives. I had a house and farm, and most of my property was rendered sacred or, as it is called in the country, tabooed, so that any person injuring it might be destroyed.

The old mother took me to her house, and we had much conversation respecting the sandal wood that I had agreed with her son for; she wept much during our conversation, and anxiously spoke of Riceammong's principal wife. You know, said she, that she paid great attention to the white people, that she fed them, and clothed them. Alas! unless some of her friends rescue her, she must follow my son to the grave. I know of no friend she has in the world, added she, embracing me, but yourself: are you willing to save her? I would do my utmost to save her. Run then, said she, hastily; wait not a moment, there is still a chance of her life being preserved.—I was ignorant what it was necessary for me to do to effect the purpose, and enquired of the mother; she added quickly. You know that you have the authority of a chief; bring to the place of funeral a valuable present, hold it up in your hands, on your knees repeat the words: I beg the life of this woman; and her life may be spared. But, continued the old woman quickly, if you save her, you will have a right to her. I do not wish any person to possess the widow of my son. I told her I only wished to save her life; when she embraced me weeping, and I went away. I had unfortunately nothing on shore with me sufficiently valuable for the purpose. I therefore ran down to the boat, to go off to the brig, which was thirty miles distant: we pulled on board as fast as possible, and I took one of the largest whales teeth, which I knew to be more valued there than gold. With a fresh boat's crew we pulled back again; I was certain there was not a moment to spare; on my reaching the shore I leaped out of the boat, and ran to the spot where the ceremony would take place. The *caloo*, however, was my enemy; indeed he was the enemy of all the white people; he had even predicted that the increased intercourse with the whites would endanger the nation. Hearing what I had intended to do, he had hastened the ceremony. He was a man apparently above the ordinary occurrences of life; whether through hypocrisy or a real hardness of heart, he seemed to be bereft of the ordinary affections of men; and I am inclined to think much instigated by hatred towards the white people, he had, under the cloak of religion, already bereft the widow of Riceammong of life. The mother had endeavoured with all her power to prolong the time; the widow also, equally anxious to escape, had used her utmost efforts to avoid the fatal cord; but all was in vain. The priest, with a look of sanctity, explained to the people that it was necessary; that men only had a right to interfere in these concerns; that it was the law, and that he was determined for reasons known only to himself, that the usual sacrifice should take place immediately. It was therefore done as he had commanded, and the widow of Riceammong was strangled about a quarter of an hour before I arrived with the whale's tooth. My departed friend had three wives, two of whom were strangled; the third was saved by the influence of her relations, who were persons of great influence.

When I saw the bodies together, and that I had endeavoured in vain to save the widow, I was excessively agitated, and, in the first impulse of my disappointment, went to the corpse of the widow and kissed it. The *caloo* was standing near it; he was a man that could contain his passions; I knew of his hostility towards me; I upbraided him with the strongest expressions I could think of; but, smothering every mark of passion, he merely answered coolly, it is the law.

Further Reading

These texts are both republished in E. Im Thurn and Leonard Wharton, eds., *The Journal of William Lockerby, Sandalwood Trader in the Fijian Islands . . . with Other Papers* (London: Hakluyt Society, 1925), though the evangelical framing of the Patterson texts is omitted. H. E. Maude's essay, "Beach-combers and Castaways," in his *Of Islands and Men* (Melbourne: Oxford University Press, 1968), remains the single most valuable survey of the genre and includes a useful bibliographic appendix. Some of the accounts of individual suffering may profitably be compared with Mungo Park's experiences; his narrative, *Travels into the Interior of Africa* (London: Eland, 1983), would certainly have been read by many beachcomber editors if not beachcombers, and may have influenced the composition of some texts.

WILLIAM MARINER

Missiles and Missives

. . . .

WILLIAM MARINER (1791–1853) was making a first voyage as captain's clerk aboard the privateering and whaling vessel *Port-au-Prince* when his ship was captured in the Ha'apai Islands in December 1806. Half the crew was massacred: others took up residence among the Tongans. Mariner, however, was singled out for special favor by Fīnau 'Ulukālala II and was adopted by one of the ruler's wives. Using the weapons confiscated from the *Port-au-Prince*, he assisted Fīnau in extending his power throughout Tonga. In 1807 Fīnau attacked and destroyed the fortress of Nuku'alofa at Tongatabu. Rather than following Mariner's advice to proceed with an invasion of Tongatabu, Fīnau rebuilt the fortress and left it in the hands of Tākai of Pea, the island's most powerful chief, who defiantly burned the fortress while he was still in sight of the flames. Fīnau then became implicated in intrigues that led to the death of the chief Tupouniua, to whom he had delegated the government of Vava'u. The people of Vava'u rebelled, constructing a fortress at Feletoa from which to resist Fīnau. After a period of indeterminate warfare he negotiated a peace, and then he treacherously attacked the most powerful Vava'u warriors, who were clubbed to death or drowned.

When 'Ulukālala died in 1809 he was succeeded by his son Moengāngongo, who also made a favorite of Mariner. In his *Account of the Tonga Islands*, Mariner contrasts the characters of the two rulers: where 'Ulukālala II is the fierce warrior, Moengāngongo is presented as a man of intellect and sentiment, who has spent his youth traveling within Polynesia and learning from the practices of his neighbors, particularly the Samoans. Fīnau's successor delegated the rule of the Ha'apai islands to chief Tupouto'a and concentrated his attentions on Vava'u, encouraging cultivation rather than warfare. Mariner enjoyed a privileged life with Moengān-gongo, until he was eventually picked up by a brig, the *Favourite*, which took him to Macao. He made his passage back to London aboard an East India merchant ship, arriving in June 1811.

Mariner's *Account of the Tonga Islands* was actually composed by John Martin, a doctor who met Mariner some years after his return to England and became fascinated by the tale of his experiences. As he explained in an introduction to the volume:

> To my inquiries respecting his intentions of publishing, [Mariner] replied, that having necessarily been, for several years, out of the habit either of writing or reading, or of that turn of thinking requisite for composition and arrangement, he was apprehensive his endeavours would fail in doing that justice to the work which I seemed to think its importance demanded: he modestly proposed, however, to submit the subject to my consideration for a future opportunity. (Martin 1818, 1:xxi–xxii)

The book is dedicated to Sir Joseph Banks, and its second volume makes a claim to scientific authority, offering a compendium on Tongan society, religion, knowledge, dress, domestic habits, pastimes, art, and language. Martin is concerned to represent his role as one primarily of transcription, claiming that "not one of the ensuing pages has therefore been written without Mr. Mariner's presence, that he might be consulted with regard to every little circumstance or observation that could in the smallest degree affect the turn of the subject under consideration" (Martin 1818, 1:xxiii). He nonetheless fashioned Mariner's account into an eminently literary text, with its contrasting portraits of the savagely heroic and sentimentally enlightened Tongan rulers and its digressions on the sublime aspects of the Tongan landscape. His description of a secret underwater cavern on the island of Hoonga, and its use in the elopement of a young native couple, was taken up by Byron in his *Bounty* poem "The Island." The *Account of the Tonga Islands* was the most popular and critically acclaimed of early beachcomber narratives, running to three editions in the decade after its publication.

The extract reproduced here demonstrates the role of the European as transmitter of a divided cultural legacy. The two European technologies that made the most immediate and lasting impact upon Oceanic politics were weapons and writing. By forging links with beachcombers or missionaries—the former frequently in possession of and able to operate guns, the latter able to teach reading and writing—chiefs of different islands could consolidate their power over a wider area than had hitherto proved possible. Fīnau had already embarked on a campaign of usurpation before Mariner arrived in Tonga—in the account of George Vason he is introduced as one of the assassins of Tuku'aho. In the civil strife that followed

Tuku'aho's death he was driven from Tongatabu and made his base in the Ha'apai islands, from where he made raids upon Tongatabu. According to I. C. Campbell, "the seizure of the *Port-au-Prince* was at least the third attempt to acquire foreign weapons and men to operate them, in anticipation of their usefulness in breaking the political deadlock. [Attacks had been made on the *Duke of Portland* in 1802, and the *Union* in 1804, both at Tongatapu.]" (Campell 1976, 306–7). The extract illustrates the impact made upon Fīnau's campaign by the muskets and carronades from the *Port-au-Prince*, which are credited with enabling him to destroy the fortress at Nuku'alofa. Traditional Tongan weapons—the club, of which Mariner lists six types in his vocabulary, and fighting spears, both of which would have been crafted from toa wood (Ferdon 1987, 259)—take on a subsidiary role in this account, proving effective once the guns have done their damage. Yet while this text is typical of many early accounts of contact in its assumption that such technologies have a revelatory potential for Pacific islanders, it in fact registers a range of Tongan responses to the new weapons. An implicit distinction is made between the defeated enemy, who endows bullets with magical powers of movement, and the more skeptical Fīnau, who questions whether the gun is ideally suited to the Tongan mode of warfare.

In the second section of the extract Fīnau surrenders skepticism in his fascination with the practice of writing. Martin describes a series of tests that the chief employs to demonstrate the power of print to convey meaning, and he records his naive semiotic queries regarding the relationship between sign and signifier. There is, however, a telling parallel between Fīnau 's experiments and certain tests that Martin describes as having been set up to establish the authenticity of Mariner's account. In his introduction he writes of Mariner:

> His memory is very retentive, and his account of things is exceedingly correct and uniform: of this I have had numberless proofs, and one in particular I shall mention. I happened to mislay the English version which he had written out at his leisure, of the speech of Finow the king on first coming into power: after a lapse of a few weeks, not finding it, I was under the necessity of requesting him to write another, which he did in the same method as before, by calling to his mind the original Tonga in which it was spoken. Sometime afterwards I found the first, and was much pleased to discover so little difference between them, that they appeared almost like copies, which sufficiently evinced the correctness with which he remembered the original Tonga, and at the same time furnished an instance of the characteristic uniformity of his expression in his own language. (Martin 1818, I: xxxvii–xxxviii)

As well as reading between versions of Mariner's account, Martin compares it with other accounts from the Pacific, such as the recently published voyage of beachcomber Archibald Campbell, and, after the second edition, with the testimony of fellow *Port-au-Prince* survivor Jeremiah Higgins. He includes Mariner's written commentary on specific passages from Campbell's text, which are paginated to enable cross-reference. Discussing orthographic discrepancies between the two accounts, Martin notes: "The king's name, here spelt '*Tamaahmaah*,' is pronounced by Mr. Mariner, and is expressed by our orthography Tămmeahmēha. . . . The editor, Mr. Smith, in note, p. 210, remarks the different modes of spelling and pronouncing this name, employed by different travellers, and that the C and the T are scarcely to be distinguished in the pronunciation of the language." Although the discrepancies testify to misconstruction by the unaccustomed British ear, Mariner explains the problem as one of transmission rather than reception: "The fact is, there are few of the natives but who have lost some of their front teeth, owing to an absurd custom of knocking them out as a sacrifice. . . . The consequence is, that their pronunciation, to the ears of a foreigner, is exceedingly indistinct: they often confound the *r* and the *l*, possibly from this cause; but their indiscriminate use of the hard *c* and the *t*, Mr. Mariner is convinced, arises from this source" (Campbell 1816, 13; Martin 1818, 1:xxii). Mariner's account produces a disabled native subject, whose cultural practices are mutually conflicting: self-mutilation hindering oral communication. Higgins in turn is brought in to read and verify Mariner's account, Martin asserting that "the information obtained from Higgins must undoubtedly be considered valuable, if only regarded as generally corroborative, and in a few instances somewhat corrective of Mr. Mariner's statements." Yet, as the following extract shows, Mariner and Higgins have been involved before this in an act of deceptive corroboration. If Martin's obsessive concern for authenticity mirrors Fïnau's games of verification, they remain, perhaps, equally open to manipulation. — VANESSA SMITH

. . . .

John Martin, *An account of the natives of the Tonga Islands, in the South Pacific Ocean. With an original grammar and vocabulary of their language. Comp. and arranged from the extensive communications of Mr. William Mariner, several years resident in those islands*, 2nd edition, 2 vols. (London: John Murray, 1818).

« FROM VOLUME I, CHAPTER 3. »

Mr. Mariner and those of his companions who were with him at the island of Lefooga, (and were four in number,) received orders from the king to prepare for the usual annual attack upon the island of Tonga, and to get ready four 12 pound carronades. They immediately set to work, to mount them upon new carriages with high wheels, made by the native carpenters, under their directions. This being done, Finow expressed his opinion, that the gun was an instrument not well fitted (being too unwieldy) for their mode of warfare, which consisted in sudden attacks and retreats, according to circumstances, rather than in a steady engagement. He very readily entered into an acknowledgment of the advantages of a steady contest, but was apprehensive that his men would not easily be brought to stand it. Mr. Mariner and his companions, however, promised that they and their countrymen (who were dispersed upon other islands,) would remain in the front of the battle with their four guns, provided the Tonga people would agree to stand fast and support them. The king assented to this on the part of his men, and a few days afterwards, when he reviewed them, he signified his wishes, and they swore to fulfil their duty.

In the mean time the Englishmen employed themselves in collecting the shot which the natives had brought from on board, but which they had thrown aside, not being able to shape them for any common purpose. They also cut up a quantity of sheet lead, and made it up in rolls to be used as shot. During this time every preparation was also making [sic] by the natives for the approaching war: they repaired the sails of their canoes, collected their arrows, spears, and clubs; and the women employed themselves in packing up bales of gnatoo[1] mats, &c. . . .

All things being now prepared for the invasion of Tonga, the gods were invoked; and the priests assured Finow of success. The large canoes of Lefooga, about fourteen in number, were then launched, which, with Toobō Nuha's fleet from Vavaoo, made together about fifty sail. Orders were sent by Finow to all the Hapai islands to make the island of Namooca the place of general rendezvous. These fifty sail under the direction of Finow, four of the largest having each a carronade on board, proceeded towards the appointed place; but on account of contrary winds were obliged to put into Wiha. Here Finow took an opportunity to review his men, most of them being painted and drest after the warlike manner of the Fiji islands. They paraded up and down for some time, brandishing their clubs and spears, and exhibiting a sort of sham fight. Finow sat with several other chiefs in the house on the malāi.[2] Each warrior of note ran singly close up to Finow, and striking his club violently on the ground,

1. Gnatoo, a sort of cloth made of the bark of the Chinese paper mulberry tree.
2. The malāi is a grass-plat, about three acres in extent, with a house on it, and is used for various public purposes, as in the present instance; there are generally four or five of them on each island. As Vavaoo is comparatively a large island, it has fourteen or fifteen.

cried out "this is the club for ————," mentioning the name of some individual enemy whom he meant particularly to seek out and engage; others running up in the same way, exclaimed, "Fear not, Finow; no sooner shall we land at Tonga than here is the club with which I will kill any one who dares to oppose us." Finow and the chiefs thanked them for their sentiments of love and loyalty, and then he addressed them in a speech to the following purpose: "Be brave in battle; fear not death: it is far better to die in war than to live to be assassinated at home, or to perish by a lingering disease."

After remaining a day and a night at this island, they again put to sea with the additional force of six canoes, and made sail for Namooca, where they arrived in a few hours. Here they had another review like the former; and after remaining two days, sailed with all the rest of the forces of the confederate islands, amounting in all to about one hundred and seventy canoes, direct for the island of Tonga. Owing to the calmness of the weather, they did not reach their destination the same evening in sufficient time to land, but went on shore at a small island close by, called Pāngaimōtoo, where they passed the night.

Before morning, several presents were brought to Finow and his chiefs, by the people living at a consecrated place on the island of Tonga, called Mafanga. Mafanga is a piece of ground about half a mile square, situated on the western part of the island. In this spot are the graves where the greatest chiefs from time immemorial have been buried, and the place is therefore considered sacred; it would be a sacrilege to fight here, and nobody can be prevented from landing: if the most inveterate enemies meet upon this ground, they must look upon each other as friends, under penalty of the displeasure of the Gods, and consequently an untimely death, or some great misfortune. There are several of these consecrated places on different islands.

The following morning, Finow with several of his chiefs and matabooles landed at Mafanga: they immediately proceeded to his father's grave, (Mr. Mariner being also with them) to perform the ceremony of Toogi. All who went for this purpose put on mats instead of their usual dress, and wreaths made of the leaves of the ifi tree round their necks (significant of respect and humility). They sat down cross-legged (the usual way of sitting) before the grave; Finow, as well as the rest, beating their cheeks with their fists for about half a minute, without speaking a word. One of the principal matabooles then addressed the spirit of Finow's father to the following purpose: "Behold the man (meaning Finow) who has come to Tonga to fight his enemies: be pleased with him, and grant him thy protection; he comes to battle, hoping he is not doing wrong; he has always held Tooitonga[3] in the highest respect, and has attended to all religious ceremonies with exactness." One of the attendants then went to Finow, and received from him a piece of cava root, which he laid down on the raised mount before the Fytoka (burying place). Several others, who had pieces of cava root in their bosoms, went up to the grave in like manner and deposited them. The ceremony being thus finished, Finow and his friends returned to the beach, where a large root of cava was brought to them as a present, by the chief of the consecrated place, on which they regaled.

During this time, the greater part of the forces in the canoes employed themselves in preparing for battle, again painting their bodies and faces after various fanciful forms. The enemy on shore were also in a state of preparation: they shouted the war-whoop, and ran up and down the beach with furious gestures; splashing up the water with their clubs, brandishing them in the air, flourishing their spears, and bidding bold defiance to their invaders.

Finow and his attendants having returned on board, the whole fleet proceeded to a neighbouring fortress called Nioocalofa, the strongest, though not the largest, in the whole island. As it will be proper to understand the usual form and construction of these Tonga fortresses, we shall give a general description of them, taking that of Nioocalofa as a model for the rest.

The fortress of Nioocalofa is situated on the western coast of the island, about one hundred yards distant from the water's edge, occupying about four or five acres of ground. It consists, in the first place, of a strong wall or fencing of reeds, something like wicker-work, supported on the inside by upright posts, from six to nine inches in diameter, and situated a foot and a half distant from each other; to which the reed-work is firmly lashed by tough sinnet, made of the husk of the cocoa-nut. This fencing is about nine feet in height, the post rising about a foot higher: it has four large entrances, as well as several small ones, secured on the inside by horizontal sliding pieces, made of the wood of the cocoa-nut tree. Over each door, as well as at other places, are erected platforms even with the top of the fencing, supported chiefly on the inside, but projecting forward to the extent of two or three feet: these platforms are about nine feet square, and situated fifteen yards distant from each other; and as they are intended for the men to stand on, to shoot arrows, or throw down large stones, they are also defended in front, and half way on each side, by a reed-work six feet high,

3. Tooitonga is a great chief, supposed to be descended from a God.

with an opening in front, and others on either hand, for the greater convenience of throwing spears, &c. The lower fencing has also openings for a similar purpose. On the outside is a ditch of nearly twelve feet deep, and as much broad; which, at a little distance, is encompassed by another fencing similar to the first, with platforms, &c. on the outside of which there is a second ditch. The earth dug out of these ditches forms a bank on each side, serving to deepen them. Opposite each large doorway, there is no ditch dug. The inner and outer fencings are ornamented profusely with white shells. Some of these fortifications are square, others round. That of Nioocalofa was round.

« FROM VOLUME I, CHAPTER 4. »

Finow being arrived with the whole of his fleet off Nioocalofa, and having with him, besides Mr. Mariner, fifteen other Englishmen, eight of whom were armed with muskets, he proceeded to land his troops under cover of a fire of musketry, which speedily drove almost all the enemy who had sallied forth back into the garrison. The first fire killed three, and wounded several; and a repetition of it threw them into such dismay, that in five minutes only forty of the bravest remained to molest them; and these began to retire, as the forces of Finow increased on the beach. In the mean while, the carronades were dismounted from their carriages, slung on poles, and conveyed over a shallow reef to the shore. The whole army being landed, and the guns again mounted, the latter were drawn up before the garrison, and a regular fire was commenced. Finow took his station on the reef, seated in an English chair, (from the Port au Prince) for his chiefs would not allow him to expose his person on shore. The fire of the carronades was kept up for about an hour: in the mean while, as it did not appear to do all the mischief to the exterior of the fortress, owing to the yielding nature of its materials, that the king expected, he sent for Mr. Mariner, and expressed his disappointment: the latter replied, that no doubt there was mischief enough done on the inside of the fort, wherever there were resisting bodies, such as canoes, the posts and beams of houses, &c.; and that it was already very evident the besieged had no reason to think slightly of the effect of the artillery, seeing that they had already greatly slackened their exertions, not half the number of arrows being now discharged from the fort; arising, in all probability, from the number of the slain, or of those who had fled up into the country. It was now resolved to set fire to the place; for which purpose a number of torches were prepared and lighted, and an attack was made upon the outer fencing; it was found, however, but weakly defended, and was soon taken: for the door-posts being shot away, an easy entrance was obtained. A considerable portion of the inner fencing was now found undefended, and towards this place a party rushed with lighted torches, whilst the enemy were kept in play elsewhere: the conflagration spread rapidly on every side; and, as the besieged endeavoured to make their escape, their brains were knocked out by a party of the besiegers, stationed at the back of the fort for the purpose. During this time the guns kept up a regular fire with blank cartridges, merely to intimidate the enemy. The conqueror, club in hand, entered the place in several quarters, and slew all they met, men, women, and children. The scene was truly horrible. The war-whoop shouted by the combatants, the heart-rending screams of the women and children, the groans of the wounded, the number of the dead, and the fierceness of the conflagration, formed a picture almost too distracting and awful for the mind steadily to contemplate. Some, with a kind of sullen and stupid resignation, offered no resistance, but waited for the hand of fate to dispatch them, no matter in what mode: others, that were already lying on the ground wounded, were stuck with spears, and beaten about with clubs by boys who followed the expedition to be trained to the horrors of war, and who delighted in the opportunity of gratifying their ferocious and cruel disposition. Every house that was not on fire was plundered of its contents; and the conquerors made a considerable booty of bales of gnatoo, mats, &c.[4]

In a few hours, the fortress of Nioocalofa, which had obstinately and bravely defended every attack for eleven years, or more, was thus completely destroyed. When Finow arrived upon the place, and saw several canoes which had been hauled up in the garrison, shattered to pieces by the shot, and discovered a number of legs and arms lying around, and about three hundred and fifty bodies stretched upon the ground, he expressed his wonder and astonishment at the dreadful effect of the guns. He thanked his men for their bravery, and Mr. Mariner and his companions in particular, for the great assistance rendered by them.

A few of the enemy, who had escaped the general slaughter, were taken prisoners. They gave a curious description of the effect of the guns. They

---

4. In this affair one of Finow's men, a native of Fiji, had made himself a sort of breast-plate of an earthenware fish-strainer, such as is laid in the bottom of dishes when fish is brought to table, which he had procured from the Port au Prince; but unluckily it happened that an arrow pierced him directly through the hole, which is commonly in the middle of such strainers: the wound laid him up eight months, and he never afterwards, in Mr. Mariner's time, was able to hold himself perfectly erect.

FIG. 9. *Mr. Mariner in the Costume of the Tonga Islands*. Engraved by [?] Bragg and published by J. Murray (London, 1816, 21.3 x 14.3 cm). By permission of the National Library of Australia.

declared, that, when a ball entered a house, it did not proceed straight forward, but went all round the place, as if seeking for men to kill; it then passed out of the house and entered another, still in search of food for its vengeance, and so on to a third, &c.; sometimes it would strike the corner-post of a house, and bring it all down together. The chiefs, seeing all this dreadful mischief going forward, rendered still more tremendous by their own imaginations, sat in consultation, upon one of the large canoes just mentioned, and came to a determination to rush out upon the white men, and take possession of the guns: this was scarcely resolved upon, when a shot struck the canoe on which they were sitting, and shattered it to pieces. This so damped their courage, that they ran for security to one of the inner houses of the garrison, when their distress was much increased by finding their men deserting the place, and running up into the country. Thus every thing was going to destruction within, although, without, the damage appeared in Finow's eyes so inconsiderable; but he had formed his judgment of the effect of the guns by their effect upon the fencing. . . .

Mr. Mariner, having heard that European ships more frequently touched at Tonga than at any of the other islands, had written, while yet at Tonga, an English letter (with a solution of gunpowder and a little mucilage for ink), on some paper which one of the natives had had a long time in his possession, and addressed it to whomsoever it might be, stating the circumstances of his situation, and that of his companions. This letter he had confided to the care of the chief of Mafanga, (the consecrated place formerly mentioned) with directions to give it to the captain of any ship that might arrive at Tonga. Tooi Tooi (the Sandwich islander) having somehow heard of this letter, mentioned it to Finow, and represented it to be a notice to European ships of the fate of the Port au Prince, and a request to take revenge for the destruction of her crew. Finow immediately sent for the letter and obtained it, under some specious pretext, from the chief of Mafanga. When it was put into his hands he looked at it on all sides; but not being able to make any thing of it, he gave it to Jeremiah Higgins, who was at hand, and ordered him to say what it meant: Mr. Mariner was not present. Higgins took the letter, and translating part of it into the Tonga language, judiciously represented it to be merely a request to any English captain that might arrive to interfere with Finow for the liberty of Mr. Mariner and his countrymen: stating that they had been kindly treated by the natives, but, nevertheless, wished to return, if possible, to their native country. This was not indeed the true substance of the letter, but it was what was least likely to give offence: and the chief accordingly remarked that it was very natural for these poor fellows to wish to go back to their native country and friends.[5]

This mode of communicating sentiments was an inexplicable puzzle to Finow; he took the letter again and examined it, but it afforded him no information. He considered the matter a little within himself; but his thoughts reflected no light upon the subject. At length he sent for Mr. Mariner, and desired him to write down something: the latter asked what he would choose to have written; he replied, put down me: he accordingly wrote "Feenow" (spelling it according to the strict English orthography): the chief then sent for another Englishman who had not been present, and commanding Mr. Mariner to turn his back and look another way, he gave the man the paper, and desired him to tell what that was: he accordingly pronounced aloud the name of the king, upon which Finow snatched the paper from his hand, and, with astonishment, looked at it, turned it round, and examined it in all directions: at length he exclaimed, "This is neither like myself nor any body else! where are my legs? how do you know it to be I?" and then, without stopping for any attempt at an explanation, he impatiently ordered Mr. Mariner to write something else, and thus employed him for three or four hours in putting down the names of different persons, places, and things, and making the other man read them. This afforded extraordinary diversion to Finow, and to all the men and women present, particularly as he now and then whispered a little love anecdote, which was strictly written down, and audibly read by the other, not a little to the confusion of one or other of the ladies present: but it was all taken in good humour, for curiosity and astonishment were the prevailing passions. How their names and circumstances could be communicated through so mysterious a channel, was altogether past their comprehension. . . . Mr. Mariner in vain attempted to explain. He had yet too slender a knowledge of their language to make himself clearly understood: and, indeed, it would not have been an easy matter to have explained the composition of elementary sounds, and of arbitrary signs expressive of them, to a people whose minds were already formed to other modes of thinking, and whose language had few expressions but what concerned the ordinary affairs of life. The only rational mode would have been, to have invented a system of spelling, and to have gone through the usual routine of teaching

5. The letter in fact was an advice to European ships to go to the Hapai Islands in preference to the Island of Tonga, as being a better place for victualling: advising at the same time, not to suffer many of the natives to be on board at once, lest they should meet with the same fate as the Port au Prince, but, if possible, to make some of the chiefs prisoners and keep them as hostages, till Mr. Mariner and his companions were delivered up.

it. Finow, at length, thought he had got a notion of it, and explained to those about him that it was very possible to put down a mark or sign of something that had been seen both by the writer and reader, and which should be mutually understood by them: but Mr. Mariner immediately informed him, that he could write down any thing that he had never seen: the king directly whispered to him to put Toogoo Ahoo (the king of Tonga, whom he and Toobō Nuha had assassinated many years before Mr. Mariner's arrival). This was accordingly done, and the other read it; when Finow was yet more astonished, and declared it to be the most wonderful thing he had ever heard of. He then desired him to write "Tarky," (the chief of the garrison of Bea, whom Mr. Mariner and his companions had not yet seen; this chief was blind in one eye). When "Tarky" was read, Finow inquired whether he was blind or not; this was putting writing to an unfair test! and Mr. Mariner told him that he had only written down the sign standing for the sound of his name, and not for the description of his person. He was then ordered in a whisper to write, "Tarky, blind in his left eye," which was done, and read by the other man to the increased astonishment of every body. Mr. Mariner then told him that, in several parts of the world, messages were sent to great distances through the same medium, and being folded and fastened up, the bearer could know nothing of the contents, and that the histories of whole nations were thus handed down to posterity, without spoiling by being kept (as he chose to express himself). Finow acknowledged this to be a most noble invention, but added, that it would not at all do for the Tonga islands, that there would be nothing but disturbances and conspiracies, and he should not be sure of his life, perhaps, another month. He said, however, jocosely, that he should like to know it himself, and for all the women to know it, that he might make love with less risk of discovery, and not so much chance of incurring the vengeance of their husbands.

Further Reading

Histories that cover the period of Mariner's residence in Tonga and employ Martin's account as source material include Sione Lātūkefu, *Church and State in Tonga: The Wesleyan Methodist Missionaries and Political Development, 1822–1875* (Canberra: Australian National University Press, 1974); Edwin N. Ferdon, *Early Tonga, As the Explorers Saw It, 1616–1810* (Tucson: University of Arizona Press, 1987); and I. C. Campbell, *Island Kingdom: Tonga Ancient and Modern* (Christchurch: Canterbury University Press,

1992). Archibald Campbell's voyage, to which Martin refers, is documented in *A voyage round the world, from 1806 to 1812 . . . with an account of the present state of the Sandwich Islands, and a vocabulary of their language* (Edinburgh: Archibald Constable and Company, 1816). Neil Rennie, *Far-Fetched Facts: The Literature of Travel and the Idea of the South Seas* (Oxford: Clarendon Press, 1995), examines the literary impact of Mariner's story. Vanessa Smith, *Literary Culture and the Pacific: Nineteenth-Century Textual Encounters* (Cambridge: Cambridge University Press, 1998), discusses Martin's text as a beachcomber narrative.

17

WILLIAM ELLIS

Unutterable Practices

. . . .

WILLIAM ELLIS (1794–1872) arrived in Eimeo (Mo'orea) in February 1817 with his wife and daughter, as part of a group of eight missionaries (also including John Williams) who constituted the second "generation" of London Missionary Society activity in Polynesia. He had received training as a printer while in England and brought with him that significant instrument of evangelism, the printing press, which was set up in the district of Afareaitu. Pomare II took a close interest in the establishment of the press and was invited to print the first sheet, and subsequently to advise on Scripture translation. A spelling book and Tahitian catechism were printed, followed by the Gospel of Luke and a hymn book. In mid-1818 Ellis moved to Huahine in the Leeward Isles, taking the press with him. The complexities of his role as printer—the literal bearer of the biblical Word to the Pacific islands—emerge in *Polynesian Researches*, where Ellis discusses the implication of the press in Pomare's theater of power, methods of charging for printed texts, and the capacity for mnemonics and mimicry displayed by islanders eager to acquire knowledge of reading (V. Smith 1998, 70–81). In 1822 Ellis joined the London Missionary Society deputation's visit to Honolulu, accompanying a party of nine converts from the Society Islands. He was invited to join the missionaries who were establishing a base in Hawaii under the auspices of the American Board of Commissioners for Foreign Missions. He moved to Hawaii in February 1823 and spent his time there preaching, translating, and traveling until September 1824, when he departed due to his wife's ill-health. He returned to England, where he wrote *Polynesian Researches*, and became foreign secretary of the London Missionary Society from 1832–41. Later in life he served as a missionary in Madagascar.

Ellis's *Polynesian Researches* has been recognized since the time of its publication as one of the most detailed and ethnographically sophisticated documents of early contact Polynesia. Rod Edmond points to the work's impact on literary figures of such varying traditions as Herman Melville, Robert Southey, Wilkie Collins, and Victor Segalen (Edmond 1997, 104–5), while Christopher Herbert sees Ellis's text as a prime example of the way early missionaries to Polynesia worked through existential dilemmas that were later to be enacted in the methodology of anthropological fieldwork (Herbert 1991, 150–203). Herbert notes that missionary accounts played a conflicted dual role, as both records of vanishing societies and triumphalist narratives of the victory of Christian practices over traditional lifeways. He cites *Polynesian Researches*, in particular, as demonstrating an intricate awareness of the systematic interconnection of Tahitian material culture, social practices, and religious belief, which nonetheless produces an unresolved contest between rejection and identification, repulsion and desire, in describing the operation of these systems.

This conflicted representation is exemplified in this passage, in which Ellis describes the practices of the Arioi cult of the Society Islands. The Arioi was a society dedicated to "Oro, the most important god in the Tahitian pantheon." They traveled throughout the island group, staging performances and receiving tribute from local populations. The society represented a paradoxical combination of license and restriction. Ellis describes its members as "privileged libertines" who engaged in a variety of unnameable sexual practices, but they were also bound rigidly to abstain from reproduction, an injunction that was adhered to through the practice of infanticide. By recuperating infanticide to the same types of unregenerate impulse as acts of sexual license, Ellis shifts attention from the aspect of sacrifice it entails. But Alfred Gell has argued that infanticide was the "penalty" of admission to the Arioi cult, whose sociological motivation "was to impose a massive restraint on the reproduction of rank in the Society Islands" (Gell 1993, 147). The degree to which the Arioi were legitimated by Tahitian society provides another point of ambivalence in Ellis's account. The cult is presented on the one hand as the apotheosis of unregenerate heathenism, and on the other as offering a politicized critique of Tahitian priestly religion. Greg Dening describes the Arioi as "the only group in the islands who called on loyalties wider than tribal and local divisions. . . . They would play the clown to established authority: they overturned the rules of proper behaviour, and danced and played without responsibility" (Dening 1996, 131). Their capacities as mimics endow the Arioi with an unstable subjectivity, which threatens to disrupt Ellis's portrayal of certain members' unproblematic shifts of identity from "docile" and "devoted" disciples of the heathen cult to consummate Christian converts.

Ellis's attack on the Arioi is two pronged. He offers a direct, materialist critique of the iniquities involved in maintaining the society, invoking the image of the desolated garden to portray not only the locust-like greed of the itinerant performers, but to hint further at the travesty of their legitimated nonproductivity, and at their post-lapsarian sinfulness. He also makes persistent oblique references to the moral crimes of the members. At these points the carefully maintained tension between the voices of missionary and ethnographer, destroyer and preserver of traditional Tahitian practices, breaks down. The missionary declares his allegiances: demonstratively balking at an act of description, while producing a site of resonant unutterability in an otherwise discursive text. As Rod Edmond has pointed out, Ellis's discussion of Arioi sexuality is a developed example of "the trope of preterition—the figure by which attention is drawn to something while professing to omit it—to which *Polynesian Researches* often resorts when faced with the untranslatable" (Edmond 1998, 158). This evasive descriptive technique is recurrent in nineteenth-century travelers' texts from Tahiti, where Europeans confronted sexual practices—for instance, those of the *mahus*, or Tahitian "third sex"—that were perceived to be unmentionable; and missionary discourse, registering a special sensitivity in the presence of sin, was above all characterized by such gaps and elisions. However, Ellis's extreme outburst toward the end of this passage, in which he rails against "abominable, unutterable" practices "which the mind cannot contemplate without pollution and pain" articulates a fear of contamination from which the ethnographic equilibrium of his account of the Arioi fails to recover. — VANESSA SMITH

. . . .

William Ellis, *Polynesian Researches, During a Residence of Nearly Six Years in the South Sea Islands*, 2 vols. (London: Fisher, 1829).

« VOLUME I, CHAPTER 12, PP. 311–28. »

The greatest source of amusement to the people, as a nation, was most probably the existence of a society, peculiar to the islands of the Pacific, if not to the inhabitants of the southern groups. This was an institution called the Areoi society. Many of the regulations of this body, and the practices to which they were addicted, cannot be made public, without violence to every feeling of propriety; but, so far as it can be consistently done, it seems desirable to give some particulars respecting this most singular institution. Although I never met with an account of any institution analogous to this, among the barbarous nations in any parts of the world, I have reason to believe it was not confined to the Society group, and neighbouring islands. It does not appear to have existed in the Marquesas or Sandwich Islands; but the Jesuit Missionaries found an institution, bearing a striking resemblance to it, among the inhabitants of the Caroline or Ladrone Islands; a privileged fraternity, whose practices were, in many respects, similar to those of the Areois of the southern islands. They were called *uritoy*, which, omitting the *t*, would not be much unlike *areoi*. A greater difference exists in the pronunciation of words known to be radically the same.

How long this association has existed in the South Sea Islands, we have no means of ascertaining with correctness. According to the traditions of the people, its antiquity is equal to that of the system of pollution and error with which it was so intimately allied; and, by the same authority, we are informed that there have been Areois almost as long as there have been men. These, however, were all so fabulous, that we can only infer from them that the institution is of ancient origin. According to the traditions of the people, Taaroa created, and, by means of Hina, brought forth, when full-grown, Orotetefa and Urutetefa. They were not his sons; *oriori* is the term employed by the people, which seems to mean *create*. They were called the brothers of Oro, and were numbered among the inferior divinities. They remained in a state of celibacy; and hence the devotees were required to destroy their offspring. The origin of the Areois institution is as follows.

Oro, the son of Taaroa, desired a wife from the daughters of Taata, the first man; he sent two of his brothers, Tufarapainuu and Tufarapairai, to seek among the daughters of man a suitable companion for him; they searched through the whole of the islands, from Tahiti to Borabora, but saw no one that they supposed fit to become the wife of Oro, till they came to Borabora. Here, residing near the foot of Mouatahuhuura, *red-ridged mountain*, they saw Vairaumati. When they beheld her, they said one to the other, This is the excellent woman for our brother. Returning to the skies, they hastened to Oro, and informed him of their success; told him they had found among the daughters of man a wife for him, described the place of her abode, and represented her as a *vahine purotu aiai*, a female possessed of every charm. The god fixed the rainbow in the heavens, one end of it resting in the valley at the foot of the red-ridged mountain, the other penetrating the skies, and thus formed his pathway to the earth.

When he emerged from the vapour which, like a cloud, had encircled the rainbow, he discovered the dwelling of Vairaumati, the fair mistress of the cottage, who became his wife. Every evening he descended on the rainbow, and returned by the same pathway on the following morning to the heavenly regions. His wife bore a son, whom he called *Hoa-tabu-i-te-rai*, friend, sacred to the heavens. This son became a powerful ruler among men.

The absence of Oro from his celestial companions, during the frequent visits he made to the cottage of Vairaumati in the valley of Borabora, induced two of his younger brothers, Orotetefa and Urutetefa, to leave their abode in the skies, and commence a search after him. Descending by the rainbow in the position in which he had placed it, they alighted on the world near the base of the red-ridged mountain, and soon perceived their brother and his wife in their terrestrial habitation. Ashamed to offer their salutations to him and his bride without a present, one of them was transformed on the spot into a pig, and a bunch of *uru*, or red feathers. These acceptable presents the other offered to the inmates of the dwelling, as a gift of congratulation. Oro and his wife expressed their satisfaction at the present; the pig and the feathers remained the same, but the brother of the god assumed his original form.

Such a mark of attention, on such an occasion, was considered by Oro to require some expression of his commendation. He accordingly made them gods, and constituted them Areois, saying, *Ei Areoi orua i ie ao nei, ia noaa ta orua tuhaa*: Be you two Areois in this world, that you may love your portion, (in the government, &c.) In the commemoration of this ludicrous fable of the pig and the feathers, the Areois, in all the taupiti, and public festivals, carried a young pig to the temple; strangled it, bound it in the *ahu haio*, (a loose open kind of cloth,) and placed it on the altar. They also offered the red feathers, which they called the *uru maru no te Areoi*; the shadowy uru of the Areoi, or the red feathers of the party of the Areoi.

It has been already stated that the brothers, who were made gods and kings of the Areois, lived in celibacy; consequently they had no descendants. On this account, although they did not enjoin celibacy upon their devotees, they prohibited their having any offspring. Hence, one of the standing regulations of this institution was, the murder of their children. The first company, the legend states, were nominated, according to Oro's direction, by Urutetefa and Orotetefa, and comprised the following individuals: Huatua, of Tahiti; Tauraatua, of Moorea, or Eimeo; Temaiatea, of Sir Charles Sander's Island; Tetoa and Atae, of Huahine; Taramanini and Airipa, of Raiatea; Mutahaa, of Tahaa; Bunaruu, of Borabora; and Marore, of Maurua. These individuals, selected from the different islands, constituted the first Areoi society. To them, also, the gods whom Oro had placed over them delegated authority, and gave permission to admit to their order all such as were desirous to unite with them, and consented to murder their infants.[1] These were always the names of the principal Areois in each of the islands; and were borne by them in the several islands at the time of their renouncing idolatry; when the Areois name, and Areois customs, were simultaneously discontinued.

It is a most gratifying fact, that some of those who bore these names, and were ringleaders in all the vice and cruelty connected with the system, have since been distinguished for their active benevolence, and moral and exemplary lives. Auna, one of the first deacons in the church at Huahine, one of the first native teachers sent out by that church to the heathen, and who has been the minister of the church in Sir Charles Sander's Island, an indefatigable, upright, intelligent, and useful man, as a Christian Missionary in the South Sea Islands, was the principal Areoi of Raiatea. He was the Taramanini of that island, until he embraced Christianity.

They were a sort of strolling players, and privileged libertines, who spent their days in travelling from island to island, and from one district to another, exhibiting their pantomimes, and spreading a moral contagion throughout society. Great preparation was necessary before the *mareva*, or company, set out. Numbers of pigs were killed, and presented to Oro; large quantities of plantains and bananas, with other fruits, were also offered upon his altars. Several weeks were necessary to complete the preliminary ceremonies. The concluding parts of these consisted in erecting on board their canoes, two temporary maraes, or temples, for the worship of Orotetefa and his brother, the tutelar deities of the society. This was merely a symbol of the presence of the gods: and consisted principally in a stone for each, from Oro's marae, and a few red feathers from the inside of the sacred image. Into these symbols the gods were supposed to enter when the priest pronounced a short *ubu*, or prayer, immediately before the sailing of the fleet. The numbers connected with this fraternity, and the magnitude of some of their expeditions, will appear from the fact of Cook's witnessing, on one occasion, in Huahine, the departure of seventy canoes filled with Areois.

On landing at the place of destination, they proceeded to the residence of the king or chief, and presented their *marotai*, or present; a similar offering was also sent to the temple and to the gods, as an acknowledgment for the preservation they had experienced at sea. If they remained in the

---

1. The above is one of the most regular accounts of the origin of the Areois institution, extant among the people. Mr. Barff, to whom I am indebted for it, received it from Auna, and Mahine the king of Huahine.

neighbourhood, preparations were made for their dances and other performances.

On public occasions, their appearance was, in some respects, such as it is not proper to describe. Their bodies were painted with charcoal, and their faces, especially, stained with the *mati*, or scarlet dye. Sometimes they wore a girdle of the yellow *ti* leaves; which, in appearance, resembled the feather girdles of the Peruvians, or other South American tribes. At other times they wore a vest of ripe yellow plantain leaves, and ornamented their heads with wreaths of the bright yellow and scarlet leaves of the *hutu*, or *Barringtonia*; but, in general, their appearance was far more repulsive than when they wore these partial coverings.

Upaupa was the name of many of their exhibitions. In performing these, they sometimes sat in a circle on the ground, and recited, in concert, a legend or song in honour of their gods, or some distinguished Areoi. The leader of the party stood in the centre, and introduced the recitation with a sort of prologue, when, with a number of fantastic movements and attitudes, those that sat around began their song in a low and measured tone and voice; which increased as they proceeded, till it became vociferous and unintelligibly rapid. It was also accompanied by movements of the arms and hands, in exact keeping with the tones of the voice, until they were wrought to the highest pitch of excitement. This they continued, until, becoming breathless and exhausted, they were obliged to suspend the performance.

Their public entertainments frequently consisted in delivering speeches, accompanied by every variety of gesture and action; and their representations, on these occasions, assumed something of the histrionic character. The priests, and others, were fearlessly ridiculed in these performances, in which allusion was ludicrously made to public events. In the taupiti, or oroa, they sometimes engaged in wrestling, but never in boxing; that would have been considered too degrading for them. Dancing, however, appears to have been their favourite and most frequent performance. In this they were always led by the manager or chief. Their bodies, blackened with charcoal, and stained with mati, rendered the exhibition of their persons on these occasions most disgusting. They often maintained their dance through the greater part of the night, accompanied by their voices, and the music of the flute and the drum. These amusements frequently continued for a number of days and nights successively at the same place. The upaupa was then *hui*, or closed, and they journeyed to the next district, or principal chieftain's abode, where the same train of dances, wrestlings, and pantomimic exhibitions, was repeated.

Several other gods were supposed to preside over the upaupa, as well as the two brothers who were the guardian deities of the Areois. The gods of these diversions, according to the ideas of the people, were monsters in vice, and of course patronized every evil practice perpetrated during such seasons of public festivity.

Substantial, spacious, and sometimes highly ornamented houses, were erected in several districts throughout most of the islands, principally for their accommodation, and the exhibition of their performances. The house erected for this purpose, which we saw at Tiataepuaa, was one of the best in Eimeo. Sometimes they performed in their canoes, as they approached the shore; especially if they had the king of the island, or any principal chief, on board their fleet. When one of these companies thus advanced towards the land, with their streamers floating in the wind, their drums and flutes sounding, and the Areois, attended by their chief, who acted as their prompter, appeared on a stage erected for the purpose, with their wild distortions of person, antic gestures, painted bodies, and vociferated songs, mingling with the sound of the drum and the flute, the dashing of the sea, and the rolling and breaking of the surf, on the adjacent reef; the whole must have presented a ludicrous imposing spectacle, accompanied with a confusion of sight and sound, of which it is not very easy to form an adequate idea.

The above were the principal occupations of the Areois; and in the constant repetition of these, often obscene exhibitions, they passed their lives, strolling from the habitation of one chief to that of another, or sailing among the different islands of the group. The farmers did not in general much respect them; but the chiefs, and those addicted to pleasure, held them in high estimation, furnishing them with liberal entertainment, and sparing no property to detain them. This often proved the cause of most unjust and cruel oppression to the poor cultivators. When a party of Areois arrived in a district, in order to provide daily a sumptuous entertainment for them, the chief would send his servants to the best plantations in the neighbourhood; and these grounds, without any ceremony, they plundered of whatever was fit for use. Such lawless acts of robbery were repeated every day, so long as the Areois continued in the district; and when they departed, the gardens often exhibited a scene of desolation and ruin that, but for the influence of the chiefs, would have brought fearful vengeance upon those who had occasioned it.

A number of distinct classes prevailed among the Areois, each of which was distinguished by the kind or situation of the tatauing on their bodies. The first or highest class was called *Avae parai*, painted leg; the leg being completely blackened from the foot to the knee. The second class was called *Otiore*, both arms being marked, from the fingers to the shoulders. The third class was denominated *Harotea*, both sides of the body, from the arm-pits downwards, being marked with tatau. The fourth class, called *Hua*, had only two or three small figures, impressed with the same material, on each shoulder. The fifth class, called *Atoro*, had one small stripe, tataued on the left side. Every individual in the sixth class, designated *Ohe-mara*, had a small circle marked round each ankle. The seventh class, or *Poo*, which included all who were in their noviciate, was usually denominated the *Poo faarearea*, or pleasure-making class, and by them the most laborious part of the pantomimes, dances, &c. was performed; the principal or higher orders of Areois, though plastered over with charcoal, and stained with scarlet dye, were generally careful not to exhaust themselves by physical effort, for the amusement of others.

In addition to the seven regular classes of Areois, there were a number of individuals, of both sexes, who attached themselves to the dissipated and wandering fraternity, prepared their food and their dresses, performed a variety of servile occupations, and attended them on their journeys, for the purpose of witnessing their dances, or sharing in their banquets. These were called Fauaunau, because they did not destroy their offspring, which was indispensable with the regular members.

Although addicted to every kind of licentiousness themselves, each Areoi had his own wife, who was also a member of the society; and so jealous were they in this respect, that improper conduct towards the wife of one of their own number, was sometimes punished with death. This summary and fatal punishment was not confined to their society, but was sometimes inflicted, for the same crime, among other classes of the community.

Singular as it may appear, the Areoi institution was held in the greatest repute by the chiefs and higher classes; and, monsters of iniquity as they were, the grand masters, or members of the first order, were regarded as a sort of superhuman beings: they were treated with a corresponding degree of veneration by many of the vulgar and ignorant. The fraternity was not confined to any particular rank or grade in society, but was composed of individuals from every class. But although thus accessible to all, the admission was attended with a variety of ceremonies; a protracted noviciate followed; and it was only by progressive advancement, that any were admitted to the superior distinctions.

It was imagined that those who became Areois were generally prompted or inspired to adopt this course by the gods. When any individual therefore wished to be admitted to their society, he repaired to some public exhibition, in a state of apparent *neneva*, or derangement. He generally wore a girdle of yellow plantain or *ti* leaves round his loins; his face was stained with *mati*, or scarlet dye; his brow decorated with a shade of curiously platted yellow cocoa-nut leaves; his hair perfumed with powerfully scented oil, and ornamented with a profusion of fragrant flowers. Thus arrayed, disfigured, and adorned, he rushed through the crowd assembled round the house in which the actors or dancers were performing, and, leaping into the circle, joined with seeming frantic wildness in the dance or pantomime. He continued in the midst of the performers until the exhibition closed. This was considered an indication of his desire to join their company; and if approved, he was appointed to wait, as a servant, on the principal Areois. After a considerable trial of his natural disposition, docility, and devotedness, in this occupation, if he persevered in his determination to join himself with them, he was, inaugurated with all the attendant rites and observances.

This ceremony took place at some taupiti, or other great meeting of the body, when the principal Areoi brought him forth arrayed in the *ahu haio*, a curiously stained sort of native cloth, the badge of their order, and presented him to the members who were convened in full assembly. The Areois, as such, had distinct names, and, at his introduction, the candidate received from the chief of the body, the name by which in future he was to be known among them. He was now directed, in the first instance, to murder his children; a deed of horrid barbarity, which he was in general too ready to perpetrate. He was then instructed to bend his left arm, and strike his right hand upon the bend of the left elbow, which at the same time he struck against his side, whilst he repeated the song or invocation for the occasion; of which the following is a translation.

"The mountain above, *moua tabu*,[2] sacred mountain. The floor beneath *Tamapua*,[3] projecting point of the sea. *Manunu*, of majestic or kingly bearing forehead. *Teariitarai*,[4] the splendour in the sky. I am such a one, (pronouncing his new Areoi name,) of the mountain huruhuru." He was then commanded to seize the cloth worn by the chief woman present, and by this act he completed his initiation, and became a member, or one of the seventh class.

The lowest members of the society were the principal actors in all their exhibitions, and on them chiefly devolved the labour and drudgery of

2. The conical mountain near the lake of Maeva.
3. The central district on the borders of the lake, lying at the foot of the mountain.
4. The hereditary name of the king or highest chief of Huahine.

dancing and performing, for the amusement of the spectators. The superior classes led a life of dissipation and luxurious indolence. On this account, those who were novices continued a long time in the lower class; and were only admitted to the higher order, at the discretion of the leaders or grand masters.

The advancement of an Areoi from the lower classes, took place also at some public festival, when all the members of the fraternity in the island were expected to be present. Each individual appointed to receive this high honour, attended in the full costume of the order. The ceremonies were commenced by the principal Areoi, who arose, and uttered an invocation to *Te buaa ra*, (which, I presume, must mean the sacred pig,) to the sacred company of *Tabutabuatea*, (the name of all the principal national temples) belonging to Taramanini, the chief Areoi of Raiatea. He then paused, and another exclaimed, Give us such an individual, or individuals, mentioning the names of the party nominated for the intended elevation.

When the gods had been thus required to sanction their advancement, they were taken to the temple. Here, in the presence of the gods, they were solemnly anointed, the forehead of each person being sprinkled with fragrant oil. The sacred pig, clothed or wrapped in the *haio* or cloth of the order, was next put into his hand, and offered to the god. Each individual was then declared, by the person officiating on the occasion, to be an Areoi of the order to which he was thus raised. If the pig wrapped in the sacred cloth was killed, which was sometimes done, it was buried in the temple; but if alive, its ears were ornamented with the *orooro*, or sacred braid and tassel, of cocoa-nut fibre. It was then liberated, and being regarded as sacred, or considered as belonging to the god to whom it had been offered, it was allowed to range the district uncontrolled till it died.

The artist or priest of the tatau was now employed to imprint, in his unfading marks, the distinctive badges of the rank or class to which the individuals had been raised. As this operation was attended with considerable suffering to the parties invested with these insignia of rank, it was usually deferred till the termination of the festival which followed the ceremony. This was generally furnished with an extravagant profusion: every kind of food was prepared, and large bales of native cloth were also provided, as presents to the Areois, among whom it was divided. The greatest peculiarity, however, connected with this entertainment was, that the restrictions of tabu, which prohibited females, on pain of death, from eating the flesh of the animals offered in sacrifice to the gods, were removed, and they partook, with the men, of the pigs, and other kinds of food considered sacred, which had been provided for the occasion. Music, dancing, and pantomime exhibitions, followed, and were sometimes continued for several days.

These, though the general amusements of the Areois, were not the only purposes for which they assembled. They included

'All monstrous, all prodigious things.'

And these were abominable, unutterable; in some of their meetings, they appear to have placed their invention on the rack, to discover the worst pollutions of which it was possible for man to be guilty, and to have striven to outdo each other in the most revolting practices. The mysteries of iniquity, and acts of more than bestial degradation, to which they were at times addicted, must remain in the darkness in which even they felt it sometimes expedient to conceal them. I will not do violence to my own feelings, or offend those of my readers, by details of conduct, which the mind cannot contemplate without pollution and pain. I should not have alluded to them, but for the purpose of shewing the affecting debasement, and humiliating demoralization, to which ignorance, idolatry, and the evil propensities of the human heart, when uncontrolled or unrestrained by the institutions and relations of civilized society and sacred truth, are capable of reducing mankind, even under circumstances highly favourable to the culture of virtue, purity, and happiness.

In these pastimes, in their accompanying abominations, and the often-repeated practices of the most unrelenting, murderous cruelty, these wandering Areois passed their lives, esteemed by the people as a superior order of beings, closely allied to the gods, and deriving from them direct sanction, not only for their abominations, but even for their heartless murders. Free from labour or care, they roved from island to island, supported by the chiefs and the priests; and were often feasted with provisions plundered from the industrious husbandman, whose gardens were spoiled by the hands of lawless violence, to provide their entertainments, while his own family was not infrequently deprived thereby, for a time, of the means of subsistence. Such was their life of luxurious and licentious indolence and crime. And such was the character of their delusive system of superstition, that, for them, too, was reserved the Elysium which their fabulous mythology taught them to believe, was provided in a future state of existence, for those so preeminently favoured by the gods. . . .

These are some of the principal traditions and particulars relative to this singular and demoralizing institution, which, if not confined to the Georgian and Society Islands, appears to have been patronized and carried to a greater extent there than among any other islands of the Pacific. Considering the imagined source in which it originated, the express appointment of Oro, their powerful god, the antiquity it claimed, its remarkable adaptation to the indolent habits and depraved uncontrolled passions of the people, the sanction it received here, and the prospect it presented to its members of the perpetuity, in a future state, of gratifications most congenial to those to whom they were exhibited, the Areoi institution appears a master-piece of satanic delusion and deadly infatuation, exerting an influence over the minds of an ignorant, indolent, and demoralized people, which no human power, and nothing less than a Divine agency, could counteract or destroy.

Further Reading

Ellis also wrote *Narrative of a Tour Through Hawaii, or, Owhyhee; with Remarks on the History, Traditions, Manners, Customs and Language of The Inhabitants of the Sandwich Islands* (London: H. Fisher, Son, and P. Jackson, 1826)—Robert Louis Stevenson takes issue with aspects of his travel reportage in *In the South Seas*—and a strident defense of missionary activity, titled *A Vindication of the South Sea Missions from the Misrepresentations of Otto von Kotzebue, captain in the Russian navy* (London: Frederick Westley and A. H. Davis, 1831). Alfred Gell, *Wrapping in Images: Tattooing in Polynesia* (Oxford: Clarendon Press, 1993), offers a detailed analysis of the politics of the Arioi society. Christopher Herbert, *Culture and Anomie: Ethnographic Imagination in the Nineteenth Century* (Chicago: University of Chicago Press, 1991); Rod Edmond, *Representing the South Pacific: Colonial Discourse from Cook to Gauguin* (Cambridge: Cambridge University Press, 1997), and "Translating Cultures: William Ellis and Missionary Writing," in *Science and Exploration in the Pacific: European Voyages to the Southern Oceans in the Eighteenth Century*, ed. Margarette Lincoln (Suffolk and Rochester, N.Y.: Boydell and Brewer, 1998); and Vanessa Smith, *Literary Culture and the Pacific: Nineteenth-Century Textual Encounters* (Cambridge: Cambridge University Press, 1998), include detailed discussion of *Polynesian Researches*.

JOHN WILLIAMS

Property and Providence

. . . .

JOHN WILLIAMS (1796–1839) was raised in Tottenham, north of London, and apprenticed to an ironmonger before he entered the ministry. In 1816 he was selected by the London Missionary Society to join the South Seas mission. He married Mary Chawner, a member of his church, and they departed London, arriving in Mo'orea in November 1817. They stayed for a year, learning the language, and then moved to Raiatea, where they helped establish a mission settlement with the authorization of the ruling chief, Tamatoa. A priority for Williams was the instruction of the islanders in a variety of trades and crafts: carpentering, boat-building, forging, sugar-boiling, sewing, and bonnet-making (Daws 1980, 32). On a trip to Sydney he purchased a ship of about seventy tons, called the *Endeavour*, partly from an advance that was to be paid back by the chiefs at Raiatea from the profits of trade. He had written to the directors of the London Missionary Society suggesting that they unite with representatives of the other main Protestant missionary groups—the Wesleyans and the Church Missionary Society—to explore and eventually allocate for conversion the different island groups of Polynesia. He made initial trips to the Cook Islands and Tubuai, before being forced to sell the vessel to pay off its purchase.

In 1827 Williams went to Rarotonga, where he set about building a ship with which to carry out his plan to expand missionary enterprise in the Pacific. The construction of this vessel, from local materials and using makeshift tools, is a mythologized moment both in Williams's autobiography and in contemporary and recent accounts of his life (Prout 1843; Sunderland and Buzacott 1866; Gunson 1972; Daws 1980). The ship was given an evangelical name: *The Messenger of Peace*. After a trial voyage to the island of Aitutaki, the Williamses returned in it to Raiatea. In 1830 Williams set off for Samoa, traveling via Mangaia, Niue, and Tonga. In Tongatabu, a Samoan chief, Fauea, was taken aboard, who acted as mediator upon the ship's arrival in Savaii. The extract here includes the passages in which Fauea features in Williams's *Narrative of Missionary Enterprises in the South Seas* and highlights his ambivalent role as cross-cultural informant. Fauea warned Williams that he might expect to encounter opposition from the despotic chief and high priest Tamafainga (Lei'ataua Tonumaipe'a Tamafaigā). However, on arriving off the coast of Savaii the party learned that Tamafaigā had died: Williams took this as a providential sign. They sailed on to Sapapalii, the district of Malietoa Vaiinupō, a principal chief. Gifts were exchanged, including a musket, and Malietoa expressed willingness to accept Christian teachers and adopt Christian practice as soon as he had finished engaging in war in Upolu. This war was to secure Malietoa's succession to the supreme position of *tafa'ifā* left vacant by the death of Tamafaigā. Williams made a second voyage to Samoa in 1832, consolidating his influence in the island group.

This influence was always more ambivalent than Williams allowed. His triumphalist account of the victory of the Christian word in Samoa takes little account of local agendas in shaping attitudes to imported religion. In fact, boundaries of missionary influence came to reflect preexisting political divisions between different Polynesian chiefdoms. Malietoa Vaiinupō exploited the missionaries' understanding of unified rule to instate himself in the European imagination as sole ruler preparatory to consolidating his influence in Samoa. He became the privileged Samoan recipient of European firearms and hardware, which in turn increased his prestige throughout the island. The Methodist missionary George Brown subsequently commented: "The consequence was that any chief who had a white man living with him could have a 'lotu' of his own 'just like Malietoa'" (Rev. George Brown, Mitchell Library MS 1119). Other chiefs, seeking similarly enhancing foreign connections, authorized beachcombers to act as their own "spiritual" directors, and a number of indigenous cargo cults and sailors' sects sprang up here and in other areas of Polynesia at this time, the most successful Samoan version being the cult of Siovili (Freeman 1959).

Williams and his family made a return visit to England in 1834, where he became an instant celebrity, occupying his time with public speaking, supervising the printing of Polynesian gospels and tracts, and writing his best-selling *Narrative of Missionary Enterprises*, which was published in 1837. He headed a public campaign that raised money for the purchase and outfitting of a ship, the *Camden*, and returned aboard this vessel to Upolu, where he established his new base. Late in

1839, the *Camden* departed on the first missionary expedition to Melanesia. Williams and his party of British and Polynesian teachers visited Futuna and Tanna in the New Hebrides. On November 20 they reached Erromango, where Williams crossed the beach and attempted initial communication. He and another missionary, James Harris, were killed by the islanders who had assembled to meet them, for reasons that remain as complex, though less subsequently theorized, as those that motivated the death of Cook. Williams's remains were eventually returned to Samoa and buried at Apia. He was eulogized after his death in both public and missionary presses.

Missionary Enterprises is a work of triumphalist missionary confidence. Williams displays an absolute faith in his gifts as an interpreter—of events, of symbols, and of languages, of providence and divine will. As the title implies, missionary work is for Williams a type of business venture, and property figures as a key signifier in his narratives of conversion. Objects, both European and indigenous, are appropriated to his message, often throwing up contradictions that the text does not pause to register. His willful blindness to the contradictory significations that buttress his evangelism, his desire to translate before he possesses fluency, and his overwhelming exegetical conviction are all the product of his faith in an ultimate providential design. As the extract indicates, all things great and small can be recuperated to providence. Weather conditions, local events, even murder are made sense of as divine manifestations, while European objects serve in Williams's account as the metonyms of providence—samples offered to the islanders of the good life that lies ahead of them under Christianity.

In this extract, Williams finds himself in a situation of dependence upon the local informant, Fauea, who acts as mediator and translator between himself and the Samoans. Fauea is a privileged reader, transmitting an authoritative account of an unfamiliar society. This produces a struggle for power within the narrative, as Williams attempts to compensate for his immediate cultural disadvantage by asserting the superiority of European material goods and technologies. He quotes several "testimonials" made by Fauea and other Samoans to the wonders of European clothing and property. These purported quotations can only be ventriloquized, since they record a moment when Williams is unfamiliar with the language he claims directly to transcribe (Ralston 1985, 311). His concern to emphasize a distinction between native naivety and European know-how implicates Williams in the same worship of technology that he ascribes to Samoans. By employing the witness of property, he risks implicating his spiritual message in economic politics. His concluding observations about the possible motivations for Fauea's enthusiastic support of his mission to Samoa concede this to some extent, acknowledging that local issues of prestige may have played a part in the reception of his mission. Yet Williams's confidence that dubious instruments such as Fauea can nonetheless serve evangelical purposes is further evidence of his commitment to the providential thesis. — VANESSA SMITH

. . . .

John Williams, *A Narrative of Missionary Enterprises in the South Sea Islands, with Remarks upon the Natural History of the Islands, Origin, Languages, Traditions and Usages of the Inhabitants* (London: John Snow, 1837).

« CHAPTER 17, PP. 306–7. »

A man came to us, and stated that he was a chief of the Navigators Islands; that he was related to the most influential families there; that he had been eleven years absent from his home, and was anxiously desirous of returning; and, having heard of our intention to convey the Gospel to his countrymen, he offered, if we would take him with us, to employ his utmost influence with his relatives, the chiefs, and with his countrymen generally, to induce them to receive the teachers kindly, and attend to their instructions. This we considered a most favourable incident; but, as so many represent themselves as of greater importance than they really are, we determined to inquire into the truth of his statements before we complied with his request, and desired him to come again to us on the following morning. As Tupou, the king, and others confirmed what he had said, and also informed us that his wife was a Christian, and that he, although not having made a public profession of Christianity, was frequent in his attendance on the means of grace, and decidedly friendly to the *lotu*,[1] we determined to make the best use we could of an instrument which God had thus placed at our disposal; and therefore, when he came to us the next day, we received him with respect, made him a trifling present, and informed him of our willingness to take him, with his wife and family, to his native land. He left us much delighted, and went home to prepare for his journey. His name was *Fauea*. He appeared to be an active, intelligent man, and proved to us an invaluable acquisition. During the week we were much engaged in preparing and fitting boarding nettings to our vessel, which consist of nets, three or four yards deep, made of rope about the thickness of the little finger, which are fastened to upright supporters all round the vessel, to prevent the natives from coming on board. . . .

1. A name for the new religion.

FIG. 10. *The Rev. John Williams on board ship with native implements, in the South Sea Islands.* Watercolor by Henry Anelay (c. 1838, 42.5 x 33.5 cm). By permission of the National Library of Australia.

« CHAPTER 29, PP. 324–40. »

We now again bent our course for the Navigators or Samoa Islands. Fauea, the chief, was in high spirits, from the prospect of speedily seeing his home, from which he had been so long absent; yet there appeared an expression of great anxiety in his countenance. We had not been long at sea, when he came and sat himself down by my side, and said that he had been thinking of the great work before us, and although he had no doubt but that the chiefs would gladly receive us, and the common people all readily attend to Christian instruction, yet there was a person there, called Tamafainga, and if *he* opposed us, he feared that our progress would be impeded. I asked him who this Tamafainga was; when he informed me that he was the man in whom the *spirit* of the gods dwelt; that he was the terror of all the inhabitants; and that, if he forbade it, the people universally would be afraid to place themselves under our instruction. This was rather discouraging information; we had, however no alternative but to proceed, looking to God alone for guidance, protection, and success. We glided pleasantly along for some little time, with a fair wind; but it soon became adverse, and we encountered, for forty-eight hours, a most furious storm, which rent our sails, and crippled us exceedingly. An influenza also broke out among our people, which laid aside nearly all on board; and it was not until the seventh day after leaving Lefuga, in the month of August, 1830, that the cloud-capped mountains of the beautiful Island of Savalii, which is the largest of the Navigators group, were descried. As the wind still blew furiously, and all our people were ill, we determined, if possible, to find an anchorage, and ran to the leeward side of the island for the purpose; but could not succeed. As soon, however, as we neared the shore, a number of natives came off to us in their canoes, of whom Fauea asked a variety of questions, to all of which he received satisfactory answers. At length, with a tremulous voice, as if afraid to hear the reply, he said, "And where is *Tamafainga?*" "Oh!" shouted the people, with evident delight, "He is dead, he is dead! He was killed only about ten or twelve days ago!" Frantic with joy at this unexpected intelligence, Fauea leaped about the vessel, and ran towards me, shouting, "*Ua mate le Devolo, ua mate le Devolo;*" "The devil is dead, the devil is dead! our work is done: the devil is dead!!" Astonished at this singular exclamation, I inquired what he meant? when he replied, "The obstacle we dreaded is removed: Tamafainga is dead; they have killed him: the people now will all receive the lotu." On hearing this we could not be otherwise than deeply affected with the seasonable interposition of a gracious Providence; and we were encouraged to hope that the time to favour the people, yea, the set time, was come. And here appears to me the most remarkable feature in this providence. Had this individual been put to death a month or two prior to our arrival, time would have been afforded for the chiefs of the various districts and islands to have met, and nominated a successor, who, from the nature of his office, would of necessity have opposed our designs; but as he had been killed only a few days, the time had not been sufficient to convene a meeting, and consequently there was no person in possession of that important office.

From this intercourse we were convinced that Fauea was really a chief; for his countrymen addressed him as such, the common people kissed his hands, and the chiefs saluted him by rubbing noses.

Finding ourselves sixty or eighty miles to leeward of the residence of Malietoa, the principal chief of the settlement which we intended to make our head-quarters, we had to beat against a very strong wind; and on Sabbath-day, being thoroughly exhausted, our people all ill, and our sails much torn, we determined, if possible, to find an anchorage; and, for that purpose, sailed into several bays, but without success. At length we thought we had succeeded, and dropped our anchor, hoping to enjoy a quiet night, to rest ourselves and our sick people, and after employing a day or two in repairing the damages which the vessel had sustained in the gale, to prosecute our voyage. As soon as the anchor was dropped a number of natives come off to us, bringing with them females, and articles for barter. Fauea informed them that, as ours was *e vaa lotu*, a praying ship, women would not be received; and that, as it was *le aso sa*, a sacred day, they must bring off food, and other articles for sale, in the morning. This was to them extraordinary information. Fauea, however, gave them to understand who we were, and what was the object of our visit; and having gathered them in a circle around him, on the quarter-deck of our little ship, he informed them of the number of islands which had become Christian, naming Tahiti, Rarotonga, Tongatabu, and others; and then specified some of the advantages which the inhabitants of those islands were deriving from the introduction of this new religion; —to all of which they listened with great interest, and expressed considerable pleasure at the prospect of being instructed, especially if by so doing an end would be put to their fearful wars. "Can the religion of these wonderful *papalangis*[2] be any thing but wise and good?" said our friend to his naked countrymen, who by this time had filled the deck, and who, with outstretched necks and gaping mouths, were eagerly catching the words as they fell from his lips: "Let us look at *them,* and then look at ourselves; their heads are covered, while ours are exposed to the heat of the sun and the wet of the rain; their bodies are clothed all over with beautiful cloth, while we have nothing but a bandage of leaves around our waist; they have clothes upon their very feet, while ours are like the dogs'; —and then look at their axes, their scissors, and their

2. Foreigners.

other property, how rich they are!" They all appeared to understand and appreciate this reasoning, and gazed on us with great interest and surprise. Some of them then began to examine the different parts of our dress, when, not meeting with any repulse, one pulled off my shoe. Startled at the appearance of the foot with the stocking on, he whispered to Fauea, "What extraordinary people this *papalangis* are; they have no toes as we have!" "Oh!" said our facetious friend, "did I not tell you that they had clothes upon their feet? feel them, and you will find that they have toes as well as ourselves." On finding out the secret, he was exceeding delighted, and began chattering away to his countrymen about the wonderful discovery he had made. All of them then came round us, and in a moment the other shoe was off, and both my own feet and those of my excellent brother underwent a thorough examination. . . .

By ten o'clock, we reached the settlement of Sapapalii, where we intended to commence our labours, and to which Fauea belonged. In all our conversations with that individual, we were impressed with his intelligence, shrewdness, and good sense, but never more so than on the morning we arrived at the place of our destination, when he lead us to a private part of the vessel, and requested us to desire the teachers, not to commence their labours among his countrymen by condemning their canoe races, their dances, and other amusements, to which they were much attached, lest, in the very onset, they should conceive a dislike to the religion which imposed such restraints. "Tell them," said he, "to be diligent in teaching the people, to make them *wise*, and then their hearts will be afraid, and they themselves will put away that which is evil. Let the 'Word' prevail, and get a firm hold upon them, and then we may with safety adopt measures, which at first would prove injurious." Thus we were constrained to admire the goodness of God, in providentially bringing to us an individual, whose character and connexions so admirably fitted him to advance the objects we had in view.

Our vessel was soon surrounded by canoes, and the deck crowded with natives, who were so agile, that they climbed, like monkeys, over our boarding nettings, although these were ten feet in depth. At length we welcomed on board *Tama le langi*, son of the skies, the brother of Malietoa, the principal chief of Sapapalii, and relative of Fauea. After the usual salutations, we requested Fauea to state to his relative the object of our visit, and also our wish immediately to land our people, with their wives and families, many of whom were suffering severely from long confinement in the vessel. A consultation was then held by the chiefs as to what should be done, when it was determined to send forthwith a messenger to Upolu, the seat of war, to inform Malietoa of our arrival, and to request his presence as soon as possible. It was also arranged that the teachers and Fauea should accompany Tamalelangi to the shore, and return on the following morning, if every thing was favourable, for their families and property. A canoe was accordingly despatched to Upolu for Malietoa, and the teachers accompanied his brother to the settlement. The pleasing prospect of accomplishing the object of our voyage, excited feelings of the liveliest gratitude, and we followed our friends with fervent prayer that God would graciously allow us to realize all the bright anticipations, which the occurrences of that eventful day had led us to indulge.

An interesting incident occurred in the course of the day, which gave us rather an exalted idea of the character of the people. Tamalelangi, and his brother, not knowing who we were, had brought off some pigs, bananas, and cocoa-nuts for sale; but, on seeing his relative Fauea, and on being informed of the kindness he had received from us, and the object of our visit, he ordered the pigs, with every thing in his canoes, to be arranged on the deck, and then presenting them to us, stated, that had they known us, they should not have brought off any thing for sale; and that in the morning they would bring a more abundant supply. Every canoe around the ship followed his example.

Our wishes were realized, and a full reward for all our perplexity, anxiety, and toil was granted, when, early on the following morning, the teachers returned from the shore, accompanied by the noble young chief, and about fifty canoes. They gave us the most flattering account of their reception, and seemed elated beyond measure with the prospect of success. In about two hours, the eight teachers, five women, and ten children, took their property with them, and left the vessel grateful and rejoicing. The poor heathen were as much delighted as themselves. Thus auspiciously, in the month of August, 1830, was this important Mission commenced.

As we were expecting Malietoa from Upolu, we could not accompany the teachers, but promised to come on shore, either in the evening or on the following morning. While we were engaged in lading the canoes, our attention was arrested, by observing the mountains on the opposite shore enveloped in flames and smoke; and when we inquired the cause of it, were informed, that a battle had been fought that very morning, and that the flames which we saw were consuming the houses, the plantations, and the bodies of the women, children, and infirm people who had fallen into the hands of their sanguinary conquerors. Thus, while we were landing the messengers of the Gospel of peace on the one shore, the flames of a dev-

astating war were blazing on the opposite; and under these striking circumstances, was this interesting Mission commenced.

This disastrous war was occasioned by the death of Tamafainga; for although all parties heartily rejoiced at the event, yet, as he was related to the
most influential families in the islands, they were bound, by the custom of
the country, to avenge it. Several skirmishes had already taken place, and a
general and terrible encounter was expected in a few days. It appeared that
the people of Upolu, wearied with the outrages and oppressions of this
tyrannical monster, whose rapacious grasp neither wives, daughters, nor
property escaped, who had power of life and death, and who was actually
worshipped as a god, had waylaid and murdered him.

About four o'clock in the afternoon, in a heavy shower of rain, the celebrated old chieftain Malietoa arrived. He appeared about sixty-five years
of age, stout, active, and of commanding aspect. Fauea saluted him with
the greatest possible respect, bowing sufficiently low to kiss his feet, and
making his child kiss even the soles of his feet. He was immediately invited into the cabin; and having no clothing except the girdle of ti leaves,
worn by the people generally, and being excessively cold and wet, we gave
him a large piece of Tahitian cloth in which he wrapped himself, and with
which he appeared much pleased. We then stated our object to him. With
this he professed to be highly delighted, and said that he had heard of the
lotu, and being desirous of instruction, was truly glad that we had come to
impart it. We expressed our deep regret at finding him engaged in so sanguinary a war, and inquired whether these differences could not be settled
amicably, and the dreadful contest terminated. He replied, that as a person
related to himself, and to all the principal chiefs had been killed, they must
avenge his death; and that if he left the war unfinished, and his enemies
unsubdued, he should be degraded in the estimation of his countrymen as
long as he lived; but he promised that he would take care there should be
no more war after the present; and that as soon as it was terminated he
would come and place himself under the instruction of the teachers. He
informed us, that he had met the enemy early in the morning, when an encounter ensued, in which he drove the opposing party into the mountains,
burnt their houses, and desolated their plantations, the destructive blaze of
which we had seen, while, assisted by Tamalelangi, we were landing the
Missionaries on the opposite shore. How differently were these two brothers employed at the same moment—the one with his ferocious warriors,
dealing misery and destruction upon the objects of their savage
vengeance—the other, with his delighted people, conveying to their shores,
with expressions of frantic joy, those who would teach them the principles,

and impart to them the blessings of the Gospel of peace! We advanced every argument we could command, to induce the old chieftain to make peace, but he persisted in declaring that he could not do otherwise than prosecute the war, until he had conquered his enemies. We then made him a present of two strings of large blue beads, which the natives prize above every other article, an axe, a chisel, a knife, and some Tahitian cloth, after which he took his leave, promising to come off in the morning, with his largest and best canoe, to convey us to shore. . . .

The scene which presented itself on our landing was unique, and most remarkable. The natives had kindled a large fire to serve as a beacon, and multitudes had supplied themselves with torches of dry cocoa-nut, and other leaves, to conduct us to the chief's dwelling. A passage was opened for us through the dense crowd, who were kept in order by a sort of native police, armed with spears and clubs, and stationed there for the purpose; and though we compassionated the unlucky sufferers, we were not a little amused to witness the severe blows which were occasionally dealt out by these officials, upon the thick craniums of those who transgressed their orders. In the meantime, some were busily employed in supplying the fire, some in conveying various articles from the boat, others in carrying them to our lodgings, whilst a crowd, anxious to testify their good feelings, as soon as orders were given, rushed into the water to haul up the boat. The majority, however, had enough to do to gaze upon the wonderful strangers, and for this purpose they climbed the cocoa-nut and other trees, upon the trunks and branches of which they were seen in clusters, by the red glare of the fire and the torches, peeping with glistening eyes and wondering look, from amongst the rich dark foliage which surrounded them.

In these circumstances we proceeded to pay our respects to Malietoa. Mr. Barff and myself had each a guard of honour, nor did we meet again until we arrived at the chief's residence. The natives vied with each other to show us every possible attention, some by carrying flambeaux, while others with their formidable weapons kept all intruders at a respectful distance. As we were walking along, having intimated to the young chief that I was exceedingly fatigued from labouring the whole day in the boat, he uttered something to his people, and, in an instant, a number of stout fellows seized me, some by my legs, and others by my arms, one placing his hand under my body, another, unable to obtain so large a space, poking a finger against me, and thus, sprawling at full length upon their extended arms and hands, I was carried a distance of half a mile, and deposited safely and carefully in the presence of the chief, and his principal wife, who, seated on a fine mat, received us with all the etiquette of heathen royalty. A beautiful mat having been spread for us, we squatted down upon it, and stated to his majesty, that we had not come to transact business with him then, but simply to pay our respects before we retired to rest. He expressed himself pleased to see us, gave us a cordial welcome to the shores of Savaii, and requested that we would take up our abode at his house; but, as our people were so unwell, and our stay would be short, we begged to be allowed, while we remained, to reside with them. On going from the house of Malietoa to that allotted by his brother for the residence of the teachers, we passed a dancing-house, in which a number of performers were entertaining a large company of spectators. On looking in, we observed two persons drumming on an instrument formed of a mat wound tight round a framework of reeds, and six young men, and two young women, jumping about with great violence, and making motions with their hands and feet in time with the drummers, while others contributed to the rude harmony, by singing a song in honour of the arrival of "the two great English chiefs." We saw nothing bordering upon indecency in the performance, which, however, required so much exertion, that the bodies of both the males and females were streaming with perspiration.

On arriving at the teachers' residence, we were grieved to find most of them suffering from influenza. Two of these we bled, and administered to others such medicines as we thought would afford them relief. They were delighted with the treatment they had received from the people generally, and with the circumstance that although their property had been distributed in many different canoes, and conveyed from them by various hands, not a single article was missing. At first, indeed, the teachers had endured considerable apprehension about their children, some of whom were not brought to them until several hours after their arrival. Upon inquiry, however, they found, that those natives who had been so fortunate as to obtain a child to bring on shore, instead of carrying it direct to it[s] parents, first took it to their own residence, killed a pig, prepared an oven of food, gave the child a thorough good "feeding" of the best they could procure, and having kept it as long as they dared, they brought it to the anxious parents. All this was most delightful intelligence, and our hearts must have been insensible indeed, if it had not excited feelings of the liveliest gratitude. . . .

« CHAPTER 20, PP. 353–66. »

. . . Having thus given a brief and hasty account of the principal events which occurred during our first voyage to the Navigators or Samoa Islands, it may neither be uninteresting nor unprofitable to pause, and erect an Ebenezer of praise to that God who protected our lives, directed our course, and opened before us so "great and effectual a door:" thus permitting us to realize more than the full accomplishment of our most sanguine expectations! We scarcely expected to secure any more than a safe and peaceable settlement for our teachers; and even that had not been obtained on the first visit at any other islands where Missionaries had been previously established. In some places, indeed, the teachers landed at the peril of their lives; and in almost all the Hervey Islands, they were plundered and ill used; while here, they were welcomed with open arms, both by chiefs and people, who vied with each other in expressions of kindness and delight! Instead of losing their property, four excellent dwellings were given to them, and the very best and largest house in the settlement was set apart for public worship and instruction. In addition to this, we ourselves were permitted to land in safety, and to live amongst the people, not only without molestation and dread, but distinguished by every mark of their attention and respect, and importuned by neighbouring chiefs to furnish them also with Missionaries. Thus auspiciously was this interesting and important Mission commenced, through the merciful interposition of an overruling Providence, who is pleased to make use of human instrumentality in accomplishing his mightiest works. No doubt much of this success was attributable, under God, to Fauea, with whom we met so providentially, and who was so admirably adapted to further our important embassy. His relationship to the principal chiefs was a circumstance of no small moment, for it was almost certain that had we not met with him, we should not have gone to the place we did, and of course should not have known Malietoa. He was a man of great decision, and not easily diverted from his purpose. Having once expressed my fear lest Malietoa and his countrymen should not receive the teachers, he replied: "If they do not receive them kindly and treat them well, I will go to a strange land and die there." Fauea also possessed such soundness of judgement and fluency of speech as would rivet the attention of listening multitudes for hours together, and always secure him the victory in a dispute. After reaching his home, he and his wife were constantly engaged in describing the triumphs of the Gospel at Tongatabu, where Tupou, the greatest chief in the island, had embraced it, and at the Haapai Islands, where all the people had become Christians. Facts, so well attested and so forcibly described, had immense weight with the natives. Of this we had an interesting proof. When they were told by him, that those who had embraced this religion, could communicate their thoughts to each other at a distance, and while residing even at a remote island, they flocked to the teachers' houses to learn this mysterious art, many of them coming eight or ten times each day, to be taught their letters.

We considered that Fauea's wife possessed more principle than her husband, who was an ambitious and aspiring man, and evidently promoted our designs, chiefly on account of the temporal advantages which would result from the introduction of Christianity among his people. He had also penetration enough to see that his family would be raised in the estimation of his countrymen, by forming an intimacy with *English chiefs*; and that his name would be transmitted to posterity as the person who conducted the Missionaries to their islands. But whatever his motives and character might have been, his zealous and unceasing endeavours eminently forwarded our designs. All these circumstances considered, we cannot but conclude, that, in first going to Tongatabu, we were led by an unerring hand, and that our meeting unexpectedly with such an efficient assistant as Fauea, was a remarkable and interesting intimation of Providence that the set time for God to accomplish his purposes of mercy to the Samoa islands was come.

Further Reading

Richard M. Moyle, ed., *The Samoan Journals of John Williams, 1830 and 1832*, (Canberra: Australian National University Press, 1984), provides a less edited version of Williams's Samoan encounters. Ebenezer Prout's early, hagiographic biography, *Memoirs of the Life of the Rev. John Williams* (London: John Snow, 1843), and the more recent and critical biographical portrait in Gavan Daws, *A Dream of Islands: Voyages of Self-Discovery in the South Seas* (New York and London: W. W. Norton, 1980), both offer insights into Williams's life and character. Background to his missionary enterprise can be found in Niel Gunson, *Messengers of Grace: Evangelical Missionaries in the South Seas, 1797–1860* (Melbourne: Oxford University Press, 1978). Gunson discusses the building of the *Messenger of Peace* in "John Williams and His Ship: The Bourgeois Aspirations of a Missionary Family," in *Questioning the Past: A Selection of Papers in History and Government*, ed. D. P. Crook (Brisbane: University of Queensland Press, 1972). The Samoan political background to Williams's missionary encounter is set out in R. P. Gilson, *Samoa 1830 to 1900: The Politics of a Multi-cultural Community* (Melbourne: Oxford University Press, 1970). Recent discussions of Williams's role include Christopher Herbert, *Culture and Anomie: Ethno-*

graphic Imagination in the Nineteenth Century (Chicago: University of Chicago Press, 1991); Rod Edmond, *Representing the South Pacific: Colonial Discourse from Cook to Gauguin* (Cambridge: Cambridge University Press, 1997); and Vanessa Smith, *Literary Culture and the Pacific: Nineteenth-Century Textual Encounters* (Cambridge: Cambridge University Press, 1998).

19

DAVID DARLING

Tapu *and Conceit in the Marquesas*

· ·

IN MOST PARTS OF POLYNESIA, the efforts of the London Missionary Society paid off in mass conversions sooner or later. In the Marquesas Islands, repeated efforts failed. In 1797–99, William Pascoe Crook had done well to preserve himself; later, he and David Darling both tried to introduce indigenous Tahitian teachers, who soon abandoned their activities. The most sustained attempt involved Darling and two younger missionaries, John Rodgerson and George Stallworthy, who arrived at Vaitahu, a harbor of frequent resort on the island of Tahuata, late in 1834. Darling was to remain for a year to help establish the station; he did so and was then glad to leave; Rodgerson and his wife left in 1837; Stallworthy remained until 1841.

Darling's discomfort at Vaitahu had a number of causes. He considered himself the senior member of the group and resented Mrs. Rodgerson's expectation that he would contribute to domestic tasks, which he felt intruded into the precious time that he could dedicate to more important matters such as linguistic inquiries. Although Darling was certainly a committed missionary, it is difficult to avoid reading his journal without a sense that his pessimism concerning the prospects for the Marquesan mission led him to indulge an enthusiasm for ethnological and linguistic inquiry: as time passed, his diary reports steadily more numerous and more extensive inquiries into Marquesan traditions, rituals, and customs. The "Remarks about the Marquesas Islands" appended to his journal, and presumably composed on his return to Tahiti, convey something of the variety and specificity of his observations, albeit here presented synthetically and shorn of the circumstances that gave rise to his generalities.

Darling may have known something of the Marquesan beliefs and practices around *tapu* from Crook and would have understood something of the cognate notions in the Society Islands (where he had worked since 1817). At any rate his passage on a dimension of Polynesian culture that Europeans found consistently unintelligible is exemplary. Darling appreciated that *tapu* was not simply "taboo," that it involved much more than proscription. Some combination of sacredness and separateness was evidently vital, that was bewilderingly various in its application: some things and people were sometimes *tapu*, others were always *tapu;* in some cases proscriptions were reciprocal (men did not wear women's cloth, women did not wear men's), in other cases they were not (men could smoke tobacco obtained by women, women could not smoke that obtained by men); *tapu* might be applied to places, activities, times, people, and objects. Admittedly Darling does not appear to have grasped the underlying principles of the "system" (which cannot be reconstructed today to a degree that fully accounts for the complexities of reported practice). Essentially, activities connected with any sort of growth, production, or life-giving activity entailed the presence of deities, and a condition of contagious sacredness, that had to be contained or separated from those persons less sacred. If Darling's account is no clearer or more complete than those of most previous and subsequent commentators, it can also be said to fail in a more positive sense, in that he is unable to impose a simple evangelical condemnation of the "system." Though missionaries were generally in the business of documenting indigenous religion in order to lampoon and subvert it, Darling like many others said too much rather than too little. His description partially sustains the thesis that *tapu* is a contrivance of men in the interest of men, but what he records makes it plain that the notions and usages cannot be reduced to an instrument of female denigration.

Darling finds that the real obstacle to the mission's progress is the "conceit" of the Marquesans, their sense that their own order of things was preferable to any possible alternative. The fact that such chauvinism might be manifest is an extraordinary testament to local resilience, given the very considerable depopulation that had taken place over the decades prior to Darling's sojourn. What is most troubling, for him, is not the fact that the Marquesans do not appear to be likely to adopt Christianity, but the evident point that they would do so for sufficient property: the Marquesans only needed to be convinced that religion was as authentic as a musket. — NICHOLAS THOMAS

. . . .

David Darling, *Remarks about the Marquesas, September 1835*. London Missionary Society, South Seas Journals, Council for World Mission Archive, School of Oriental and African Studies, London.

The Marquesans have no regular forms of worship amongst them; they have gods many and lords many, but they pay them no manner of worship in a regular way. They believe in one god called *Tiki* who made man and the dry land as they say—but there are an endless variety of gods as they call them, who are said to be the fathers from whom all things come, who produced all things that exist. There is a different being or god who presides over every different thing; such as *Atea* and *Atanua* are over the sea; Tonofiti is the god of Havaii or the invisible world; *Tu* is the god of war; *Tikoke* of the *koinas* or feasts; *Tea* the god of the sun, and Kupenu of the moon. Tamatua or *Momea* causes the breadfruit to grow. The principal *vanana* or worship is paid to the god of the breadfruit; and in consequence (as they say) of their praying to the god of the *Mei* or breadfruit it grows.

Every valley has a different god which the people [of] that valley believe in. The god sometimes used to come and take up his abode in the bodies of men: then these men were considered as gods, and all the *Heanas* or men killed in war were taken to them to be presented to the god. Sometimes the god was seen to depart from one place to another when he was offended on any account; it was only those that were *Tauâ Etuas* that went up into the heavens at death, then they became gods; all other persons went down to *Hav[a]ii* at death. *Havaii* is the Hades or invisible state of the dead. The Marquesans have many traditions about *Havaii*; the door to it (they say) is down through the sea a little way beyond Ohivahoa, and that the splash of the sea can be seen when a spirit descends. In Havaii there are different rooms or fields called little hills, where the dead reside in different companies according to the manner of their deaths, and their standing in this life; such as all that are killed in war by a shot from a musket live together; all that die through falling from rocks are living together, and all that die of disease of the same kind go together; those that have much property given and put with them at their death obtain an inside residence; whilst those that are poor and have no friends to give property with them are left out side of the palaces in *Havaii*.

The Marquesans have no idea of any state of punishment whatever after death. They have no knowledge of a Resurrection, no idea of a body coming to life again after it dies in this world, nor will the[y] believe any thing about a resurrection at present. [I]t is not easy however to get a correct account of their belief in this respect as different parties tell different stories about the nature of their faith respecting the existence of departed spirits, this is the most correct that I could obtain.

The *Tapu* System

This is Satan's strong hold in all the Marquesan islands almost every thing has a *tapu* attached to it less or more. The Tapu is the making of a thing or person sacred, or separating them from another thing or person, a prohibition, the breaking of which is often punished with death, but sometimes only with disease according to the natives account.

The *Tapus* are connected almost with every thing they do: sometimes they are only for a time and then removed, other *Tapus* are continual, such as sacred places called *taha tapu*, the women are never allowed to go on sacred ground or enter a sacred house called *fae tapu*. Tapus are attached to persons, to food, to times, and to things. Many persons are *tapu* made so on particular occasions, some few are always so:—these *tapus* allow the men to do what the women are not allowed to do; and to go where women cannot or at least dare not go; there is a great deal of ceremony about the food at the Marquesas, many kinds the women are not allowed to touch, the men alone can eat it, other kinds are eaten by both sexes, sometimes together and at other times separately: even in the making of the *Maa* or sour breadfruit the men have pits in many instances different from the women in which they keep their food.

All the Koinas or ceremonies at feasts are all attended with *tapus* of different kinds, and lasts for days, and sometimes for weeks together, at these times the men are very strick [*sic*] in the observance of the *tapu*, they never go to their own homes all the time the *tapu* lasts, and they keep themselves from their wives. Some *tapus* are on account of rank, and some are from a kind of sacredness with reference to the gods; there are *tapus* also which to the time a child is born; and to different periods of life, and also some at the time of death.

Almost all things have *tapu* about them: such as the building of a house; the learning of a song or tradition; the getting of the body tatood or marked with the *tatau* &c. The fire that cooks the mens food must not be taken to light the fire with for cooking the womens food; the men may eat the womens food, but the women must not eat that which belongs to the men, or that which is cooked or beat up by the men; the [men] may smoke tobacco that is got by the women, but the women may not smoke that which belongs to the men or is got by them. The women must not wear any of the cloth that has been worn as under garments by the men. The men never wear any belonging to the women; the men are so particular in this respect that they always burn all their old rags in case the women should get hold of them and wear them, they think they would then be overtaken with disease.

The Marquesans never killed their children as the Tahitians used to do. Infanticide was never practised among them; they are very fond of their children; it is a very general custom with them to adopt the children of others as their own, and bring them up as such. It is said that formerly persons never died of disease, all that died except of old age, either died in war or by the sorcery called *Kaha*: all the diseases that now take off both young and old have been introduced by vessels that have touched at the islands at different times, and are now very extensive on all the islands. Death by the *kaha* was very common, and was performed in several ways, but death was almost always certain, and was accompanied with very great pain. It is affirmed that by getting hold of the spittle, or something that belonged to a person, the sorcerers could so work with that something that the object of their wrath would soon be dead. Such was Satan's power among these people.

The Marquesas islands produce nearly the same kinds of food as the Society Islands do: the breadfruit is of a very fine quality, and grows very large; it is taken great care of, and is regularly made into *Maa*, that is sour paste; in this state it keeps in the pits as long as they please: the mountain plantains are not so numerous as they are at Tahiti; but cocoa-nuts, Bananas, and most other kinds of food are plentiful; there are no reefs round any of the islands; all round is a bold rocky shore, and there is no low land excepting in the vallies, in some of these there is a sandy beach, but generally a great surf lashing on the shore. The people all live in the vallies; there is nothing but barren and bare ridges of hills between most of the vallies, which run from the higher mountains to the shore, and ends in high bluff rocks.

The Marquesans are very idle, they care very little for anything besides muskets and powder, they will hardly work for anything else, excepting tobacco which is in great demand of late years; they sleep all the middle of the day, and are awake most of the night; they do not allow the sun to shine much upon them; and often carry a large *Vahana* leaf over their heads, both men and women; they are also excessively fond of anointing themselves with Turmeric mixed with a kind of oil, it cleans and whitens their skin. The Marquesans are also somewhat different in their manner of living from the Tahitians; they in general roast their breadfruit instead of baking it in an oven, when it is done they break it up in a round wooden dish in cold water, and all that are to partake sit around the dish and take it out with their hands in mouthfuls at a time, and bolt it down without any ceremony. The Tahitians spread a table with leaves on the floor and everyone takes his own breadfruit. When the breadfruit is out of season at the Marquesas they cook large ovens of sour breadfruit, what is called *Maa*, and keep it for a week in this cooked state, mixing and beating it up as the[y] want it in their wooden dishes for use; of this kind of food their is never any scarcity; they use it until the season of breadfruit returns, and what is left remains in the pits, and the new *Maa* is put on the top of the old, thus it keeps for many years.

The Marquesan houses are of a particular form; they are more like half houses than anything else; the back side is nearly perpendicular and the front side only is of a roof pitch; they are in general covered with *au mei*, that is the leaves of the breadfruit tree; some of the chiefs houses are covered in the front side with what is called the leaf of the Vahana tree, which grows somewhat like the cocoa nut tree; there is very little of the [?] to be got, such as they make the thatch of at Tahiti. The inside of the houses is very different from the Tahitian houses; the Marquesan houses in general are not more that 8 or 9 feet wide; four feet is left along the back side for a sleeping place, there is a kind of pillow laid from one end to the other close to the back of the house, the remaining 4 or 5 feet toward the front side is paved with large smooth stones, in the place that is not paved there is a mat for sleeping on; their bodies lay on the mat, but their legs and feet on the pavement, they sleep in a row all along from one end to the other both sexes.

The dress of the Marquesans is peculiar, the men are dressed in general when they have a clean *hami* or girdle with the ends behind and before hanging down to the ground, and a *Tahû* or fan in their hands, and a head dress of hair, feathers, or shells on their heads; and a long string of whales teeth either cut up or whole around their necks; the beards of the old men are in general left to grow long and the hair of the head is all cut off excepting two tuffs that are left and tied up like two horns on the top of the head; the men are very fond of letting their beards grow long in order to leave the hair as a Legacy to the children or grand children. The long white hair of the beard of an old man is thought much off, a musket is the price of it when it is sold: it is worn as an ornament on the head at all the *koinas* or on feast days: the bodies and legs of the men are left all bare and anointed with the turmeric and oil until they shine again. The women dress differently: they have an under garment round them like a petticoat and a large white cloth over their shoulders which covers all their body so that no part of their skin can be seen but their feet and head. They have a very fine white cloth like gauze which they put round their heads in the form of a cap called *pae*; with this they cover and [?] up their hair which is always long in different forms according to the taste or fancy of the individuals. The women also wear the ornaments of hair feathers and shells round their heads and the whales teeth round their necks when they go to look at the *Koinas*. The *koina* are performed at the place of public resort called the Tohua which is in every district. At these *koinas* there are in general three drums in the centre of the Tohua which is a square place fitted up with stones for the men to sit on and large stones set for them to place their backs against, the women are never allowed to go within this square; when they perform the men sit all round and the drums in the middle are beat with the hands not with sticks: all the men then chant or sing in a humming tone and clap their hands with great spirit for hours together. One man or two sometimes dance about dressed all over, head, arms and legs with hair tied in tuffs their dancing is nothing or less than a wild jumping and leaping about: the women sit out side of the square and look on; sometimes they join among themselves in chanting humming and clapping their hands. These songs are in general Traditions or something respecting their families, or lands, or old customs. Some koinas are performed on some special occasions, some are for obtaining property, and others only for pastime, young and old all attend these *koinas* or Marquesan plays.

There are two classes of players who perform at the *koinas*; one class are called *kaiois* who perform on all occasions at home or in the neighbouring districts; the other class is called *Hoki*, they are a select party who go about to others islands or districts on purpose to perform in order to collect property from the places where the[y] act their plays; they are something different from the *Arioi* who existed at Tahiti formerly; they do not keep up any order of persons for the purpose, but only select a number at the time they determine to [on] these excursions; the greater part of their time is spent in this way about these *koinas* as they are called.

The chiefs at the Marquesas do not seem to have much power, farther than over their own dependants, such as their own families and a few others who hold their land under them; in each valley are three, four, five or more chiefs of equal power and authority; most of the people are masters of their own land and seem to pay no regular acknowledgment to their chiefs, as they do at Tahiti. The chiefs often feast together, and the[y] call themselves by the name of *Huepo* that is those that have their faces black all over with the *tatooing*, they are those that fight most in the wars, being the *aitos* as the[y] are termed they are sought after by the principal chiefs as their associates at all times.

One of the most filthy and disgusting things to be seen among them is a custom they have of taking [?] the vermin out of each others heads, and giving them to the person from whose head they come who eats them; they say that as they have been biting them they must eat them, this is the general reason that is given for this filthy practice; this was also done at other islands formerly to a great extent.

Wars

The wars at the Marquesas are frequent, and seem to arise out of the state of the islands; as on each of the islands there are two parties, there are a certain number of vallies that are on friendly terms with each other and form a party the remaining vallies join together and are friendly, thus forming two different parties always at variance with each other on each island; this is the present state on all the islands; those that are friendly together visit each other, but if any of the other party should happen to come amongst them they are seized and in general killed and eaten this always causes a fresh war, which continues until some are killed on both sides; then a peace is made for a while, but a lasting union never takes place; whenever some fresh crime is committed by either party then they go to war again. Sometimes there are two different parties in the same valley and they often fight against each other. On the island of Tahuata one of the two parties have been brought under and are in a measure subject to the other, as most of the old warriors have died and as Iotete the present chief of Vaitahu has influence amongst both parties, which is one principal reason why there has been no wars for years back on that island when *Tetupa* was alive the great cannibal chief of the party that used to be opposed to Vaitahu party and used to fight with them.

Iotete is in general for peace, and dislikes war very much; he never was known to indulge in devouring his enemies, as most of the other chiefs of the other islands do. Tetupa who belonged to the opposition party on Tahuata, who is now dead, used to eat and devour all the enemy's party that he could get hold off.

The first person slain in war is called *Heana*, and was taken to the *Taha Tapu*, the place where it is said the gods reside, and is taken there by some one of a few old priests or sacred persons that remain, these places are in each valley and are said to be some where up at the [foot] of the mountains, but the common people never attempt to go near it; they believe that the power of the gods would destroy them as they went near the place, no one they say ever came back again that attempted to go; there are a certain class that are Tapu for the purpose of going to the place, but the[y] seldom or never go now; all respect for the gods seems to be lost sight of only as far as it serves the purposes of the men in keeping the women in a kind of low degraded state.

The Language at the Marquesas differs very much from the Tahitian although it is a dialect of the same language; there are many words nearly the same; they discard some letters such as the *r* which the Tahitians use very frequently and adopt others which is not at all used by the Tahitians; like the [Tahitians] they put the substantive before the adjective; as *enata meitai* a good man, but the[y] also put the substantive before the verb, which the Tahitians seldom or never do; a Tahitian would say:

Tahitian   { e hoo te buaa
              { buy the pig
Marquesan   { te buaka e hoo
              { the pig buy
Tahitian   { E Bure i te Etua
              { pray to God
Marquesan   { i te Etua e Bue
              { to God pray
Marquesan   { i te vai kaukau
              { in the water wash
Tahitian   { e hopu i te vai or papa
              { wash in the water

and so on in a great number of peculiarities of construction: also in the application of the pronouns and prepositions which are mostly different from the Tahitian.

Many words are used differently at the different islands in the Windward and Leeward groups of the Marquesas.

The Marquesan dialect is not so soft a Language as the Tahitian, there being a much more frequent use of the consonants, especially of the letter *k* which is not in the Tahitian. It has the same peculiarity as the Tahitian in never allowing two consonants to come together, nor a syllable to end without a vowel; it is copious, and you can convey your ideas very direct; it is also figurative, the natives are fond of using comparisons, there is no difficulty in making known the Gospel in it, yet it is barren of course of some very essential words necessary to be used in preaching the word of God which must be supplied.

One great difficulty to be contended with is the conceit the people seem to have of their own system as being better than any thing else that can be taught them, and it is only from a difference of property and appearance which foreigners make amongst them, which makes them think that their circumstances are better not because they think at present that the word of God which been taken to them is better than their former faith of things; many of them might be brought over to do any thing, or to adopt almost any system of things, for certain kinds of property they would do so just to please, and in order to get the property.

The Marquesans think themselves perfectly safe at death, they have no fear of any punishment after death; they do believe that they have souls and that is all, they do not seem to care any thing about them, so that they can get what the body requires. Whilst I was at Vaitahu I was often astonished to witness the indifference which they manifested to all spiritual things, whilst at the same time they confessed that they believed them to be true. All this proves the truth of the word of God, that all men are dead in trespasses and sins; and that nothing but the word of God applied by the Spirit of God can enlighten the minds of dead sinners.

This ought to excite all the friends of Missionaries, and Missionaries themselves, to be more and more fervent at a throne of Grace for the out pouring of the Holy Spirit of God upon the labours of all the Missionaries that have gone or that may go forth among the heathens; God must work [in?] them and by them or the work will not be done. The harvest truly *is* great but the labourers *are* few; pray ye therefore the Lord of the harvest that he would send forth labourers into his harvest.[1]

The above Journal is what was written down every day whilst I resided at the island of Tahuata, relating simple occurrences as they took place. The Remarks which I have made are all founded upon facts, that came under my own observation, and inquiries.

David Darling
Missionary
Tahiti.

To the Directors
    of the London
    Missionary Society
    London

(copied out January 1836)

1. Luke X. 2.

Further Reading

On the background to London Missionary Society activity in Tahiti, see Niel Gunson, *Messengers of Grace* (Melbourne: Oxford University Press, 1978); for the Marquesas in the period and the missionary efforts, see Greg Dening, *Islands and Beaches* (Melbourne: Melbourne University Press, and Honolulu: University of Hawaii Press, 1980); and Nicholas Thomas, *Marquesan Societies* (Oxford: Oxford University Press, 1990).

ABBY JANE MORRELL

Philanthropic Sympathy and the Interests of Commerce

. . . .

ABBY JANE WOOD was born into a New York maritime family in 1809 and married her cousin Benjamin Morrell in 1824. Her husband had at this stage already completed the first of his trading voyages to the Pacific Ocean. In the early years of their marriage he embarked on two further voyages while his bride remained at home and bore him a son. It appeared that Abby had consigned herself to the life of a sailor's wife, a circumscribed sentimental narrative predicated upon waiting for her husband's returns with, in her case, an intense erotic anticipation: "for many nights my dreams were of him, on a boundless ocean, tossed by storms or engulfed in the deep. To these gradually succeeded dreams of his being wrecked on desolate islands, and subject to all the violence of savage men" (A. J. Morrell 1833, 16). When he embarked upon his fourth voyage in 1829, however, she broke this pattern and insisted on accompanying him on a two-year journey that took them throughout the Pacific in search of seal skins, bêche-de-mer, and other luxury commodities. In order to travel she had to leave her infant son in the care of her mother, thereby risking being perceived as an unnatural parent, whose ties with her husband even outweighed the bond with her offspring.

Her account of the journey labors to deflect this charge in contradictory fashion, on the one hand by emphasizing her newlywed, girlish status, and on the other hand by finding alternative objects for her maternal sympathy: the unregenerate seaman and the heathen savage. Her text is proffered as a feminine version of and supplement to her husband's narrative of his four voyages, which was written after her own account but published in the preceding year. Benjamin Morrell makes empirical claims for his narrative: he is "the discoverer of countries the very existence of which was before unknown to the civilized world"; writing is the mere medium by which he performs the task "of increasing [the] stock of geographical knowledge, and adding much to the accumulated treasures of cosmographical science" (B. Morrell 1832, ix). Abby Morrell's apologetic self-presentation, on the other hand, "as I have seen much and suffered much, I have been advised to give my narrative to my friends through the press, hoping it might afford some amusement to them as well as profit to myself" (A. J. Morrell 1833, 13), conforms to what Deirdre Coleman describes as "the convention of the essentially private, financially [motivated], and reluctant woman writer" (Coleman 1999, 4). Yet her narrative is not without its own sphere of purpose. Abby initially justifies her presence within the masculine world of the ship and the subsequent publication of her story by becoming an advocate of the sailor, a role that she equates with the infantile rather than the maternal, depicting herself, somewhat absurdly, as the lisping spokeschild of maritime welfare:

> It has been said, that when Napoleon was brooding over his disasters no one dared approach him but a pet child, who played around him and induced him to take nourishment and repose. Let the public therefore consider me in the capacity of the child; and if there be any force in my suggestions they will go for what they are worth; if there be none, why they will pass off with a smile. (A. J. Morrell 1833, vii–viii)

At the conclusion of the volume she reaches a feminine philanthropic maturity, figuring as the universalized bride of the ocean, "wedded to the seas as much as the Chief of Venice was wedded to the Adriatic" and, by embracing the cause of the heathen native, claiming sisterhood with conservative and sentimentalist female intellectuals such as "Hannah More, Miss Edgeworth, Mrs Hemans,—and our own countrywomen, Mrs Sigourney and Miss Sedgwick" (A. J. Morrell 1833, 226).

Abby's feminine presence on board the trading ship serves the further purpose of reconciling commerce with sympathy, two potentially conflicting terms that have already achieved synthesis within her marriage. She is represented, in both her own and her husband's accounts, as a softening and feminizing influence on the shipboard world. Benjamin writes, "I found my own mental temperament much improved by the influence of her society; her sweetly smiling vivacity and exuberance of spirits operated on my own feelings like a charm," and he depicts her as busy with a range of appropriate feminine tasks: "I was now very much amused with the curiosity, vivacity, and activity of my wife, who was almost constantly on deck, with her drawing apparatus, sketching different views of the islands as we passed them; . . . she flitted about the vessel like some ethereal form from a higher sphere" (B. Morrell 1832, 418). Within her narrative, Abby deploys a variety of current literary discourses from the sublime to the sentimental to ameliorate and dignify a fairly brutal story of commercial gain. Her disquisitions on taste in this extract, buoyed by quotations from Gay's urban georgic "Trivia" and Thomas Moore's orientalist epic "The Fire-Worshippers," play out late eighteenth-century debates about the relationship between luxury and corruption. In this context, the limitations of Benjamin Morrell's nominating imperative are shown up with comic effect: whether he figures as a heavy-handed second Crusoe, christening the kidnapped natives "Sunday and Monday," or as a politic designator of new landscapes: "My husband named this promontory Woodbury's Cape, in honour of the then Chairman of Naval Affairs in Congress, now Secretary of the Navy of the United States"; his terminology offers a bathetic contrast to Abby's purple diction.

In justifying the commercial project of her voyage, Abby Morrell employs a pseudo-scientific and ethnographic language whose effect borders on the parodic. Her lengthy discussion of the origins of amber, for instance, confuses two substances with purely etymological kinship: amber and ambergris. In listing the natural productions of each location she visits, she develops a conventional account of the Pacific island as a site of luxuriant natural abundance into a catalog of commodities for an expanding global market. Her husband's activities clearly involve plunder rather than trade: they are referred to in her narrative simply as "collecting." While her thesis is the advancement of civilization through commercial venture, her meditation on the bird of paradise threatens to undermine the Enlightenment telos of her argument by introducing notions of a Romantic idyll inevitably destroyed by progress. Yet this very instability of reference also introduces complexity into her discussion of the Melanesian people she encounters on the voyage. In a period where the concern to classify and heirarchize Melanesian and Polynesian islanders dominated discussion of the region, and only a year after Dumont D'Urville had attempted definitively to categorize Melanesians as darker, less socialized, and more intellectually degraded versions of their Polynesian counterparts (D'Urville 1832), Morrell, viewing Melanesian cultures through the lens of commerce, relativizes canons of taste and pays tribute to the physical attractiveness of Melanesian people, the strength of their family ties, and the complexity of their art. — VANESSA SMITH

. . . .

Abby Jane Morrell, *Narrative of a Voyage to the Ethiopic and South Atlantic Ocean, Indian Ocean, Chinese Sea, North and South Pacific Ocean, in the Years 1829, 1830, 1831* (New York: J. and J. Harper, 1833).

« CHAPTER 4, PP. 73–86. »

We now shaped our course for New-Ireland, and continued our way through St George's Channel, which is formed by the west side of New-Ireland and the east side of New-Britain. This channel is safe, or it seemed so to us at least, and has been described as one of the most beautiful on the globe; and I think it is. The hills on each side are lofty, and the descent to the sea is gentle and regular. The forests are of the most massy growth, and greatly diversified by various kinds of trees, intermingled with luxuriant flowers and fruit trees. The air, as you sail along in a fine day, is aromatic with the nutmeg and other spicy groves. These islands are said to be not only abounding in the productions of nature, but capable of raising almost every thing in the known world. The biche-de-mer, hawksbill tortoise-shell, red coral, ambergris, and no doubt many other things, are found here, such as pearl-shell and sandal-wood; for it seems to be law of nature, that where she shows her kindnesses she outpours them in great abundance. The natives visited us, bringing plenty of fruits and fowls, which we purchased for a few pieces of iron hoops and some trinkets. Few people that I have seen are better formed than these islanders; they are dark, stout built, and are susceptible of becoming the most civilized in the Eastern world, I should think. In the course of the day we had ample opportunity to form an opinion of them; and after a short time one gets into a habit of forming more correct opinions in an hour than could be made up in a day, when first launched into a world of wonders.

We landed on New-Britain, and found a great variety of birds, some of beautiful plumage, and others of most melodious notes. Hogs and dogs are also found here, and are plentiful to a great extent. The fish are remarkably fine around the island. In fine, these people seemed to me to be the happiest of all the race of wild men I had ever seen. It is amusing to think how soon we become enamoured with the thought of natural society, and in moments of contemplation wish to be found among people of a primitive cast. The thousand evils of social life crowd upon us when we look at these forests and their inhabitants; there is no vulgar wretchedness, as seen in crowded cities—no squalid diseases; there is nothing of aristocratic contumely, and the laws of nature are only slightly regulated by convention or necessity.

From here we sailed to examine the north cape of New-Britain. We were visited by the inhabitants, who seemed of a much more savage nature than those of New-Ireland. The shores are surrounded with coral reefs, about eight or ten miles from them. Arrowsmith's charts, my husband said, were pretty correct; but he regretted very much that he could not spare time to give a more correct one. It is wonderful to me that they are so correct as we find them, so little time could be bestowed upon the subject. We continued to keep near the shore for some time, having now and then a little difficulty with the natives; for they thought our vessel so small that a crew of one or two canoes would take her with ease; we had only to splash the water about them, however, with a cannon shot or two, to make them keep at a fearful distance. There is something terrible to a savage ear in the sound of big guns, and I know not whose ear ever gets familiar to the roar of a full-mouthed battery. I must confess, though I thought myself quite brave, that I always trembled a little to hear a great gun fired, and to feel the tremulous motion of the ship at its recoil. Fortunately we were not obliged to sacrifice any of the natives for our safety, as we could get along without proceeding to such extremities. Half the blood that has been spilt in the world might have been avoided by prudence and moral reflection. The natives often act from ignorance, and a natural love of gain or power; and the civilized man turns his rage upon the poor wretches, as if they were as able to reason as an enlightened European. If we had a hold on their affections, I have no doubt that we should find them strong and permanent; for they have but few conventional reasons to break in upon a course of nature, and as far as I have watched the operations of nature, the savage loves his offspring as much as civilized man. But it is in vain to moralize, for this will not change habits, manners, or morals. Oh! for that blessed day when civilization, attended by all the Christian virtues, shall reach the isles of the sea, and make glad all the nations of the earth. I am no enthusiast; but when I see what has been done at New-Zealand, I do not despair, in my time, of hearing that these very places I have attempted faintly to describe have felt the benign influences of our holy religion.

We crossed the straits, and came close under the northern shore of an island, which lies nearly in the centre of the strait. It is of some size and my husband called it Dampier's Island, in honour of the discoverer of it. The natives came off to see us, and were very cautious; but by coaxing them with the show of trinkets, we got them alongside. While with us, they discovered more than ordinary curiosity, for savages; they examined every thing about the vessel, were curious to know the uses of the chain cables and anchors, the great guns, and every thing on board. They offered us various articles, which we purchased, such as fishing gear, spears, war clubs, and pearl-shells; as also some of their household implements, such as knives and other instruments made of pearl-shell, and of no ordinary workmanship. They presented us some elegant spears, with pearl-shell heads, and ornamented in fine style with carving and feathers of the birds of paradise. The wooden part of these spears is of excellent heavy dark wood, resembling ebony; and the carving upon them is often really curious, and bespeaks an advance in the arts hardly believed to exist in savage life. It would not be saying enough to call them ingenious; they are tasteful. It is astonishing to those who think all barbarous nations are only on an equality, in the arts, with our North American Indians, to witness such specimens of skill in carving and ornamenting their works of war, or of taste. The villages of these islanders are laid out upon the sides of the hills, and their dwellings are shaded by the lofty cocoanut and bread-fruit trees. They seem to live happily among themselves, and to enjoy every hour of their existence; and as far as I am able to judge, the extent of human life is as great in these climates as in any part of the world. I saw no victims of disease, nor any instances of decrepitude.

On the 12th of November we left Dampier's Island, with fair weather and a fine breeze. We sailed at the rate of thirteen miles an hour, assisted by the current, and soon reached the north of Long Island, which is less elevated than the one we had just left. We saw only a few wigwams along the shore, and some natives; but we could not conveniently land, and kept on our course until we had passed the western end of Long Island, and thence proceeded to the coast of New-Guinea.

All these seas are dangerous, by reason of the coral reefs, and navigators should be on their guard, as they are liable to be suddenly run upon. The mariner is not much assisted by soundings, for these reefs arise from deep water, thrown up by volcanic power, and come from the depths of the ocean.

We now reached De Kay's Bay, the entrance to which is in latitude 5° 39' south, and longitude 146° 2' east. The villages around these shores are numerous and pleasant. The natives have the negro cast of features, and they are shrewd, although their appearance is as savage as well could be. They are not in person like the negro, for they are well formed in their limbs; but no one, on looking at them, could confide in them for an instant. Their instruments of war make them formidable. They are expert in the use of the bow, and send their arrows with great directness and force.

They are extremely adroit in catching fish, which is a considerable part of their employment.

The heads of the natives are decorated with the plumage of the bird of paradise, of many species. We saw many flocks of these birds soaring high above the water; they float along as a tuft of feathers. They are of all sizes, from that of a pigeon to the diminutive form of a sparrow. The noise they make in the air is not at all melodious; it is a sort of chattering, without a distinct note. They look splendid in the sun, and some of the most diminutive are not the least beautiful. Fancy has given these birds properties which nature never did; but nothing can look more beautiful than they do when floating along with all the colours of the rainbow in the rays of the sun. They have such an abundance of feathers compared to their corporeal weight, that it is easy for them to keep on the wing; and therefore the fabulist and romantic have made them live for ever in flight; but reason and examination have proved this false. It is certain, I believe, that they flourish only near the equator, and cannot endure the slightest chill. They live among the flowers and sandal-wood. Delicate things of nature are generally grouped together.

The race of men, however, must make an exception to this rule. Whatever pride may say, or think, the beauties of nature in the wilds of the world were made without any regard to proud man, for nature often revels in beauties, and unveils her charms to the most ecstatic extent, where man is ignorant and savage; and man is often greatest where nature is steril and iron-bound. No bird of paradise ever spread its wings on the hills of North America, or on the mountains of Switzerland or Scotland, where man has reached the highest moral and intellectual perfection. And even when civilized man takes possession of the bowers of Eden, he does not suffer the original features of nature to remain, but sacrifices every grace and beauty to the rigid laws of utility and productiveness. The most lovely streams in our own country, adorned with dashing falls and pure water, are not suffered to run on in their natural course, but are stopped and tortured to turn a millwheel, or dammed up to move off obliquely and fill a canal. The aborigines look with pity on these tasteless occupants of their soil, and sigh to think that power and prosperity do not suffer the lovely face of nature to remain as it was in the days of their fathers. But utility should be paramount to taste in a world whose object is gain.

On Saturday, the 13th of November, we kept the mainland close on board of us, being obliged to sheer off sometimes to clear the coral reefs. In the afternoon we were close to a headland that seemed hanging over the sea. Between this and the seashore, however, there were many huts of the natives in the midst of beautiful groves of cocoanut-trees. My husband told me to put the name of this cape, which is in latitude 4° 59' south, and longitude 145° 16' east, in my journal as Cape Livingston, in honour of Edward Livingston, Esq., Secretary of State.

About six leagues from the cape, N.N.E., lies a small volcanic island. At night the prospect was indeed sublime; the flames were bursting from the crater, and ascending much higher than those of Ætna or Vesuvius, as those bursts of smoke and fire have been described to us. The flames reached at least, as I had been taught to measure distances with my eye since I have been on the voyage, a thousand feet in height. It was as light as if ten thousand lamps were suspended over our deck; and the stones cast up appeared like myriads of red-hot shot thrown in the night at incalculable distances. I gazed on this scene as one of wonderful sublimity, and thought how impotent language was to convey a full and competent idea of it. The next day, following the course of the island of Papua, we passed six other volcanic islands, all of which were in full blast.

What a scene for the poet! If those of antiquity roused all their energies and exhausted their powers of language on Ætna, whose fires were almost burnt out when they wrote, how would they have communicated to the world their impressions of these numerous mountains of infernal smoke and fire, which seemed, as it were, in the first stage of their wrath! How small seems the power of man, when we contemplate these wonders of nature, and ask for what uses they were formed! After the wonder has passed over us, we begin to see their uses; they are the engines of the Almighty in planting islands in the midst of the seas. By volcanic power masses of the bottom of the ocean are thrown up, the lava is spread abroad to a greater or less extent, and on its surface a soil is formed; and by some inscrutable law of nature trees grow up, birds and animals are found upon it, and man, self-wise man, wonders and puzzles his head to tell why all this is, and makes a thousand fanciful conjectures upon what he calls the philosophy of the matter, and talks learnedly upon the nature of things. But after all, he knows but little about it. Although in our common course of life, in the midst of society, we know, when we reason, that God is everywhere, yet we soon see so much of the works of man that there is a sort of belief in our minds that man has much to do with all affairs in this world, and seems to divide the empire of it with its Creator. But on the widespread ocean, where nature is every thing, and man is nothing, we enter, as it were, the depths of Omnipotence, and adore his majesty and power as the Being who said, and still says, in the burning mountain as in the burning bush, I AM that I AM; and who is there then that would not turn aside to see this great sight?

My husband named this promontory Woodbury's Cape, in honour of the then Chairman of Naval affairs in Congress, now Secretary of the Navy of the United States. Five miles from the cape is a fine spacious harbour, of sufficient depth of water between the rocks, but the course is narrow and winding.

The next day, November 15th, we passed another headland, which was called Cape Decatur, in honour of Capt. Stephen Decatur, formerly of the United States' navy. This day and the following we were visited by many of the natives, but were cautious of them, as we had suffered so much from their treachery.

We fell in with numerous islands, but I do not recollect that my husband gave them a name, or that they had already had one given them. They lie low, and are surrounded by a coral reef. Here there is plenty of biche-de-mer, pearls, tortoise, and oysters. Of this place I had neither latitude nor longitude given me, and I have never inquired the cause, but I could easily conjecture it. From these islands the natives came off to us in great numbers in large canoes. They made an attempt to get us on the coral reef, by making their canoes fast to the schooner and paddling towards the shore; but the wind being brisk, they could not make any headway. Their lines soon parted, and in their rage they shot their arrows at the schooner. A few guns were fired over their heads to frighten them, and make them understand the power of those they attempted to assail. The report that came from the cannon astounded them, and many leaped into the sea for safety. We had already had enough of blood, and were unwilling to shed it. A boat was lowered while they were in confusion, and one of the natives picked up. We took him away for the purpose of educating him, by giving him an opportunity of seeing civilization, and then returning him to his native country. After we had taken our prisoner, they made the best of their way to the shore. These islands are all thickly wooded; the cocoa-nut trees are lofty and fruitful, and as large as any I ever saw, and bread-fruit trees are in great profusion. The natives dress with coral necklaces, feathers in their hair, and numerous other ornaments, which give them quite a stylish appearance. Tortoise-shell and mother-of-pearl are profuse in these ornaments, and they bear the marks of opulence in all those things which we think of importance. Their dress is nothing more than an apron about their loins, formed of several kinds of materials, as they can afford, according to their rank. These natives are well formed and muscular, and their features are manly; they are unlike any other tribe in these seas. There are one or two passages through the reefs, and after getting within them you find good anchorage.

While here, my husband purchased several pieces of *ambergris* of the natives. I examined this wonderful substance very attentively. Its colour is a darkish yellow, resembling very closely a mass of bees-wax. It had insects and beaks of birds in it, and burned very clear, as much so as bees-wax. When rubbed, it emits a perfume generally much admired. It was taken from the water, on which it was floating, about one-third of it above the surface. Numerous accounts have been given of its nature and origin. It has been said that it grows in the intestines of the spermaceti whale. It is true that it is often found in the whale, but generally in those that are poor and unhealthy. The whalers, I find, have a general impression that it originates there from the feeding of the whale on certain fish called squids. The orientals, however, had no such idea of its origin; they considered it as a sea mushroom, which, growing on the bottom of the sea, was by time or accident rooted up, and coming to the surface grew harder by partial exposure to the sun. Others would say that it grows on the rocks, and is washed off in storms and driven near the islands, where it is picked up by the natives. Some suppose it is wax, or a honey-comb, which, by dropping into the sea, undergoes a chymical change; while some contend that it is a bituminous matter, that comes from the bottom of the sea. There are not a few who think that it is the excrement of certain fish; but the poets of the East say that is a gum from the tears of certain consecrated sea-birds.

"Around thee shall glisten the loveliest *amber*
That ever the sorrowing sea-bird hath wept,
And many a shell in whose hollow-wreathed chamber
We Peris of ocean by moonlight have slept."

Whatever may be its origin or creation, it certainly has for many centuries been held in high estimation as a perfume and for ornaments, and its use has generally been confined to the rich and powerful. Large pieces of it have lately been found, and when we consider the purposes for which it has been used,—particularly as a perfume,—the price of it is astonishing. My husband, who has been much in these seas, and often made it a matter of traffic, is of the opinion that the natives of these islands have a correct idea of the substance; viz. that it is made by an insect at the bottom of the sea, and accumulates for years; and that sea-birds devour it when within their reach, which accounts for their bills being found in it. The birds, being attracted by its glutinous qualities, strike their beaks too deep to extricate themselves, and their bodies decay, while the bony parts of their beaks remain. The sperm-whale is a ravenous animal, and he may root it up and swallow it; and this, perhaps, is one mode by which the God of nature intended that the leviathan of the ocean should be destroyed. That it is formed in the whale seems unnatural in many respects; the places, too, where it is found in the most abundance, do not abound in sperm-whales, and I have never read that it was found in any other kinds of whales.

There is no accounting for the arbitrary laws of fashion; once a man of fashion in England, and in most cities on the Continent, must have an amber-headed cane, if he carried one at all. Gay, in his Trivia, alludes to this matter of fashion:—

"If the strong cane support thy walking hand,
Chairmen no longer shall the wall command;
Even sturdy carmen shall thy nod obey,
And rattling coaches stop to make thee way.
This shall direct thy cautious tread aright,
Though not one glaring lamp enliven night.
Let beaux their canes, with *amber tipp'd*, produce,
Be theirs for empty show, but thine for use."

Since the days of the rage for tulips in Holland, and their high prices, there has not been a more decidedly mere creature of fashionable imagination that that of a partiality among the rich for amber, whether dug from the mines, or found in another form floating upon the water, or torn from the murdered whale. It is, perhaps, the only way that commerce can be sustained, to supply the whims of the opulent as well as the honest wants of the community: the artificial wants of society support a great proportion of the people of every country.

We left these islands with a fine breeze, and soon found ourselves near another one, low and uninhabited, and within a coral reef. Not far from this we discovered another island not laid down on any chart we had on board. Here we were visited by the natives, and found them, like most of these aborigines, dangerous to deal with. These groups are thinly inhabited. I am fully of opinion that numerous islands, containing articles of valuable commerce, are still to be found in these seas; it cannot be that half of them are yet discovered.

On 26th of November we took the tradewinds in latitude 6° 0', and longitude 144° 55', and between this and New-Britain we discovered the islands from which we took two natives, whom my husband named SUNDAY and MONDAY. On the 27th we crossed a coral reef of several miles in circumference, with from three to ten fathoms of water on it. From hence we steered for the St. Bernardino, which we entered on the 9th December, and the next day touched at Port of Santa Sinto, and took in a supply of provisions, of which we were in great want, as we had been on short allowance for many days, which I feared would create some disturbance on board; but when the sailors and Manilla men saw that we in the cabin were on allowance also, they were kept quiet as lambs—so easy is it to govern others when we can govern ourselves. During our whole cruise from Manilla we had no sickness, or none to speak of,—one man only requiring medicine. This was effected, in these warm and often sickly climes, by keeping all in a state of cleanliness, without the use of ardent spirits, and never suffering the crew, in any case, to be long idle. Vinegar is an excellent thing for keeping a vessel sweet, and we used it freely.

Further Reading

Benjamin Morrell's companion volume to Abby's account is *A Narrative of Four Voyages to the South Sea, North and South Pacific Ocean, Chinese Sea, Ethiopic and Southern Atlantic Ocean, Indian and Antarctic Ocean from the year 1822 to 1831* (New York: Harper, 1832; reprint, Upper Saddle River, N.J.: Gregg Press, 1970). Deirdre Coleman looks at strategies of narration open to the female voyager in her introduction to *Maiden Voyages and Infant Colonies: Two Women's Travel Narratives of the 1790s* (London: Leicester University Press, 1999). Markman Ellis discusses the relationship between sentimental rhetoric and commerce in *The Politics of Sensibility: Race, Gender and Commerce in the Sentimental Novel* (Cambridge: Cambridge University Press, 1996). Dumont D'Urville's theories on Pacific race were published in "Sur les îles du Grand Océan," *Bulletin de la Société de Géographie* 17 (1832): 1–21. For a discussion of the Melanesia/Polynesia distinction in early and recent Pacific ethnography, see Nicholas Thomas, "The Force of Ethnology: Origins and Significance of the Melanesia/Polynesia Division," *Current Anthropology* 30 (1989): 27–41.

21

MARY WALLIS

Among the Cannibals

. . . .

EUROPEAN WOMEN other than missionary wives played limited roles in cross-cultural encounters in the Pacific until the second half of the nineteenth century, when the growth of beach settlements in places such as Honolulu and Levuka in Fiji saw larger numbers of resident white women. Earlier, however, captains of trading vessels had occasionally been accompanied by their wives; though few wrote, the narratives of Abby Jane Morrell and Mary Wallis are of interest for offering distinct perspectives upon trading activities and indigenous sociality, as well as for their apologia (female authorship required special justification if it was not to appear unseemly) and their modes of narration.

Mary Wallis's book was based on a six-year voyage in the *Zotoff*, which was engaged in the Fiji–Manila bêche-de-mer trade, during a period of increasing conflict in Fiji. Long-running dynastic conflicts among the most potent of the indigenous polities—Bau, Rewa, and Viwa, which were clustered around southeastern Viti Levu—had escalated; warfare was fueled in part by considerable injections of trade goods and muskets. At the same time, Methodist missionaries, who derived some support from visiting traders, were placing increasing pressure upon chiefs to convert to Christianity and abandon customs such as polygyny and widow-strangling: the hierarchical structure of Fijian culture and society was well understood, and it was evident that little would be gained by proselytizing among common people, who would not *lotu* (join the Church) until their chiefs did so. Mrs. Wallis became informally but actively associated with the mission and spent a good deal of time at mission stations, particularly with John and Hannah Hunt, while her husband was cruising within the group to obtain bêche-de-mer. She was regarded as sufficiently important by Fijians for her name to be adopted and in-corporated—still today in Fiji there are many women named Merewalesi.

Although Methodist missionaries in Fiji were later prolific—Thomas Williams and James Calvert's *Fiji and the Fijians* (1858) became a classic of mis-sionary literature—little had appeared by 1850. In her preface, Wallis justified her publication with extracts from a letter from Calvert, who noted that the public lacked any full account of "the present abominations of cannibal Feejee" (Wallis 1851, iv). In his introduction, the Reverend C. W. Flanders of Concord, New Hampshire, drew attention to the marvelous and seemingly hyperbolic character of some passages in *Life in Feejee*, while suggesting that it could be safely assumed that she never succumbed to the temptation to exaggerate or fictionalize what she had witnessed. In his endorsement of the book, he placed particular emphasis upon Wallis's style, which he found to be distinguished by "a pleasantry in the manner of narration" that gave the train of facts and incidents the character of "a moving panorama." The striking feature of this delineation was evidently its ab-solute contrasts:

> And, then, there is a change of character, so graphically described, that, while we see a difference in the parts performed, we can hardly persuade ourselves that the different parts are performed by the same persons. Here, the ferocious islander appears with his formidable war-club—and there it is exchanged for the implement of husbandry. Here, descending with savage cries upon a neigh-bouring island to murder its unsuspecting inhabitants—and there assembled with them in the same sanctuary, listening to the words of eternal life. Here, around the burning pile, feasting upon the flesh of their slaughtered captives—and there around the communion-table, celebrating the dying love of Him in whom they have believed. (in Wallis 1851, xi)

The problem of plausibility that dogs earlier voyage accounts is evoked here not in order to suggest that Wallis's stories are in fact unbelievable, but rather to heighten the dramatic juxtapositions between seemingly incommensurable fea-tures of Fijian life. The succession of examples is carefully chosen, since the first draws attention to a contradiction in Fijian natures—between the ferocious war-rior and the industrious agriculturalist. The wholly commendable practice of cul-tivation is not the result of any missionary intervention, but attests rather to the divided nature of the Fijian character and its potential for uplift. Had Fijians been pure cannibals with no redeeming features, it would have been more difficult to imagine any transformation of them, any reform through conversion. The solution to the incommensurability to which Flanders draws attention is the work of di-vine intervention, channeled through missionary agency.

On the face of it, it is puzzling to find Wallis's style commended, since what her journal seems to lack is any polish or refinement. The text is presented as what it may well be, a direct transcription of a diary, in which entries are of highly uneven length, often bearing the character of casual jottings that do not follow one from another and that are frequently highly particular. Whether this was deliberate or not, it does have the effect of stressing the sheer incongruities of darkness and light that energize Wallis's pious narrative. She evokes morally polarized but socially proximate conditions, which are evidently characteristic of the active face of missionary effort and the transitional moments around scenes of conversion. Among the most dramatic of these are those associated with widow-strangling (compare the extract in chapter 15). While drawing attention to what she saw as other dimensions of female degradation in Fiji, Wallis does not, in the case referred to here, attempt to present the woman as an unwitting victim, but acknowledges her apparent wish to be strangled so that she may join her husband.

Not all readers found Mrs Wallis's moralization of Fijian life plausible; one copy of the book bears a contemporary inscription characterizing the author as "a greater cannibal than those she describes." — NICHOLAS THOMAS

. . . .

Mary Wallis, *Life in Feejee or, Five Years Among the Cannibals* (Boston: William Heath, 1851).

« CHAPTER 3, PP. 64–70. »

[February] 23 [1845]. We learn that a town belonging to Rewa has been destroyed by Bau. Six men were killed, who were taken to Bau and eaten.

Mrs. Jaggar, Mrs. Watsford and myself, have commenced teaching a class of girls to sew; one teaching one week, and the other the next, and so on. Mrs. Hunt does not join us at present, on account of ill health.

24. Namosimalua has beaten two of his women most unmercifully, for some trifling fault. None seem to like him or respect his character. Many of his women are pious, but cannot enjoy the privileges of the church while living in a state of concubinage, and this they are compelled to do, as he will not release them. He is neither Christian nor heathen. He has renounced many of his heathen practices, given up cannibalism, has no confidence in heathen gods, believes in the only true God, but neither loves nor serves Him.

March 8. The solemn notes of a bell are now sounding in my ears. Some one is about to be laid in his last resting-place on earth. How many times has the bell of my own church tolled since I left my native land! Many of my own loved friends, from whom I parted in the full glow of health, may be resting in the cold grave. I am 15,000 miles from home.

16. Capt. Stratton has sailed for Sydney, and taken letters to forward to England and America. The white men living at this place, of whom there are several, procured rum from Capt. S., and had a grand time last night. They sent for Verani, and invited him to join them; this he refused, telling them that he did not wish to get drunk, that it was bad to do so. They told him that the drink they offered him was not rum, but wine, which the missionaries had given to a sick woman, wife of one of the tempters. Verani thought it no harm to drink wine, and soon they all became drunk together.

21. Verani came to Mr. Jaggar, and inquired why religious services were to be held on this day. He was told that it was "Good Friday," the day on which it was supposed that Jesus Christ died. "Then this shall be the day on which I will lotu," said Verani; and in accordance with this resolution, he attended the morning prayer meeting, and on his knees, publicly renounced heathenism. It appears that the mind of this chief has been much exercised upon the subject of religion for some two or three months past, but he has had much to struggle against. He has fully believed, that unless he repented of his sins, and loved God, he could not be happy in another world. If he became a Christian, however, he must not only brave the resentment of Thakombau, which is no slight thing, but he must give up all which is dear to a heathen; and in return he sees in prospect no earthly reward. He knows that those who become Christians, gain no riches from the missionaries; but are taught how to gain the "pearl of great price," and that is all. He could not expect to gain any thing from the masters of trading vessels, either, for these, with but very few exceptions, prefer to have nothing to do with Christianity, or Christians. It may be seen from this, that he is now willing to give up all for the salvation of his soul. He has learned to read, and has many times of late sat up all night with a teacher, talking about religion.

The Lasakaus have at length accomplished their purpose. Nalela was killed last night in Bau. Navinde has been here very often since the pretended reconciliation, and used every means to convince Nalela of his sincerity. Nalela has, however, declined going to Bau to live, but occasionally visited there. Last night, as he was sitting in the "*buri*," he was shot. The Marama and others of his women have gone to Bau, where it is most likely that some of them will be strangled. Namosimalua looks dark, and says that Bau is determined to kill off the old chiefs, and his turn will soon come. He has sent to Bau to ask if this is intended as an insult to Vewa. If so, they may come on; Vewa is ready to meet them.

Last evening Vewa received a present of several muskets and kegs of powder from Thakombau. This was, that he might receive the news of the morning with "a good mind." Bau has as much to do with the affair as Lasakau.

22. Nalela went to Bau the day before he was killed, to see Navinde, who, they pretended, was sick. He spent his first night there safely, and avowed his intention of remaining the second. During the day, some friend secretly warned him of his danger, and advised his return to Vewa immediately. He disregarded the friendly warning and decided to remain, thinking, perhaps, if they were determined to kill him, they might as well accomplish their purpose at once. He had been a prisoner for three years, and had now tasted again the sweets of liberty, rendered doubly dear, no doubt, by being so long deprived of them. In the evening, Nalela, with his father, Navinde, and others, were seated in the great "*buri*" of Bau, drinking yanggona, and enjoying a social chat, when suddenly the report of a musket was heard, and Nalela fell. Navinde sprung to his feet, and struck the fallen chief several blows with his club. The poor old father of Nalela said to him, "Oh, do not do that, he will die with the shot." With the fury of a demon, Navinde turned, and struck the old man so violently that he fell to the ground a corpse. In the morning Tanoa was told of the death of Nalela. "Very good," said the king, "send to Vewa that his wife may come and kiss the body of her husband." She found his body exceedingly mutilated—the heart, liver and tongue had been devoured.

23. The chiefs of Bau would not consent to strangle any of the women that had belonged to Nalela, as they wished to have him feel the effects of their hatred in the next world. After having shot and clubbed him out of this world, they mean to starve him in the next, by not allowing any woman to go with him to do his cooking. The Marama, after returning from Bau, went to Namosimalua, and said, "Come, strangle me quick, that my spirit may go with the spirit of Nalela, and comfort him, he is even now faint for food." Namosi is Christian enough to refuse her request. She then applied to Verani, who said, "No, you must not be strangled, for you can do no good to Nalela where he is; you must live and repent of your sins, that when you die, you may go to heaven." "Ah!" she exclaimed, in accents of the deepest woe, "it is true that no one loves me. There was one that loved me, but they have killed him, and there is not one left that loves

me enough to send me to him. You are my brother, but you do not love me. I will starve myself."

The manner of strangling the females when a chief dies, is as follows:— The woman first kisses the corpse, then hastens to the house of her nearest male relative, or in his absence, to the chief, and says, "I wish to die, that I may go where my husband is. Love me, and make haste to strangle me, that I may hasten and overtake him." The relatives applaud her resolution, and direct her to bathe herself. Her ablutions being accomplished, her female friends accompany her to the house of the deceased with all despatch, and dress and decorate her for the journey which she is about to undertake. Her mother, if alive, spreads a mat for her to sit upon. All, then, give her their parting salutation. While some rejoice at, and commend her heroism, occasionally there are some whose feelings recoil at the apparatus of death, and by such persons (but the number is comparatively few), the murderous cord is touched with a trembling hand, or seized with the grasp of a maniac. The widow summons all her energy, and surrenders herself to her murderers. The willing victim is placed in the lap of a female, and a piece of native cloth is folded so as to make a strong cord, which is placed round her neck. A knot is tied on each side of the windpipe, and the two ends are made to pass each other in opposite directions; and while one woman is pressing down her head, and another holding her hand over her mouth and nostrils, five or six men take hold of each end of the cord, and pull it till the two ends meet, or pass each other. The work of death is violent, brief and certain. The body is soon stretched on the mat a breathless corpse. The cord is left about her neck, the ends unfolded and tied in a knot. The body is then rubbed over with tumeric, and placed by the side of the dead chief. The friends of the chief then present a whale's tooth to her nearest male relative, and say, "*A kennai sere, ni wa ni kuna.*"—"This is the untying of the cord of strangling." The cord is then untied, and left loose about her neck. She is buried in the same grave with her husband. If the chief is of very high rank, several women are thus sacrificed.

24. Mr. Hunt has visited at the house of the murdered chief. He did not see the widow, but found the other women making a great noise. It is the custom to burn the houses of deceased chiefs, with every thing they contain; but Verani would not allow it in this case. The widow has, however, burned and broken many articles, and the last accounts stated that she was hard at work in accomplishing the ruin of a pair of strong scissors.

Nalela was a very wicked, blood-thirsty tyrant. Although while a prisoner at Vewa, in constant fear and real danger, yet he omitted no opportunity of showing his *amiable character*. He was a "vasu" to Vewa, and exercised his power with the younger portion of the population in the most despotic manner.

Not long since, Masapai told one of his men to take a pig belonging to himself, to another island, which he named. Nalela heard of it, and determined to kill the man who had executed the orders of Masapai. Mr. Hunt heard of the affair, and *"soroed"* to the chief in time to save the life of the young man. *"To soro,"* is to take a present to the offended party, and say *"Au soro,"* "I ask pardon."

25. Last evening being fine, and lighted by the full, unclouded moon, Mr. and Mrs. Watsford and myself walked to the spacious mansion of the Turaga-lavu. The prospect from the elevation where this mansion is located, is extensive and beautiful, either by sunlight or moonlight. I love beautiful prospects, rich and charming scenery, but fail in any attempt to describe it. As we reached the dwelling of the chief, we heard the sound of prayer. When it was ended, Namosi and Vatai came forth. We remarked that we had come to look at the bright moon, the sparkling waters, and the lands of Feejee. Namosi said, "The sun is true, the moon is true and the stars are true, for they were made by the true God." Vatai said, "Many have been the days of my foolishness, when I did not know the true God. I believed in the gods of Feejee. When the lands trembled, I believed that the god Dengai turned over in his cave, and that caused the earth to shake."

Further Reading

The full text of Wallis's book has been republished in facsimile by Gregg Press (New York, 1967) and by the Fiji Museum (1983). A separate journal by Wallis has recently been published as *The Fiji and New Caledonia Journals of Mary Wallis* (Suva: Institute of Pacific Studies, 1994). The most illuminating discussion of Fijian history in the period appears in a number of essays by Marshall Sahlins, notably "Other Times, Other Customs," in *Islands of History* (Chicago: University of Chicago Press, 1985); and "The Discovery of the True Savage," in *Dangerous Liaisons*, ed. Donna Merwick (Parkville: Department of History, University of Melbourne, 1994).

22

FREDERICK MANING

Tapa *and* Muru *in New Zealand*

. . . .

FREDERICK MANING (1812–83) described himself as a pakeha Maori, a term applied to traders who were adopted by a *hapu* (or subtribe) in New Zealand and
typically given hospitality, protection, and a wife in return for organizing the exchange of raw materials (in this case timber) for European goods (especially muskets). Born in Dublin of Anglo-Irish parentage, Maning grew up in Tasmania and
moved to the Hokianga harbor of the North Island of New Zealand in 1833, when
he was twenty-two years old. Although he always regarded himself as a gentleman, he entered into a relationship whose indignity he was quite prepared to acknowledge. His worth was weighed in muskets, he confesses, and he was referred
to by the chief of the Te Hikutu as "my pakeha." His position was ill-defined from
a European point of view, for he was like a beachcomber to the extent that he took
a native wife and was entirely dependent on the goodwill of the *hapu* who "owned"
him; and like a settler to the extent that he bought land and established himself in
the region as a prominent trader. Presumably it was this amphibian status he was
trying to defend when he spoke against the Treaty of Waitangi in 1840, believing
that a formal annexation and settlement of New Zealand by Great Britain was
neither in his interest nor that of the Maori. Although later he supported the Europeans in their wars with the Maori and eventually became a judge of the Native
Land Court, Maning was unremitting in his hostility to missionaries, and indeed
toward any ameliorative view of colonization. He was convinced that settlement
could only be successful if Maori resistance was utterly crushed, an opinion he
tried to illustrate in his other major publication, *A History of the War in the North*,
which he wrote during Hone Heke's campaign of 1845–46.

Maning published *Old New Zealand* in 1863 in the same spirit that Twain would compose *Life on the Mississippi*, commemorating a vivid period of early settlement, before respectability and religion had largely abolished the risk of frontier life. And like Twain, Maning's confident prose style reflects a delight in conversation, an art in which he shone. *Old New Zealand* is a tour de force, exploiting the digressive technique and buttonholing manner of the Romantic essayists who owed a good deal to Sterne, an author whose Irish origins and rare improvisational talents clearly appealed to Maning too. However, Maning is probably best remembered for his ethnographic anecdotes. His story of the slave who died when he realized he had eaten food reserved for a chief reappears in both Frazer's *The Golden Bough* (1925) and Freud's *Totem and Taboo* (1919). In this extract Maning is discussing a variation of *tapu* called *tapa*, and *muru*, the custom of pillaging people who have had bad luck. All are cognate conditions of attraction or repulsion with regard to food and artifacts, depending on the degree of *mana* of the person who confronts them. Butler was to remember the passage on *muru* when he was writing *Erewhon* (1872), the story of a New Zealand utopia where misfortune is treated as a crime. — JONATHAN LAMB

. . . .

The following extracts are courtesy of Alex Calder, ed., *Old New Zealand, and Other Writings,* by F. E. Maning (London: Leicester University Press, 2001); this new edition is based on the so-called second edition of Maning's *Old New Zealand* (Auckland: Robert J. Creighton and Alfred Scales, 1863; page references are to this 1863 edition).

« CHAPTER 12, PP. 175–78. »

There was a kind of variation on the *tapu*, called *tapa*, of this nature. For instance, if a chief said, 'That axe is my head', the axe became his to all intents and purposes, except, indeed, the owner of the axe was able to break his 'head', in which case, I have reason to believe, the *tapa* would fall to the ground. It was, however, in a certain degree necessary to have some legal reason, or excuse, for making the *tapa*; but to give some idea of what constituted the circumstances under which a man could fairly *tapa* anything, I must needs quote a case in point.

When the Ngapuhi attacked the tribe of Ngati Wakawe, at Rotorua, the Ngati Wakawe retired to the island of Mokoia in the lake of Rotorua, which they fortified, thinking that, as the Ngapuhi canoes could not come nearer than Kaituna on the east coast, about thirty miles distant, that they in their island position would be safe. But in this they were fatally deceived, for the Ngapuhi dragged a whole fleet of war canoes over land. When, however, the advanced division of the Ngapuhi arrived at Rotorua, and encamped on the shore of the lake, Ngati Wakawe were not aware that the canoes of the enemy were coming, so every morning they manned their large canoes, and leaving the island fort, would come dashing along the shore deriding the Ngapuhi, and crying, '*Ma wai koe e kawe mai ki Rangitiki?*'—'Who shall bring you, or how shall you arrive, at Rangitiki?' Rangitiki was the name of one of their hill forts. The canoes were fine large ornamented totara canoes, very valuable, capable of carrying from fifty to seventy men each, and much coveted by the Ngapuhi. The Ngapuhi of course considered all these canoes as their own already, but the different chiefs and leaders, anxious to secure one or more of these fine canoes for themselves and people, and not knowing who might be the first to lay hands on them in the confusion of the storming of Mokoia, which would take place when their own canoes arrived, each *tapa'd* one or more for himself, or—as the native expression is—*to* himself. Up jumped Pomare, and standing on the lake shore in front of the encampment of the division of which he was leader, he shouts—pointing at the same time to a particular canoe at the time carrying about sixty men—'That canoe is my backbone'. Then Tareha, in bulk like a sea elephant, and sinking to the ancles in the shore of the lake, with a hoarse, croaking voice roars out, 'That canoe! my skull shall be the baler to bale it out'. This was a horribly strong *tapa*. Then the soft voice of the famous Hongi Ika, surnamed 'The eater of men', or *Hongi kai tangata*, was heard, 'Those two canoes are my two thighs'. And so the whole flotilla was appropriated by the different chiefs. Now it followed from this that in the storming and plunder of Mokoia, when a warrior clap't his hand on a canoe and shouted, 'This canoe is mine', the seizure would not stand good if it was one of the canoes which were *tapa-tapa*, for it would be a frightful insult to Pomare to claim to be the owner of his 'backbone', or to Tareha to go on board a canoe which had been made sacred by the bare supposition that his 'skull' should be made a vessel to bail it with. Of course the first man laying his hand on any other canoe and claiming it secured it for himself and tribe, always provided that the number of men there present representing his tribe or *hapu* were sufficient to back his claim and render it dangerous to dispossess him. I have seen men shamefully robbed, for want of sufficient support, of their honest lawful gains, after all the trouble and risk they had gone to in killing the owners of their plunder. But dishonest people are to be found almost everywhere, and I will say this, that my friends the Maoris seldom act against law, and always try to be able to say what they do is 'correct'—(*tika*).

« CHAPTER 7, PP. 105–13. »

There were in the old times two great institutions, which reigned with iron rod in Maori land—the *Tapu* and the *Muru*. *Pakehas* who knew no better, called the *muru* simply 'robbery', because the word *muru*, in its common signification, means to plunder. But I speak of the regular legalised and established system of plundering as penalty for offences, which in a rough way resembled our law by which a man is obliged to pay 'damages'. Great abuses had, however, crept into this system—so great, indeed, as to render the retention of any sort of movable property almost an impossibility, and to in a great measure discourage the inclination to labour for its acquisition. These great inconveniences were, however, met, or in some degree softened, by an expedient of a peculiarly Maori nature, which I shall by-and-by explain. The offences for which people were plundered were sometimes of a nature which, to a mere *pakeha*, would seem curious. A man's child fell in the fire and was almost burnt to death. The father was immediately plundered to an extent that almost left him without the means of subsistence: fishing nets, canoes, pigs, provisions—all went. His canoe upset, and he and all his family narrowly escaped drowning—some were, perhaps, drowned. He was immediately robbed, and well pummelled with a club into the bargain, if he was not good at the science of self-defence— the club part of the ceremony being always fairly administered one against one, and after fair warning given to defend himself. He might be clearing some land for potatoes, burning off the fern, and the fire spreads farther than he intended, and gets into a *wahi tapu* or burial-ground. No matter whether any one has been buried in it or no for the last hundred years, he is tremendously robbed. In fact, for ten thousand different causes a man might be robbed; and I can really imagine a case in which a man for scratching his own head might be legally robbed. Now as the enforcers of this law were also the parties who received the damages, as well as the judges of the amount, which in many cases (such as that of the burnt child) would be everything they could by any means lay hands on, it is easy to perceive that under such a system personal property was an evanescent sort of thing altogether. These executions or distraints were never resisted. Indeed in many cases, as I shall explain by-and-by, it would have been felt as a slight, and even an insult, *not* to be robbed; the sacking of a man's establishment being often taken as a high compliment, especially if his head was broken into the bargain; and to resist the execution would not only have been looked upon as mean and disgraceful in the highest degree, *but it would have debarred the contemptible individual from the privilege of robbing his neighbours*, which was the compensating expedient I have alluded to. All this may seem a waste of words to my *pakeha* Maori readers, to whom these things have become such matters of course as to be no longer remarkable; but I have remembered that there are so many new people in the country who don't understand the beauty of being knocked down and robbed, that I shall say a few more words on the subject.

The tract of country inhabited by a single tribe might be say from forty to a hundred miles square, and the different villages of the different sections of the tribe would be scattered over this area at different distances from each other. We will by way of illustrating the working of the *muru* system take the case of the burnt child. Soon after the accident it would be heard of in the neighbouring villages; the family of the mother are probably the inhabitants of one of them; they have, according to the law of *muru*, the first and greatest right to clean out the afflicted father—a child being considered to belong to the family of the mother more than to that of the father—in fact it is their child, who the father has the rearing of. The child was moreover a promising lump of a boy, the making of a future warrior, and consequently very valuable to the whole tribe in general, but to the mother's family in particular. 'A pretty thing to let him get spoiled'. Then he is a boy of good family, a *rangatira* by birth, and it would never do to let the thing pass without making a noise about it. That would be an insult to the dignity of the families of both father and mother. Decidedly, besides being robbed, the father must be assaulted with the spear. True, he is a famous spearman, and for his own credit must 'hurt' some one or another if attacked. But this is of no consequence; a flesh wound more or less deep is to be counted on; and then think of the plunder! It is against the law of *muru* that any one should be killed, and first blood ends the duel. Then the natural affection of all the child's relations is great. They are all in a great state of excitement, and trying to remember how many canoes, and pigs, and other valuable articles, the father has got: for this must be a clean sweep. A strong party is now mustered, headed probably by the brother of the mother of the child. He is a stout chap, and carries a long tough spear. A messenger is sent to the father, to say that the *taua muru* is coming, and may be expected to-morrow, or the next clay. He asks, 'Is it a great taua?' 'Yes; it is a very great *taua* indeed'. The victim smiles, he feels highly complimented, he is then a man of consequence. His child is also of great consideration; he is thought worthy of a large force being sent to rob him! Now he sets all in motion to prepare a huge feast for the friendly robbers his relations. He may as well be liberal, for his provisions are sure to go, whether or no. Pigs are killed and baked whole, potatoes are piled up in great heaps, all is made ready, he looks out his best spear, and keeps it always ready in his hand. At last the *taua* appears on a hill half a mile off; then the whole fighting men of the section of the tribe of which he is an important member, collect at his back, all armed with spear and club, to show that they could resist, if they would—a thing, however, not to be thought of under the circumstances. On comes the *taua*. The mother begins to cry in proper form; the tribe shout the call of welcome to the approaching robbers; and then with a grand rush, all armed, and looking as if they intended to exterminate all before them, the *kai muru* appear on the scene. They dance the war dance, which the villagers answer with another. Then the chief's brother-in-law advances, spear in hand, with the most alarming gestures. 'Stand up!—stand up! I will kill you this day', is his cry. The defendant is not slow to answer the challenge. A most exciting, and what to a new *pakeha* would appear a most desperately dangerous fencing bout with spears instantly commences. The attack and defence are in the highest degree scientific; the spear shafts keep up a continuous rattle; the thrust, and parry, and stroke with the spear shaft follow each other with almost incredible rapidity, and are too rapid to be followed by an unpractised eye. At last the brother-in-law is slightly touched; blood also drops from our chief's thigh. The fight instantly ceases; leaning on their spears, probably a little badinage takes place between them, and then the brother-in-law roars out, '*murua! murua! murua!*' Then the new arrivals commence a regular sack, and the two principals sit down quietly with a few others for a friendly chat, in which the child's name is never mentioned, or the enquiry as to whether he is dead or alive even made. The case I have just described would, however, be one of more than ordinary importance; slighter 'accidents and offences' would be atoned for by a milder form of operation. But the general effect was to keep personal property circulating from hand to hand pretty briskly, or indeed to convert it into public property; for no man could say who would be the owner of his canoe, or blanket, in a month's time. Indeed, in that space of time, I once saw a nice coat, which a native had got from the captain of a trading schooner, and which was an article much coveted in those days, pass through the hands, and over the backs, of six different owners, and return, considerably the worse for wear, to the original purchaser; and all these transfers had been made by legal process of *muru*. I have been often myself paid the compliment of being robbed for little accidents occurring in my family, and have several times also, from a feeling of politeness, robbed my Maori friends, though I can't say I was a great gainer by these transactions. I think the greatest haul I ever made was about half a bag of shot, which I thought a famous joke, seeing that I had sold it the day before to the owner for full value. A month after this I was disturbed early in the morning, by a voice shouting 'Get up!—get up! I will kill you this day. You have roasted my grandfather. Get up!—*stand up!*' I, of course, guessed that I had committed some heinous though involuntary offence, and the 'stand up' hinted the immediate probable consequences; so out I turned, spear in hand, and who should I see, armed with a bayonet on the end of a long pole, but my friend the sometime owner of the bag of shot. He came at me with pretended fury, made some smart bangs and thrusts, which I parried, and then explained to me that I had 'cooked his grandfather'; and that if I did not come down handsome in the way of damages, deeply as he might regret the necessity, his own credit, and the law of *muru*, compelled him either to sack my house or die in the attempt. I was glad enough to prevent either event, by paying him two whole bags of shot, two blankets, divers fishhooks, and certain figs of tobacco, which he demanded. I found that I had really and truly committed a most horrid crime. I had on a journey made my fire at the foot of a tree, in the top of which the bones of my friend's grandfather had once been deposited, but from which they had been removed ten years before; the tree caught fire and burnt down: and I, therefore, by a convenient sort of figure of speech, had 'roasted his grandfather', and had to pay the penalty accordingly.

Further Reading

For an account of New Zealand contemporary with Maning's, see Richard Taylor, *Te Ika a Maui: or, New Zealand and its Inhabitants* (London: Wertheim and Macintosh, 1855), which deals, among other things, with Hone Heke, *tapu*, the folly of Wakefield's planned settlement of New Zealand, and "the fearful state of depravity which prevailed amongst all ranks in the early days of the colony" (283). The most recent account is James Belich, *Making Peoples: A History of New Zealand* (Auckland: Penguin, 1996). For Maning, consult the entry in the *Dictionary of New Zealand Biography*, vol. 1, ed. W. H. Oliver and Claudia Orange (Wellington: Allen and Unwin and Department of Internal Affairs, 1990); and Alex Calder, ed., *Old New Zealand and Other Writings*, by F. E. Maning (London: Leicester University Press, 2001).

part three

Literary Travelers

Introduction

The colonial transformation of the Pacific's political geography was nothing if not uneven. However, the broad pattern over the second half of the nineteenth century was certainly one of increasing dominance by colonial powers. More frequent visits by naval as well as trading vessels, more securely established missions, and larger numbers of settlers—in the context of severe and sometimes catastrophic indigenous depopulation, together with the erosion of indigenous political forms—led to a new environment, quite different to that from which the texts in the first two parts of this anthology emerged. Missionaries were no longer tentatively attempting to establish new social orders, highly conscious of their daily dependence upon chiefs; rather, they were entrenched and often were well-placed to manage indigenous relations with other foreigners, able to manipulate chiefs more than they themselves were locally manipulated. After 1860 beachcombers in most of the larger archipelagoes of the central and eastern Pacific were no longer beyond European law; rather, this domain was dominated by trading companies, businessmen, and recognized consuls.

The actual extension of colonial government was, however, more often than not a drawn-out process. In Hawaii, for example, by 1840 the American settlers dominated the Hawaiian rulers, and in 1848 they forced Kamehameha III to alienate the bulk of Hawaii's land, dispossessing the commoner population at a stroke. Yet annexation by the United States, mooted much earlier, did not finally take place until 1898. In Fiji, the numbers of settlers and missionaries were low—totaling only a few hundred—up to the early 1860s, when a cotton boom led to a dramatic increase. Attempts were made locally by settlers to establish European forms of government, headed by the preeminent chief Cakobau; these led eventually to cession to Britain in 1874. Tahiti had been annexed by the French much earlier, in 1842. Although these circumstances were very different, they created, by the 1870s and 1880s, broadly similar conditions. In particular, they made it possible for European visitors to move and settle relatively freely. Although various forms of imposed change, incursions upon sovereignty, and the expropriation of land were continually resisted, Polynesians were not, in general, liable to threaten individual travelers. The Pacific was not yet within the reach of regular or organized tourism, but there began to be scope for travel that was essentially recreational.

In the 1860s, Mark Twain visited Hawaii on one of the first regular services; by the late 1880s, Robert Louis Stevenson found Hawaii overrun by tourists and could only find the genuinely strange and exotic in far more remote Kiribati. Constance Gordon-Cumming traveled in newly pacified Fiji in the mid-1870s, fully exploiting the literary potential of the fact that cannibalism and warfare had only recently been suppressed. By the time the Stevensons visited the Marquesas, the much-reduced local population had been dominated for decades by Catholic missionaries. Although anti-colonial resistance appears to have motivated some late outbreaks of cannibalism in the 1860s, Fanny Stevenson's appeal to the trope is romantic and nostalgic. Henry Adams's fascinating dialogues with the Tahitian aristocrats, the Arii Taimai and her son Tati Salmon, similarly reflect a colonial situation in which indigenous culture is very much the object of what became known as salvage ethnography. Louis Becke's own experiences in the Pacific had been in less secure situations. Although his story harks back to the disorder of the 1860s and 1870s, the conditions he described remained prevalent in the western Pacific until much later. At the end of the nineteenth century, many peoples in the Solomon Islands and in much of Papua New Guinea had experienced no contact or only minimal contacts with Europeans; they remained attached to local religions until much later, and in some cases they have resisted Christianity up to the present. They continued to be hostile to traders or controlled the terms of trade. These parts of the Pacific remained inaccessible to recreational travelers until well into the twentieth century.

The literary traveler does not constitute a particular type, with a distinctive approach to writing about Oceania. There are notable differences between the voices in this section, ranging as they do from Gordon-Cumming's secure and optimistic sense of colonial hierarchy and progress to Becke's cynical evocation of hybridity. Some writers' texts were deeply inflected by indigenous conversations and were, in effect, characterized by the multivocality that is often assumed to be a new trend in postmodernist ethnographic writing. Others are far more superficial. Yet the writers represented in this section were mainly authors who were self-consciously seeking audiences quite different from those addressed by missionaries and those composing ships' logs. Though these texts are produced from experience on the beach, the beach for most of these writers was experienced with the object of a text in mind.

23

MARK TWAIN

A Yankee at the Court of Captain Cook

MARK TWAIN (the nom de plume of Samuel Langhorne Clemens, 1835–1910) arrived in Hawaii in March 1866 on the second voyage of the *Ajax*, the newly inaugurated steamer service between San Francisco and Hawaii. He had been commissioned by the Sacramento *Union*, a leading newspaper self-styled "the friend of the common people" (Frear 1947, 94), to spend a month in the Sandwich Islands as a traveling correspondent. In the event, he remained for four months, visiting the three larger Hawaiian islands of Oahu, Maui, and Hawaii and writing twenty-five letters for the *Union*. The material became the basis for a popular series of lectures upon his return to the United States and was partially incorporated, with elaborations, into his travelogue novel *Roughing It* (1872).

Twain's brief from the *Union* was to report on the burgeoning Hawaiian sugar trade, or as he expressed it, "to write up sugar," though he also "threw in a good deal of extraneous matter that hadn't anything to do with sugar" (Frear 1947, 115). Like Stevenson after him, Twain did not simply record impressions: he researched widely among the existing literature of the islands. This included, according to Walter Frear, reading histories,

some by Hawaiians; studying the lexicon and phrase book, examining defunct as well as surviving newspapers, including Hawaiian, and even vol. 2 of the Supreme Court Reports, published during his visit, governmental reports, statistics, archives, the sugar and whaling industries, social, religious, political, educational, industrial, racial and hygienic conditions, the Hawaiian Board of Missions, the Hawaiian Mission's Children's Society . . . , the status and salaries of clergymen, the various religious denominations, . . . Hawaiian mythology and traditions. (Frear 1947, 23)

Frear suggests that Twain made himself familiar with the whole text of Hawaiian society, yet this purported penchant for factual detail did not produce the negative response elicited by Stevenson's early South Seas letters to the New York *Sun* (chapter 25). In part this reflected the particular commercial and political interest and investment of Twain's West Coast American readership in the Hawaiian kingdom. From mid-1842 the United States had virtually extended the Monroe Doctrine over the Hawaiian islands. The majority of settlers in Hawaii were American, and Twain dwelt on the resources of the island and advocated annexation. He was also less scrupulous in the presentation of his facts than Stevenson, peppering his letters liberally with unlikely anecdotes and bigoted asides (reiterating what one critic refers to as "the Yankee dominated crudities of Honolulu" [Steegmuller 1951, ix]), and devising a fictional sidekick, Brown, as a butt of humor and to provide some limited self-reflexive commentary.

This extract describes Twain's visit to Kealakekua Bay and his response to the British commemoration of Cook at the site of his death. Twain favors American sources on Cook: his version falls into a tradition of Yankee skepticism that began with the cited account by Lieutenant John Ledyard, corporal of the marines on Cook's third voyage. *John Ledyard's Journal of Captain Cook's Last Voyage* (1783) offered the least mitigating portrait of the explorer's death in the voyage literature; Gananath Obeyesekere, the most recent representative of the skeptical tradition, claims that Ledyard has been dismissed by Cook scholars in the hagiographic mode as "that nasty Connecticut Yankee" (Obeyesekere 1992a, 71). Twain encountered Ledyard's text extracted within James Jackson Jarves's *History of the Hawaiian or Sandwich Islands* (1843), of which he made substantial use (Frear 1947, 156–63). Jarves also drew on translations from "Ka Mooolelo Hawaii," a collection of texts on Hawaiian history written by scholars of the missionary seminary at Lahainaluna. These documents, which were in turn heavily influenced by the American missionary context in which they were produced, represented Cook as having colluded with his purported reception in Hawaii as the god Lono in order to elevate his personal status and exploit Hawaiian hospitality. Despite the irreverent criticisms of missionary literature he voices in the extract through his alter ego Brown, Twain thus becomes a vessel for a distilled missionary version of Hawaiian history. Twain's version of the Cook/Lono story further signals its derivation from missionary sources in conflating the myths of the god Lono and the Hawaiian chief Lono-i-ka-makahiki, whose legendary history is recorded at the end of the extract (Sahlins 1985, 115; Obeyesekere 1992a, 154). Although his account of Cook is in the debunking tradition, Twain's skepticism is not directed toward the phenomenon of Cook's premortem apotheosis, which has more recently become the topic of vigorous contestation between anthropologists Marshall Sahlins and Gananath Obeyesekere. For Twain, following "Ka Mooolelo Hawaii," Cook's claim to divinity is surrendered at the moment of death, when he betrays his mortality with a wince of human pain (Jarves 1843, 127–28).

Twain's account of the death of Cook is more than a simple retailing of the anti-British sentiments of American missionaries. It is carefully framed as a meditation on tradition itself; an acutely self-reflexive discussion of the complex layerings that constitute historical memory. The historical record is depicted via a series of memorials that move from the natural to the manmade, and from the sublime to the ridiculous. The impressions of tree forms retained by the lava of the Kona coast give way to the overinscribed tree-stump, first imprinted by the cannon of Cook's ship and subsequently by the captains of visiting ships; this in turn finds a debased reflection in the "ample hog-pen" where Cook's remains were burned, declared by Twain to be "not properly a monument, since it was erected by the natives themselves, and less to do honor to the circumnavigator than for the sake of convenience in roasting him"; here, by contrast, inscription has become "so defaced [by the elements] as to render it illegible." Inseparable from these historical palimpsests are the types of tourist who are their projected audience: the "school-boy" reader, the visitor of sites, and, figured through the increasingly ludicrous interventions of Brown, the avid collector of curios. Amid these competing versions of history, Twain reports that he has attempted his own type of reenactment: a gesture of identification with the imperial narrative of Cook's death, which has resulted in a bathetic act of discovery: simply, "I discovered that I could not do it." For the romance of the dying explorer/god he purports to substitute a value-free, plain-style "unvarnished history"; a claim to neutrality that displays the hallmarks of the Yankee tradition to which Twain's account belongs. — VANESSA SMITH

Mark Twain, letters to the *Sacramento Union*, published between August 24 and September 29, 1866; reprinted in Walter Francis Frear, *Mark Twain and Hawaii* (Chicago: Lakeside Press, 1947, pp. 372–92).

Nineteenth letter to the *Sacramento Union*, published August 24 and 25, 1866.

« KONA (SANDWICH ISLANDS), JULY 1866 »

STILL IN KONA—CONCERNING MATTERS AND THINGS ... We passed several sugar plantations—new ones and not very extensive. The crops were, in most cases, third rattoons. Almost everywhere on the island of Hawaii sugar-cane matures in twelve months, both rattoons and plant, and although it ought to be taken off as soon as it tassels, no doubt, it is not absolutely necessary to do it until about four months afterward. In Kona, the average yield of an acre of ground is two tons of sugar, they say. This is only a moderate yield for these islands, but would be extraordinary for Louisiana and most other sugar growing countries. The plantations in Kona being on pretty high ground—up among the light and frequent rains—no irrigation what-ever is required.

In Central Kona there is but little idle cane land now, but there is a good deal in North and South Kona. There are thousands of acres of cane land unoccupied on the island of Hawaii, and the prices asked for it range from one dollar to a hundred and fifty an acre. It is owned by common natives, and is lying "out of doors." They make no use of it whatever, and yet, here lately, they seem disinclined to either lease or sell it. I was frequently told this. In this connection it may not be out of place to insert an extract from a book of Hawaiian travels recently published by a visiting minister of the gospel:

"Well, now, *I* wouldn't, if I was you."

"Brown, I *wish* you wouldn't look over my shoulder when I am writing; and I wish you would indulge yourself in some little respite from my affairs and interest yourself in your own business sometimes."

"Well, I don't care. I'm disgusted with these mush-and-milk preacher travels, and I wouldn't make an extract from one of them. Father Damon has got stacks of books shoemakered up by them pious bushwhackers from America, and they're the flattest reading—they are sicker than the smart things children say in the newspapers. Every preacher that gets lazy comes to the Sandwich Islands to 'recruit his health,' and then he goes back home and writes a book. And he puts in a lot of history, and some legends, and some manners and customs, and dead loads of praise of the missionaries for civilizing and Christianizing the natives, and says in considerable chapters how grateful the savage ought to be; and when there is a chapter to be filled out, and they haven't got anything to fill it out with, they shovel in a lot of Scripture—now *don't* they? You just look at Rev. Cheever's book and Anderson's—and when they come to the volcano, or any sort of heavy scenery, and it is too much bother to describe it, they shovel in another lot of Scripture, and wind up with 'Lo! what God hath wrought!' Confound their lazy melts! Now, I wouldn't make extracts out of no such bosh." . . .

NATURE'S PRINTED RECORD IN THE LAVA At four o'clock in the afternoon we were winding down a mountain of dreary and desolate lava to the sea, and closing our pleasant land journey. This lava is the accumulation of ages; one torrent of fire after another has rolled down here in old times, and built up the island structure higher and higher. Underneath, it is honey-combed with caves; it would be of no use to dig wells in such a place; they would not hold water—you would not find any for them to hold, for that matter. Consequently, the planters depend upon cisterns.

The last lava flow occurred here so long ago that there are none now living who witnessed it. In one place it inclosed and burned down a grove of cocoa-nut trees, and the holes in the lava where the trunks stood are still visible; their sides retain the impression of the bark; the trees fell upon the burning river, and becoming partly submerged, left in it the perfect counterfeit of every knot and branch and leaf, and even nut, for curiosity seekers of a long distant day to gaze upon and wonder at.

There were doubtless plenty of Kanaka sentinels on guard hereabouts at that time, but they did not leave casts of their figures in the lava as the Roman sentinels at Herculaneum and Pompeii did. It is a pity it is so, because such things are so interesting, but so it is. They probably went away. They went away early, perhaps. It was very bad. However, they had their merits; the Romans exhibited the higher pluck, but the Kanakas showed the sounder judgment.

As usual, Brown loaded his unhappy horse with fifteen or twenty pounds of "specimens," to be cursed and worried over for a time, and then discarded for new toys of a similar nature. He is like most people who visit these Islands; they are always collecting specimens, with a wild enthusiasm, but they never get home with any of them.

CAPTAIN COOK'S DEATH-PLACE   Shortly we came in sight of that spot whose history is so familiar to every school-boy in the wide world—Kealakekua Bay—the place where Captain Cook, the great circumnavigator, was killed by the natives nearly a hundred years ago. The setting sun was flaming upon it, a Summer shower was falling, and it was spanned by two magnificent rainbows. Two gentlemen who were in advance of us rode through one of these, and for a moment their garments shone with a more than regal splendor. Why did not Captain Cook have taste enough to call his great discovery the Rainbow Islands? These charming spectacles are present to you at every turn; they are as common in all the islands as fogs and wind in San Francisco; they are visible every day, and frequently at night also—not the silvery bow we see once in an age in the States, by moonlight, but barred with all bright and beautiful colors, like the children of the sun and rain. I saw one of them a few nights ago. What the sailors call "rain-dogs'—little patches of rainbow—are often seen drifting about the heavens in these latitudes, like stained cathedral windows.

Kealakekua Bay is a little curve like the last kink of a snail shell, winding deep into the land, seemingly not more than a mile wide from shore to shore. It is bounded on one side—where the murder was done—by a little flat plain, on which stands a cocoanut grove and some ruined houses; a steep wall of lava, a thousand feet high at the upper end and three or four hundred at the lower, comes down from the mountain and bounds the inner extremity of it. From this wall the place takes its name, *Kealakekua*, which in the native tongue signifies "The Pathway of the Gods." They say (and still believe, in spite of their liberal education in Christianity) that the great god *Lono,* who used to live upon the hillside, always traveled that causeway when urgent business connected with heavenly affairs called him down to the seashore in a hurry.

As the red sun looked across the placid ocean through the tall, clean stems of the cocoanut trees, like a blooming whiskey bloat through the bars of a city prison, I went and stood in the edge of the water on the flat rock pressed by Captain Cook's feet when the blow was dealt that took away his life, and tried to picture in my mind the doomed man struggling in the midst of the multitude of exasperated savages—the men in the ship crowding to the vessel's side and gazing in anxious dismay toward the shore—the—But I discovered that I could not do it.

It was growing dark, the rain began to fall, we could see that the distant Boomerang was helplessly becalmed at sea, and so I adjourned to the cheerless little box of a warehouse and sat down to smoke and think, and wish the ship would make the land—for we had not eaten much for the ten hours and were viciously hungry.

THE STORY OF CAPTAIN COOK Plain unvarnished history takes the romance out of Captain Cook's assassination, and renders a deliberate verdict of justifiable homicide. Wherever he went among the islands he was cordially received and welcomed by the inhabitants, and his ships lavishly supplied with all manner of food. He returned these kindnesses with insult and ill-treatment.

When he landed at Kealakekua Bay, a multitude of natives, variously estimated at from ten to fifteen thousand, flocked about him and conducted him to the principal temple with more than royal honors—with honors suited to their chiefest god, for such they took him to be. They called him Lono—a deity who had resided at that place in a former age, but who had gone away and had ever since been anxiously expected back by the people. When Cook approached the awe-stricken people, they prostrated themselves and hid their faces. His coming was announced in a loud voice by heralds, and those who had not time to get out of the way after prostrating themselves, were trampled under foot by the following throngs. Arrived at the temple, he was taken into the most sacred part and placed before the principal idol, immediately under an altar of wood on which a putrid hog was deposited. "This was held toward him while the priest repeated a long and rapidly enunciated address, after which he was led to the top of a partially decayed scaffolding. Ten men, bearing a large hog and bundles of red cloth, then entered the temple and prostrated themselves before him. The cloth was taken from them by the priest, who encircled Cook with it in numerous folds, and afterward offered the hog to him in sacrifice. Two priests, alternately and in unison, chanted praises in honor of Lono, after which they led him to the chief idol, which, following their example, he kissed." He was anointed by the high priest—that is to say, his arms, hands and face, were slimed over with the chewed meat of a cocoanut; after this nasty compliment, he was regaled with awa manufactured in the mouths of attendants and spit out into a drinking vessel; "as the last most delicate attention, he was fed with swine meat which had been masticated for him by a filthy old man."

These distinguished civilities were never offered by the islanders to mere human beings. Cook was mistaken for their absent god; he accepted the situation and helped the natives to deceive themselves. His conduct might have been wrong, in a moral point of view, but his policy was good in conniving at the deception, and proved itself so; the belief that he was a god saved him a good while from being killed—protected him thoroughly and completely, until, in an unlucky moment, it was discovered that he was only a man. His death followed instantly. Jarves, from whose history, principally, I am condensing this narrative, thinks his destruction was a direct consequence of his dishonest personation of the god, but unhappily for the argument, the historian proves, over and over again, that the false Lono was spared time and again when simple Captain Cook of the Royal Navy would have been destroyed with small ceremony.

The idolatrous worship of Captain Cook, as above described, was repeated at every heathen temple he visited. Wherever he went the terrified common people, not being accustomed to seeing gods marching around of their own free will and accord and without human assistance, fled at his approach or fell down and worshipped him. A priest attended him and regulated the religious ceremonies which constantly took place in his honor; offerings, chants and addresses met him at every point. "For a brief period he moved among them an earthly god—observed, feared and worshipped." During all this time the whole island was heavily taxed to supply the wants of the ships or contribute to the gratification of their officers and crews, and, as was customary in such cases, no return expected. "The natives rendered much assistance in fitting the ships and preparing them for their voyages."

At one time the King of the island laid a tabu upon his people, confining them to their houses for several days. This interrupted the daily supply of vegetables to the ships; several natives tried to violate the tabu, under threats made by Cook's sailors, but were prevented by a chief, who, for thus enforcing the laws of his country, had a musket fired over his head from one of the ships. This is related in "Cook's Voyages." The tabu was soon removed, and the Englishmen were favored with the boundless hospitality of the natives as before, except that the Kanaka women were interdicted from visiting the ships; formerly, with extravagant hospitality, the people had sent their wives and daughters on board themselves. The officers and sailors went freely about the island, and were everywhere laden with presents. The King visited Cook in royal state, and gave him a large number of exceeding costly and valuable presents—in return for which the resurrected Lono presented His Majesty a white linen shirt and a dagger—an instance of illiberality in every way discreditable to a god.

"On the 2d of February, at the desire of his commander, Captain King proposed to the priests to purchase for fuel the railing which surrounded the top of the temple of *Lono!* In this Cook manifested as little respect for the religion in the mythology of which he figured so conspicuously, as scruples in violating the divine precepts of his own. Indeed, throughout his voyages a spirit regardless of the rights and feelings of others, when his own were interested, is manifested, especially in his last cruise, which is a blot upon his memory."

Cook desecrated the holy places of the temple by storing supplies for his ships in them, and by using the level grounds within the inclosure as a general workshop for repairing his sails, etc.—ground which was so sacred that no common native dared to set his foot upon it. Ledyard, a Yankee sailor, who was with Cook, and whose journal is considered the most just and reliable account of this eventful period of the voyage, says two iron hatchets were offered for the temple railing, and when the sacrilegious proposition was refused by the priests with horror and indignation, it was torn down by order of Captain Cook and taken to the boats by the sailors, and the images which surmounted it removed and destroyed in the presence of the priests and chiefs.

The abused and insulted natives finally grew desperate under the indignities that were constantly being heaped upon them by men whose wants they had unselfishly relieved at the expense of their own impoverishment, and angered by some fresh baseness, they stoned a party of sailors and drove them to their boats. From this time onward Cook and the natives were alternately friendly and hostile until Sunday, the 14th, whose setting sun saw the circumnavigator a corpse.

Ledyard's account and that of the natives vary in no important particulars. A Kanaka, in revenge for a blow he had received at the hands of a sailor (the natives say he was flogged), stole a boat from one of the ships and broke it up to get the nails out of it. Cook determined to seize the King and remove him to his ship and keep him a prisoner until the boat was restored. By deception and smoothly-worded persuasion he got the aged monarch to the shore, but when they were about to enter the boat a multitude of natives flocked to the place, and one raised a cry that their King was going to be taken away and killed. Great excitement ensued, and Cook's situation became perilous in the extreme. He had only a handful of marines and sailors with him, and the crowd of natives grew constantly larger and more clamorous every moment. Cook opened the hostilities himself. Hearing a native make threats, he had him pointed out, and fired on him with a blank cartridge. The man, finding himself unhurt, repeated his threats, and Cook fired again and wounded him mortally. A speedy retreat of the English party to the boats was now absolutely necessary; as soon as it was begun Cook was hit with a stone, and discovering who threw it, he shot the man dead. The officer in the boats observing the retreat, ordered the boats to fire; this occasioned Cook's guard to face about and fire also, and then the attack became general. Cook and Lieutenant Phillips were together a few paces in the rear of the guard, and perceiving a general fire without orders, quitted the King and ran to the shore to stop it; but not being able to make themselves heard, and being close pressed upon by the chiefs, they joined the guard, who fired as they retreated. Cook having at length reached the margin of the water, between the fire and the boats, waved with his hat for them to cease firing and come in; and while he was doing this a chief stabbed him from behind with an iron dagger (procured in traffic with the sailors), just under the shoulder-blade, and it passed quite through his body. Cook fell with his face in the water and immediately expired.

The native account says that after Cook had shot two men, he struck a stalwart chief with the flat of his sword, for some reason or other; the chief seized and pinioned Cook's arms in his powerful gripe, and bent him backward over his knee (not meaning to hurt him, for it was not deemed possible to hurt the god *Lono,* but to keep him from doing further mischief) and this treatment giving him pain, he betrayed his mortal nature with a groan! It was his death-warrant. The fraud which had served him so well was discovered at last. The natives shouted, "He groans!—he is not a god!" and instantly they fell upon him and killed him.

His flesh was stripped from the bones and burned (except nine pounds of it which were sent on board the ships). The heart was hung up in a native hut, where it was found and eaten by three children, who mistook it for the heart of a dog. One of these children grew to be a very old man, and died here in Honolulu a few years ago. A portion of Cook's bones were recovered and consigned to the deep by the officers of the ships.

Small blame should attach to the natives for the killing of Cook. They treated him well. In return, he abused them. He and his men inflicted bodily injury upon many of them at different times, and killed at least three of them before they offered any proportionate retaliation.

MARK TWAIN

Twentieth Letter to the *Sacramento Union*,
published August 30 and September 1, 1866.

« KEALAKEKUA BAY (S. I.), 1866 »

GREAT BRITAIN'S QUEER MONUMENT TO CAPTAIN COOK   When I digressed from my personal narrative to write about Cook's death I left myself, solitary, hungry and dreary, smoking in the little warehouse at Kealakekua Bay. Brown was out somewhere gathering up a fresh lot of specimens, having already discarded those he dug out of the old lava flow during the afternoon. I soon went to look for him. He had returned to the great slab of lava upon which Cook stood when he was murdered, and was absorbed in maturing a plan for blasting it out and removing it to his home as a specimen. Deeply pained at the bare thought of such a sacrilege, I reprimanded him severely and at once removed him from the scene of temptation. We took a walk then, the rain having moderated considerably. We clambered over the surrounding lava field, through masses of weeds, and stood for a moment upon the doorstep of an ancient ruin—the house once occupied by the aged King of Hawaii—and I reminded Brown that that very stone step was the one across which Captain Cook drew the reluctant old king when he turned his footsteps for the last time toward his ship.

I checked a movement on Mr. Brown's part: "No," I said, "let it remain; seek specimens of a less hallowed nature than this historical stone."

We also strolled along the beach toward the precipice of Kealakekua, and gazed curiously at the semicircular holes high up in its face—graves, they are, of ancient kings and chiefs—and wondered how the natives ever managed to climb from the sea up the sheer wall and make those holes and deposit their packages of patrician bones in them.

Tramping about in the rear of the warehouse, we suddenly came upon another object of interest. It was a cocoanut stump, four or five feet high, and about a foot in diameter at the butt. It had lava bowlders piled around its base to hold it up and keep it in its place, and it was entirely sheathed over, from top to bottom, with rough, discolored sheets of copper, such as ships' bottoms are coppered with. Each sheet had a rude inscription scratched upon it—with a nail, apparently—and in every case the execution was wretched. It was almost dark by this time, and the inscriptions would have been difficult to read even at noonday, but with patience and industry I finally got them all in my note-book. They read as follows:

"Near this spot fell CAPTAIN JAMES COOK, The Distinguished Circumnavigator, who Discovered these islands A. D. 1778. His Majesty's Ship Imogene, October 17, 1837."

"Parties from H. M. ship Vixen visited this spot Jan. 25, 1858."

"This sheet and capping put on by Sparrowhawk, September 16, 1839, in order to preserve this monument to the memory of Cook."

"Captain Montressor and officers of H. M. S. Calypso visited this spot the 18th of October, 1858."

"This tree having fallen, was replaced on this spot by H. M. S. V. Cormorant, G. T. Gordon, Esq., Captain, who visited this bay May 18, 1846."

"This bay was visited, July 4, 1843, by H. M. S. Carysfort, the Right Honorable Lord George Paulet, Captain, to whom, as the representative of Her Britannic Majesty Queen Victoria, these islands were ceded, February 25, 1843."

After Cook's murder, his second in command, on board the ship, opened fire upon the swarms of natives on the beach, and one of his cannon balls cut this cocoanut tree short off and left this monumental stump standing. It looked sad and lonely enough out there in the rainy twilight. But there is no other monument to Captain Cook. True, up on the mountain side we had passed by a large inclosure like an ample hog-pen, built of lava blocks, which marks the spot where Cook's flesh was stripped from his bones and burned; but this is not properly a monument, since it was erected by the natives themselves, and less to do honor to the circumnavigator than for the sake of convenience in roasting him. A thing like a guideboard was elevated above this pen on a tall pole, and formerly there was an inscription upon it describing the memorable occurrence that had there taken place; but the sun and the wind have long ago so defaced it as to render it illegible.

Twenty-first letter to the *Sacramento Union*,
published September 6 and 8, 1866.

« KEALAKEKUA BAY (S. I.), JULY 1866 »

A LUCRATIVE OFFICE When I woke up on the schooner's deck in the morning, the sun was shining down right fervently, everybody was astir, and Brown was gone—gone in a canoe to Captain Cook's side of the bay, the Captain said. I took a boat and landed on the opposite shore, at the port of entry. There was a house there—I mean a foreigner's house—and near it were some native grass huts. The Collector of this port of entry not only enjoys the dignity of office, but has emoluments also. . . .

THE HOLY PLACE Two hundred yards from the house was the ruins of the pagan temple of Lono, so desecrated by Captain Cook when he was pretending to be that deity. Its low, rude walls look about as they did when he saw them, no doubt. In a cocoanut grove near at hand is a tree with a hole through its trunk, said to have been made by a cannon ball fired from one of the ships at a crowd of natives immediately after Cook's murder. It is a very good hole. . . .

THE SHAMELESS BROWN I got uneasy about Brown finally, and as there were no canoes at hand, I got a horse whereon to ride three or four miles around to the other side of the bay and hunt him up. As I neared the end of the trip, and was riding down the "pathway of the gods" toward the sea in the sweltering sun, I saw Brown toiling up the hill in the distance, with a heavy burden on his shoulder, and knew that canoes were scarce with him, too. I dismounted and sat down in the shade of a crag, and after a while—after numerous pauses to rest by the way—Brown arrived at last, fagged out, and puffing like a steamboat, and gently eased his ponderous burden to the ground—the cocoanut stump all sheathed with copper memorials to the illustrious Captain Cook.

"Heavens and earth!" I said, "what are you going to do with that?"

"Going to do with it!—lemme blow a little—lemme blow—it's monstrous heavy, that log is; I'm most tired out—going to do with it! Why, I'm going to take her home for a specimen."

"You egregious ass! March straight back again and put it where you got it. Why, Brown, I am surprised at you—and hurt. I am grieved to think that a man who has lived so long in the atmosphere of refinement which surrounds me can be guilty of such vandalism as this. Reflect, Brown, and say if it be right—if it be manly—if it be generous—to lay desecrating hands upon this touching tribute of a great nation to her gallant dead? Why, Brown, the circumnavigator Cook labored all his life in the service of his country; with a fervid soul and a fearless spirit, he braved the dangers of the unknown seas and planted the banner of England far and wide over their beautiful island world. His works have shed a glory upon his native land which still lives in her history to-day; he laid down his faithful life in her service at last, and unforgetful of her son, she yet reveres his name and praises his deeds—and in token of her love, and in reward for the things he did for her, she had reared this monument to his memory—this symbol of a nation's gratitude—which you would defile with unsanctified hands. Restore it—go!"

"All right, if you say so; but I don't see no use of such a spread as you're making. I don't see nothing so very high-toned about this old rotten chunk. It's about the orneryest thing for a monument I've ever struck yet. If it suits Cook, though, all right; I wish him joy; but if I was planted under it I'd highst it, if it was the last act of my life. Monument! it ain't fit for a dog—I can buy dead loads of just such for six bits. She puts this over Cook—but she put one over that foreigner—what was his name?—Prince Albert—that cost a million dollars—and what did *he* do? Why, he never done anything—never done anything but lead a gallus, comfortable life, at home and out of danger, and raise a large family for Government to board at £300,000 a year apiece. But with this fellow, you know, it was different. However, if you say the old stump's got to go down again, down she goes. As I said before, if it's your wishes, I've got nothing to say. Nothing only this—I've fetched her a mile or a mile and a half, and she weighs a hundred and fifty I should judge, and if it would suit Cook just as well to have her planted up here instead of down there, it would be considerable of a favor to me."

I made him shoulder the monument and carry it back, nevertheless. His criticisms on the monument and its patron struck me, though, in spite of myself. The creature has got no sense, but his vaporings sound strangely plausible sometimes.

In due time we arrived at the port of entry once more.

MARK TWAIN.

Twenty-second letter to the *Sacramento Union*,
published September 22 and 29, 1866.

« KEALAKEKUA BAY (S. I.), JULY 1866 »

THE ROMANTIC GOD LONO I have been writing a good deal, of late, about the great god Lono and Captain Cook's personation of him. Now, while I am here in Lono's home, upon ground which his terrible feet have trodden in remote ages—unless these natives lie, and they would hardly do that, I suppose—I might as well tell who he was.

The idol the natives worshiped for him was a slender, unornamented staff twelve feet long. Unpoetical history says he was a favorite god on the island of Hawaii—a great king who had been deified for meritorious services—just our own fashion of rewarding heroes, with the difference that we would have made him a Postmaster instead of a god, no doubt. In an angry moment he slew his wife, a goddess named Kaikilani Alii. Remorse of conscience drove him mad, and tradition presents us the singular spectacle of a god traveling "on the shoulder;" for in his gnawing grief he wandered about from place to place boxing and wrestling with all whom he met. Of course this pastime soon lost its novelty, inasmuch as it must necessarily have been the case that when so powerful a deity sent a frail human opponent "to grass" he never came back any more. Therefore, he instituted games called makahiki, and ordered that they should be held in his honor, and then sailed for foreign lands on a three-cornered raft, stating that he would return some day, and that was the last of Lono. He was never seen any more; his raft got swamped, perhaps. But the people always expected his return, and they were easily led to accept Captain Cook as the restored god.

THE POETIC TRADITION But there is another tradition which is rather more poetical than this bald historical one. Lono lived in considerable style up here on the hillside. His wife was very beautiful, and he was devoted to her. One day he overheard a stranger proposing an elopement to her, and without waiting to hear her reply he took the stranger's life and then upbraided Kaikilani so harshly that her sensitive nature was wounded to the quick. She went away in tears, and Lono began to repent of his hasty conduct almost before she was out of sight. He sat him down under a cocoanut tree to await her return, intending to receive her with such tokens of affection and contrition as should restore her confidence and drive all sorrow from her heart. But hour after hour winged its tardy flight and yet she did not come. The sun went down and left him desolate. His all-wise instincts may have warned him that the separation was final, but he hoped on, nevertheless, and when the darkness was heavy he built a beacon fire at his door to guide the wanderer home again, if by any chance she had lost her way. But the night waxed and waned and brought another day, but not the goddess. Lono hurried forth and sought her far and wide, but found no trace of her. At night he set his beacon fire again and kept lone watch, but still she came not; and a new day found him a despairing, broken-hearted god. His misery could no longer brook suspense and solitude, and he set out to look for her. He told his sympathizing people he was going to search through all the island world for the lost light of his household, and he would never come back any more till he found her. The natives always implicitly believed that he was still pursuing his patient quest and that he would find his peerless spouse again some day, and come back; and so, for ages they waited and watched in trusting simplicity for his return. They gazed out wistfully over the sea at any strange appearance on its waters, thinking it might be their loved and lost protector. But Lono was to them as the rainbow-tinted future seen in happy visions of youth—for he never came.

Some of the old natives believed Cook was Lono to the day of their death; but many did not, for they could not understand how he could die if he was a god.

Further Reading

The latter section of Twain's *Roughing It* (1872; reprint, London and New York: Penguin, 1981) is based on his letters from Hawaii, cut and polished for book publication. The letters were not otherwise published in book form during Twain's lifetime. They were collected in *Letters from the Sandwich Islands: Written for the* Sacramento Union *by Mark Twain*, ed. G. Ezra Dane (Stanford: Stanford University Press, 1938), though the editor of this volume excluded those letters that concerned trade in the islands, arguing that these commercial reports lacked any literary value. Walter Francis Frear's compendious *Mark Twain and Hawaii* (Chicago: Lakeside Press, 1947) gives exhaustive background information about Twain's visit to Hawaii and the publication history of the letters, which are fully reproduced in an appendix. Twain's main historical source on Hawaii was James Jackson Jarves's *History of the Hawaiian or Sandwich Islands* (Boston: Tappan and Dennet, 1843); this incorporated translated extracts from "Ka Mooolelo Hawaii" written by scholars of the Lahainaluna Seminary, of which the most recent edition is Dorothy M. Kahananui, ed., *Ka Mooolelo Hawaii, Hawaiian Language Reader, Based on Sheldon Dibble, Ka Mooolelo Hawaii,* (Honolulu: University of Hawaii Press, 1984). The debate between Marshall Sahlins and Gananath Obeyesekere over the paradigm of Cook's premortem apotheosis can be followed through several volumes: Sahlins, *Historical Metaphors and Mythical Realities: Structure in the Early History of the Sandwich Islands Kingdom* (Ann Arbor: University of Michigan Press, 1981); Sahlins, *Islands of History* (London: Tavistock, 1985); Obeyesekere, *The Apotheosis of Captain Cook: European Mythmaking in the Pacific* (Princeton: Princeton University Press, 1992); and Sahlins, *How Natives Think: About Captain Cook, for Example* (Chicago: University of Chicago Press, 1995).

24
———

CONSTANCE FREDERIKA
GORDON-CUMMING
Quite Alone in a Mountain Village

. . . .

THOUGH CONSTANCE FREDERIKA GORDON-CUMMING (1837–1924) is today less well-known than Mary Kingsley and Isabella Bird, she was hardly a less significant Victorian lady traveler and travel writer. Her accounts of essentially recreational journeys in South Asia, North America, the Pacific, and elsewhere were popular and were frequently reprinted over the last three decades of the nineteenth century. Her writing is polished and literary; she evokes natural beauty and the variety of scenery, the dignity and oddity in turn of indigenous individuals, and the attractiveness of indigenous artifacts that are appropriated by her as "curiosities"; she is quick to distinguish between the aesthetically appealing in pre-Christian indigenous culture and the deplorable inauthenticity of acculturation, manifest in trade artifacts. Her presence in Fiji was intimately connected with the early years of British rule there: her relative, the first governor, Sir Arthur Hamilton Gordon, asked her to serve as his wife's companion, and she was thus a member of the governor's household while in Fiji over 1875–77. And yet she moved about a good deal, sometimes with Lady Gordon, and sometimes with missionaries or independently. It is not surprising that she responds to Fijians in terms that were shared by Gordon, who also saw parallels between Fijian life and that of earlier Britons, and who also took great interest in Fijian material culture.

In her study of women's travel writing, *Discourses of Difference* (1991), Sara Mills juxtaposes "the discourses of colonialism" and "the discourses of femininity"; the former requires an authoritative, intrepid narrator, while the latter entails passivity and interest in human relationships. In the case of Mary Kingsley, among others, Mills finds that these discourses are both drawn upon, and in some respects subverted (1991, chapter 6 passim). Something like this clash might be identified in Gordon-Cumming, but her text undermines the strong distinction between the discourses that is a predicate of this analysis. Her attitude toward Fijians is often sentimental and affectionate, but frequently also renders them childlike, comical, or ludicrous, like Reuben's "exceedingly fat wife" mentioned below. Even when she is drawing attention to the dignity of senior men, Gordon-Cumming characterizes them as picturesque; this is affirmative but does not go far toward acknowledging them as complex, fully human characters, as distinct from the scenery of amusement and observation. This interest in "relationships" cannot simply be opposed to an authoritative colonialist attitude, since the relationships are conceived of in sentimental yet patently paternalistic, or maternalistic, terms. The colonialism in Gordon-Cumming's narrative cannot be ascribed to her partial embrace of a "colonial discourse" that is otherwise in tension with her representation of her femininity; nor would it be apt to characterize her first-person sentimentality as a feminine modality of colonial discourse: as we have seen in previous extracts, the thematization of particular relationships, and for that matter of the passivity of the traveler, were not gender specific, either in the experience of travel or in its narration.

Gordon-Cumming's emphasis upon her absolute safety in parts of Fiji, which had only very recently adopted Christianity and rejected practices such as cannibalism, draws attention to the new effectiveness of British rule, and the book does have something of the form of an advertisement for the colony: the personal letters that make up the substance of the book are preceded by a succinct account of the circumstances of cession to Britain and followed up with an appendix on aspects of the colonial administration. But Gordon-Cumming's interest in arousing the fascination of a metropolitan readership leads her to accentuate both the negative and positive dimensions of her story. As in other literature of the period, much is made of cannibalism (which had, in fact, been more widely practiced in Fiji than in most other societies, especially during the mid-nineteenth-century escalation of warfare), yet much is also made of the congenial character of colonial domesticity and of the intimacies that emerge between members of the British elite and Fijian aristocrats. The paradox is epitomized in the very title of the book, which appears on decorated bindings of some early editions with a prominent "cannibal fork," a horrifying variant upon a harmless domestic implement and almost an emblem of Fiji at the time. This notion of being "at home" among cannibals was the droll, almost bizarre, motif of Gordon-Cumming's book. — NICHOLAS THOMAS

.   .   .   .

FIG. 11. *Rewa, December 1875.* Watercolor by Constance F. Gordon-Cumming. By permission of Cambridge University Museum of Archaeology and Anthropology.

C. F. Gordon-Cumming, *At Home in Fiji*, 5th ed. (Edinburgh: Blackwood, 1885).

« CHAPTER 9, PP. 80–82. »

NAKORO VATU (THE STONE TOWN)
December 19, 1875.

DEAREST JEAN,—You will have heard from Eisa of our start from Rewa. Now we are a long way up the river, and indulging in a sort of continuous picnic, which is full of interest to me, though very difficult to describe so as to convey to you any idea of its fascination to one actually living in it.

The stream, of course, narrowed rapidly as we ascended, and in doing so gained immensely in interest. Gradually we approached beautiful mountain-ranges, and whenever we landed and ascended even the smallest rising ground, we found ourselves encircled by a panorama of rare loveliness. But of course, so long as we were on the water-level our horizon was bounded by the river-banks, and after a while the mere loveliness of vegetation became almost monotonous, and we found ourselves gliding unheeding past forests of tree-ferns and grand old trees, festooned with a network of lianas, rich and rare, such as a few days previously would have driven us into ecstasies of delight. Here and there, where some quiet pool in a rocky stream offered a tempting bathing-place, we called a halt, and therein revelled, while the boatmen were boiling the kettle and preparing breakfast or lunch in some shady nook at a respectful distance. No words can describe to you how delicious are such impromptu bathes in clear sparkling streams, embowered in exquisite ferns, which meet overhead, throwing a cool shade on the water, and forming a lovely tracery, through which you get glimpses of the bluest sky. And the light that does reach you is mellowed, and the colour of the great fronds is like that tender green of beech-woods in early spring; and the water is so fresh and delightful that you would fain prolong your bathe all day.

We halted several days at Navounindrala, where the river branches off into two heads, the Wai Nimala and the Wai Nimbooco, both too shallow at this season to admit of the large boat going any further; so, leaving it at the junction, we transferred our three selves to one very large canoe, while two ordinary ones carried our necessary goods. Thenceforward we paddled and poled by turns, as occasion demanded; and when any difficulty arose in ascending rapids, we invariably found ready helpers willing to lend us their aid.

We first proceeded up the Wai Nimbooco, sleeping at various villages, in which no white women had previously set foot; nor, indeed, any white teacher, for it is only a year since these people were cannibal and heathen. The first native teachers sent to them died in the measles, and those now sent to replace them are men from the Windward Isles, half Tongan, and they find great difficulty in mastering the mountain dialect, which differs greatly from that of Bau and other coast districts. But the people seem eager to make the very most of their small advantages, and everywhere we find flourishing schools and most devout congregations; and our party receives cordial welcome, the villagers crowding round to shake hands, foreign fashion I certainly prefer this to having my hand sniffed impressively!

In some villages the people brought very curious bowls, clubs, and spears for sale, and I have greatly enlarged my collection. Some of the wood-carving is so fine that it fills me with wonder, when I remember that hitherto the only implements of these artists have been stone-axes, and rats' or sharks' teeth to do the finer work. Imagine the patience and contrivance which every carved spear-head represents. I bought several very tall carved walking-sticks, used by the old men, which I think some of you will like to adopt as alpenstocks, though you can never hope to look as picturesque as the fine old men who brought them to me. They generally ask for large strong knives, or so many fathoms of very wide strong white calico, in preference to money, and are very discriminating as to quality, having learnt by sad experience how worthless are the cheap Manchester fabrics sent to these isles for trade with natives—mere whitened shams, made up with dressing, and useless when washed. . . .

« CHAPTER IO, PP. 90–91. »

On great festivals the family jewels are all displayed. They consist of necklaces of whales' teeth rudely fastened together with sinnet, or else most carefully cut into long curved strips like miniature tusks, highly polished, and strung together in the form of a great collar, which is worn with the curved points turning outwards like a frill. The average length of each tooth is about six inches; but some necklaces, which are treasured as heirlooms, are nearly double this size, and all the teeth are beautifully regular. Their effect when worn by a chief in full dress is singularly picturesque, though scarcely so becoming as the large curved boar's tooth, which sometimes forms an almost double circle, and is worn suspended from the neck, the white ivory gleaming against the rich brown skin.

The most artistic and uncommon ornament of a Fijian chief is a breastplate from six to ten inches in diameter, made of polished whale's tooth, sliced and inlaid with pearly shell, all most beautifully joined together. These, like all native work, whether wood-carving or ivory, not only claim admiration, but fill me with wonder at the patient ingenuity which could possibly produce such results with the tools hitherto possessed by these people, to whom metals were unknown, whose axes and hatchets were made of smooth and beautifully polished greenstone (precisely similar to the celts of our forefathers, and how they made these is to me incomprehensible). I have bought several tied with coarse sinnet to a rude handle of wood cut in the form of a bent knee. When the stone axe had accomplished the first rough shaping of the form required, a skilfully used firestick next came into use, and then a lump of mushroom coral, or a piece of the rough skin of the sting-ray, stretched on wood, acted as a rasp or file. A fine polish was attained by patient friction with pumice-stone and cocoa-nut oil. The only other tools of the Fijian workman consisted of broken shells, the teeth of rats and fishes, or the sharp spines of the echini, set in hard wood. Yet with these rude implements these untutored savages (if so we should call them) produced forms so artistic, and carving so elaborate and graceful, as must excite the keen admiration of all lovers of art.

But alas for the vulgarising influence of contact with white men! Already the majority of the islanders have sold their own admirable ornaments, and wear instead trashy English necklaces, with perhaps a circular tin looking-glass attached, or an old cotton-reel in the ear instead of a rudely carved ear-ring. In the more frequented districts this lamentable change thrusts itself more forcibly on the attention, as almost all the fine old clubs and beautifully carved spears have been bought up, and miserable sticks and nondescript articles—including old European battle-axes—take their place. . . .

« CHAPTER 12, PP. 107–8. »

QUITE ALONE IN A MOUNTAIN VILLAGE—RETURN TO REWA—BASALTIC PILLARS—REWA POTTERY—BAU—NEW YEAR'S EVE—KING THAKOMBAU AS AN ELDER OF THE WESLEYAN CHURCH—PRE-CHRISTIAN TIMES.

NAKAMEROUSI, Monday, *Dec. 27.*

DEAREST NELL—I must begin a letter to you to-night, for the strangeness of the situation exceeds any I have yet happened on. I have left the Langhams at Nirukuruku, and am here quite by myself, very much at home in a Fijian hut, and surrounded by natives, most of whom were, till within the last two years, uncompromising cannibals, and who, moreover, have never before beheld the face of a white woman!

The way it came about was this. When we were going up the river in hot haste, and with no time to loiter by the way, the village of Nakamerousi had attracted my especial admiration. It is perched on a steep bank, and looks right along a broad reach of the river to a beautiful mountain-range. Being anxious to secure a sketch from that point, it was agreed that I should take advantage of the return thither of Reuben, the native teacher, who, with the help of Joshua, one of the boatmen, accordingly paddled me down in a small canoe. Great was the astonishment of the villagers, and still greater that of Reuben's exceedingly fat wife, in whose house I am spending the night. We made great friends, though I could hardly utter a word of Fijian, and probably few of those around me had ever heard a word of English.

As seen from outside, this house promised well, but on entering I perceived that the first effort of civilisation had not improved the ordinary home. For the teachers have been encouraged to show the advantages of a separate sleeping-room, by having a third of the house screened off with a reed partition, but so little do they appreciate the innovation that they generally convert the inner room into a store-room for yams or lumber. So it is in this case. However, the kind fat old lady resigned the post of honour for my benefit, and here I have hung up my plaid-curtain and mosquito-net, thereby greatly interesting a crowd of spectators, who had previously watched the wonderful process of consuming chocolate and biscuits. One kind woman has brought water in a bamboo, and therewith filled my big brass basin (the old companion of my happy tent-life in the Himalayas).

Now a party of laughing brown children are holding up small torches of blazing bamboo, by the light of which I am writing; but the illumination seems to me so likely to end in a general blaze that I will not be responsi-ble for it. And so good night. The girls are greatly delighted with my hair-brushes, especially my tooth-brush. I shall have to keep jealous guard lest they experiment with it! They themselves use wooden combs, sometimes ornamented with coloured string and beads.

Really these falling sparks are too dangerous. Good night again.

Further Reading

Gordon-Cumming's other Pacific travel books include *Fire Fountains* (on Hawaii, 1883) and *A Lady's Cruise in a French Man o' War* (1882). The initial phases of British rule in Fiji and the interest in artifacts in the governor's household are discussed in Nicholas Thomas, *Entangled Objects* (Cam-bridge, Mass.: Harvard University Press, 1991), chapter 4; Claudia Knap-man discusses Gordon-Cumming and Lady Gordon briefly in *White Women in Fiji 1835–1930* (Sydney: Allen and Unwin, 1986), which is pri-marily concerned with settler women. Sara Mills's *Discourses of Difference: An Analysis of Women's Travel Writing and Colonialism* (London: Routledge, 1991) was one of the first critical studies of this area; more recent work in-cludes Susan Morgan, *Place Matters: Gendered Geography in Victorian Women's Travel Books about Southeast Asia* (New Brunswick, N.J.: Rutgers University Press, 1996). There is as yet no comparable book-length study of women's writing in the Pacific.

25

ROBERT LOUIS STEVENSON

Belated First Contact

. . . .

ROBERT LOUIS STEVENSON (1850–94) spent the last six years of his life either traveling or in residence in Oceania. He gave up a position of celebrity in English and American literary circles to settle permanently on an estate in Samoa, Vailima, where he found the climate beneficial to his health, the mail service adequate to continued literary production, and contemporary chiefly culture and rivalries reminiscent of the Scottish romance tradition that his writing had helped to revive. His publication proceeded with unabated intensity from the Pacific: he continued to write romances, poetry, adventure stories, and travel narratives, and also expanded into realist prose, history, oral-style tale, and fable in response to the challenges offered by the subject matter and local narrative traditions that he encountered. The variations in his writing formula did not always meet with a positive reception from publishers, audiences, and critics. *In the South Seas*, from which this extract is taken, received criticism when it was published in its earliest form from, among others, Stevenson's wife Fanny (see chapter 26), who argued that the book was in effect a scholarly synthesis, failing to meet its readers' desires for accounts of the romantic and exotic.

When Stevenson first departed San Francisco for the Marquesas with his family in June 1888, his American agent had obtained a commission from the *New York Sun* for a series of letters describing his anticipated adventures in the South Seas, also to be serialized in the English press. Stevenson worked on the draft of a travel account during both his journey on the yacht *Casco*, which took the party through French Polynesia and to Hawaii, and his travels on the trading steamer

Equator, among the atolls of Micronesia. This was printed as a copyright edition, *The South Seas*, in November 1890, which was sent on to the *Sun* for serialization. The paper refused to print this text, claiming that it was not in the letter format they had commissioned. *In the South Seas* did not in fact appear in book form during Stevenson's lifetime, and evolved in its contents and order of arrangement throughout the early years of its publication (Swearingen 1980, 143).

In the South Seas is as much a commentary on the desires that inform encounters with exotic cultures, textual and actual, as it is a compendium of travel. The early chapters of the book deal with Stevenson's travels in the Marquesas and among the islands of the Tuamotu archipelago—regions in which he is able to locate the evocative traces of cannibalism and savagery. In the third section of the book, however (one not consistently published as part of *In the South Seas*), he reaches Hawaii, an effectively Americanized group of islands, where he initially searches in vain for traces of the strange and authentic. Attempting to differentiate his own experience from that of the tourist multitude, he chooses to visit Hookena on the Kona coast of Hawaii, "a village uninhabited by any white, the creature of pure native taste," and finds himself in the equivalent of "a well-to-do western hamlet in the United States" (Stevenson 1924a, 179). The legacy of worship and mythologization attributed to Captain Cook, which Mark Twain had skeptically assessed some years earlier (chapter 23), seems to offer a measure for the failed originality of Stevenson's experience. As he goes unnoticed in a society that replicates American dress, housing, and cuisine, he measures the difference between his own reconstructed first-contact scenario and Cook's initial cross-cultural encounter. His search for the exotic is doubly nostalgic: he elegizes not only the disappearance of the Hawaiian heroes of old, but equally the first visitor's privileged experience of objectification within the Hawaiian metaphoric imagination. He regrets a range of possibilities of reappraisal opened up by early contact with other cultures: the fascination that European objects held before they became domesticated, the novelties initially suggested by different bodies and their costumings.

From Hawaii Stevenson boarded a trading steamer for the Gilbert Islands (Kiribati), staying first at Butaritari and then finally locating in the "quarantined" island of Abemama ("Apemama") something akin to the unique contact experience he had been seeking. Abemama was the realm of the absolute monarch, Tem Binoka ("Tembinok'"), whose father, Tem Baiteke, established a regime unique in nineteenth-century Polynesia. According to the Pacific historian H. E. Maude, Tem Baiteke and his son "maintained the political, economic, and social integrity of their territory from the beginnings of European contact to virtually the end of the nineteenth century, selecting and accepting from the European only such ideas and material goods as appeared to them of value, and these strictly on their own terms and not those dictated by the dominant race" (Maude 1973, 223). As Stevenson reports, Europeans resided in Abemama on sufferance and only for specified periods; trade and importation were strictly controlled, and foreign innovations were either prohibited or made the prerogative of the ruler. Tem Binoka's ambitions were only checked when he ventured into empire-building and export.

Tem Binoka's island offers Stevenson unexplored literary territory. He describes Abemama as "a close island, lying there in the sea with closed doors; the king himself, like a vigilant officer, ready at the wicket to scrutinise and reject intrenching visitors. Hence the attraction of our enterprise; not merely because it was a little difficult, but because this social quarantine, a curiosity in itself, has been the preservative of others" (Stevenson 1924a, 83). Yet Abemama is not simply a preserve of cultural authenticity. Tem Binoka is a "trader king" whose desire for foreign souvenirs reflects Stevenson's own enthusiasm for genuine cultural encounter. The items that Stevenson collected during his Pacific travels—Polynesian necklaces, fans, combs, currency, domestic utensils, and items of dress—were, like the soap, waistcoats, and stoves purchased by Tem Binoka, everyday items rendered significant by cultural difference. In Tem Binoka's cabinet of European curiosities the quotidian is placed under scrutiny: Stevenson experiences the defamiliarization he had missed in his visit to Hawaii. Although he portrays Tem Binoka as, to an extent, the victim of foreign trading agendas, he also depicts traders pushed to the extremes of inventiveness in order to accommodate their products to the king's taste, and recognizes the surreal eclecticism of Tem Binoka's museum of European trade articles, his transgression of the distinctions between use and exchange values.

In achieving a semblance of that first contact that he has repeatedly sought, however, Stevenson becomes implicated in a regime of power that is a microcosm of the colonial. Tem Binoka dresses up as the imperialist, supervising the building of Equator city, the Stevensons's compound, in costume: "a pith helmet on his head, a meerschaum pipe in his mouth" (Stevenson 1924a, 287). As guest of the king, Stevenson finds he has limited contact with Tem Binoka's subjects: "We saw but little of the commons of the isle . . . Many villagers passed us daily going afield; but they fetched a wide circuit round our tapu, and seemed to avert their looks" (Stevenson 1924a, 305). Having desired to play first author, he suspects instead that he has become the subject of an imperial minidrama: distanciated from, rather than in contact with, island life. — VANESSA SMITH

Robert Louis Stevenson, *In the South Seas: Being an Account of Experiences and Observations in the Marquesas, Paumotus, and Gilbert Islands in the Course of Two Cruises, on the Yacht 'Casco' (1888) and the Schooner 'Equator' (1889)* (London: William Heinemann, 1924).

« FROM PART 3, THE EIGHT ISLANDS, CHAPTER I, »
THE KONA COAST.

It was on a Saturday afternoon that the steamer *Hall* conveyed me to Hookena. She was charged with tourists on their way to the volcano; and I found it hard to justify my choice of a week in an unheard-of hamlet, rather than a visit to one of the admitted marvels of the world. I do not know that I can justify it now and to a larger audience. I should prefer, indeed, to have seen both; but I was at the time embarrassed with arrears of work; it was imperative that I should choose; and I chose one week in a Kona village and another in the lazaretto, and renounced the craters of Maunaloa and Haleakala. For there are some so constituted as to find a man or a society more curious than the highest mountain; some, in whom the lava foreshores of Kona and Kaū will move as deep a wonder as the fiery vents that made them what they are.

The land and sea breezes alternate on the Kona coast with regularity; and the veil of rain draws up and down the talus of the mountain, now retiring to the zone of forests, now descending to the margin of the sea. It was in one of the latter and rarer moments that I was set on board a whale boat full of intermingled barrels, passengers, and oars-men. The rain fell and blotted the crude and sombre colours of the scene. The coast rose but a little way; it was then intercepted by the cloud: and for all that appeared, we might have been landing on an isle of some two hundred feet of elevation. On the immediate foreshore, under a low cliff, there stood some score of houses, trellised and verandahed, set in narrow gardens, and painted gaudily in green and white; the whole surrounded and shaded by a grove of cocoa-palms and fruit trees, springing (as by miracle) from the bare lava. In front, the population of the neighbourhood were gathered for the weekly incident, the passage of the steamer; sixty to eighty strong, and attended by a disproportionate allowance of horses, mules, and donkeys; for this land of rock is, singular to say, a land of breeding. The green trees, the painted houses, the gay dresses of the women, were everywhere relieved on the uncompromising blackness of the lava; and the rain, which fell unheeded by the sightseers, blended and beautified the contrast.

The boat was run in upon a breaker, and we passengers ejected on a flat rock where the next wave submerged us to the knees. There we continued to stand, the rain drenching us from above, the sea from below, like people mesmerised; and as we were all (being travellers) tricked out with the green garlands of departure, we must have offered somewhat the same appearance as a shipwrecked picnic.

The purser spied and introduced me to my host, ex-judge Nahinu, who was then deep in business, despatching and receiving goods. He was dressed in pearl-grey tweed like any self-respecting Englishman; only the band of his wide-awake was made of peacock's feather.— "House by and by," said he, his English being limited, and carried me to the shelter of a rather lofty shed. On three sides it was open, on the fourth closed by a house; it was reached from without by five or six wooden steps; on the fourth side, a further flight of ten conducted to the balcony of the house; a table spread with goods divided it across, so that I knew it for the village store and (according to the laws that rule in country life) the village lounging-place. People sat with dangling feet along the house verandah, they sat on benches on the level of the shed or among the goods upon the counter; they came and went, they talked and waited; they opened, skimmed, and pocketed half-read, their letters; they opened the journal, and found a moment, not for the news, but for the current number of the story: me thought, I might have been in France, and the paper the *Petit Journal* instead of the *Nupepa Eleele*. On other islands I had been the centre of attention; here none observed my presence. One hundred and ten years before, the ancestors of these indifferents had looked in the faces of Cook and his seamen with admiration and alarm, called them gods, called them volcanoes; took their clothes for a loose skin, confounded their hats and their heads, and described their pockets as a "treasure door, through which they plunge their hands into their bodies and bring forth cutlery and necklaces and cloth and nails," and to-day the coming of the most attractive stranger failed (it would appear) to divert them from Miss Porter's *Scottish Chiefs:* for that was the novel of the day.

My host returned, and led me round the shore among the mules and donkeys to his house. Like all the houses of the hamlet, it was on the European or, to be more descriptive, on the American plan. The parlour was fitted with the usual furniture and ornamented with the portraits of Kamehameha the third, Lunalilo, Kalakaua, the queen consort of the isles, and Queen Victoria. There was a Bible on the table, other books stood on a shelf. A comfortable bedroom was placed at my service, the welcome afforded me was cordial and unembarrassed, the food good and plentiful. My host, my hostess; his grown daughters, strapping lasses; his young hopefuls, misbehaving at a meal or perfunctorily employed upon their school-books: all that I found in that house, beyond the speech and a few exotic dishes on the table, would have been familiar and exemplary in Europe.

I walked that night beside the sea. The steamer with its lights and crowd of tourists was gone by; it had left me alone among these aliens, and I felt no touch of strangeness. The trim, lamp-lit houses shining quietly, like villas, each in its narrow garden; the gentle sound of speech from within; the room that awaited my return, with the lamp, and the books, and the spectacled householder studying his Bible:—there was nothing changed; it was in such conditions I had myself grown up, and played, a child, beside the borders of another sea. And some ten miles from where I walked, Cook was adored as a deity; his bones, when he was dead, were cleansed for worship; his entrails devoured in a mistake by rambling children.

« FROM PART 5, THE GILBERTS—APEMAMA, CHAPTER I, »
THE KING OF APEMAMA: THE ROYAL TRADER.

There is one great personage in the Gilberts: Tembinok' of Apemama: solely conspicuous, the hero of song, the butt of gossip. Through the rest of the group the kings are slain or fallen in tutelage: Tembinok' alone remains, the last tyrant, the last erect vestige of a dead society. The white man is everywhere else, building his houses, drinking his gin, getting in and out of trouble with the weak native governments. There is only one white on Apemama, and he on sufferance, living far from court, and hearkening and watching his conduct like a mouse in a cat's ear. Through all the other islands a stream of native visitors comes and goes, travelling by families, spending years on the grand tour. Apemama alone is left upon one side, the tourist dreading to risk himself within the clutch of Tembinok'. And fear of the same Gorgon follows and troubles them at home. Maiana once paid him tribute; he once fell upon and seized Nonuti: first steps to the empire of the archipelago. A British warship coming on the scene, the conqueror was driven to disgorge, his career checked in the outset, his dear-bought armoury sunk in his own lagoon. But the impression had been made; periodical fear of him still shakes the islands: rumour depicts him mustering his canoes for a fresh onfall; rumour can name his destination; and Tembinok' figures in the patriotic war-songs of the Gilberts like Napoleon in those of our grandfathers.

We were at sea, bound from Mariki to Nonuti and Tapituea, when the wind came suddenly fair for Apemama. The course was at once changed;

all hands were turned-to to clean ship, the decks holystoned, the cabin washed, the trade-room overhauled. In all our cruising we never saw the *Equator* so smart as she was made for Tembinok'. Nor was Captain Reid alone in these coquetries; for, another schooner chancing to arrive during my stay in Apemama, I found that she also was dandified for the occasion. And the two cases stand alone in my experience of South Sea traders.

We had on board a family of native tourists, from the grandsire to the babe in arms, trying (against an extraordinary series of ill-luck) to regain their native island of Peru[1]. Five times already they had paid their fare and taken ship; five times they had been disappointed, dropped penniless upon strange islands, or carried back to Butaritari, whence they sailed. This last attempt had been no better starred; their provisions were exhausted. Peru was beyond hope, and they had cheerfully made up their minds to a fresh stage of exile in Tapituea or Nonuti. With this slant of wind their random destination became once more changed; and like the Calendar's pilot, when the "black mountains" hove in view, they changed colour and beat upon their breasts. Their camp, which was on deck in the ship's waist, re-sounded with complaint. They would be set to work, they must become slaves, escape was hopeless, they must live and toil and die in Apemama, in the tyrant's den. With this sort of talk they so greatly terrified their chil-dren, that one (a big hulking boy) must at last be torn screaming from the schooner's side. And their fears were wholly groundless. I have little doubt they were not suffered to be idle; but I can vouch for it that they were kindly and generously used. For, the matter of a year later, I was once more shipmate with these inconsistent wanderers on board the *Janet Nicoll*. Their fare was paid by Tembinok'; they who had gone ashore from the *Equator* destitute, reappeared upon the *Janet* with new clothes, laden with mats and presents, and bringing with them a magazine of food, on which they lived like fighting cocks throughout the voyage; I saw them at length repatriated, and I must say they showed more concern on quitting Ape-mama than delight at reaching home.

We entered by the north passage (Sunday, September 1st), dodging among shoals. It was a day of fierce equatorial sunshine; but the breeze was strong and chill; and the mate, who conned the schooner from the cross-trees, returned shivering to the deck. The lagoon was thick with many-tinted wavelets; a continuous roaring of the outer sea overhung the an-chorage; and the long, hollow crescent of palm ruffled and sparkled in the wind. Opposite our berth the beach was seen to be surmounted for some

1. In the Gilbert Group.

distance by a terrace of white coral, seven or eight feet high and crowned in turn by the scattered and incongruous buildings of the palace. The village adjoins on the south, a cluster of high-roofed maniap's. And village and palace seemed deserted.

We were scarce yet moored, however, before distant and busy figures appeared upon the beach, a boat was launched, and a crew pulled out to us bringing the king's ladder. Tembinok' had once an accident; has feared ever since to intrust his person to the rotten chandlery of South Sea traders; and devised in consequence a frame of wood, which is brought on board a ship as soon as she appears, and remains lashed to her side until she leave. The boat's crew, having applied this engine, returned at once to shore. They might not come on board; neither might we land, or not without danger of offence; the king giving pratique in person. An interval followed, during which dinner was delayed for the great man; the prelude of the ladder, giving us some notion of his weighty body and sensible, ingenious character, had highly whetted our curiosity; and it was with something like excitement that we saw the beach and terrace suddenly blacken with attendant vassals, the king and party embark, the boat (a man-of-war gig) come flying towards us dead before the wind, and the royal coxswain lay us cleverly aboard, mount the ladder with a jealous diffidence, and descend heavily on deck.

Not long ago he was overgrown with fat, obscured to view, and a burthen to himself. Captains visiting the island advised him to walk; and though it broke the habits of a life and the traditions of his rank, he practised the remedy with benefit. His corpulence is now portable; you would call him lusty rather than fat; but his gait is still dull, stumbling, and elephantine. He neither stops nor hastens, but goes about his business with an implacable deliberation. We could never see him and not be struck with his extraordinary natural means for the theatre: a beaked profile like Dante's in the mask, a mane of long black hair, the eye brilliant, imperious, and inquiring: for certain parts, and to one who could have used it, the face was a fortune. His voice matched it well, being shrill, powerful, and uncanny, with a note like a sea-bird's. Where there are no fashions, none to set them, few to follow them if they were set, and none to criticise, he dresses—as Sir Charles Grandison lived—"to his own heart." Now he wears a woman's frock, now a naval uniform; now (and more usually) figures in a masquerade costume of his own design: trousers and a singular jacket with shirt tails, the cut and fit wonderful for island workmanship, the material always handsome, sometimes green velvet, sometimes cardinal red silk. This masquerade becomes him admirably. In the woman's frock he looks ominous and weird beyond belief. I see him now come pacing towards me in the cruel sun, solitary, a figure out of Hoffmann.

A visit on board ship, such as that at which we now assisted, makes a chief part and by far the chief diversion of the life of Tembinok'. He is not only the sole ruler, he is the sole merchant of his triple kingdom, Apemama, Aranuka, and Kuria, well-planted islands. The taro goes to the chiefs, who divide as they please among their immediate adherents; but certain fish, turtles—which abound in Kuria,—and the whole produce of the cocoa-palm, belong exclusively to Tembinok'. "A' cobra berong me," observed his majesty with a wave of his hand; and he counts and sells it by the houseful.[2] "You got copra, king?" I have heard a trader ask. "I got two, three outches,"[3] his majesty replied: "I think three." Hence the commercial importance of Apemama, the trade of three islands being centred there in a single hand; hence it is that so many whites have tried in vain to gain or to preserve a footing; hence ships are adorned, cooks have special orders, and captains array themselves in smiles, to greet the king. If he be pleased with his welcome and the fare he may pass days on board, and every day, and sometimes every hour, will be of profit to the ship. He oscillates between the cabin, where he is entertained with strange meats, and the trade-room, where he enjoys the pleasures of shopping on a scale to match his person. A few obsequious attendants squat by the house door, awaiting his least signal. In the boat, which has been suffered to drop astern, one or two of his wives lie covered from the sun under mats, tossed by the short sea of the lagoon, and enduring agonies of heat and tedium. This severity is now and then relaxed and the wives allowed on board. Three or four were thus favoured on the day of our arrival: substantial ladies airily attired in *ridis*. Each had a share of copra, her *peculium*, to dispose of for herself. The display in the trade-room—hats, ribbons, dresses, scents, tins of salmon—the pride of the eye and the lust of the flesh—tempted them in vain. They had but the one idea—tobacco, the island currency, tantamount to minted gold; returned to shore with it, burthened but rejoicing; and late into the night, on the royal terrace, were to be seen counting the sticks by lamplight in the open air.

The king is no such economist. He is greedy of things new and foreign. House after house, chest after chest, in the palace precinct, is already crammed with clocks, musical boxes, blue spectacles, umbrellas, knitted

2. Copra: the dried kernel of the cocoa-nut, the chief article of commerce throughout the Pacific Islands.

3. Houses.

waist-coats, bolts of stuff, tools, rifles, fowling-pieces, medicines, European foods, sewing-machines, and, what is more extraordinary, stoves: all that ever caught his eye, tickled his appetite, pleased him for its use, or puzzled him with its apparent inutility. And still his lust is unabated. He is possessed by the seven devils of the collector. He hears a thing spoken of, and a shadow comes on his face. "I think I no got him," he will say; and the treasures he has seem worthless in comparison. If a ship be bound for Apemama, the merchant racks his brain to hit upon some novelty. This he leaves carelessly in the main cabin or partly conceals in his own berth, so that the king shall spy it for himself. "How much you want?" inquires Tembinok', passing and pointing. "No, king; that too dear," returns the trader. "I think I like him," says the king. This was a bowl of gold-fish. On another occasion it was scented soap. "No, king; that cost too much," said the trader; "too good for a Kanaka." "How much you got? I take him all," replied his majesty, and became the lord of seventeen boxes at two dollars a cake. Or again, the merchant feigns the article is not for sale, is private property, an heirloom or a gift; and the trick infallibly succeeds. Thwart the king and you hold him. His autocratic nature rears at the affront of opposition. He accepts it for a challenge; sets his teeth like a hunter going at a fence; and with no mark of emotion, scarce even of interest, stolidly piles up the price. Thus, for our sins, he took a fancy to my wife's dressing-bag, a thing entirely useless to the man, and sadly battered by years of service. Early one forenoon he came to our house, sat down, and abruptly offered to purchase it. I told him I sold nothing, and the bag at any rate was a present from a friend; but he was acquainted with these pretexts from of old, and knew what they were worth and how to meet them. Adopting what I believe is called "the object method," he drew out a bag of English gold, sovereigns and half-sovereigns, and began to lay them one by one in silence on the table; at each fresh piece reading our faces with a look. In vain I continued to protest I was no trader; he deigned not to reply. There must have been twenty pounds on the table, he was still going on, and irritation had begun to mingle with our embarrassment, when a happy idea came to our delivery. Since his majesty thought so much of the bag, we said, we must beg him to accept it as a present. It was the most surprising turn in Tembinok's experience. He perceived too late that his persistence was unmannerly; hung his head a while in silence: then, lifting up a sheepish countenance, "I 'shamed," said the tyrant. It was the first and the last time we heard him own to a flaw in his behaviour. Half an hour after he sent us a camphor-wood chest, worth only a few dollars—but then heaven knows what Tembinok' had paid for it.

Cunning by nature, and versed for forty years in the government of men, it must not be supposed that he is cheated blindly, or has resigned himself without resistance to be the milch-cow of the passing trader. His efforts have been even heroic. Like Nakaeia of Makin, he has owned schooners. More fortunate than Nakaeia, he has found captains. Ships of his have sailed as far as to the colonies. He has trafficked direct, in his own bottoms, with New Zealand. And even so, even there, the world-enveloping dishonesty of the white man prevented him; his profit melted, his ship returned in debt, the money for the insurance was embezzled, and when the *Coronet* came to be lost, he was astonished to find he had lost all. At this he dropped his weapons; owned he might as hopefully wrestle with the winds of heaven; and like an experienced sheep, submitted his fleece thenceforward to the shearers. He is the last man in the world to waste anger on the incurable; accepts it with cynical composure, asks no more in those he deals with than a certain decency of moderation: drives as good a bargain as he can; and when he considers he is more than usually swindled, writes it in his memory against the merchant's name. He once ran over to me a list of captains and supercargoes with whom he had done business, classing them under three heads: "He cheat a litty"—"He cheat plenty"—and "I think he cheat too much." For the first two classes he expressed perfect toleration; sometimes, but not always, for the third. I was present when a certain merchant was turned about his business, and was the means (having a considerable influence ever since the bag) of patching up the dispute. Even on the day of our arrival there was like to have been a hitch with Captain Reid: the ground of which is perhaps worth recital. Among goods exported specially for Tembinok' there is a beverage known (and labelled) as Hennessy's brandy. It is neither Hennessy, nor even brandy; is about the colour of sherry, but is not sherry; tastes of kirsch, and yet neither is it kirsch. The king, at least, has grown used to this amazing brand, and rather prides himself upon the taste; and any substitution is a double offence, being at once to cheat him and to cast a doubt upon his palate. A similar weakness is to be observed in all connoisseurs. Now, the last case sold by the *Equator* was found to contain a different and I would fondly fancy a superior distillation; and the conversation opened very black for Captain Reid. But Tembinok' is a moderate man. He was reminded and admitted that all men were liable to error, even himself; accepted the principle that a fault handsomely acknowledged should be condoned; and wound the matter up with this proposal: "Tuppoti[4] I mi'take, you 'peakee me. Tuppoti you mi'take, I 'peakee you. Mo' betta."

4. Suppose.

After dinner and supper in the cabin, a glass or two of "Hennetti"—the genuine article this time, with the kirsch bouquet,—and five hours' lounging on the trade-room counter, royalty embarked for home. Three tacks grounded the boat before the palace; the wives were carried ashore on the backs of vassals; Tembinok' stepped on a railed platform like a steamer's gangway, and was borne shoulder-high through the shallows, up the beach, and by an inclined plane, paved with pebbles, to the glaring terrace where he dwells.

Further Reading

Stevenson's Pacific fictions include *Island Nights' Entertainments* (London: Hogarth, 1987); *The Wrecker* (London: Cassell, 1893); and "The Ebb-Tide," published in *Dr Jekyll and Mr Hyde and other stories* (London: Penguin, 1987). (The latter two were cowritten by Stevenson's stepson, Lloyd Osbourne.) His history of the Samoan wars, "A Footnote to History," the only section of the *South Seas* material published during Stevenson's lifetime, is reprinted in *Vailima Papers* (London: Heinemann, 1924). His private correspondence from the period covered by *In the South Seas* is collected in *The Letters of Robert Louis Stevenson*, ed. Bradford A. Booth and Ernest Mehew, vol. 6 (New Haven: Yale University Press, 1995). Stevenson's Pacific writing is discussed in detail in Vanessa Smith, *Literary Culture and the Pacific: Nineteenth-Century Textual Encounters* (Cambridge: Cambridge University Press, 1998). H. E. Maude's essay "Baiteke and Binoka of Abemama: Arbiters of change in the Gilbert Islands" is in *Pacific Island Portraits,* ed. J. W. Davidson and Deryck Scarr (Canberra: Australian National University Press, 1973). Freud discusses defamiliarization in "A Disturbance of Memory on the Acropolis," in *Character and Culture,* trans. James Strachey (New York: Collier Books, 1963). Articles on tourism and the desire for authenticity include Dean MacCannell, "Staged Authenticity: Arrangements of Social Space in Tourist Settings," *American Journal of Sociology* 79, no. 3 (1973): 589–603; and John Frow, "Tourism and the Semiotics of Nostalgia," *October* 57 (1991): 121–51.

26

FANNY VAN DER GRIFT STEVENSON

Cannibal Fashions

. . . .

FANNY STEVENSON (1840–1914), an American by birth, traveled to the Pacific with her second husband, Robert Louis Stevenson, and her son Lloyd Osbourne in 1888. The party toured Polynesia and Micronesia, first in a luxury yacht and then a trading steamer, and eventually settled on a four hundred acre property, Vailima, above the town of Apia on the island of Upolu, Samoa, becoming interested observers of Samoan chiefly and colonial rivalries. In taking up the different roles of grand tourist, trader traveler, settler, and political enthusiast, the Stevensons sampled the gamut of perspectives available to the late nineteenth-century traveler in the region, and their writings reflect these shifting points of view. Fanny was a driving force behind the organization both of the initial trip to the islands and their subsequent travels throughout the Pacific and domestic life in Samoa, motivated by her expressed concern for her husband's health. She remained in Samoa and Hawaii for some years after his death, eventually selling the Vailima estate in 1897. Her ashes were returned to Upolu by her daughter and buried next to Stevenson on Mount Vaea.

Fanny Stevenson's Pacific writings consist of a travel account, *The Cruise of the Janet Nichol*, reworked from diary entries and published in the year of her death; further diary entries, some of which were published in 1956 as *Our Samoan Adventure*; and correspondence. Their author has received a mixed press, represented either as a source of nurturing strength and encouragement to her husband or, more commonly, as a neurotic, unfulfilled writer who subsisted off her husband's reputation. Both these portraits are unselfconsciously gendered and figure Fanny's limited corpus as at best an adjunct to her husband's oeuvre. During Stevenson's lifetime Fanny was an active and sometimes outspoken critic of his work, and she had clear ideas of what she felt to be lacking in her husband's descriptions of Pacific societies. In a letter to Sidney Colvin from Honolulu, dated May 21, 1889, she summed up her misgivings about the text that would eventually evolve into *In the South Seas*, arguing that

> Louis has the most enchanting material that any one ever had in the whole world for his book, and I am afraid he is going to spoil it all. He has taken it into his Scotch Stevenson head, that a stern duty lies before him, and that his book must be a sort of scientific and historical impersonal thing, comparing the different languages (of which he knows nothing, really) and the different peoples, the object being to settle the question as to whether they are of common Malay origin or not. . . . And I believe there is no one living who has got so near to them, or who understands them as he does. Think of a small treatise on the Polynesian races being offered to people who are dying to hear about Ori a Ori, the making of brothers with cannibals, the strange stories they told, and the extraordinary adventures that befell us;—suppose Herman Melville had given us his theories as to the Polynesian language and the probable good or evil results of the missionary influence instead of *Omoo* and *Typee*. (Booth and Mehew, 303–4)

Fanny's complaint was that Stevenson seemed to be approaching his task as ethnographer rather than author, surrendering his powers of elaboration and invention to the faithful description of what he regarded as transient societies. In the letter to Colvin reproduced here, she writes the kind of story she would have liked Stevenson to tell, replete with salacious descriptions of cannibalism, and detailing the accoutrements of otherness.

Fanny's letter is not merely a romanticized appendix to Stevenson's scholarly compendium. Juxtaposed with her husband's travel notes, it offers a commentary on the gendering of travel as experience and as discourse, making explicit the different things that men and women saw in crossing cultures. Fanny has a privileged access, for instance, to the relationship between custom and fashion, which informs her witty observations on the ontological resonance of a simple change of costume. She interrogates essentialist notions of savagery, reflecting on the ways that dress, objects, and posturings position individuals in the theater of cultural exchange. Licensed by her travels outside the Victorian cultural milieu, Fanny is

shown here undergoing a reciprocal role change from civilized to savage, delighting in a conventionally masculine hardihood and enjoyment of the grotesque.
— VANESSA SMITH

. . . .

« MRS. R. L. STEVENSON, LETTER TO SIDNEY COLVIN »
Scribner's Magazine 75, NO. 4 (APRIL 1934): 408–10.

TAIOHAE, HIVA OA, MARQUESAS ISL.
August 1888.

DEAR AND NEVER FORGOTTEN CUSTODIAN,

Oh that you and a few—a very few—friends were with us in these enchanted Isles to stay for ever and ever, and live and die with these delightful miscalled savages. That they are cannibals may be true, but that is only a freak of fashion like the taste for decayed game, and not much more unpleasant. Last evening we had a savage queen to dine with us; I say savage, because her son, who came with her, continually referred to themselves as "we savages." The old lady has presided at many a sacrificial feast, and ordered many a poor wretch to instant execution, and yet a more gracious affection-compelling person I do not expect to see until I again meet Lady Shelley, of whom she greatly reminded us. Not a word of any tongue could she speak but her own, and she was deaf besides, but we managed to pass more than three hours very pleasantly in her charming society. She wore a white dress made like a nightgown, of very fine material, no underclothes, and a white china crape shawl heavily embroidered and fringed. Her hands and what could be seen of her feet and legs were elaborately tattooed. Even Mrs. Stevenson has grown to dislike the look of untattooed hands. The queen, they say, is entirely covered with the most beautiful tattooing that has ever been done in the Islands. On Monday next Stanislas, the heir apparent, has invited us to a picnic. We are to go on horses, natives having gone on ahead to prepare a meal. I am rather curious as to what will take place, as the point of interest, a balancing rock, has been tabooed for many years, though it stands in full sight of the village, and even Stanislas has never been near it. He made a little speech to us last evening thanking us formally for our sympathetic treatment of "his savages."

It was a sad business when we left Anahoe. We had eight particular friends there whom, I suppose, we shall never see again. When we first ar-

FIG. 12. Mr. and Mrs. Robert Louis Stevenson in company with Nan Tok and Natakanti on Butaritari Island. Published in Fanny Stevenson, *The Cruise of the "Janet Nichol" Among the South Sea Islands* (London: Chatto and Windus, 1915). By permission of the National Library of Australia.

rived there they swarmed over the vessel like flies, clothed in breech-cloths and tattooing only. For their farewell visit the beachcomber had made them all white trousers and shirts. Every man was as clean as a new pin, and shining with cocoanut oil, their finger nails, even, as carefully looked after as our own. We gave them what keepsakes we could find among our things, and they presented us with tapa cloth beaten out of tree bark, oranges, cocoa-nuts prepared for drinking, some rare shells, and to Lloyd one of them gave a carving done on the bone of one of his ancestors. We had gingerbread and a glass of rum all round, the whole party took a last walk through the vessel, we shook hands, and parted. Hoka, the most beautiful dancer and the most graceful person I have ever seen, dropped all his usual airs and graces and sat most of the time staring on the floor, just as we do when we are very unhappy and distressed, sighing heavily; when he had shaken hands he turned his head away, and never once looked back. Typee, the chief, on the contrary, stood up in the midst of his men, waving his hands and making gestures of farewell as long as he could see us. As the canoe went off the captain saluted Typee, when all the men uncovered.

Our cannibal friend Koamoa was, I am sorry to say, too drunk to come aboard, and was left on the beach hanging over the branch of a tree. It seems that a Corsican had come over in a boat with a demijohn of rum, which was more than the old chief could stand. Our own Hoka, I fear, believes in eating one's enemies. He had had a quarrel with the Corsican who called him "cochon" and "sauvage." Hoka's reply was "you are more of a savage than I am," whereupon the man struck him a boxer's blow, of which Hoka had no understanding. He said he was going to get a gun soon, and then he could go over to the island where the Corsican lives and shoot him, after which he meant to cut off and eat one of his arms. In the next island we are going to visit, a man whom the whole population hated was killed for vengeance. The question was how should every man have a taste of his enemy without the authorities finding it out. This was solved by filling match-boxes with the cooked flesh, and passing them round. I think the combination of the civilized match-box and the "long pig" very interesting. Three months ago, a little boy was called for at the school by a couple of people who were decoying him into a quiet spot for the purpose of killing and eating him, but he descried their evil intention in time to call for help. Three of the townspeople have lately disappeared mysteriously; they are supposed to have fallen victims to private vengeance. Lloyd has had given him by a native woman an ornament to wear in the war dance. It is composed of locks of women's hair made into a sort of gigantic fringe. As many as ten women were killed to make this ghastly adornment, their bodies being cooked for the dancers' feast.

I am glad to tell you that quite suddenly Louis's health took a change for the better, and he is now almost as well as he ever was in his life. It has been a mistake about the cold places; warmth and hot sun is what he needs. Certainly we have found the right place for him; and we both love it. It is hard that we should ever have to go away. Stanislas says that Dominique is still better, and if we conclude to come back here to stay that is the island for us. I think it is very nice of Stanislas to praise another island when he would so much like to have us here. Our next point is Hiva oa, for which we start in three days, taking with us a most delightful person called Frère Michel, who builds churches not to be conceived of. I have made careful drawings of one which will delight your soul, and fill you with pleased laughter. My dearest love to you all, best beloved friends. Louis is away walking in the hills, Lloyd playing on the fiddle.

Ever yours affectionately,
F. V. DE G. STEVENSON
A sudden shower has blotted my letter almost out.

Further Reading

For further writing on Pacific subjects by Fanny Stevenson, see Fanny and Robert Louis Stevenson, *Our Samoan Adventure*, ed. Charles Neider (London: Weidenfeld and Nicolson, 1956); Mrs. R. L. Stevenson, *The Cruise of the 'Janet Nichol' among the South Sea Islands: A Diary by Mrs. Robert Louis Stevenson* (New York: Charles Scribner's Sons, 1914; London: Chatto and Windus, 1915); and Bradford A. Booth and Ernest Mehew, eds., *The Letters of Robert Louis Stevenson*, vol. 6 (New Haven: Yale University Press, 1995). Alexandra Lapierre, *Fanny Stevenson: Muse, Adventuress and Romantic Enigma*, trans. Carol Cosman (New York: Carol and Graf, 1995; London: Fourth Estate, 1995), though in part a fictional meditation, is the most recent and sustained biographical work on Fanny Stevenson.

27

Henry Adams/Ari'i Taimai

"That Link of History"

. . . .

HENRY ADAMS (1838–1918) traveled to the Pacific in August 1890, accompanied by his friend the artist John La Farge. Adams had just completed his nine-volume *History of the United States during the Administrations of Jefferson and Madison* and was suffering from grief occasioned by the suicide of his wife in 1885. He and La Farge spent some time in Samoa, visiting the Stevensons at Vailima, and early in 1891 were in Tahiti, where they befriended Tati Salmon, chief of the Teva. In letters to Mabel Hooper La Farge, Adams described his visit to Tati Salmon's home at Papara:

> Tati is quite unlike our Samoan chiefs. He is half English, and lives like us, talking English, and living in a European house, or something like it . . . He was very kind indeed, and so was his old mother, the chiefess of the Teva clan, who is a pure native and speaks no foreign language. She is sixty-eight years old, and refuses to sit at table with us, but sits on the floor in the old native way, and is a very great person indeed. In the evenings we lay down on the mats about her, and she told us of the old Taïti people, who were much more interesting than now. She told us, too, long native legends about wonderful princesses and princes, who did astonishing things in astonishing ways, like Polynesian Arabian Nights. (Cater 1947, 240, cf. 246)

Adams claimed to find in Tati Salmon and his mother living embodiments of old and new Tahiti. He took notes from the stories that "Grandmamma Hinarii" told him, her daughter Marau Taaroa acting as interpreter, and worked them into a book, *Memoirs of Marau Taaroa, Last Queen of Tahiti*, which he had privately printed in 1893. He wrote to John Hay that he "sent to Marau a small volume of her *Memoirs*, hoping to encourage the family to supply more material; for I really enjoy writing that link of history" (Cater 1947, 304–5). She responded with annotations and corrections that were incorporated into the enlarged *Memoirs of Arii Taimai E Marama of Eimeo, Teriirere of Tooarai, Teriinui of Tahiti, Tauraatua I Amo*, which Adams also had privately printed in Paris in 1901. Scrupulous proofing was typical of Adams: his biographer writes of "The exactness with which Adams worked and his manner of absorbing himself in the minutest details, . . . also with the correction of proof" (Cater 1947, liv). Incorporating Marau's interventions into his text, however, was not simply further evidence of his fastidiousness in print: it enabled a continued dialogue with the oral historical tradition that she represented. The effect of this dialogue is apparent in the changed order of the opening chapters. The 1893 edition begins with the history of Tahiti sifted from European accounts. Dense quotation from the voyage literature acts as a framing device for the narrated history of the Teva clan. In the 1901 edition, the interpolated European accounts are pushed back to the sixth chapter, and the framework of the history becomes the story of the Teva.

At the same time, Adams did not intend a sense of this dialogue to rupture his text. As Greg Dening has pointed out, Adams "maintained the fiction that it was Arii Taimai's pen that had written the memoirs" (Dening 1996, 164). Dening refers to the *Memoirs* as translation: it is certainly a piece of consummate ventriloquism. The writing of the memoirs offers the highly literate Adams the opportunity to play oral ethnographic informant; the liberal republican to comment on kingship; the white male historian to dress up as a Tahitian queen and write a history motivated by female power. He tells us of the difficulties of translating a Tahitian tongue he doesn't in fact speak: "Poetry is not supposed in any language to have an exact equivalent in prose, and I do not pretend to give an English equivalent for anything Tahitian" (Adams 1901, 25–26). He laughs at the English infatuation with divine right: "Every Englishman in those days took comfort, when wandering over the world, in the faith that kings and queens were part of the divine system, and that no intelligent race could hold up its head without them" (Adams 1901, 65). And he represents Tahitian women as supreme historical agents:

> Women played an astonishing part in the history of the island. In the absence of sons, daughters inherited chieferies and property in the lands that went with the chief's names or titles, and these chiefesses in their own right were much the same sort of personages as female sovereigns in European history; they figured as prominently in island politics as Catherine of Russia, or Marie Theresa of Austria, of Marie Antoinette of France, or Marie Louise of Parma, in the

politics of Europe. A chiefess of this rank was as independent of her husband as of any other chief; she had her seat, or throne, in the Marae even to the exclusion of her husband; and if she were ambitious she might win or lose crowns for her children, as happened with Wallis's friend Oberea, our great aunt Purea, and with her niece Tetuanui reiaiteatea, the mother of the first King Pomare. (Adams 1901, 10)

The extract reproduced here narrates probably the most famous of the Tahitian histories of powerful women: the story of Purea. The existing historical record of Purea is a multifaceted and often contradictory one (Dening 1996, 147–56), and the Adams/Ari'i Taimai version contributes to the complexity of her portrayal, representing her both through Tahitian genealogy and legend and as European literary construct. This interweaving of sources is apparent even at the level of diction: the Marae Purea builds for her son is introduced as the relativized concept of a "pyramid"; but then a district is said to occupy "the tail of the fish," a casual reference to a Tahitian metaphor introduced at the beginning of the history: "The island of Tahiti is shaped like an hour-glass or figure of 8; but as the natives knew neither hour-glasses nor figures, they used to call the island a fish, because it had a body and a tail" (Adams 1901, 1). The history of Purea is presented as one of mutual appropriation: Purea manipulates the Europeans' desire to perceive her as Tahitian "queen" in the interests of her overweening ambitions for her son Teri-irere, and in turn she becomes an object of European literary discourse. At the same time, her role upon the stage of European politics is depicted as an active one: her historical influence extends to the metropolis. Ari'i Taimai's presentation of her Tahitian history as a history of female protagonists sets the scene for the final chapters of her volume, in which she recuperates her own ambiguous role in reconciling Queen Pomare IV to French rule during the colonial crisis of 1842 as another stage in an ongoing story of the feminine strategic manipulation of cross-cultural politics.

The writing of the *Memoirs* gave Adams insight into his own historical practice. The "histories" he produced subsequently, *Mont-Saint-Michel and Chartres: A Study in Twelfth-Century Unity* (1904) and *The Education of Henry Adams* (1907), were less conventional, more self-reflective works than his earlier history of American politics. After the publication of the 1893 edition, Adams wrote to John Hay, "It shows me, too, why I loathe American history. Tahiti is all literary. America has not a literary conception. One is all artistic. The other is all commercial. Both are about equally bankrupt. That is their only marked resemblance" (Cater 1947, 305). Debate about the different types of history appropriate to metropolitan and "peripheral" societies has been ongoing in the twentieth century, often tinged by the assumption that island history lies outside the stream of global events. In the

Memoirs of Arii Taimai, the weaving of Tahitian events back into the tapestry of European politics undermines this claim. Adams's refusal to disentangle his own voice from the narrating voice of Ari'i Taimai allows her to emerge as a critically acute historical commentator, reflecting not only upon events, but on the modes of discourse through which events are represented as history. — VANESSA SMITH

. . . .

[Henry Adams] *Memoirs of Arii Taimai E Marama of Eimeo, Teriirere of Tooarai, Teriinui of Tahiti, Tauraatua i Amo* (Paris, 1901).

« CHAPTER 5, PP. 40–46. »

If a family must be ruined by a woman, perhaps it may as well be ruined thoroughly and brilliantly by a woman who makes it famous. Te vahine Airorotua i Ahurai i Farepua, and most of the other highest connections in the island, was a very great lady. Standards of social rank differ a little in different countries and times, but in any country or time a woman would meet with consideration when she and her husband could control a hundred thousand people; when she could build a pyramid for her child, and take for him the produce of a swarming country; when she was handsome, with manners equal to the standard of countries where the manners of Europe would be considered barbarous; and finally, when she had an unbroken descent from chiefs as far back as human society existed; and the consideration would not be the less because, like a large proportion of the more highly educated ladies and gentlemen of Europe, her views on some points of morality were lax and her later career disastrous.

Airorotua, familiarly called Purea, was a daughter of Terii vaetua, chief of Tefana i Ahurai or Faaa, the tail of the fish, close to the modern Papeete and partly including it. The district of Faaa, though it contained only about seven miles of seacoast, was for many reasons very important. It stood, as an independent little nation, between the great Teva alliance on the south, the Porionuu and te Aharoa on the east, and the large island of Eimeo or Moorea, some twelve miles to the west. As Tefana leaned toward Papara or against it, the chiefs of Papara were apt to be less anxious about their enemies or more anxious to win friends. At the time when Amo married Purea, in the middle of the last century, Tefana was particularly strong in its connections.

Terii vaetua, Purea's father, had married one of the Vaiari family—Te vahine Airoro anaa te arii ote maevarau of Vaiari, marae Farepua, born literally in the purple or scarlet of the Ura. They had seven children: (1) Tepau i Ahurai, known in the English books of travel as Tubourai Tamaide; (2) Terai mateata; (3) Hituterai; (4) Te vahine Airorotua, or Oberea, Berea, Purea; (5) Teihotu; (6) Auri; (7) Mareiti. Of these seven children three were persons of no small concern to us—Purea, Teihotu, and Auri. Purea married the chief of Papara and became mother of Teriirere; Teihotu married Vavea of Nuurua and was grandfather of King Pomare; Auri married Tetuaraenui of the Punaauia and Vaiari families and was grandfather of Marama. Thus King Pomare was second cousin of my mother, Marama Arii manihinihi, and as in Tahiti cousins are regarded as brothers and sisters, Pomare always called my mother sister, which had a curious effect on our lives and fortunes.

With such connections as her father and mother and husband gave her, Purea had no serious rival in the island, and when her son Teriirere was born, somewhere about the year 1762, he became at once the most important person in the world in the eyes of his mother and of Tahiti. The son always superseded the father, whose authority after the birth of a child was merely that of guardian. As often happened, Tevahitua took a new name from the child, and called himself Amo, the winker, from a habit of winking which seems to have amused him in the infant Teriirere. The same cause that superseded the father gave the mother often an increase of influence and freedom from restraint. Purea, after the birth of Teriirere, was emancipated, and the relation between her and Amo was from that time a political rather than a domestic one. They were united only in the interests of Teriirere.

They then asserted the child's supremacy by undertaking what no other great chief had ever attempted, and what still strikes us with astonishment as it struck Captain Cook and Sir Joseph Banks in 1769. They not only imposed a general *Rahui* for the child's benefit, as Tavi of Tautira did for his unfortunate son a hundred years before; but they also began a new Marae for Teriirere, in which he was to wear the Maro, and they set their people to work on the enormous task of piling up the pyramid at Mahaiatea which was an exhibition of pride without a parallel in Polynesia.

This was more than Purea's female relations could bear, and it set society in a ferment. The island custom provided more than one way of dealing with pride. Though Purea and Teriirere were admitted to be political superiors, they were socially no better than their cousins, and custom required that if during a *Rahui* any relative or guest of equal rank should come to visit the chief who had imposed it, the *Rahui* was broken, and the guest received by courtesy all that the *Rahui* had produced. Such an attempt to break the *Rahui* was of course an act which could not be ventured by any ordinary chief within the direct control of Papara; but Tefana i Ahurai was independent, and if Purea's own family chose to set up such a claim, Purea would resist it at her peril. Not even she could afford such a quarrel.

The first person who undertook to break the *Rahui* was probably Purea's sister-in-law, no doubt the wife or widow of Teihotu, on behalf of her son, Terii vaetua. She set out from Faaa in her double-canoe, with the house or tent, called *fare-oa*, in the prow, which only head-chiefs could use; and a crew of fifty men or more paddled this barge of state, with all the show of a royal ceremony, along the coast to Papara, some twenty miles away, until, opposite to the Point of Mahaiatea, they turned in to an opening in the reef which had on some pretext become sacred, and was known as the sacred pass, through which only sacred chiefs might go. Purea was then living on the Point, and probably was superintending the work on her great Marae. She came out on the beach, and as the double canoe, with its royal tent, passed through the opening and drew towards the land she hailed it:

"Who dares venture through the sacred pass? Know they not that the Tevas are under the sacred *Rahui* for Teriirere i Tooarai? Not even the cocks may crow or the ocean storm."

"It is Terii vaetua, Arii of Ahurai."

"How many more royal heads can there be? I know none but Teriirere i Tooarai. Down with your tent!"

The Ahurai chiefess wept and cut her head with the shark's tooth till blood flowed down her face, which was the custom of women in sign of great emotion, and meant in thi[s] instance revenge as well as grief; but Purea was inexorable, and Terii vaetua was obliged to turn round and go home like any ordinary stranger.

The quarrel, once begun, was extended by another of the Ahurai family, a woman who proved to be more than Purea's equal in most forms of energy. She was Purea's niece, the daughter of Teihotu and sister of the insulted Terii vaetua. Her name was Tetuanui rea i te Raiatea, and she was or became the wife of Tunuieaiteatua i Tarahoi, Cook's friend Otoo, and the missionaries' friend Pomare. A very famous woman in Tahitian history, much talked about by Captain Bligh in 1788 and by the missionaries as Iddeah, Tetuanui i Nuurua was not even mentioned by Wallis or Cook, although the latter, in 1774, frequently mentions "Tarevatoo, the king's younger brother," whom I take to be Terii vaetua, the king's brother-in-law, who had begun the attempt to break the *Rahui*. Indeed, Cook never saw even Pomare until August, 1773, when Pomare was already thirty years old.

After the repulse of Terii vaetua, this sister undertook to pursue the quarrel. The matter had become uncommonly serious, for a feud between Papara and Ahurai might upset the whole island. Nothing more would then be needed to overthrow the Papara supremacy than the alliance of Ahurai and the Purionuu with Vehiatua, whose fortunes had been made a hundred years before by a similar combination to break a similar *Rahui*. Tradition has preserved the precise words used by the family to avert the peril into which Purea's pride and temper were pushing them.

Tetuanui in her turn made her appearance in the state canoe off the point of Mahaiatea, and as she approached the beach was received by Purea with the same order, "Down with your tent!" Tetuanui came ashore and sat on the beach and cut her head with the shark's tooth till the blood flowed down into a hole she dug to receive it. This was her protest in form; an appeal to blood. Unless it were wiped away it must be atoned by blood.

Then the high-priest Manea interposed. Manea was Amo's younger brother, from whom we are directly descended in the fourth generation, and probably we owe our existence in a double sense to him, for his act wiped out the blood-feud as far as his own descendants were concerned.

"Hush, Purea! Whence is the saying, 'The pahus (drums) of Matairea call Tetunai for a Maro-ura for Teriirere i Tooarai. Where wilt thou wear the Maro-ura? In Nuura and Ahurai. One end of the Maro holds the Purionuu; the other end the Tevas; the whole holds the Oropaa.'"

Manea quoted the maxim of family statecraft in vain. Purea replied only that she was going to allow no rivalry to her son. "I recognize no head here but that of Teriirere." Then Manea dried the blood of Tetuanui with a cloth, wiping away the feud as far as he was concerned; and so long are these things remembered that forty years afterwards, when the Purionuu savagely raided Papara, Manea's great-grandchildren were supposed to have been spared in memory of Manea's act.

This scene must have occurred at about the time when Wallis discovered the island, and had he taken forty-eight hours to make the visit to Papara which Purea invited him to make, perhaps he might have seen the preparations for the great feast at which Teriirere i Tooarai was to wear the Maro-ura for the first time in his great new Marae at Mahaiatea. Thus far I have had to depend mainly on tradition, but here Captain Wallis and Captain Cook begin their story from the European stand-point.

« CHAPTER 6, PP. 55–56. »

The natural goodness of the human heart and the moral blessings of a state of nature were the themes of all Rousseau's followers, and at that time all Europe was following Rousseau. The discovery of Tahiti, as Wallis and Commerson painted it, was the strongest possible proof that Rousseau was right. The society of Tahiti showed that European society had no real support in reason or experience, but should be abolished, with its absurd conventions, contrary to the natural rights and innate virtue of man. The French philosophers seriously used Tahiti for this purpose, and with effect, as every one knows. Wallis's queen played a chief part in the European play, by exciting interest and sympathy; for the years before and after 1770 were sentimental, and, between Diderot's Orou and Goethe's Werter, the sentimental princess of Hawkesworth's voyages was at home. As the queen, according to our family record, was our great-great-grandaunt Purea, or rather the wife of our great-great-granduncle, and as I know something about Tahitian women, and especially about this one by tradition, I will not deny that perhaps Dr. Hawkesworth may have added some color of rose to the story that Wallis had to tell; but this has nothing to do with the curious accident that Tahiti really influenced Europe, and that our great-great-grandaunt, "my princess, or rather, queen", was, without her own knowledge or consent, directly concerned in causing the French Revolution and costing the head of her sister queen, Marie Antoinette.

As Diderot and Commerson show, the interest felt in France for the state of nature in Tahiti was largely caused by the eternal dispute about marriage and the supposed laxity of Tahitian morals in regard to the relations of men and women. I say "supposed" because no one knows how much of the laxity was due to the French and English themselves, whose appearance certainly caused a sudden and shocking overthrow of such moral rules as had existed before in the island society; and the "supposed" means that when the island society as a whole is taken into account, marriage was real as far as it went, and the standard rather higher than that of Paris; in some ways extremely lax, and in others strict and stern to a degree that would have astonished even the most conventional English nobleman, had he understood it. The real code of Tahitian society would have upset the theories of a state of nature as thoroughly as the guillotine did; but, when seen through the eyes of French and English sailors, who had not the smallest sense of responsibility, and would not have been sorry to overthrow all standards, Tahiti seemed to prove that no standard was necessary, which made the island interesting to philosophers and charming to the French people, never easy under even the morality recognized at Paris. So there again our aunt Purea, Wallis's queen, played a part in the drama, for, in an island which seemed to have no idea of morals, she was a model of humanity, sentiment, and conduct—the flower of a state of nature.

Of course the sentiment of Hawkesworth, and the Cytherean tastes of Bougainville and Commerson, did not please every one, least of all in England, where French philosophy and shepherdesses were rarely welcome. A friend has given me a quotation from Horace Walpole, who wrote to one of his correspondents in 1773: "I hope you are heartily provoked at the new Voyages, which might make one a good first mate, but tell one nothing at all. Dr. Hawkesworth is still more provoking. An old black gentlewoman of forty carries Captain Wallis across a river when he was too weak to walk, and the man represents them as a new edition of Dido and Æneas." Whatever pleased the French was pretty sure to displease the English, and so, from the first, Tahiti took a French color which ended by deciding its fate; and there, too, our aunt Purea unconsciously may have been a chief agent in causing the sentimental attachment which brought the French squadrons seventy years later to our shores.

Further Reading

Letters relating to Adams's stay in Tahiti and an extended biographical essay are published in Harold Dean Cater, ed., *Henry Adams and His Friends: A Collection of His Unpublished Letters* (Boston: Houghton Mifflin, 1947). John La Farge's account of the trip has been republished as *An American Artist in the South Seas* (1914; reprint, London: KPI, 1987). Greg Dening meditates on the role of Purea in "Possessing Tahiti," *Performances* (Chicago: University of Chicago Press, 1996) and "The Hegemony of Laughter: Purea's Theatre," in *Pacific Empires*, ed. Alan Frost (Melbourne: Melbourne University Press, 1999). Debate about Pacific historiography is discussed in Robert Borofsky and Alan Howard, "The Early Contact Period," *Developments in Polynesian Ethnology* (Honolulu: University of Hawaii Press, 1989); Nicholas Thomas, "Partial Texts: Representation, Colonialism and Agency in Pacific History," *The Journal of Pacific History* 25, no. 2 (1990); and Vanessa Smith, *Literary Culture and the Pacific: Nineteenth-Century Textual Encounters* (Cambridge: Cambridge University

Press, 1998). Niel Gunson assesses the value of the *Memoirs* as historical document in "A Note on the Difficulties of Ethnohistorical Writing, with Special Reference to Tahiti," *Journal of the Polynesian Society* 72, no. 4 (December 1963): 415–19.

28

LOUIS BECKE

The Ebbing of the Tide

. . . .

CONRAD'S *Heart of Darkness* (1902) is famous for its pessimistic account of colonialism; it is sometimes seen to have inaugurated a critical understanding of empire. The selections from eighteenth-century texts we have included here make it clear, however, that travel, exploration, and colonization were regarded as fraught projects, and as projects prone to failure, from a much earlier date. That said, a distinct attitude does emerge in the late nineteenth century, defined by a vigorous skepticism toward both imperial and evangelical propaganda. From the 1870s on, fantastic accounts of the "prospects" of Fiji and other Pacific islands were in circulation, most particularly in Australia, where colonial nationalism and what might be called regional sub-imperialism became closely connected; writers such as Louis Becke (1855–1913) derided these visions, as they did the evocations of model Christian communities in the islands that were proffered by mission societies. For Becke, commercial projects were typically failures, and white men in the South Seas were typically degenerate, while indigenous Christians embraced piety rather than morality.

Becke stowed away in a vessel bound for Samoa in 1872, to spend the better part of the following twenty years working in the Pacific as a trader, labor recruiter, and supercargo. This experience, together with work in the Australian outback and on the goldfields, gave him a wealth of material that he drew upon when he began to write, after settling in Sydney in 1892. He wrote over thirty books and much journalism before his death in 1913. Although he lapsed into formulae, Becke's early stories remain notable for their deft and condensed evocation of the culture of the late nineteenth-century beach.

Although the social dynamics of these milieux differ from those we have described for the late eighteenth and early nineteenth centuries (in the sense that traders were often established residents with at least some contact with commercial shipping), self-preservation was nevertheless an issue. The trader, like the beachcomber, was apt to be assimilated to some degree into local mores, a process that was now figured paradigmatically through cross-racial sexuality and conjugality, which is shown to have varying outcomes in Becke's tales. If his traders are avowedly flawed characters, they are often decent ones, whose downfall follows from the genuinely evil propensities of other indigenous or nonindigenous actors. In "Kennedy the Boatsteerer" the fatal clash is with custom, with the "law" of tabu, here resolutely reified as ineradicable superstition. The plot, in which the white man attempts to escape in a canoe with his tabooed native lover, was to become something of a cliché of South Seas literature; it was the basis, for example, of the Flaherty/Murneau film *Tabu*. Becke exempts no one on the beach from the corruption that appears to follow from cross-cultural entanglement. He projects no amelioration of social conditions, no reform through Christianity or the further extension of commerce, but instead simply presents the indeterminate and often vicious morality of a beach marked by the sapping of energies, by the ebbing of the tide. — NICHOLAS THOMAS

. . . .

Louis Becke, *The Ebbing of the Tide: South Seas Stories* (London: T. Usher Unwin, 1895).

« "KENNEDY THE BOATSTEERER," PP. 93–100. »

STEERING north-west from Samoa for six or seven hundred miles you will sight the Ellice Group—low-lying, palm-clad coral atolls fringed on the lee with shimmering sandy beaches. On the weather-side, exposed to the long sweep of the ocean-rollers, there are but short, black-looking reefs backed by irregular piles of loose, flat, sea-worn coral, thrown up and accumulating till its surface is brushed by the pendant leaves of the cocoanuts, only to be washed and swirled back seawards when the wind comes from the westward and sends a fierce sweeping current along the white beaches and black coral rocks alike.

Twenty-three years ago these islands were almost unknown to any one save a few wandering traders and the ubiquitous New Bedford whaler. But now, long ere you can see from the ship's deck the snowy tumble of the surf on the reef, a huge white mass, grim, square, and ugly, will meet your eye— white-washed walls of a distressful ghastliness accentuated by doors and windows of the deadliest black. This cheerful excrescence on the face of suffering nature is a native church.

The people have mostly assimilated themselves, in their manners and mode of life generally, to the new order of things represented by the fear-ful-looking structure aforementioned. That is to say, even as the Tongan and Fijian, they have degenerated from a fierce, hardy, warlike race into white-shirted, black-coated saints, whose ideal of a lovely existence is to have public prayer twice a day on week-days and all day on Sundays. To them it is a good thing to get half a dollar from the white trader for a sick fowl—which, when bought, will be claimed by another native, who will have the white man fined two dollars for buying stolen property. Had the white man paid a dollar he had done wisely—that coin sometimes goes far in the Tokelaus. For instance, the truly unctuous native Christian may ask a dollar for two fowls, but he will also lease out his wife for a similar amount. Time was, in the Ellices, when the undue complaisance of a mar-ried woman meant a sudden and inartistic compression of the jugular, or a swift blow from the heavy, ebony-wood club of the wronged man. Nowa-days, since the smug-faced native teacher hath shown them the Right Way, such domestic troubles are condoned by—a dollar. That is, if it be a genuine American dollar or two British florins; for outraged honour would not accept the cast-iron Bolivian money or the poor silver of Chili and Peru. And for a dollar the native "Christian" can all but pay for a nicely-bound Bible, printed in the Samoan tongue, and thus, no doubt, out of evil would come good; for he could, by means of his newly-acquired purchase, picture to his dusky mate the terrors that await those who look upon strange men and *tupe fa'apupula* (bright and shining money).

But I want to tell about Kennedy. Kennedy the Boatsteerer he was called; although twenty years had passed and gone since that day at Wallis Island when he, a bright-eyed, bronze-faced lad—with the fighting-blood of the old Puritan Endicotts running like fire through his veins despite his New England bringing-up—ran his knife into a shipmate's heart and fled for ever from all white associations. Over a woman it was, and only a copper-coloured one at that; but then she was young and beautiful, with dreamy, glistening eyes, and black, wavy hair, ornamented with a wreath of orange-flowers and coil upon coil of bright-hued *sea sea* berries strung together, hanging from her neck and resting upon her dainty bosom.

Standing at the doorway of his house, looking over the placid waters at the rising sun, Kennedy folds his brawny arms across his bare, sun-tanned chest and mutters to himself, in his almost forgotten mother-tongue: "Twenty years, twenty years ago! Who would know me there now? Even if I placarded my name on my back and what I did, 'taint likely I'd have to face a grand jury for running a knife into a mongrel Portuguee, way out in the South Seas a score of years ago . . . Poor little Talamalu! I paid a big price for her—twenty years of wandering from Wallis Island to the Bonins; and wherever I go that infernal story follows me up. Well, I'll risk it anyhow, and the first chance that comes along I'll cut Kanaka life and drinking ship's rum and go see old dad and mum to home. Here, Tikena, you Tokelau devil, bring me my toddy."

A native, clad in his grass *titi*, takes from a wooden peg in the house wall two shells of toddy, and the white wanderer takes one and drinks. He is about to return the other to the man when two girls come up from the beach with their arms around each other's waists, Tahiti fashion, and one calls out with a laugh to "leave some in the shell." This is Laumanu, and if there is one thing in the world that Jake Kennedy cares for above himself it is this tall girl with the soft eyes and lithe figure. And he dreams of her pretty often, and curses fluently to think that she is beyond his reach and is never likely to fill the place of Talamalu and her many successors. For Laumanu is *tabu* to a Nuitao chief—that is, she has been betrothed, but the Nuitao man is sixty miles away at his own island, and no one knows when he will claim his *avaga*. Then the girl gives him back the empty toddy-shell, and, slyly pinching his hand, sails away with her mate, where-upon the susceptible Kennedy, furious with long disappointment, flings himself down on his bed of mats, curses his luck and his unsuspecting rival at Nuitao, and finally decides not to spring a surprise on "dad and mum" by going "hum" for a considerable number of years to come.

Mr. Jake Kennedy at this time was again a widower—in the widest sense of the word. The last native girl who had occupied the proud position of *Te avaga te papalagi* (the white man's wife) was a native of the island of Maraki—a dark-skinned, passionately jealous creature, who had followed his fortunes for three years to his present location, and then developed *mal-du-pays* to such an extent that the local priest and devil-catcher, one Pare-vaka, was sent for by her female attendants. Pare-vaka was not long in making his diagnosis. A little devil in the shape of an octopus was in Tenenapa's brain. And he gave instructions how to get the fiend out, and also further instructions to one of the girl attendants to fix, point-upwards, in the sick woman's mat the *foto*, or barb of the sting-ray. So when Kennedy, who, in his rough, careless way, had some faint fondness for the woman whom three years ago he went mad over, heard a loud cry in the night and was told that Tenenapa was dead, he did not know that as the sick woman lay on her side the watchers had quietly turned her with her face to the roof, and with the needle pointed *foto* pierced her to the heart. And old Pare-vaka rejoiced, for he had a daughter who, in his opinion, should be *avaga* to the wealthy and clever white man, who could *tori nui* and *sisi atu* (pull cocoanuts and catch bonito) like any native; and this Tenenapa—who was she but a dog-eating stranger from Maraki only fit for shark's meat? So the people came and brought Kennedy the "gifts of affliction" to show their sympathy, and asked him to take a wife from their own people. And he asked for Laumanu.

There was a dead silence awhile, and then a wild-looking creature with long white hair falling around his shoulders like a cloak, dreading to shame the *papalagi* before so many, rose to his feet and motioned them away. Then he spoke: "Forget the words you have said, and take for a wife the girl from the house of Pare-vaka. Laumanu is *tabu*, and death walks behind her." But Kennedy sulked and wanted Laumanu or none.

And this is why he feels so bad to-day, and the rum keg gives him no consolation. For the sweet-voiced Laumanu always runs away from him when he steps out from his dark little trade-room into the light, with unsteady steps and a peculiar gleam in his black eye, that means mischief—rude love to a woman and challenge to fight to a man.

Lying there on his mat, plotting how to get possession of the girl, there comes to him a faint cry, gradually swelling in volume until every voice in the village, from the full, sonorous tones of the men to the shrill treble of the children, blend together: "*Te vaka motu! Te vaka motu!*" (a ship! a ship!). Springing up, he strides out, and there, slowly lumbering round the southwest end of the little island, under cruising canvas only, he sees her. One quick glance shows her to be a whaler.

In ten minutes Kennedy is in a canoe, flying over the reef, and in as many more alongside and on deck. The captain is an old acquaintance, and while the boats are sent ashore to buy pigs and poultry, Kennedy and he have a long talk in the cabin. Then the skipper says, as he rises, "Well, it's risky, but it's a smart way of earning five hundred dollars, and I'll land you and the creature somewhere in the Carolines."

The whaler was to lie off and on all night, or until such time as Kennedy and the girl came aboard in a canoe. To avert suspicion, the captain was to remain ashore with his boat's crew to witness a dance, and, if all went well, the white man was to be aboard before him with Laumanu and stow her away, in case any canoes came off with the boat.

The dance was in full swing when Kennedy, stripped to the waist, with a heavy bag of money in his left hand and a knife in his right, took a long farewell of his house and stepped out into the silent groves of coco-palms. A short walk brought him to a salt lagoon. On the brink he stood and waited, until a trembling, voiceless figure joined him from out the depths of the thick mangroves. Hand-in-hand they fled along the narrow, sandy path till they reached the beach, just where a few untenanted thatched huts stood on the shingle. Between these, covered over with cocoanut branches, lay a canoe. Deftly the two raised the light craft and carried it down to the water that broke in tender, rippling murmurs on the white sand. And with Laumanu seated for'ard, gazing out beyond into the blackness before them, he urged the canoe seawards with quick, nervous strokes. Far away to the westward he could see the dull glimmer of the whaleship's lights.

The mate of the *Essex* was leaning over the rail, drowsily watching the phosphorescence in the water as the ship rolled gently to the ocean swell, when a cry came from for'ard: "A heavy squall coming down, sir, from the land!" And it did come, with a swift, fierce rush, and so strong that it nearly threw the old whaler over on her beam-ends. In the midst of the hum and roar of the squall some one in the waist of the ship called out something about a canoe being alongside. The mate's comment was brief but vigorous, and the matter was speedily forgotten. Then the rain fell in torrents, and as the ship was made snug the watch got under shelter and the mate went below to get a drink of rum, and curse his captain for loafing ashore, watching naked women dancing.

Three miles further out a canoe was drifting and tossing about with outrigger carried away. Now and then, as a big sea lifted her, the stern would rise high out of the water and the sharp-nosed whaleback for'ard go down as if weighted heavily. And it was—with a bag of dollars lashed underneath. When in the early morning the whaleship sighted the drifting speck, floating on the bosom of a now placid sea, the thoughtful Down-East skipper—observant of the canoe's bows being under water—lowered a boat and pulled over to it. He took the bag of dollars and muttering something about "rather thinking he was kinder acquainted with the poor man's people," went back to the ship and stood away on his course in pursuit of his greasy vocation.

And Kennedy and the girl! Go some night and watch the dark-skinned people catching flying-fish by the light of *au lama* torches. Look over the side of the canoe and see those swarms of grim, grey devils of the tropic sea that ever and anon dart to the surface as the paddlers' hands come perilously near the water, and wonder no longer as to the fate of Kennedy the Boatsteerer and his Laumanu.

Further Reading

Becke's stories were collected in a number of volumes, of which *Pacific Tales* (1897) has been most recently reprinted (London: KPI, 1987). A. Grove Day's *Louis Becke* (New York: Twayne, 1966) is a dated but informative biography; postcolonial critical assessments include Robert Dixon, *Writing the Colonial Adventure: Race, Gender and Nation in Anglo-Australian Popular Fiction, 1875–1914* (Cambridge: Cambridge University Press, 1995); for discussion of Becke's trading activities, letters to his mother, and evocations of masculine identity and degeneration in the Pacific, see Nicholas Thomas and Richard Eves, *Bad Colonists: The South Seas Letters of Vernon Lee Walker and Louis Becke* (Durham: Duke University Press, 1999).

Bibliography

Abbott, John Lawrence. 1982. *John Hawkesworth: Eighteenth-Century Man of Letters*. Madison: University of Wisconsin Press.

[Adams, Henry]. 1901. *Memoirs of Arii Taimai e Marama of Eimeo, Teriirere of Tooarai, Teriinui of Tahiti, Tauraatua i Amo*. Paris: n.p.

Adams, Percy, ed. 1988. *Travel Literature Through the Ages*. New York: Garland.

———. 1962. *Travellers and Travel Liars*. Dover: New York.

Anderson, Adam. 1825. *The South Sea Bubble*. London: Thomas Boys.

Anson, George. 1776. *Voyage Round the World*. London: W. Bowyer et al.

Armitage, David. 1992. "The Cromwellian Protectorate and the Language of Empire." *The Historical Journal* 35, no. 3: 531–56.

Arnold, Joseph. 1820. "Captain Richard Siddons' Experiences in Fiji 1809–15." *Gentleman's Magazine* 90: 184–85, 211–31, 297–300.

Autograph Letters, Original Manuscripts, Books, Portraits and Curios from the library of the late Robert Louis Stevenson consigned by the present owner Mrs Isobel Strong. 1914. New York: Anderson Auction Company.

Awnsham and J. Churchill, comps. 1704. *Collection of Voyages and Travels*. 4 vols. London: Awnsham and J. Churchill.

Ayres, Philip. 1694. *The Voyages and Adventures of Captain Bartholomew Sharp*. London.

Barker, Francis, et al., eds. 1982. *1789: Reading Writing Revolution: Proceedings of the Essex Conference on the Sociology of Literature, July 1981*. Colchester: University of Essex.

Beaglehole, J. C. 1947. *The Exploration of the Pacific*. 2nd edition. London: A. and C. Black.

Becke, Louis. 1895. *The Ebbing of the Tide: South Seas Stories*. London: T. Fisher Unwin.

———. 1897. *Pacific Tales*. London: T. Fisher Unwin. Reprint, London: KPI, 1987.

Belich, James. 1996. *Making Peoples: A History of New Zealand*. Auckland: Penguin.

Bligh, William. 1790. *A Narrative of the Mutiny on Board His Majesty's Ship the Bounty and subsequent voyage of part of the crew in the ship's boat from Tofoa, one of the Friendly Islands, to Timor, a Dutch settlement in the East Indies*. London: G. Nicol.

————. 1792. *A Voyage to the South Seas, undertaken by command of His Majesty, for the purpose of conveying the breadfruit tree to the West Indies in His Majesty's Ship the* Bounty. London: G. Nicol.

Bligh, William. 1937. *A Voyage in the* Resource *from Coupang to Batavia, together with the Log of his Subsequent Passage to England in the Dutch packet* Vlydt *and his remarks on Morrison's Journal*. London: Golden Cockerel Press.

Boon, James A. 1982. *Other Tribes, Other Scribes: Symbolic Anthropology in the Comparative Study of Cultures, Histories, Religions, and Texts*. Cambridge: Cambridge University Press.

————. 1985. "Anthropology and Degeneration: Birds, Word and Orangutans." In *Degeneration: The Dark Side of Progress*, ed. J. Edward Chamberlin and Sander L. Gilman. New York: Columbia University Press.

Boorstin, Daniel J. 1985. *The Discoverers*. New York: Vintage.

Booth, Bradford A., and Ernest Mehew, eds. 1995. *The Letters of Robert Louis Stevenson*. 7 vols. New Haven: Yale University Press.

Borland, Francis. 1715. *Memoirs of Darien*. Glasgow.

Borofsky, Robert, and Alan Howard. 1989. *Developments in Polynesian Ethnology*. Honolulu: University of Hawaii Press.

Bougainville, Louis de. 1772. *A Voyage Round the World*. Translated by Johann Reinhold Forster. London: J. Nourse and T. Davies.

[Bulkeley, John]. 1745. *A Voyage to the South Seas 1740–1744*. London: R. Walker.

Burgh, James. 1764. *An Account of the First Settlement, Laws, Form of Government and Politics of the Cessares*. London: J. Payne et al.

Burney, Fanny. 1907. *The Early Diary of Fanny Burney, 1768–78*. 2 vols. Edited by Annie Raine Ellis. London: George Bell.

Burney, James. 1975. *With Captain James Cook in the Antarctic and Pacific: The Private Journal of James Burney, Second Lieutenant of the Adventure on Cook's Second Voyage, 1772–1773*. Edited and introduced by Beverley Hooper. Canberra: National Library of Australia.

————. 1803–16. *A Chronological History of the Discoveries in the South Sea or Pacific Ocean*. 5 vols. London: Luke Hansard.

Butler, Samuel. 1962. *Erewhon and Erewhon Revisted*. London: Dent.

Byron, John. 1768. *An Account of the Great Distresses on the Coasts of Patagonia*. London: S. Baker and G. Leigh.

Calder, Alex, ed. 2001. *Old New Zealand and Other Writings*. London: Leicester University Press.

Calder, Alex, Jonathan Lamb, and Bridget Orr, eds. 1999. *Voyages and Beaches: Pacific Encounters, 1769–1840*. Honolulu: University of Hawaii Press.

Campbell, Archibald. 1816. *A voyage round the world, from 1806 to 1812 . . . with an account of the present state of the Sandwich Islands, and a vocabulary of their language*. Edinburgh: Archibald Constable and Company.

Campbell, I. C. 1976. "European Transculturalists in Polynesia, 1789–ca.1840." Ph.D. diss., University of Adelaide.

————. 1992. *Island Kingdom: Tonga Ancient and Modern*. Christchurch: Canterbury University Press.

Campbell, John, ed. 1764. *Navigantium atque Itinerantium Bibliotheca; or, A Complete Collection of Voyages and Travels*. 2 vols. London: T. Osborne.

Camoens, Luis Vaz de. 1952. *The Lusiads*. Translated by William C. Atkinson. Harmondsworth: Penguin.

Canny, Nicholas, ed. 1998. *The Origins of Empire: British Overseas Enterprise to the Close of the Seventeenth Century*. Oxford: Oxford University Press.

Carter, Elizabeth. 1817. *Letters from Mrs. Elizabeth Carter, to Mrs. Montagu, Between the Years 1755 and 1800*. 3 vols. London: F. C. and J. Rivington.

Cater, Harold Dean, ed. 1947. *Henry Adams and His Friends: A Collection of His Unpublished Letters*. Boston: Houghton Mifflin.

Cathcart, Michael, et al. 1990. *Mission to the South Seas: The Voyage of the* Duff, *1796–1799*. Melbourne: Department of History, University of Melbourne.

Claeys, Gregory. 1994. *Utopias of the British Enlightenment*. Cambridge: Cambridge University Press.

Coleman, Deirdre. 1999. *Maiden Voyages and Infant Colonies: Two Women's Travel Narratives of the 1790s*. London: Leicester University Press.

Cook, James. 1955. *The Journals of Captain James Cook on His Voyage of Discovery*. Vol. 1, *The Voyage of the Endeavour 1768–71*. Edited by J. C. Beaglehole. Cambridge: Hakluyt Society, extra series no. 34.

Cook, James, and James King. 1784. *A Voyage to the Pacific Ocean 1776-80*. 3 vols. London: W. and A. Strahan.

Cooke, Edward. 1712. *A Voyage to the South Sea*. London: B. Lintot.

Cowley, William Ambrosia. 1683. The Voyage of William Ambrosia Cowley, Mariner, from the Capes of Virginia to the South Sea. Sloane MS 54. British Library, London.

Coyer, G. F. 1767. *A Letter to Dr Maty*. London: T. Beckett and P. A. de Hondt.

————. 1752. *A Supplement to Lord Anson's Voyage Round the World*. London: A. Millar, J. Whiston and B. White.

Crook, D. P., ed. 1972. *Questioning the Past: A Selection of Papers in History and Government*. Brisbane: University of Queensland Press.

Dalrymple, Alexander. 1767. *An Account of Discoveries in the South Pacific previous to 1764*. London.

————. 1773. *A Letter to Dr Hawkesworth*. London: J. Nourse, T. Payne, Brotherton and Sewell, B. White, J. Robson, P. Elmsly, T. Davies and S. Leacroft.

————. 1773. *Mr Dalrymple's Observations on Dr Hawkesworth's Preface to the Second Edition*. London.

Dampier, William. 1729. *A Collection of Voyages*. 4 vols. London: J. and J. Knapton.

————. 1697–1703. *A New Voyage Round the World*. London: James Knapton.

————. 1927. *A New Voyage Round the World*. Edited by N. M. Penzer. Introduction by Sir Albert Gray. London: Argonaut Press.

————. 1703. *A Voyage to New Holland, &c*. London: James Knapton.

Dane, G. Ezra, ed. 1938. *Letters from the Sandwich Islands: Written for the Sacramento Union by Mark Twain.* Stanford: Stanford University Press.

Darling, David. 1836. Remarks about the Marquesas. South Seas Journals, London Missionary Society archive, Council for World Mission collection, School of Oriental and African Studies, London.

Davidson, J. W., and Deryck Scarr, eds. 1973. *Pacific Island Portraits.* Canberra: Australian National University Press.

Davis, J. C. 1981. *Utopia and the Ideal Society.* Cambridge: Cambridge University Press.

Daws, Gavan. 1980. *A Dream of Islands: Voyages of Self-Discovery in the South Seas.* New York and London: W. W. Norton.

Day, A. Grove. 1966. *Louis Becke.* New York: Twayne.

Defoe, Daniel. 1712. *An Essay on the South-Sea Trade by the Author of the Review.* London: J. Baker.

———. 1725. *A New Voyage Round the World.* London: A. Bettesworth.

———. 1719. *Robinson Crusoe.* London.

Dening, Greg. 1980. *Islands and Beaches: Discourse on a Silent Land.* Melbourne: Melbourne University Press, and Honolulu: University of Hawaii Press.

———, ed. 1974. *The Marquesan Journal of Edward Robarts, 1797–1824.* Canberra: Australian National University Press.

———. 1992. *Mr Bligh's Bad Language: Passion, Power and Theatre on The* Bounty. Cambridge: Cambridge University Press.

———. 1996. *Performances.* Chicago: University of Chicago Press.

Denoon, Donald, and Stewart Firth. 1997. *The Cambridge History of the Pacific Islanders.* Cambridge: Cambridge University Press.

Diderot, Denis. 1992. "Supplement au voyage de Bougainville." In *Political Writings,* ed. John Hope Mason and Robert Wokler. Cambridge: Cambridge University Press.

Dixon, Robert. 1995. *Writing the Colonial Adventure: Race, Gender and Nation in Anglo-Australian Popular Fiction, 1875–1914.* Cambridge: Cambridge University Press.

Dunphy, Jocelyn. 1982. "Insurrection and Repression: Bligh's 1790 *Narrative of the Mutiny on Board H. M. Ship Bounty."* In *1789: Reading Writing Revolution: Proceedings of the Essex Conference on the Sociology of Literature,* ed. F. Barker et al., 281–301. Colchester: University of Essex.

D'Urville, Dumont. 1832. "Sur les îles du Grand Océan." *Bulletin de la Société de Géographie* 17: 1–21.

Edmond, Rod. 1997. *Representing the South Pacific: Colonial Discourse from Cook to Gauguin.* Cambridge: Cambridge University Press.

———. 1998. "Translating Cultures: William Ellis and Missionary Writing." In *Science and Exploration in the Pacific: European Voyages to the Southern Oceans in the Eighteenth Century,* ed. Margarette Lincoln. Suffolk and Rochester, N.Y.: Boydell and Brewerx.

Ellis, Markman. 1996. *The Politics of Sensibility: Race, Gender and Commerce in the Sentimental Novel*. Cambridge: Cambridge University Press.

Ellis, William. 1826. *Narrative of a Tour Through Hawaii, or, Owhyhee; with Remarks on the History, Traditions, Manners, Customs and Language of The Inhabitants of the Sandwich Islands*. London: H. Fisher, Son, and P. Jackson.

———. 1829. *Polynesian Researches, During a Residence of Nearly Six Years in the South Sea Islands*. London: Fisher.

———. 1831. *A Vindication of the South Sea Missions from the Misrepresentations of Otto von Kotzebue, captain in the Russian navy*. London: Frederick Westley and A. H. Davis.

An Enquiry into the Causes of the Miscarriage of the Scots Colony at Darien, or, an Answer to a Libel Entitled, A Defence of the Scots Abdicating Darien. 1700. Glasgow.

Escobar, Arturo, and Sonia E. Alvarez, eds. 1992. *The Making of Social Movements in Latin America: Identity, Strategy and Democracy*. Boulder: Westview.

Exquemelin, Alexandre Olivier. 1684–85. *Bucaniers of America*. 2nd ed. London: W. Crooke.

Fausett, David. 1993. *Writing the New World: Imaginary Voyages and Utopias of the Great Southern Land*. Syracuse: University of Syracuse Press.

Ferdon, Edwin N. 1987. *Early Tonga, As the Explorers Saw It, 1616–1810*. Tucson: University of Arizona Press.

Ferguson, Adam. 1980. *An Essay on the History of Civil Society*. New Brunswick, N.J.: Transaction.

Forster, George. 2000. *A Voyage Round the World*. Ed. N. Thomas and O. Berghof. Honolulu: University of Hawaii Press. Originally published 1777 (London: B. White).

Forster, Johann Reinhold. 1996. *Observations Made During a Voyage Round the World*. Edited by Nicholas Thomas, Harriet Guest, and Michael Dettelbach. Honolulu: University of Hawaii Press. Originally published 1778 (London: G. Robinson).

Frear, Walter Francis. 1947. *Mark Twain and Hawaii*. Chicago: Lakeside Press.

Freeman, J. D. 1959. "Joe the Gimlet or Siovili Cult: An Episode in the Religious History of Early Samoa." In *Anthropology in the South Seas: Essays Presented to H.D. Skinner*, ed. J. D. Freeman and W. R. Geddes. New Plymouth: Thomas Avery.

Frezier, Amedee. 1717. *A Voyage to the South-Sea*. London: Jonah Bowyer.

Freud, Sigmund. 1963. *Character and Culture*. Translated by James Strachey. New York: Collier Books.

Frost, Alan, ed. 1999. *Pacific Empires*. Melbourne: Melbourne University Press.

Frow, John. 1991. "Tourism and the Semiotics of Nostalgia." *October* 57: 121–51.

Gallagher, Robert E. ed. 1964. *Byron's Journal of His Circumnavigation, 1764–66*. Cambridge: Hakluyt Society.

Garrett, John. 1982. *To Live Among the Stars: Christian Origins in Oceania*. Geneva: World Council of Churches.

Gell, Alfred. 1993. *Wrapping in Images: Tattooing in Polynesia*. Oxford: Clarendon Press.

Gilson, R. P. 1970. *Samoa 1830 to 1900: The Politics of a Multi-cultural Community*. Melbourne: Oxford University Press.

Gordon, Eleanora. 1984. "Scurvy and Anson's Voyage." *American Neptune* 44, no. 3: 155–66.

Gordon-Cumming, Constance F. 1883. *Fire Fountains: The Kingdom of Hawaii, its Volcanoes, and the History of its Missions*. Edinburgh: W. Blackwood.

———. 1882. *A Lady's Cruise in a French Man-of-War*. Reprint, New York: Praeger, 1970.

Greenblatt, Stephen. 1980. *Renaissance Self-Fashioning*. Chicago: Chicago University Press.

Guest, Harriet. 1992. "Curiously Marked: Tattooing, Masculinity, and Nationality in Eighteenth Century British Perceptions of the South Pacific." In *Painting and the Politics of Culture: New Essays on British Art, 1700–1850*, ed. John Barrell. Oxford: Oxford University Press.

———. 1989. "The Great Distinction: Figures of the Exotic in the Work of William Hodges." In *New Feminist Discourses: Critical Essays on Theories and Texts*, ed. Isobel Armstrong. London: Routledge.

Gunson, Niel. 1972. "John Williams and His Ship: The Bourgeois Aspirations of a Missionary Family." In *Questioning the Past: A Selection of Papers in History and Government*, ed. D. P. Crook. Brisbane: University of Queensland Press.

———. 1978. *Messengers of Grace: Evangelical Missionaries in the South Seas, 1797–1860*. Melbourne: Oxford University Press.

———. 1963. "A Note on the Difficulties of Ethnohistorical Writing, with Special Reference to Tahiti." *Journal of the Polynesian Society* 72, no. 4: 415–19.

Hacke, William. 1699. *A Collection of Voyages*. London: James Knapton.

Hakluyt, Richard. 1600. *Voyages of the English Nation*. 3 vols. London: George Bishop.

Haweis, Rev. Thomas. N.d. A Collection of 38 Draft Letters and Manuscripts many of which are in hand of the Rev. Thomas Haweis, dealing with the early missions to the South Seas, and including diaries sent by the missionaries to the London Missionary Society. Mitchell MS 4910X 1,2. Mitchell Library, Sydney.

Hawkesworth, John. 1773. *An Account of the Voyages and Discoveries in the Southern Hemisphere*. 3 vols. London: W. Strahan and T. Cadell.

Herbert, Christopher. 1991. *Culture and Anomie: Ethnographic Imagination in the Nineteenth Century*. Chicago: University of Chicago Press.

Herder, Johann Gottfried. 1800. *Outlines of a Philosophy of the History of Man*. Translated by T. Churchill. New York: Bergman.

Herries, Walter. 1700. *A Defense of the Scots Abdicating Darien*. Glasgow.

Heylyn, Peter. 1667. *Cosmographie*. London: Philip Chetwode.

Im Thurn, E., and Leonard Wharton, eds. 1925. *The journal of William Lockerby, Sandalwood Trader in the Fijian Islands . . . with Other Papers*. London: Hakluyt Society.

Jarves, James Jackson. 1843. *History of the Hawaiian or Sandwich Islands*. Boston: Tappan and Dennet.

Journal of a Voyage Round the World in the Dolphin. 1767. London: M. Cooper.

Kahananui, Dorothy M., ed. 1984. *Ka Mooolelo Hawaii, Hawaiian Language Reader Based on Sheldon Dibble, Ka Mooolelo Hawaii*. Honolulu: University of Hawaii Press.

Keate, George. 2001. *An Account of the Pelew Islands*. Edited by Karen Nero and Nicholas Thomas. London: Cassells Academic/Leicester University Press. Originally published 1788 (London: G. Nicol).

Knapman, Claudia. 1986. *White Women in Fiji 1835–1930*. Sydney: Allen and Unwin.

La Farge, John. 1914. *An American Artist in the South Seas*. London: Grant Richards. Reprint, London: KPI, 1987.

Lamb, Jonathan. 1994. "Circumstances Surrounding the Death of John Hawkesworth." In *The South Pacific in the Eighteenth Century: Narratives and Myths*, ed. Jonathan Lamb, Robert P. Macubbin, and David F. Morrill. Special issue of *Eighteenth-Century Life* 18, no. 3: 97–113.

Lapierre, Alexandra. 1995. *Fanny Stevenson: Muse, Adventuress and Romantic Enigma*. Translated by Carol Cosman. New York: Carol and Graf; London: Fourth Estate.

Lātūkefu, Sione. 1974. *Church and State in Tonga: The Wesleyan Methodist Missionaries and Political Development, 1822–1875*. Canberra: Australian National University Press.

Lazarus, Neil. 1990. *Resistance in Postcolonial African Fiction*. New Haven: Yale University Press.

Lincoln, Margarette, ed. 1998. *Science and Exploration in the Pacific: European Voyages to the Southern Oceans in the Eighteenth Century*. Suffolk and Rochester, N.Y.: Boydell and Brewer.

Lloyd, David. 1993. *Anomalous States: Irish Writing and the Post-Colonial Moment*. Dublin: Lilliput Press.

Lovett, Richard. 1899. *The History of the London Missionary Society, 1795–1895*. London: Henry Frowde.

MacCannell, Dean. 1973. "Staged Authenticity: Arrangements of Social Space in Tourist Settings." *American Journal of Sociology* 79, no. 3: 589–603.

McCutcheon, Elizabeth. 1977. "Denying the Contrary: More's Use of Litotes in Utopia." *Essential Articles for the Study of Thomas More*. Edited by Richard Standish Sylvester and Germain Marc'hadour. Hamden, Conn.: Archon.

McKeon, Michael. 1987. *The Origins of the English Novel*. Baltimore: Johns Hopkins University Press.

McPhail, Bridget. 1994. "Through a Glass, Darkly: Scots and Indians Converge at Darien." In *The South Pacific in the Eighteenth Century: Narratives and Myths*, ed. Jonathan Lamb, Robert P. Macubbin, and David F. Morrill. Special issue of *Eighteenth-Century Life* 18, no. 3: 129–47.

Mandeville, Bernard. 1924. *The Fable of the Bees*. Edited by F. B. Kay. Oxford: Clarendon Press.

Maning, F. E. 1863. *Old New Zealand.* Auckland: Robert J. Creighton and Alfred Scales.

Markley, Robert. 1994. "'So Inexhaustible a Treasure of Gold': Defoe, Capitalism, and the Romance of the South Seas." In *The South Pacific in the Eighteenth Century: Narratives and Myths,* ed. Jonathan Lamb, Robert P. Macubbin, and David F. Morrill. Special issue of *Eighteenth-Century Life* 18, no. 3: 148–67.

Marshall, P. J., and Glyndwr Williams. 1982. *The Great Map of Mankind: British Perceptions of the World in the Age of Enlightenment.* London: Dent.

Martin, John. 1818. *An account of the natives of the Tonga Islands, in the South Pacific Ocean. With an original grammar and vocabulary of their language. Comp. and arranged from the extensive communications of Mr. William Mariner, several years resident in those islands.* 2nd ed. 2 vols. London: John Murray.

Maude, H. E. 1973. "Baiteke and Binoka of Abemama: Arbiters of Change in the Gilbert Islands." In *Pacific Island Portraits,* ed. J. W. Davidson and Deryck Scarr. Canberra: Australian National University Press.

———. 1968. *Of Islands and Men.* Oxford: Oxford University Press.

Mills, Sara. 1991. *Discourses of Difference: An Analysis of Women's Travel Writing and Colonialism.* London: Routledge.

Mitchell, Timothy. 1998. *Colonising Egypt.* Berkeley: University of California Press.

Morgan, Susan. 1996. *Place Matters: Gendered Geography in Victorian Women's Travel Books about Southeast Asia.* New Brunswick, N.J.: Rutgers University Press.

Morrell, Abby Jane. 1833. *Narrative of a Voyage to the Ethiopic and South Atlantic Ocean, Indian Ocean, Chinese Sea, North and South Pacific Ocean, in the Years 1829, 1830, 1831.* New York: J. and J. Harper.

Morrell, Benjamin. 1832. *A Narrative of Four Voyages to the South Sea, North and South Pacific Ocean, Chinese Sea, Ethiopic and Southern Atlantic Ocean, Indian and Antarctic Ocean from the year 1822 to 1831.* New York: Harper. Reprint, Upper Saddle River, N.J.: Gregg Press, 1970.

Morrison, James. 1935. *The Journal of James Morrison, Boatswain's Mate of the Bounty, describing the Mutiny and Subsequent Misfortunes of the Mutineers together with an account of the Island of Tahiti.* Edited by Owen Rutter. London: Golden Cockerel Press.

Moyle, Richard M., ed. 1984. *The Samoan Journals of John Williams, 1830 and 1832.* Canberra: Australian National University Press.

Nero, Karen. 1987. "A Cherecha a Lokelii: Beads of History of Krakor, Palau 1783–1983." Ph.D. diss., University of California, Berkeley.

Obeyesekere, Gananath. 1992a. *The Apotheosis of Captain Cook: European Mythmaking in the Pacific.* Princeton: Princeton University Press.

———. 1992b. "'British Cannibals': Contemplation of an Event in the Death and Resurrection of James Cook, Explorer." *Critical Inquiry* 18, no. 4: 630–54.

Oliver, Douglas. 1974. *Ancient Tahitian Society.* 3 vols. Honolulu: University of Hawaii Press.

———. 1988. *Return to Tahiti: Bligh's Second Breadfruit Voyage.* Melbourne: Melbourne University Press.

Orange, James. 1840. *Narrative of the late George Vason, of Nottingham. One of the first missionaries sent out by the London Missionary Society, in the Ship Duff, Captain Wilson, 1796. Giving an Account of his Voyage Outward, Settlement in Tongataboo, Apostasy, Heathen Life, Escape from the Island, Return to England, Subsequent Life, and Death in 1838, aged 66 years. With a preliminary Essay, on the Geography of the South Sea Islands, also a Description of the Manners, Habits, Customs, Traditions, &c. &c. of the Inhabitants, and a succinct Account of the South Sea Island Mission.* Derby: Henry Mozley.

Pagden, Anthony. 1995a. "The Effacement of Difference: Colonialism and the Origins of Nationalism in Diderot and Herder." In *After Colonialism: Imperial Histories and Postcolonial Displacements,* ed. Gyan Prakash. Princeton: Princeton University Press.

Pagden, Anthony. 1995b. *Lords of All the World.* New Haven: Yale University Press.

Park, Mungo. 1983. *Travels into the Interior of Africa.* London: Eland.

Parmentier, Richard J. 1987. *The Sacred Remains.* Chicago: University of Chicago Press.

Patterson, Samuel. 1817. *Narrative of the Adventures and Sufferings of Samuel Patterson, Experienced in the Pacific Ocean, and Many Other Parts of the World.* Palmer, Mass.: The Press in Palmer. Reprint, Providence: Journal Office, 1825.

Piozzi, Hester. 1984. *Anecdotes of Samuel Johnson.* Gloucester: Sutton. Originally published London: Cadell, 1786.

Pratt, Mary Louise. 1992. *Imperial Eyes: Travel Writing and Transculturation.* London and New York: Routledge.

Prout, Ebenezer. 1843. *Memoirs of the Life of the Rev. John Williams.* London: John Snow.

Ralston, Caroline. 1985. "Early Nineteenth-Century Millennial Cults and the Case of Hawaii." *Journal of the Polynesian Society* 94: 307–31.

Raynal, Guillaume Thomas. 1783. *A History of the East and West Indies.* 8 vols. Translated by J. O. Justamond. London: W. Strahan and T. Cadell.

Rediker, Marcus. 1987. *Between the Devil and the Deep Blue Sea.* Cambridge: Cambridge University Press.

Rennie, Neil. 1995. *Far-Fetched Facts: The Literature of Travel and the Idea of the South Seas.* Oxford: Clarendon Press.

Robertson, George. 1948. *The Discovery of Tahiti: Journal of the Second Voyage of the Dolphin.* Edited by Hugh Carrington. London: Hakluyt Society.

Rogers, Woodes. 1712. *A Cruising Voyage Round the World.* London: A. Bell.

Rousseau, Jean-Jacques. 1803. *Eloisa: or a Series of Original Letters.* Reprint, Oxford: Woodstock, 1989.

Salmond, Anne. 1997. *Between Worlds: Early Exchanges Between Maori and Europeans, 1773–1815.* Auckland: Viking.

———. 1991. *Two Worlds: First Meetings Between Maori and Europeans, 1642–1772.* Auckland: Viking.

Sahlins, Marshall. 1992. *Anahulu: The Anthropology of History in the Kingdom of Hawaii.* Vol. 1, *Historical Ethnography.* Chicago: University of Chicago Press.

———. 1994. "The Discovery of the True Savage." In *Dangerous Liaisons: Essays in Honour of Greg Dening,* ed. Donna Merwick. Parkville: Department of History, University of Melbourne.

———. 1985. "Hierarchy and Humanity in Polynesia." In *Transformations of Polynesian Culture,* ed. Antony Hooper and Judith Huntsman. Auckland: The Polynesian Society.

———. 1981. *Historical Metaphors and Mythical Realities: Structure in the Early History of the Sandwich Islands Kingdom.* Ann Arbor: University of Michigan Press.

———. 1995. *How Natives Think: About Captain Cook, for Example.* Chicago: University of Chicago Press.

———. 1985. *Islands of History.* Chicago: Chicago University Press.

Shaftesbury, A. A. C., Lord. 1964. *Characteristics.* Indianapolis: Bobbs-Merrill.

Simson, Richard. N.d. *Observations Made During a South-Sea Voyage.* Sloane MS 86 (672). British Library, London.

Smith, Bernard. 1985. *European Vision and the South Pacific.* 2nd ed. Sydney: Harper and Row.

———. 1992. *Imagining the Pacific: In the Wake of the Cook Voyages.* Melbourne: Melbourne University Press.

Smith, Thomas. 1838. *The History and Origin of the Missionary Societies.* 2 vols. London: Thomas Kelly.

Smith, Vanessa. 1998. *Literary Culture and the Pacific: Nineteenth-Century Textual Encounters.* Cambridge: Cambridge University Press.

Smollett, Tobias. 1748. *The Adventures of Roderick Random.* Reprint (edited by Paul-Gabriel Boucé), Oxford: Oxford University Press, 1979.

———. 1768–69. *The Present State of all Nations.* 8 vols. London: R. Baldwin.

Sobell, Dava. 1995. *Longitude.* New York: Walker.

Sparrman, Anders. 1944. *A Voyage round the World with Captain James Cook in HMS* Resolution. London: Golden Cockerel.

Spate, O. H. K. 1979–88. *The Pacific Since Magellan.* 3 vols. Minneapolis: University of Minnesota Press.

Stafford, Barbara. 1984. *Voyage into Substance.* Cambridge: MIT Press.

Steegmuller, Frances. 1951. *The Two Lives of James Jackson Jarves.* New Haven: Yale University Press, 1951.

Stevenson, Fanny [Mrs. R. L. Stevenson]. 1914. *The Cruise of the 'Janet Nichol' among the South Sea Islands: A Diary by Mrs. Robert Louis Stevenson.* New York: Charles Scribner's Sons. Reprint, London: Chatto and Windus, 1915.

Stevenson, Fanny, and Robert Louis Stevenson. 1956. *Our Samoan Adventure.* Edited and with introduction and notes by Charles Neider. London: Weidenfeld and Nicolson.

Stevenson, Robert Louis. 1900. *In the South Seas: The Marquesas, Paumotus and Gilbert Islands.* Reprint, London: KPI, 1986.

———. 1924a. *In the South Seas: Being an Account of Experiences and Observations in the Marquesas, Paumotus, and Gilbert Islands in the Course of Two Cruises, on the Yacht 'Casco' (1888) and the Schooner 'Equator' (1889)*. London: William Heinemann.

———. 1924b. *Vailima Papers*. London: Heinemann.

———. 1987. *Island Nights' Entertainments*. London: Hogarth.

Stevenson, Robert Louis, and Lloyd Osbourne. 1893. *The Wrecker*. London: Cassell.

———. "The Ebb-Tide." 1987. In *Dr Jekyll and Mr Hyde and Other Stories*. London: Penguin.

Sunderland, J. P., and A. Buzacott. 1866. *Mission Life in the Islands of the Pacific*. London: John Snow.

Swearingen, Roger. 1980. *The Prose Writings of Robert Louis Stevenson: A Guide*. London: Macmillan.

Swift, Jonathan. 1971. *Gulliver's Travels*. Edited by Paul Turner. Oxford: Oxford University Press.

Taussig, Michael. 1993. *Mimesis and Alterity: A Particular History of the Senses*. London and New York: Routledge.

Taylor, Richard. 1855. *Te Ika a Maui: or, New Zealand and its Inhabitants*. London: Wertheim and Macintosh.

Thacker, Christopher. 1997. "'O Tinian! O Juan Fernandez!': Rousseau's 'Elysee' and Anson's Desert Islands." *Garden History* 5, no. 9: 41–47.

Thomas, Nicholas. 1994. *Colonialism's Culture : Anthropology, Travel and Government*. Oxford: Polity Press.

———. 1991. *Entangled Objects : Exchange, Material Culture, and Colonialism in the Pacific*. Cambridge: Harvard University Press.

———. 1989. "The Force of Ethnology: Origins and Significance of the Melanesia/Polynesia Division." *Current Anthropology* 30: 27–41.

———. 1990. *Marquesan Societies*. Oxford: Oxford University Press.

———. 1997. *In Oceania: Visions, Artifacts, Histories*. Durham, N.C.: Duke University Press.

———. 1990. "Partial Texts: Representation, Colonialism and Agency in Pacific History." *The Journal of Pacific History* 25, no. 2: 139–58.

Thomas, Nicholas, and Richard Eves. 1998. *Bad Colonists: The South Seas Letters of Vernon Lee Walker and Louis Becke*. Durham: Duke University Press.

Thomas, Nicholas, Diane Losche, and Jennifer Newell, eds. 1999. *Double Vision: Art Histories and Colonial Histories in the Pacific*. Cambridge and Melbourne: Cambridge University Press.

Thomas, Pascoe. 1745. *A True and Impartial Journal of a Voyage to the South Seas*. London: S. Birt, J. Newbery and J. Collyer.

Transactions of the Missionary Society. 1804. 2nd ed. Vol. 1. London: Bye and Law.

Trenchard, John. 1725. *Cato's Letters: or, Essays on Civil Liberty*. London: J. Walthoe.

The Travels of Hildebrand Bowman Esq. 1778. London: Strahan and Cadell.

Twain, Mark. 1872. *Roughing It*. Reprint, London and New York: Penguin, 1981.

Vason, George. 1810. *An authentic narrative of four years' residence at Tongataboo, one of the Friendly Islands, in the South Sea, by* —— *who went there in the "Duff", under Captain Wilson, in 1796*. London: Longman, Hurst, Rees, and Orme.

Wafer, Lionel. 1903. *A New Voyage and Description of the Isthmus of America*. Edited by G. P. Winship. Cleveland: Burrows. Originally published London: James Knapton, 1699.

——. 1934. *A New Voyage and Description of the Isthmus of America*. Edited by L. E. Elliott Joyce. Oxford: Hakluyt Society.

Wales, William. 1781. *An Inquiry into the Present State of Population in England and Wales*. London: J. Nourse.

——. 1778. *Remarks on Mr Forster's Account of Captain Cook's Last Voyage*. London: J. Nourse.

Wallis, Helen. 1964. "The Patagonian Giants." Appendix 1 in *Byron's Journal of His Circumnavigation 1764–1766*, ed. Robert E. Gallagher. Cambridge: Hakluyt Society.

Wallis, Mary. 1851. *Life in Feejee or, Five Years Among the Cannibals*. Boston: William Heath. Facsimile reprint, New York: Gregg Press, 1967; and Suva: Fiji Museum, 1983.

——. 1994. *The Fiji and New Caledonia Journals of Mary Wallis*. Suva: Institute of Pacific Studies.

Walpole, Horace. 1964. "An Account of the Giants Lately Discovered: In a Letter to a Friend in the Country (1766)." Appendix 3 in *Byron's Journal of his Circumnavigation 1764–1766*, ed. Robert E. Gallagher. Cambridge: Hakluyt Society.

Williams, Glyndwr. 1994. "Buccaneers, Castaways, and Satirists: The South Seas in the English Consciousness before 1750." Special issue of *Eighteenth Century Life* 18, no. 3: 114–28.

——. 1967. *Documents Relating to Anson's Voyage Round the World, 1740–44*. London: Navy Records Society.

——. 1997. *The Great South Sea: English Voyages and Encounters, 1570–1750*. New Haven: Yale University Press.

Williams, John. 1837. *A Narrative of Missionary Enterprises in the South Sea Islands, with Remarks upon the Natural History of the Islands, Origin, Languages, Traditions and Usages of the Inhabitants*. London: John Snow.

Williams, Thomas, and James Calvert. 1858. *Fiji and the Fijians*. 2 vols. Edited by George Stringer Rowe. London: Alexander Heylin.

Wilson, James. 1799. *A Missionary Voyage to the Southern Pacific Ocean, performed in the years 1796, 1797, 1798, in the Ship Duff, commanded by Captain James Wilson*. London: published for the benefit of the society, printed by S. Gosnell for T. Chapman. Reprint (with introduction by Irmgard Moschner), New York: Frederick A. Praeger, 1979.

Woodward, R. L. 1969. *Robinson Crusoe's Island: A History of the Juan Fernandez Islands*. Chapel Hill: University of North Carolina Press.

Index